The Pennsylvania State College

1853 – 1932

Interpretation and Record

The Pennsylvania State College

1853 – 1932

Interpretation and Record

Erwin W. Runkle

The Nittany Valley Society

State College

Published in the United States of America
by The Nittany Valley Society, Inc.
www.nittanyvalley.org

ISBN-10: 0-9853488-7-9
ISBN-13: 978-0-9853488-7-8

The Pennsylvania State College, 1853-1932: Interpretation and Record
Erwin W. Runkle

First Edition Hardcover

CONTENTS

PUBLISHER'S NOTE

It is with great pride and excitement that we undertake the honor of presenting this first-ever publication of Dr. Erwin Runkle's history of Penn State. All proceeds from the sale of this volume will be donated to support the Penn State Libraries (this was a corporate decision made by the Nittany Valley Society's board of directors and was not requested, authorized or endorsed by Penn State or the University Libraries).

This work, meticulously and lovingly crafted by the school's first historian, was commissioned by the University's trustees, but never approved for publication. Eventually, the time period covered here was officially and capably documented in Wayland Dunaway's "History of The Pennsylvania State College." With the presentation of this often-intimate account of early Penn State in print and digital formats, we hope to add greater depth and flavor to the telling of Penn State's story. As former trustee George Henning notes in his introduction, the author's "access and knowledge of people and documents from the formative years of the College allow him to pass along to us a first-hand view of events."

Now, Dr. Runkle's "Interpretation and Record" can take its place among the works of Dunaway, Leon Stout, Michael Bezilla, Ridge Riley, Carol Sonenklar, Darryl B. Daisey, Lou Prato and others, further enriching our understanding of the proud institution that sprung up in the "splendid isolation" of a Central Pennsylvania valley guarded by Mount Nittany.

Every effort has been made to remain faithful to the original text. In cases where reasonable judgment indicated genuine typographical error, corrections were made. Certain punctuation (dashes, ellipses) was standardized and headings were converted to sentence case to optimize the reader's ability to access and engage with the material. The rule, however, was to err on the side of preservation. The reader will no doubt discover numerous instances of unconventional and idiosyncratic spelling and syntax (e.g. commas where they do not belong or absence of them where they do) throughout the document; these are the hallmarks of Dr. Runkle's personal style.

His manuscript was composed by typewriter on standard, office-size sheets, so certain formatting—indentations, lists, tables, etc.—had to be adapted for the various print and digital versions published by The Nittany Valley Society. Here, a good faith effort was made to bridge the gaps between fidelity to the source material, accessibility for the reader and standardization across multiple publishing platforms. For example, text that was, in the original work, underlined to show emphasis has been italicized in this version to avoid confusion with hypertext in the digital formats. Dr. Runkle's original footnote numbering system, which was inconsistent and potentially confusing to readers, has been replaced with a single, standardized numeric progression, internalized and unique to this first-time printing.

Special thanks are due to Mike Furlough and Timothy Pyatt of the Penn State University Libraries, without whose help and faith this book would not be possible, and extra special appreciation goes out to Jackie Esposito, who was as invaluable a resource to this project as she has been to countless other efforts to preserve and promote the culture and history of Penn State and the Nittany Valley; all Penn Staters owe her a debt of gratitude for her exemplary work as University archivist. Thanks also to Paul Karwacki for his assistance in obtaining the images used on the front and back covers. We are also extremely grateful to George Henning, for his belief in the project and his contribution of a fresh introduction that enhances the experience of engaging with Dr. Runkle's original manuscript, as well as to Andy Nagypal, for his exceptional diligence and attention to detail during the proofing process.

Please enjoy and share Dr. Runkle's story of the University's founding and growth, with all of its attendant calamity and triumph. For every heart that truly loves the name of Dear Old State, a bountiful treasure trove awaits.

The Board of Directors of The Nittany Valley Society
at the Central Pennsylvania Festival of the Arts
July 13, 2013

FOREWORD

By George T. Henning, Jr. '63

I have been a collector of Penn State memorabilia beginning with my matriculation at Penn State in 1959 – I still have my acceptance letter and fee statements from my freshman year! As I went through my undergraduate days at Penn State, I saved a few items from events at the time. Later in the 1970s, I became a collector in earnest with the acquisition of the game ball from the VMI football game that Penn State won 21-0, signed by the entire team. I acquired the football at an auction for the benefit of a charity in State College and to my surprise later realized the ball was from the first game of my freshman year. As I had attended all the home football games during my years at Penn State, I knew I had been there!

The feeling of being connected to Penn State history by an item I acquired led me to more serious collecting. Over the years I have been able to acquire items from the original College Building (the first Old Main building) including a stairwell post and a roof tile. Other items in my collection are a bass drum used by the Air Force ROTC marching band during ROTC drills on Thursday afternoons in the 1950s and 1960s as well as magazines, newspapers, postcards and many other historical items ranging from class reunion favors to bowl game mementos. One of the most interesting items from class reunions is a Certificate of congratulations "in consideration of the sometime connection" presented to John Carothers by the Class of 1862 on the occasion of its 50th Reunion. It is signed by President Edwin Sparks and Trustee Chair James Beaver. The class invited to their 50th reunion all the entering members of the class, even those who never completed their education, many due to their participation in the Civil War, which was the case for Carothers who left classes to fight in the War, got married and never returned to school.

11

I describe my collection briefly as an introduction to my fascination with Penn State history. My wife and I enjoy sharing the collection with current students and alumni. The stairwell post stands at the bottom of a stairwell in my home. As we pass the stairwell post from the original College Building, view the Carothers certificate and envelopes stamped with early post marks of Farm School and Agricultural College, we talk about the students who walked by this post and perhaps hung on to the post as they speedily rounded the corner on their way down the stairs from the dormitory rooms on the upper floors to classes and dining areas below. What was the school like during the Civil War? What letters did students write? I enjoy speculating with the visitors about the items in the collection and I share the meager history I have of student life. As a result of publication of Dr. Runkle's book, we all have more information on the lives of the students during the College's early years and the men who participated in founding our great University. Dr. Runkle's "Interpretation and Record of The Pennsylvania State College 1853-1932" provides rare insight into the early days of Penn State and the parade of history he covers. He provides many informative details that allow us to put together a picture of the times during which the school emerged from a dream into a reality.

Dr. Runkle graduated from Yale University in 1893 with a PhD. in Philosophy and was appointed instructor in Philosophy and Ethics at Penn State the same year. He also served part-time as librarian from 1904 to 1924 when he was appointed head of the new Department of Philosophy. He continued as head of the Department until his retirement in 1935. From Runkle's text you learn that many of the faculty and staff had multiple jobs. Runkle's other duties included being the first College historian. He organized a large collection of letters, reports, manuscripts and other information pertaining to the College in order to properly recognize its history for its 50th anniversary in 1905, and is recognized as the Father of the University Archives. Dr. Runkle wrote the manuscript for this book in 1933. The English language from 80 years ago is a bit stiff to our ears today but portrays the life of a different time in history, and his words project the image of a book from a bygone era. The manuscript covers most subjects in chronological order, but as Dr. Runkle covers one subject he at times goes ahead with that story only to back up in time to begin another one. Dr. Runkle arrived at Penn State a mere 34 years after its first class was admitted. During his tenure he was able to meet many of the people involved in the early development of the College or talk to people who knew our early leaders. Dr. Runkle's access and knowledge of people and documents from the formative years of the College allows him to pass along to us a first-hand view of events.

Among the events described in the book that give insight into daily life, Dr. Runkle includes a letter from a student reminiscing of his time in the earliest years of the school when three hours of manual labor were required daily. The letter includes a description of clearing stones from the fields surrounding the College Building in preparation for planting. In one season 3,000 two-horse wagons of stone were collected! Descriptions of the College Building in the early times provide a feeling of the rustic living. We learn the coal stoves in student rooms were a response to economics rather than a point of design. The College Building was designed with three large furnaces in the basement, and the building contained flues to carry the heat to the rooms. Due to the low attendance at the school, operation of the furnaces that heated the entire building became too costly, so the students were provided with coal stoves to use in their rooms rather than operate the furnaces; without the furnaces, coal stoves also heated the classrooms.

Dr. Runkle also gives us a view of student activities which appear to have been very limited in the early years – if I performed three hours of manual labor, got up at 6:30 am for Chapel and attended classes all day I don't believe I would have energy or time for many student activities! Dr. Runkle traces the development of the first literary societies and their outgrowth, the development of intramural sports from the class scraps, and changes to Chapel attendance requirements through 1930 when the requirement was eliminated entirely. While describing the student activities, Dr. Runkle reports that in 1898 approximately 100 students and faculty traveled from State College to Bellefonte to take a train to Dickinson College to witness a debate between the two schools. He notes that the ban on dancing in College buildings was lifted in 1890! The beginning of eating clubs and fraternities, theatrical performances, newspapers and magazines and discipline are all traced by Runkle, as are the effects of the Civil War and World War I on the students and the College.

I enjoyed the sections of the book describing the development of the buildings on campus, including descriptions of buildings now long gone. The advent of tunnels to carry utilities on the campus was earlier than I would have expected. As new buildings were built the uses for the College Building changed and it became more an administrative center and classrooms. Dr. Runkle also describes the growth of the town and how College Avenue was formed. Details on the exact time and date of the arrival of the first train from Bellefonte, the earliest electronic communication and the installation of the first electric lights are included in the book.

Dr. Runkle describes in significant detail the work done by supporters of the school who worked to have the income from Pennsylvania's Morrill Land Grant Act receipts awarded to The Agricultural College of Pennsylvania. The history of the approval by the state legislature and attempts to reverse the awarding of Pennsylvania's income from the receipts of the land grant sales to The Agricultural College of Pennsylvania is much more complicated than I had previously realized. Twenty years after the first legislative approval of The Agricultural College of Pennsylvania as the land grant institution for Pennsylvania, there remained opposition to the distribution of the funds. The book describes the politics and regional disputes of the time that affected the decision to make The Agricultural College of Pennsylvania and later as the result of a name change, The Pennsylvania State College, the sole recipient of the income from the land grant receipts.

Although Dr. Runkle includes several references and examples of the school's inaccessibility, the number and frequency of visitors to the campus surprised me. Initially, the closest railroad was located in Spruce Creek, a five-hour stagecoach ride to the campus. Yet we learn that in 1857, 200 representatives of the Pennsylvania State Agricultural Society, county agricultural societies and legislators and friends met at the site of the school to elect the first Trustees and celebrated with a dinner in the College's large barn as the College Building was still under construction! The book includes facts on the Board of Trustees as it is formed and transitions through the time period of the book. As Dr. Runkle includes dedication speeches, letters of commendation, even odes written for special occasions by Fred Lewis Pattee (head of the English Department for many years and author of the school's Alma Mater), we gain more insight into the life and times that are being described and the perspective of the participants in the events of the times. Although Runkle does not spend a great deal of time on any single individual, he does provide a short biography and perspective on many names we still recognize on campus buildings and local streets.

I believe anyone who has an interest in the history of Penn State and the lives of the individuals involved will enjoy this book. Readers without a connection to Penn State will also enjoy this book, as they will learn of the life styles of college students in the last half of the 19th century and the early 20th century. I know I will be able to enjoy and share many of the items in my collection to a greater degree than I could before I read Dr. Runkle's book. It is my hope for every reader that this remarkable book can become something worth treasuring for years to come.

The Pennsylvania State College
1853 – 1932
Interpretation and Record

Erwin W. Runkle

DEDICATION

To Dr. Evan Pugh, the first President, whose scientific ideals dominated the beginnings of Penn State; who wrote the first history of the Institution, a prophet of, an exemplar in, a martyr for the cause of science in industry and in education.

1859—1864

To President George W. Atherton who made scholarship and the Penn State standard synonymous; secured legal responsibility on the part of the Commonwealth for an assumed but unrecognized obligation; established the college where it ever remains in the very heart of the people of the State.

1882—1906

To President Edwin Erle Sparks whose public address and contagious good-will gave new meaning and direction to College Extension and Publicity, and whose personal influences upon students and alumni ever ensure reverent memories and grateful honors in the history of The Pennsylvania State College.

1908—1920

To President Ralph D. Hetzel whose genius for cooperation is excelled only by his gift for leadership, and whose plans and achievements for Penn State as a public service institution are irresistibly moving toward larger and finer ends.

1927—

PREFACE

Three principles have determined the form which this record assumes. First, I have chosen, particularly in the earlier portions of the narrative, to let the actors and scenes, purposes and enactments speak for themselves. I have tacitly assumed that these original documents, addresses, letters, catalogues, reports, etc., are the institution's history writ large. Comparison and interpretation, then, are the necessary tasks which everyone must undertake who would know the spirit of The Pennsylvania State College. That I have in adequate measure succeeded in weaving the varied, oft one-sided, and even prejudiced and antagonistic threads into a coherent and vital pattern, I have not the temerity to claim. I only say that as a labor of love and in the midst of regular duties, I have earnestly tried to distill the essence of a matchless record of devotion, plan, and achievement which the founders and builders of the College have bequeathed. They have left more than a history or an institution, they have transmitted life.

A second principle has been to accept the successive administrations as more or less adequate divisions of the unfolding theme. This method has some disadvantages. Leaders fall, the life of the institution goes on. However, for that very reason, the pace is accelerated, retarded, modified or transformed by the way in which the countless cooperating activities are typified and garnered in the leader. The larger and more successful he be, the more surely is he but the embodiment of the genius of the institution's past, the converging and rallying point of the common and shared labors of the public, the Commonwealth, trustees, faculty, alumni and students.

Third, I have tried to emphasize those features of our college life that are in some sense distinctive of it. There *is* a Penn State Spirit; its "splendid isolation" has given rise to some variant types or "sports" of a sheltered environment, some strangely amorphous if conceived in a diverse setting. Always in the general stream of college life, Penn State has nevertheless had a "way of her own". That "way of her own" is of one piece, too, with the individuality, the experimental bent, the pragmatic, democratic spirit of public service which the Land-Grant Institutions, the Peoples' Colleges, the State Colleges and Universities are so abundantly realizing.

The writer thanks all who have generously aided and expresses the hope that a more vital and wide-spread interest in the unique history of The Pennsylvania State College shall ensue.

Erwin W. Runkle
State College, Pennsylvania
May 22nd, 1932.

Part I

Introductory

CHAPTER 1

The Background in Nation and State

"The significance of the Agricultural College for the whole trend of American Education was its naive effrontery in frankly seeing for life-training a new connection with real life use, and this significance exceeds in service to the nation even the weight of benefits wrought for the tilling and tiller of the soil."

President Benjamin Ide Wheeler

"The Spirit of the Land-Grant Institution is the Spirit of Service through the application of exact knowledge to the ordinary affairs of life. It began as an attempt to provide an approximate literature for the man on the farm and in the workshop... The Spirit of the Land-Grant Colleges has developed into a national system of Public Service Institutions."

Dean Eugene Davenport

"If the land-grant college fails, neither democracy's goal of education, nor education's goal of democracy will be reached."

Chancellor E.C. Elliott

Movements which have the vitality and meaning of those which led to the founding of The Pennsylvania State College are not the work of one man or group of men. Such movements lie deeper than the purposes and plans of individuals, they are the products of the common consciousness of whole peoples. A nation was becoming aware of well-nigh boundless resources in land, forest and mine; of undeveloped and unutilized wealth of raw materials for manufacture; of opportunities for trade and commerce. A whole people was becoming cognizant of its work in the world; of railroads and bridges to build, of telegraphs and telephones to perfect and to construct; of the processes of manufacture to discover and to apply.

The apprenticeship system was proving its inadequacy to the greater complexity of demands made upon it. The factory was vying with and supplanting domestic manufacture. An almost prophetic consciousness seemed to arise that with the Civil War to be fought, there would come the vastly intricate problems of industrial freedom and reconstruction. The westward movement toward the fertile plains was necessitating a changed emphasis in the eastern methods of farming, and an almost new approach in the west. In the east, it was chemistry applied to intensive production. In the west, it was machinery multiplying human labor and applied to extensive production. To cope with these changing conditions, the nation must gird herself with new educational principles, the hand must be trained with the brain, the slave of tools must become the master of tools.

These forces had their renaissance about eighteen hundred and fifty; and all over the country the leaven was at work for the education of the masses as well as the classes. A new professional, technical and industrial training was developing which would extend the learned professions from those of law, medicine and theology, so as to include the agriculturist, the engineer, the miner, the chemist, the manufacturer and the artisan.

The general government provided for training in a specific direction by the establishment of a military school at West Point in eighteen hundred and two. One of its early graduates, Captain Alden Partridge opened a military school at Norwich in which Greek and Latin were made elective. According to published announcements, the school "prepared men to become merchants, manufacturers, teachers, surveyors, engineers or soldiers". The Rensselaer Polytechnic Institute established in 1825, was the first scientific school, (not on a military basis), whose avowed purpose was "the application of science to the common purpose of life." In 1847 and following decade, the Lawrence, Sheffield, and Chandler endowments formed the nuclei for scientific and industrial training at Harvard, Yale, and Dartmouth respectively.

In these early days, the scientific school was kept distinct from the "college proper", the student of the "classics" was considered as superior to the student of the sciences. Andrew D. White writing in 1874, affirmed, "the scientific student was of a different caste. He lived in a different building, had lectures and recitations in different rooms, was instructed by different professors, was graduated at a different time and place. He was not considered as properly of the graduating class of his year. Nay, whether it was that young men taking scientific studies were considered as ipso facto lost souls, or as having no souls to be saved at all, they were not admitted to the students seats at chapel—they were practically as of an inferior order." We may read between the lines, the need of a more liberal social consciousness as well as a new economic adjustment. We may glean from the series of struggles that faced the new education, some measure of the importance of the Peoples' Colleges, the Land-Grant Colleges in justifying themselves and in establishing their mission to maintain the genuine democracy of all learning, and a genuine learning for all democracy.

The year 1850 marks a distinct period in the history of industry and in the applications of scientific study to its development. At that time, there was no railroad west of the Mississippi, and continuity of lines was apparent only on the Atlantic seaboard, and from Southern Maine to Washington, D. C. Ten years witnessed the linking of the middle west and north-west, so that, in 1860, one-third of the total mileage was in the five states of Ohio, Indiana, Illinois, Michigan, and Wisconsin. Another decade pushed the trunk line to the Pacific coast; and empire after empire of industrial achievement awaited the toil of hand and brain. Labor with such a task must be "paced by machinery," science and invention must be crafted. It is significant, too, in this connection that whereas the number of patents issued from 1840 to 1850 totaled six thousand four hundred and eighty, the number in the next decade reached twenty-eight thousand. Paraphrasing Clark,[1] we may confidently affirm that while the technology of manufactures and industry in the period of beginnings was practical rather than scientific, that few were as yet formally trained to apply generalized knowledge to productive processes, it constitutes but the prologue to the narrative of greater things that followed. In this story of industrial, commercial, and scientific expansion, the Land-Grant Colleges have had a continuous and important part.

In Education, also, the mid-century marked significant changes. "About 1850 (writes Wickersham) teachers everywhere began to feel the stir of a new life. Among them inquiry, discussion, organization for mutual improvement, movement in advance became the order of the day." Teachers' Institutes[2] were held; the *Pennsylvania School Journal* was issued and became the official organ; State Teachers organized an association. Governors Bigler and Pollock strongly favored education, and sponsored legislation that resulted in the establishment of the County Superintendency, in Normal Schools (under Dr. Burrowes), in Teachers' Institutes. Increased funds for the Common Schools were provided, School Districts were given corporate powers, a minimum school term was established, definite courses of study outlined, and finally, the separation of the Department of Schools from that of the Department of State.

The year 1850 marked a decided interest in agriculture and agricultural education. A Report upon Agricultural Education to the Legislature of Massachusetts in 1850 affirmed that in foreign countries there were twenty-two agricultural schools ranking with our best colleges and universities, in the number and scope of the sciences taught, while there were fifty-four which

---

[1] History of Manufactures in the United States 1620-1860.
Carnegie Institution Publications, #215B.
[2] One of the pioneer county institutes was held at Oak Hall, September 30th, 1850 under the initiative of Mr. W. G. Waring, later the first Superintendent of the Farmers' High School of Pennsylvania.

would compare favorably with most American Colleges. It is remarkable, continued this Report, that the United States should not contain a single institution of the kind. To remedy this situation, efforts widespread and almost simultaneous were made, so that it is largely an academic question whether to Maine, Michigan, New York, Pennsylvania, Maryland, Massachusetts, Ohio, or Illinois should go the credit for the earliest effective support to professional instruction for farmers.

It should be recorded, however, that a school for vocational training in agriculture, as developed by Fellenberg in Switzerland, was established at Bristol in Bucks County in 1831. Also James Gowen[3] opened in 1848 a school for practical farmers at Mount Airy, and it was successfully conducted for five years under the charge of one John Wilkinson. From 1850, Mr. Gowen became one of the most frequent contributors to agricultural journals in awakening the farmers to the need of agricultural schools. Under date of April 20th, 1851, he wrote to the *Farm Journal*: "Let no farmer who respects his calling or loves Pennsylvania be backward to enter this field, and having entered it, let him never think of quitting it till the work is finished, till the goal is reached, and the prize awarded—the prize an agricultural college or colleges, instituted by the State wherein every farmer's son may receive a literary and professional education compatible with the dignity of agriculture and the pre-eminence of Pennsylvania."

It is important to note, too, that the Free School Law of 1834 provided that School Boards may purchase materials and employ artisans to teach mechanic arts and where practicable agricultural pursuits. So significant is this provision that I quote Section Ten of the act entire: "Whereas manual labor may be advantageously connected with intellectual and moral instruction in some or all of the schools, it shall be the duty of school directors to decide whether such connection in their respective districts shall take place or not;

---

[3] James Gowen styled himself in his Will as "formerly merchant now farmer," having retired to rural pursuits in middle life. He was well-known as a breeder of Durham cattle and his sales were famous throughout the country. He was one of the organizers of the Pennsylvania State Agricultural Society and served also as President. He was born March 17th, 1790 and died January 8th, 1873.

and if decided affirmatively they shall have power to purchase materials and employ artisans for the instruction of the pupils in the useful branches of the mechanic arts, and where practicable, in agricultural pursuits: Provided, nevertheless, that no such connection shall take place in any common school, unless four out of the six directors of the district shall agree thereto."

The mid-century shows, too, a distinct movement toward the multiplication of organizations among the agricultural classes. The Pennsylvania State Agricultural Society was formed January 21st, 1851, the following resolutions were adopted in convention which met in the Hall of the House of Representatives:

1st. That it is expedient to establish a Pennsylvania State Agricultural Society.

2nd. That a committee on Constitution be provided.

3rd. That a committee be appointed to memorialize the Legislature for a charter and an appropriation for the purpose of the Society.

4th. That it is expedient that instruction in agriculture be introduced into the system of education in the public schools of the Commonwealth.

County Societies were urged to become auxiliary to the State Society, and from this time the needs and claims of agriculture never lacked recognition in the economic and legislative councils of the Commonwealth.

Similar organizations were already in existence or were under process of formation in other states. In 1858, a list was compiled and published in the annual Report of the United States Patent Office (Agriculture being at this time under that Division), which gives State Agricultural Societies as twenty-seven; and "boards and societies existing in the United States connected wholly or in part with agriculture" as nine-hundred-twelve. Of these one-hundred-thirty-seven were in the South, while Pennsylvania had seventy-one,

New York ninety-seven, Illinois ninety-four, Ohio and Iowa seventy-four each.

A National Agricultural Convention was held in Washington in 1852, representing twenty-three States and Territories, at which an Association was formed and the federal development of agriculture was advocated. This convention met, too, as the direct result of measures inaugurated at the First Annual Session of the Pennsylvania State Agricultural Society.

It is important to recall, as a matter of just pride to Pennsylvania, that the Pennsylvania State Agricultural Society was founded upon the initiative of that ancient and honorable organization, The Philadelphia Society for the Promotion of Agriculture. It was distinctly recommended that a Farmers' Convention be held at Harrisburg on the third Tuesday of January 1851 for the purpose of forming a State Agricultural Society, to consider the landed interests, and to devise means to promote and advance the agriculture of the Commonwealth." Reviewing the progress made in other States in organizing State Societies, New York, Ohio, Maryland, Virginia, the query is raised: "With such examples before her, and such incentives to action, is it possible that Pennsylvania will not shake off her apathy, that like a blighting mildew seems to paralyze her energies and her progress?" Continuing the appeal affirmed, "That the importance, claims and calling of so large a body of citizens as the Farmers of Pennsylvania should be so long neglected, is not only paradoxical but discreditable... if the Legislature represent all classes, and, as admitted, the Farmers are the largest, then it is plain that the Farmers are to blame, if their interests are neglected—the remedy is in their own hands, and it is their fault if they do not effectually apply it."

Centre County sent six delegates, among whom were General James Irvin, who donated the land for The Farmers' High School, and William G. Waring, the first Superintendent of the Farm School. A charter was secured from the Legislature, and a permanent organization effected with Frederick Watts as chairman, so long and so prominent as President of the Board of Trustees of the College. The Secretary, Robert C. Walker, (also a member of the first Board of Trustees of the College) reported the first annual meeting as an organization registering not the "nominal meetings of a few theorists," but a society whose "members compose two thousand and ninety of the Farmers, Mechanics, and Artisans of Pennsylvania." To show the wider outlook and interest of these pioneers, resolutions were adopted for the appointment of a State Chemist (the germ of the State Department of Agriculture); for the establishment of a national bureau of agriculture; and for the organization of a national agricultural society. The hope is expressed of cooperation with all other societies which have for their object the improvement of agriculture and the mechanic arts.

The first annual exhibition was held at Harrisburg on the last three days of October 1851, with more than twenty thousand persons in attendance. More than a hundred covered sheds were erected. Large rings for the exhibition of horses and cattle were constructed. Long houses were built for almost every variety of "feathered domestics." The "mammoth tents" from the Rochester Fair were set up for articles of usefulness, for the fine arts, ladies handiwork, luxuries of the farm, the mechanic arts and inventions, etc. Plowing matches were held, and the judges on fourteen committees awarded the prizes.

The second annual exhibition at Lancaster drew larger crowds. The exhibit of "domestic Wines" was pronounced "sparkling," and the "mountain crab-apple cider" was recommended as a "mild and pleasant drink." The big pumpkin weighed sixty-two and a half pounds, and the "best sponge cake (really fine)" came from Chester County. Dr. T. H. Burrowes (later connected with our own college at a critical period) exhibited school desks and chairs, and was awarded a diploma.

At the third exhibition in Pittsburgh in 1853, it is estimated that one hundred thousand people were present on Thursday, the big day of the Fair. Two years later the exhibition at Harrisburg was graced by the presence of the President of the United States, Franklin Pierce, who delivered an address. Governor Pollock, Ex-Governors Bigler and Porter also participated in the agricultural and industrial jubilee, the President of the Pennsylvania State Agricultural Society, James Gowen, presiding. The records of the society thus featured this gala occasion: "The people from all parts of the state, including many of the most prominent citizens of both parties gathered around the chief Magistrate in great numbers; the ladies in carriages and in the surrounding tents; the platform crowded with distinguished gentlemen of the state government; a bright sun and a bracing breeze contributed to present a scene which is not often witnessed." Under the inspiration of such a tribute to industry by both nation and state, by nature and man, the judges proceeded with the task of awarding prizes for the best entries in cattle, horses, sheep, swine, poultry, fruit, tobacco, dairy products, honey, vegetables, flowers, household manufactures, silk, domestic wines, flour, agricultural machinery and the mechanic arts generally.

Pennsylvania contributed, also, a plan for agricultural and industrial training, as well as fostered new interests by associations and exhibitions. A really remarkable and noteworthy project was outlined by Superintendent A. L. Russell. Mr. Russell was Deputy Secretary of the Commonwealth under Townsend Haines in 1846, and became his successor as Secretary and as Superintendent of the Common Schools. He was a graduate of Washington College and read law under his father, but never practiced at the bar. During the Civil War he was Adjutant General and in 1879 was appointed by President Hayes, Consul at Montevideo, Uruguay; where he died in 1885. In the seventeenth annual report of the schools of the Commonwealth, dated January 6th, 1851, Mr. Russell writes: "I desire to submit a project of an institution, allied to them (the legislative bodies) in its nature and importance, -a State institution for special instruction in the theory and practice of agriculture, and for general instruction in all the branches of a high school course. The institution should be large enough to take care of five hundred pupils, a Board of three Regents elected by popular vote, a body of land of not less than a thousand acres, eight professors and sixteen associates, Professors of English Literature and Mental Philosophy; General History and Political Economy; Mathematics; Practical Farming and Rural Architecture; Agricultural Chemistry, General Chemistry; Geology; Botany; Natural Philosophy; Mechanics and Engineering; Comparative Anatomy and ex-officio Physician of the Institution; German Language."

A quarter of a million is the proposed original outlay. Need we wonder that Mr. Russell continued: "Thus viewed we see it in fact a college, not a college in the ancient sense of the name, devoted to elegant though chiefly theoretical learning but a college devoted wholly to real and inevitably profitable knowledge."

He clearly and succinctly stated the truth underlying the "manual labor fetish" of so many of these early plans and institutions. "While it is designed that the pupils should work as practical farmers, it cannot be supposed that they should spend time, periods for study, in menial offices profitless except for the moment."

The vision of the college as a public service agency expands. "Such an institution might furnish much of the teaching material, that in other states is provided at public expense by the maintenance of Normal Schools, by making it one of the conditions on which each of the three hundred State scholars is received into the institution, that after completion of his full term therein, a certain period shall be devoted to the state in the capacity of a teacher in her common schools." Prophetically, he affirms: "In no other Atlantic State of the Union could an Agricultural School be maintained with the same advantages to the pupils as in Central Pennsylvania." Enthusiastically, he pleads: "Is not the effort due to the reputation and the hopes of the State? Massachusetts has her Harvard; Connecticut has her Yale; New Jersey has her Nassau Hall; may not Pennsylvania behold her Agricultural College, destined at no remote day, in the robustness of youth and with none of the burdens of antiquated notions to check its progress leaving these venerable competitors far behind in the race for honors which the age will award only to practical knowledge."

One cannot but be impressed, by even so brief a recital as this of the new professional sense of democracy which the mid-century heralded. Equally significant is the recognition of the inter-relation, the inevitable inter-relation of agriculture, the industries and education, as the trinity of interests, the sacred and responsible compact of this growing sense of vital democracy. The Commonwealth bears an ancient and honorable part, too, in furthering the interdependence of these activities. A pamphlet by George Logan published in

Philadelphia in 1800 is entitled, a Letter to the Citizens of Pennsylvania on the necessity of promoting Agriculture, Manufactures and the Useful Arts. He urged an association whose object shall be: "To procure from the fertile soil of Pennsylvania every production it is capable of affording, and from the labor and ingenuity of independent citizens every article of manufacture and of the useful arts necessary to render our country happy, prosperous, and truly independent." Prior to this, on February 11th, 1785, "twenty-three eminent citizens who had a propensity to agriculture met at the sign of the cock in Front Street and formed the Philadelphia Society for Promoting Agriculture." There were then, probably, but two Agricultural Societies in the Union. The seal of the society bore the motto, Venerate the Plow; and among its members were Washington, Jefferson and Franklin.

A committee of the society made a report, January 21st, 1794 toward correlating and extending the efforts now made "to acquire other useful knowledge suitable for the agricultural citizens of the State." The committee proposed to work through institutions already established; through increase of funds of the society; by fairs and premiums; by incorporation in the common schools; by action of the legislature; by courses, books, and by schoolmasters who combine the subject of agriculture with other parts of education. Of this report, Dr. A. C. True, the historian of American Agriculture affirms that it seems to have been the first formal attempt made in the United States to urge the claims of agricultural education and experiment upon the attention of a law making body.

While the chief interests of this venerable organization, venerating the plow, were commercial and social, yet it maintained that: "Many citizens have a mistaken idea that their not being agriculturists disqualifies them from being useful members of our Society. The interests of Commerce, Arts and Manufactures form, with agriculture, an indissoluble union to which citizens of every class and calling have it in their power amply to contribute."

This contribution to agriculture and to manufactures, this contribution to citizenship, to education and to social responsibility found its effective embodiment in the pioneer activities of such institutions as our own, the forerunners of our system of Peoples' Colleges, the State Colleges and Universities. It is to the history of one of these pioneers, known successively as The Farmers' High School of Pennsylvania, chartered in 1854 and rechartered in 1855; The Agricultural College of Pennsylvania, 1862; and The Pennsylvania State College, 1874, that this record of story and document is devoted.

Part II

Founding and Refounding the College

1853 – 1864

CHAPTER 2

Establishing a College by a Convention

"A new light is about to break upon the Agricultural Community" 1857

Frederick Watts, President of the Board of Trustees

1855 – 1874

"The Agricultural College of Pennsylvania has for its object to associate a high degree of intelligence with the practice of Agriculture and the Industrial arts, and to seek to make use of this intelligence in developing the Agricultural and Industrial resources of the country, and protecting its interests."

President Evan Pugh

1859 – 1864

Official recognition of these movements toward a new industrial training in both nation and state found expression in the papers of Governors William Bigler and James Pollock, the former from 1852 to 1855, and the latter from 1855 to 1858. In his inaugural address, Governor Bigler commends the organization of the Pennsylvania Agricultural Society and pledges the administration to a thoughtful and efficient support of the needs of agriculture. From his messages of succeeding years, much might with profit be quoted. There is ample proof that a new spirit was astir that was to have its echoes in legislative halls. In 1852, he writes:

"The subject of agriculture has not, it seems to me, received that attention in this state which its exceeding importance would seem to justify... The art of tilling the soil in such manner as to secure the largest yield of vegetable matter of which it is capable, and the application of the principles of science to that art, so far as indispensable to the attainment of this end, is a topic worthy of the attention of the best minds of the state. Agriculture is the primitive, as it is the most necessary, occupation of man. It was at the beginning of his existence, and is at the foundation of all of his pursuits. In this Commonwealth, it is peculiarly adapted to the soil, to the climate, and to the habits of the people, and constitutes their greatest source of wealth and happiness. It is the agriculturist who pays the largest share of the country's taxes in time of peace and furnishes the greatest number of her soldiers in time of war. It is the most steady, peaceful and dignified, as it is the least exacting, of all our good interests... But is it not astonishing, that in this progressive country of ours, so suited to agriculture, and in this age of scientific discoveries and perfection in all the arts, that no institutions to impart instruction in the science of agriculture have been established? It is true that societies have been formed in a number of the states, and exhibitions have been held calculated to awaken the people to the importance of this subject. Our State Society, organized about two years since, has held two exhibitions, which have done much good in the way of sending to all parts of the state the best breed of domestic animals, the best grains and seeds and the most approved agricultural machinery. But it seems to me that the government might justly lend her aid and countenance to this good work. In Maryland, an agricultural Chemist has been employed by the state, and I am informed that the results of his investigations have been highly satisfactory and useful to the people. Cannot the great State of Pennsylvania do as much for her farmers? She has expended a large sum in the development of her mineral resources, and has cherished her manufactures by every-proper means, and it is right that she should now do something for her agriculturists. I, therefore, respectfully recommend the appointment of an Agricultural Chemist, with a moderate salary, leaving the details of his duties to be suggested by the state and county societies."

In the Message of 1853, fuller appreciation of the new forces at work is felt: "Efforts, extensive, energetic, and highly commendable, are being made in all parts of the country to advance the interests of agriculture, by the dissemination of correct information concerning this great pursuit, and in this way bestow upon the farmer the blessings of a scientific as well as a greatly refined practical understanding of the noble work in which he is engaged... The utility of establishing an agricultural college, with a model farm attached, wherein the principles of a scientific cultivation of the soil and manual labor in academical studies, has been strongly urged upon my attention. Such an institution and system of education, it is believed, would at the same time improve the physical and moral condition of the professional and mercantile classes and promote the social and intellectual attainment of the agriculturist, mechanic and laborer, in addition to the vast benefits it would confer upon the pursuit of the farmer. These considerations and others which will doubtless be presented by the advocates of the proposed institution will commend the subject to your favorable consideration. It is believed that such an institution can be successfully organized under the auspices of the state and county societies."

The important part that Governor James Pollock took in legislation and in the work of locating and establishing the institution will presently appear. We must first trace the way in which these vague, wide-spread longings and hopes in a new form of education found legal expression, of how wishes became realities, ideals became hopes.

The following Resolutions adopted at the Second Annual Meeting of The Pennsylvania State Agricultural Society, January 18th, 1853 mark the first *official* step toward the founding of The Pennsylvania State College: Resolved, That the Pennsylvania State Agricultural Society highly approves and concurs in the recommendation of the Governor in his annual message that an institution to impart instruction in the science of Agriculture should be established, and that legislative provision be made for the appointment of a State Agricultural Chemist. Resolved that a committee of five be appointed to report at an adjourned meeting this evening, on the expediency of adopting measures for the establishment of a State Agricultural School to be called, "The Farmers' High School of the State of Pennsylvania." The chairman, the Honorable Frederick Watts, appointed Algernon S. Roberts, A. O. Hiester, James Konigmacher, James Carothers, and David Mellinger. This Committee reported the present "as an auspicious period for the introduction into the State of Pennsylvania of a scientific and practical education particularly adopted to the improvement and extension of agricultural knowledge", and recommended: "That an Agricultural Convention be held at Harrisburg, on Tuesday, the 8th of March next, to adopt measures for the establishment of an agricultural institution, to be styled, The Farmers' High School of Pennsylvania with a model farm attached thereto; and that the convention consist of as many delegates from each district as there are Senators and Representatives in the Legislature from the same; said delegates to be chosen by the Agricultural Societies, where such are located, and in other districts, by the friends of agricultural education."

The convention met in the Senate Chamber in Harrisburg, and was called to order by Simon Cameron. The officers of the State Agricultural Society present were admitted to seats in the Convention, also the Governor and Heads of Departments were invited to participate in the proceedings.

Thirty-six counties were represented, the Philadelphia Society for Promoting Agriculture had nine delegates, with such well-known names as those of Alfred L. Elwyn, John C. Cresson, Algernon S. Roberts, William M. Meredith, David Landreth, Isaac Newton, John S. Hart, Charles B. Trego, and Alfred L. Kennedy. The permanent chairman, John Strohm of Lancaster

County appointed as a committee "to prepare business for the action of the Convention", G. Blight Browne of Montgomery; A. L. Elwyn and Algernon S. Roberts of Philadelphia; Frederick Watts of Cumberland; Simon Cameron of Dauphin; Benjamin Herr of Lancaster, and H. N. McAllister of Centre. Upon motion of Mr. Roberts, John S. Hart of Philadelphia was added to the Committee.

The report was read by Frederick Watts. It outlined the proposed institution as to title, situation, quality of land, educational organization, pupils, teachers, assistants, buildings, and resources. "There is a spirit of examination abroad in the world, the committee affirmed, from whose scrutiny nothing escapes; and agriculture, which, until within a few years, was regarded as a kind of tranquil retirement for dull minds, has passed to the crucible of the chemist, the closet of the philosopher, under the close and deep examination of the man of science, and entered among the profound speculations of the political economist. The destiny of this noble art is now entirely removed from mere manual dexterity or the pursuit of old customs. Powerful and acute minds are busy with it minutely examining its practical details, in all its departments, endeavoring to break down the obstinacy of old ideas, by analysis of their truth, and form principles and philosophy from what has heretofore been but a crude mass of ill arranged and imperfectly examined assertions. It is now a progressive art, and rapidly assuming the form and condition of a science. Conscious of this, those who have the interests of agriculture at heart, have determined to propose to their fellow citizens, and the farmers of the State, a plan by which they can, not only keep pace with the general movement, but prevent themselves from falling behind other states, which are already commencing the establishment of Schools and Professorships of Agriculture."

The report as a whole is prophetic of the early organization and work of the institution which it sponsored. The location is to be accessible to markets but not near a large town. Its course of study is to be rigidly prescribed, to include a labor detail of not less than three hours daily. Its buildings and equipment are to be substantial and ample, such as would meet the approval of the constituency they are intended to serve. "Our view is to let this project have a beginning, and we have all confidence, that, under the general influence of enlightened minds, it will work itself into public favor."

There remained for this unique founding of a college by a convention, but to take the decisive step, embodied in the following resolution: "That... be a Committee whose duty it shall be to draft a bill in accordance with the principles of this report, and submit the same for the action of the Legislature." The Convention approved as such Committee, Frederick Watts of Cumberland; Simon Cameron of Dauphin; Christian Myers of Clarion; H. Jones Brooke of Delaware; and John Strohm of Lancaster.

The Convention adjourned on March 8th, and three days later a bill was introduced in the Senate, entitled an Act to establish an Agricultural School. On March 23rd, the bill was reported from the Committee on Agriculture and Domestic Manufacturers as an Act to incorporate the Farmers' High School. On April 7th, it was considered by the Senate in a Committee of the whole. It failed of passage owing to the near approach of adjournment, but also because of a feature of the bill which provided for free scholars. An interest had been awakened, however, and the Agricultural and other journals contain renewed discussions of the aims and purposes of the proposed school. Appeals for a united effort on the part of all the friends of agricultural education are made that the bill does not fail a second time. Encouragement was given to the project by a bequest of Elliott Cresson of five thousand dollars toward the erection and support of an agricultural college. Mr. Cresson, who was a member of the Philadelphia Society for Promoting Agriculture, died on February 20th, 1854.

At the session of the Legislature in 1854, an enabling act or charter was approved, and received the signature of Governor William Bigler. It provided for an institution to be known as the Farmers' High School of Pennsylvania, for a Board of Trustees composed of the President and Vice-President of the Pennsylvania State Agricultural Society and the President of the several county agricultural societies which shall at any time have been organized for more than one year. This group of some sixty-five trustees was given full power to organize the institution, secure a location, erect buildings, select a faculty, hold and transfer property in perpetuity. The sole provision for maintenance was the clause in Section Eight, that it shall be lawful for the State Agricultural Society to appropriate the sum of ten thousand dollars out of its funds.

Attempts were made to organize under this charter. It was approved on the thirteenth day of April; thirteen members constituted a quorum for the transaction of business; the trustees met on the thirteenth of June and again on the thirteenth of July but failed because of real reasons, rather than that of fate. Responsibility was so dissipated and divided that only a few of the designated trustees responded. Subject to such constant changes as these elective trustees were, it could not be expected that the necessary sacrifices would be made. Consequently no quorum was present, but a Committee was appointed to issue an Address to the People of Pennsylvania; to solicit and examine proposals for the location of the proposed school; and to secure from the next legislature an amended charter which shall remedy the manifest defects of that of 1854. This Committee consisting of Frederick Watts, Geo. W. Woodward, and A. L. Elwyn entered with enthusiasm upon their work, used the press of the state to awaken interest and crystalize sentiment. There was readily secured, too, from the legislature of 1855, a repeal of the old and the enactment of a new charter. This was approved by Governor James Pollock on February 22nd, 1855. This is, therefore, the natal day of The Pennsylvania State College, and sharing in the glory which radiates from the Father of his country.

The new charter provided for a Board of Trustees, four of whom were ex-officio, the Governor of the Commonwealth; the Secretary of the Commonwealth; the President of The Pennsylvania State Agricultural Society; and The Principal of the Institution; together with nine members named in the charter. These were Dr. A. L. Elwyn and Algernon S. Roberts of the city of Philadelphia; Hugh Nelson McAllister of Centre; Robert C. Walker of Allegheny; James Miles of Erie; John Strohm of Lancaster; A. O. Hiester of Dauphin; William Jessup of Susquehanna; and Frederick Watts of Cumberland. The successors of these charter trustees were elected by the votes of the Executive Committee of the Pennsylvania State Agricultural Society and of three representatives from each County Agricultural Society which shall have been organized at least three months preceding the time of election. The Board was empowered to organize at Harrisburg on the second Thursday of June following the passage of the Act. The Board was instructed to determine the location; by purchase, gift, grant or otherwise secure "a tract of land containing at least two hundred acres and not exceeding two thousand acres;" carry out such improvements and alterations "as will make it an institution properly adapted to the instruction of youth in the art of farming. The Board shall choose a man as Principal, a man of scientific attainments who shall be a good practical farmer, and other professors, teachers, or tutors as shall be qualified to impart to pupils under their charge, a knowledge of the English language, grammar, geography, history, mathematics, chemistry, and such other branches of natural and exact sciences as will conduce to the proper education of a farmer." The pupils are to "perform all the labor necessary in the cultivation of the farm, and shall thus be instructed and taught all things necessary to be known by a farmer."

Provision for a Treasurer of the Institution was enacted, and authority given for the payment of ten thousand dollars by the State Agricultural Society, and for such further appropriations, annually, out of their funds as will aid in the prosecution of this object. An annual report was made a duty of the Board, to be transmitted by the Pennsylvania State Agricultural Society, together with the Report of the Society, to the Legislature.

Thus the institution is launched, its immediate course charted. Certain aspects of its sailing orders are clear. It is to be an institution for the training of students in the science and art of agriculture. It is to connect with the common schools, and to embody manual labor both for its bearing upon the science and art of farming, but also as bringing the opportunities of the institution within the reach of the sons of toil. It is to be an agency of the Agricultural Society of the State (itself a child of the State) for the purposes of higher education. It is thus manifestly a public and semi-state institution from the beginning, while its incorporation under Federal Act (the Morrill Act of 1862), ratified by solemn compact with the Commonwealth of Pennsylvania renders it a public and state institution in very fact. A farm bloc, an educational farm bloc, it was; not however selfishly conceived or with even a distinct class consciousness. Its high purpose was to give to the industrial masses an opportunity to serve more adequately the country in civic affairs, in political life, in school and church. The laborer, the farmer, the artisan were to be evaluated not as class distinctions, but as an educated citizenship ready to assume a share of the burdens of democracy as well as reap the rewards.

The Board organized under the charter at Harrisburg, June 14th, 1855, by electing Governor James Pollock, Chairman, and Robert C. Walker, Secretary. With commendable dispatch, they proceeded to the consideration of a location for the institution. Previous solicitations had brought out the following proposals:

James Miles of Erie, James Irvin of Centre County, and Elias Baker of Blair County, each offered two hundred acres of land. Joseph Bailey of Perry County proposed to sell two thousand acres, and the estate of George A. Bayard of Allegheny, six hundred acres, as suitable sites. Subsequently offers were received increasing to four hundred acres the donation of Elias Baker. The Honorable Simon Cameron proposed a location in Dauphin County. Any one of three farms was tendered in Franklin County, while from Union County came an offer to sell two hundred and sixty-five acres. A second proposition from Blair County to guarantee the sum of ten thousand dollars provided their site was chosen gave added interest. Completing the list of proposals, Centre County submitted the following paper:

To the Trustees of the Farmers' High School of Pennsylvania.

Gentlemen: Whereas the citizens of Centre and Huntingdon Counties have subscribed ten thousand dollars to the Farmers' High School of Pennsylvania on condition the institution be located on the lands offered by General James Irvin of Centre County, and Whereas the subscription and standing of many of the subscribers are unknown to the Trustees, we do hereby guarantee that the sum of ten thousand dollars shall be collected and paid upon subscriptions to the Farmers' High School of Pennsylvania agreeable to the terms and conditions thereof.

12 September 1855

Signed
H. N. McAllister
James Irvin
A. G. Curtin

Here were prospective locations, easily accessible to the cities, Erie, Pittsburgh, Altoona, Harrisburg, and Chambersburg, as well as in rural central Pennsylvania. A committee consisting of Governor Pollock, Judge Watts, and Dr. Elwyn examined the sites, and reported a really wide spread interest over the State in the projected institution. They set forth the advantages and claims of the various propositions with genuine impartiality. They affirmed that no site offered was ineligible. In view of the importance of the question, and in order that any offers subsequently received may have due consideration, the committee asked to be continued, with instructions that all the "proceedings thus far be published."

At the third meeting of the Board, September 12th, 1855, the Committee completed an account of its survey. After due deliberation (Governor Pollock presiding) the following motion was made by Judge Watts: "Resolved that the adoption of the proposition of General James Irvin for the location of the Farmers' High School will best promote the interests of the Institution, and that the same is hereby adopted." Substitute motions were offered by James Gowen and A. L. Elwyn for other sites but both motions failed. Judge Watts with eminent candor and fairness moved postponement, and the appointment of a new committee consisting of James Gowen, A. O. Hiester and John Strohm to examine sites and made a report to the Board. This motion was also voted down, as was another to substitute the offer of George A. Bayard. The original resolution was thereupon decided in the affirmative.

Sentiment on location was thus by no means unanimous, but of the spirit of fairness and impartiality on the part of the Committee and of the Board of Trustees there is unquestioned evidence. The Chosen site had certainly no urban, civic or journalistic influences in its behalf. In some quarters, it was apparently felt that the location was a foregone conclusion. An illuminating note appeared in *The Pennsylvania Telegraph and Whig State Journal* of March 29th, 1854. After noting the passage of the Bill by the House incorporating the Pennsylvania Agricultural School, the rather complacent remark follows; "The location of this school will probably be at Harrisburg which will add another interesting feature to our place."

A committee was appointed consisting of Frederick Watts, H. N. McAllister, and James Miles to act with the Principal when elected in preparing the site and erecting buildings for the work of the School. The Board added the minute that Moses Thompson of Centre Furnace act with the Committee. He was an honored co-worker and efficient local agent in carrying out the plans and purposes of the Board, and also gave his business acumen and financial backing in times of need. He served the Board as Secretary from 1859 to 1865, and as Treasurer from 1867 to 1874.

The institution now had a local habitation and a name. The enterprise of the citizens of Centre County, plus its central position in the Commonwealth, perchance even the surpassing beauty of its mountains and valleys won the votes of these pioneers of a new experiment in education. The local steps in the campaign should be recorded. At a meeting of the Centre County Agricultural Society, January 24th, 1855, a resolution was presented endorsing the movement for an Agricultural High School, and urging the representatives in the Legislature to grant the charter. General James Irvin took the floor and made a vigorous speech in support of the Resolution. He fitted deeds to words by offering to donate two hundred acres of land provided the Institution be located in Centre County. On February 22nd, 1855, he communicated the offer in writing to the Executive Committee of the Pennsylvania Agricultural Society, by whom it was referred to the Board of Trustees.

On June 20th, the site was visited by the Committee of the Board (of which we have written), accompanied by other members of the Board. A cloud of witnesses must, also, have foregathered since "the Trustees and all the company repaired to the dwelling house of Moses Thompson at Centre

Furnace where one hundred and fifty persons were entertained by a sumptuous dinner prepared by Mrs. Thompson."

Was the location unwise? As late as 1881 prominent citizens of the Commonwealth so testified, and some members of the Board agreed reluctantly. In the early legislative campaigns, the location as unfortunate and inaccessible was capitalized by opponents of the college. Visiting committees deplored an adequate Baedeker to guide them to the institution which was located in Centre County near Boalsburg, Spruce Creek, Lewistown, or Bellefonte, but where were they?

An answer to some of these criticisms was made by George W. Woodward in the annual address before the Pennsylvania State Agricultural Society at Pittsburgh on October 3rd, 1856. "In the minds of some of the best friends of this enterprise serious objections are entertained to the location of the school. Centre County contains some of the best farm land and some of the best farmers in Pennsylvania. No where are better crops of wheat and corn produced than in Nittany and Penn's Valleys, and in one of the most healthful and beautiful portions of the latter is the farm school to be planted. It was the generosity of the donor which determined the location. The objections have reference principally to the want of water and the distance from railroad communication. The first of these objections I am assured can and will be obviated, and as to the latter I have never felt its force. The school will be some twenty miles from the Central Railroad, and in my judgment, that is near enough. Boys had better be away from the temptations and annoyances peculiar to railroads whilst acquiring education. And surely they can travel twenty miles without steam in pursuit of such advantages as this school is to offer." Three years later, the Editor of the *Public Ledger* in an editorial under date of March 28th, 1859 wrote: "We wish the place itself were more accessible. To call it 'near Boalsburg' is not very clear, till one knows where Boalsburg is. It is in Centre County, twelve miles from Bellefonte; but the school is not so near even Boalsburg, we believe, but that it has been necessary to establish a 'Farm School Post-Office' for its special accommodation. It is a central position, and anticipated railroads will ultimately bring it more within reach. Till then, in these days of rapid travel, twenty-five miles by stage over the 'seven mountains' from the nearest station, is a serious thing. But this once accomplished, the studious youth will find himself in an extremely beautiful and salubrious region, far from the temptations of a populous community, and with highly valuable helps and applicances for his improvement. We wish that multitudes of such might faithfully try its opportunities for themselves."

Student publications have frequently taken a fling at the "inaccessible centrality" of our location, but have ended by sober appraisement of compensating advantages, natural, social, and intellectual. Thrown upon our own resources and developing our own environment as needs arose, we have a more spontaneous and distinctive college spirit than where the economic and social environments are more powerful and compelling. Judge Watts in his famous "Barn Speech" at thee Farm School spoke wise words for all time on behalf of the Board on September 2nd, 1857: "Let there be no adverse feelings founded on local preference.

What motive could there be to induce those who examined and determined the locality of this school to do else than right? With the approval of my associates, I could gladly have taken it into my own dear valley of Cumberland, but in the exercise of a sound and clear judgment (I speak for all as an inconsiderable one only), the Board having looked over all proposed lands and considered all circumstances, believed the one chosen to be the best. It is possible that we were in fault, yet I have ever believed the selection made combined more advantages than any other offered, and I ask for myself and associates the credit at least of honest motives, and of all to consider how many of the most essential advantages of soil, surface, exposure, healthfulness, and centrality are combined in the ground we have met upon."

Let us make it unanimous by enrolling Mount Nittany, Bald Top, the beautiful valleys of Nittany and Penn upon our Faculty. Let us glory in our broad expanse of campus, as it is and as it will be no better site for men and women to grow wise and sane, to earn and learn citizenship in the industrial and social world, than here.

CHAPTER 3

Personalia of the Founders

"The secret of its success... is to be found in the indomitable perseverance of a small number of public-spirited men, who were determined it should not fail."

Dr. Evan Pugh

1862

The first Board of Trustees, the Governor of the Commonwealth, The Secretary of the Commonwealth, the President of the State Agricultural Society; and the Principal of the institution, Ex-Officio; together with nine appointees, was made up of men successful in their callings, educated professional men. They were impelled to service outside their immediate interests by their zeal for the new experiment in education. There were among them graduates of Harvard, Yale, Princeton, University of Pennsylvania, Jefferson, Dickinson, and others. Seven were lawyers, four of whom held judicial posts. There were business men of large interests. Three were primarily agriculturists. Out of the thirteen, nine were indirectly engaged in agriculture in connection with professional and business activities. The cities of Philadelphia and Pittsburgh were represented, as were the following counties, Lancaster, Susquehanna, Centre, Northumberland, Erie, Dauphin, Chester, and Cumberland.

Governor James Pollock was a warm supporter of education, and took much more than official interest in founding, locating and developing the Farmers' High School. He presided at meetings of the Board, served on committees, and sponsored both in public and private the plans and prospects of the institution. He was graduated from Princeton in 1831 and received the degree of Doctor of Laws from the same institution and also from Jefferson College. He was by profession a lawyer, and also served as President Judge. A man of large vision in the lines of the new agricultural and industrial movement, he predicted in 1848, a trunk line to the Pacific Coast in less than a quarter of a century. He served but one term as Governor, having refused a re-nomination, but his popularity was so great that upon leaving Harrisburg at the close of his administration, both Houses "adjourned and accompanied him to the cars." His life was characterized by earnest endeavor in educational and religious reforms; and the institution may well congratulate itself in having had so wise and helpful a leader on its first Board of Trustees.

Andrew G. Curtin was Secretary of the Commonwealth and Superintendent of Schools under Governor Pollock, and later Governor and Minister to Russia. As War Governor he won "renown throughout the country and added historic grandeur to the annals of his native

Commonwealth." He was closely identified with men and measures during the early years of the college; the land-grant bestowal upon it; the early struggle for ways and means.

James Gowen, as previously intimated, was a well-known friend and supporter of Agricultural training, while John Strohm, Algernon S. Roberts and Robert C. Walker were prominent business men, miller, iron master, and ship builder whose industrial achievements in the midst of increasing complexity and competition led them to advocate a new type of education.

Dr. A. L. Elwyn was of English descent, his father was born at Canterbury and was a graduate of Oxford. His son, Alfred was born at Portsmouth, New Hampshire, July 9, 1804. He attended Exeter Academy, and graduated from Harvard in 1823. He spent three years in reading medicine, continuing his studies during a three years' sojourn in England, Scotland and on the continent. He received in 1831 the degree of M. D. from the University of Pennsylvania, but never practiced his profession. He preferred outdoor life and was deeply interested in rural life and farming. He was one of the founders of the State Agricultural Society, interested in Science, one of the oldest members of the American Association for the Advancement of Science, and of the Academy of Natural Sciences. He was for many years a trustee of Girard College, and an officer of the Pennsylvania Historical Society. As a public servant and philanthropist, his work led to tangible results in the aid of the blind; in organization looking to the prevention of cruelty to animals, and to the Training School for Feeble Minded at Elwyn. His interest in farming was experimental as well as practical, and the first guano on lands in Chester County was applied by him. His taste, dignity, thorough training, and wide experience gave to his counsels a peculiar value in those early days. He resigned as trustee in 1858, but was instrumental with others, in the selection of Dr. Pugh as the first President.

William Jessup was a native of Susquehanna County, a graduate of Yale, a lawyer and judge. From 1853 to 1857 he was President of the Lackawanna Railroad, and representative of its legal relations in the city of New York. Hamilton College conferred upon him the degree of Doctor of Laws in 1848, and his own effective support of social, educational, agricultural and religious movements are continued by the honored names of two sons in educational missions at Beirut. Mr. Jessup was a vital exponent of the industrial classes, and of their right to the opportunities for training. As president of the Society for the Promotion of Agriculture and Mechanic Arts in his native county, he stated his creed thus: "I can never consent that the non-producing class shall claim in any respect a superiority over those who rise in the morning of every day to daily toil; who work laboring with their own hands."

Judge James Miles of Erie and A. O. Hiester of Dauphin served the college in much the same way. Both were trained in law and business, and both were interested in farming. Miles was engaged with his father in developing and leasing lands in Erie County. Large tracts were reclaimed from the wilderness, and opportunities for settlement effected. Hiester was interested in industrial enterprises in Harrisburg, in banking and in passenger railways, while in his country home, he enjoyed and perfected the growth of fruit and plant. Both served as trustees until their respective deaths, Miles serving thirteen years and Hiester, fifteen years. Each also had sons who were honored successors on the Board.

But the two men upon whose shoulders fell the chief burdens of the institution were Hugh Nelson McAllister and Frederick Watts. No tribute can be excessive of the self-sacrificing, self-denying, persistent, intelligent labors of these men—labors not for honor or fame, but "each for the joy of working" wrought that the ideals, hopes, and needs of the industrial classes might become vocal in this new type of institution and training.

Mr. McAllister was born in Juniata County, June 28th, 1809. He graduated at Jefferson College in 1833, read law in Bellefonte, and later attended law school in Carlisle. He practiced at the bar for thirty-eight years, everywhere respected as "honest and upright, stern for the right, for temperance, education, and reform." Governors Bigler and Curtin desired to appoint him to judicial posts, for which he was eminently fitted but he declined. Although beyond military age and with frail health, he served in the Civil War until relieved by younger men. He was one of the delegates to "reform the State Constitution" in 1873, but due to excessive strain and overwork, he became ill and died in Philadelphia, May 5th, 1873 before the convention had completed its work.

In 1859, he formed a law partnership with James A. Beaver, and thus trained a worthy successor upon whom his mantle fell in 1873. During the years 1854 to 1873, there was scarcely a day which did not have some task for the college which demanded his thought or counsel. Letters to Mr. Waring, the first Superintendent, Dr. Pugh, the first President, Trustee and Business Committee records, and even the Faculty minutes show the vital interest in and oversight of all the affairs of the institution, financial, scholastic, academic, or disciplinary. The Faculty paid tribute to his work and worth in a series of resolutions: "That the Agricultural College of Pennsylvania has experienced in his death the loss of one who by his zeal; his ungrudging sacrifice of time, money and effort in its behalf; his hopefulness in the dark hours of its history; and his influence in winning others to its support has endeared his memory not only to its Faculty and Students but also to the friends of practical education throughout the country." The Board also passed resolutions, witnessing "the valuable services which he rendered in the establishment of this Institution and the conscientious and persevering energy with which he prosecuted its objects and purposes," extolling also "our high regard for his public services and private virtues." McAllister Hall pays tribute to his memory.

Frederick Watts was another member of this first Board of Trustees without whose labors prior to the charter, and during the years of early struggle, the institution could hardly have come into existence. He was President of The Board from 1854 to 1874, the public spokesman and representative of the Institution in the Councils of the Commonwealth. He spoke with authority, because he thought and wrought with integrity. He embodied in a peculiarly effective manner the necessity of training for the agricultural and industrial workers, if they are to have their due weight and influence in the solution of the problems of democracy. For the proper balance in government, he looked away from mere class, autocratic, or paternalistic control, to mass, to democratic, to self-expressed control. Here was the "new light" upon the way in which he set out to restore to the common people their right to learn as well as earn, to rule with intelligence in industry and in legislative halls, equally with the so-called professional classes.

Frederick Watts was born May 9th, 1801 and graduated from Dickinson at the age of eighteen. He entered the office of Andrew Carothers of Carlisle as a law student, and was later admitted to partnership. He was president of the Cumberland Valley Railroad for twenty-six years. As President of the Cumberland County Agricultural Society, as well as farm manager and operator, he was actively identified with the progress of agriculture in Pennsylvania. He was a man of large vision as to its needs and possibilities. Dr. Pugh wrote in 1862, that an "Agricultural Institution of learning adapted to the wants of the farmer had been a favorite idea with the present worthy President of the Board of Trustees of the Agricultural College of Pennsylvania for twenty years before this institution was founded, but the pressing duties of public life prevented him from devoting time to the advocacy of these views, till in 1853, the subject was brought before the Pennsylvania State Agricultural Society."

In 1871, he was urged for appointment as Commissioner of Agriculture at Washington and was tendered the place by President U. S. Grant. A letter to his friend H. N. McAllister concerning the appointment shows his modest demeanor and simple, unaffected honesty. It deserves a place here for its historic value as well as its personal revelation. Under date of July 1st, 1871, he wrote: "You have doubtless seen the offer of Commissioner of Agriculture offered to me and the various reasons for it. The truth is, the President offered me the appointment which I declined pe-remptorily because I could not think of breaking up my present home connections. The offer was repeated and pressed upon me by Mr. Scott and Mr. Cameron. My friends around me whom I consulted insisted upon my acceptance, and I was prevailed upon to say—that if the President still insisted upon it I would accept and added it is greatly against my inclinations and if the President can suit himself with anybody else it will be exceedingly acceptable to me—and thus the matter now rests... I do not desire that any publicity be given to my position in the matter but I communicate to you because I know you take an interest in what concerns me."

He served with distinction for six years, and was instrumental in convening nation wide associations to give consideration to the opportunities and needs of agriculture and mechanic arts. He broadened and intensified the work of the department at Washington—signally stressing some of the scientific bearings and inaugurating a new division of forestry and forest conservation.

His business interests were engrossing, yet his philanthropic enterprises were not less so. His devotion to the college in time, care and energy would lead one to suppose that this was his chief interest. He was described as a "man of great force of character and abiding self-confidence. As a lawyer he occupied a front rank for nearly half a century." Again he was portrayed as a man of large intellect, sterling integrity, and unblemished honor. Watts Hall expresses the recognition by the Commonwealth of the significance of his labors for The Pennsylvania State College, and the College honors itself, no less than one of its real founders in Watts Memorial Hall.

The donor of the land, General James Irvin was a native of Centre County, born at Linden Hall on February 18th, 1800. As merchant and grain dealer at Oak Hall, later purchasing with his father an interest in Centre Furnace, he became a large owner of lands, mills, and furnaces. In 1840, he was elected to Congress, and his first speech was in the interest of American industries. By the Whig Party, he was put in nomination for Governor in 1847, but was defeated by Francis R. Shunk. He resumed his business interests, and in 1854, he was the proprietor of ten charcoal blast furnaces, the forge and rolling mill at Milesburg, and large landed estates. His "handsome stone mansion" was a landmark in the community, and the radiating center of generous hospitality. His spirit of helpfulness in religious, social and educational causes, together with his buoyant enterprise in turnpikes, canals, and railroads led to the depletion of his fortune. Because of the panic of 1857, he retired from active business. He died at Hecla, November 28th, 1862. He was a "gentleman of the old school" generous, large minded, public spirited.

He gave to the Farmers' High School not only of his means, but of his confident faith in the training of the worker. His presence and address helped, also, to win friends for the Farm School, and his staunch business integrity was ever at the service of the institution's credit.

Mention should be made, also, among the founders, of Edward C. Humes, Treasurer from 1855 to 1867. He built up one of the strongest banking institutions in the state. His financial backing and experience were placed freely at the disposal of the institution—baring with courage and patience large overdrafts of funds, and carrying almost single handed at times, the very honor and credit of the struggling college.

Among the administrative and educational leaders in giving form and substance to these early efforts, two are of the first importance, Superintendent W. G. Waring and Dr. Evan Pugh. The significance of the work of each appears in the story of the plant, buildings, farm and college yard, as well as in the program of student training and discipline. A few biographical facts, here will best serve to set the stage.

William G. Waring was born in England, but came to America in 1833 at seventeen years of age. In connection with earning a livelihood, he taught a night school for factory workers. Growing plants and developing nursery practice were his chief interests; his secondary enthusiasms were for teaching and teachers' institutes. He wrote much and spoke earnestly for agricultural education, aided in securing for Centre County the Farm School; laid out grounds and buildings; and carried on the operations of plant, farm and school, under the direction of the Business Committee of the Board, during the years prior to the arrival of Dr. Pugh in October 1859. He published a Fruit Growers' Handbook, bearing the imprint Boalsburg, Centre County, Pennsylvania, 1851, a Concise Manual of Directions for the Selection and Culture of the Best Hardy Fruits in the Garden or Orchard. He issued, also, a Nursery Catalogue of the Farmers' High School in 1859 which was sent to all parts of the State. Improved stocks were offered for sale; and explicit directions for planting, pruning, and growing were incorporated. This served to call attention in a practical manner to one of the means of general service the institution could render. It amply deserves the recognition as the first extension document of the College. Accompanying the circular, Professor Waring sent to editors and others interested a supplementary and explanatory letter: "This is printed separately from the general catalogue of the Institution, and will be found especially interesting and valuable to fruitgrowers, and especially to beginners who wish to know *why* and *when* the various processes of fruit and plant culture are advisable. Trees will take care of their own growth if not interfered with, and an excellent feature of this pamphlet is that of how to "let them alone." A system of characters which readily express their meaning is used to describe the chief peculiarities of the different fruits and flowers.

The Report of the President of the Board for 1857 acknowledges "the valuable services which have been rendered by Professor William G. Waring to whom has been committed the whole subject of making the necessary preparations for the future operations of the Institution." Need we wonder, therefore, that he was destined in view of this large order to "bear the Brunt" of criticism and lack of appreciation which invariably arises from conservative sources and vested interested when a new task is getting under way. That he did his work with fidelity but under difficulties which it is honorable both to the institution and to himself to have felt and expressed, the following extract from his diary bears eloquent witness[4]:

"When Mr. McAllister (Bellefonte) and Judge Watts of Carlisle began to agitate for a Farm School I assisted much by writing for different papers and helped much to get the location where it is on land offered by General Irvin. I met Judge Watts by request at Moses Thompson's and was offered the position of Superintendent of the building operations there (1856), and when the school opened I was, altho I declared I had never been inside a college, injudiciously selected as Principal of the Faculty. My retiring nature and independent unyielding ways, plain, candid, and unceremonious, soon got me into trouble with other more ambitious and envious members of the faculty,

---

[4] I am debtor to Professor J. H. Waring, a grandson of Professor W. G. Waring for the courtesy of access to this interesting document.

and with boys, many of them the worst sort expelled from other schools. Besides this, I was at home (where ever a prophet has no honor), and all the old grudges of envious and prejudiced neighbors came into play against me, and after four years of effort there—all the while supported warmly by the trustees with brief cases of exception, and after my nerves wholly gave way at Waldie's death (Dec. 4, 1859) and Melinda's increasing weakness (she died 2½ later) I resigned. The misrepresentations and ill-treatment that I—(then thin-skinned and sensitive)—underwent from some people there so weighed upon me that I never could bear to go among them again and I have not seen that region (now 1891) these 30 years. I have the satisfaction, however, of having retained the good opinion of the best people there and of having retained my own self-respect through all hardships and trials."

He resigned as Superintendent of the Farm on September 30th, 1862; while his name continues in the catalogues of 1862 to 1864 as Professor of Horticulture, and Superintendent of Nursery. That he followed with interest the affairs of the school is shown by his enthusiasm over the election of Dr. Burrowes in 1869; and in gratification at the Report of Dr. Burrowes on the yield of the Central Farm as far exceeding all others. "What a triumphant answer," he writes, "to the jealous carpers who railed so at the choice of the farm in the barren wilderness."

Easily first in importance in shaping the educational and scientific character of the institution was Dr. Evan Pugh. Portions of an address on the occasion of the one hundredth anniversary of his birth, February 29th, 1928 are here incorporated.

Evan Pugh, the fourth child and oldest son of Lewis Pugh and Mary Hutton Pugh was born at Jordan Bank, East Nottingham Township, Chester County, Pennsylvania, on February 29, 1828. He was of Welsh descent and Quaker faith. Here are the sources of that blend in Pugh's life, a rugged, energetic physique, a straight-forward common sense manner, combined with the heart of a child, and the integrity and moral robustness of mature manhood. He attended district school, but was largely educated within the family and by private tutors. His father, was a farmer-blacksmith, and ran at

Jordan Bank a two story shop, with an old fashioned tilt-hammer forge driven by water power. A repair and wheelwright establishment was located on the second floor. An accident which rendered his father blind, and his subsequent death in 1840, threw upon young Pugh a sense of responsibility for his own future. His grandfather was his guardian, and it was fondly hoped that the eldest son Evan, would eventually succeed to his father's business. Such dreams and visions he entertained but not very cordially, other ambitions and ideals were stirring in his breast. At sixteen, he was apprenticed to learn the trade of the blacksmith but continued his studies under the instruction of his aunt, a sister of his fathers. He chaffed under the interference with his studies which the apprenticeship entailed, aided as it was by the boorish, unsympathetic nature of his boss. How deep an impression these years must have made upon him, we may infer from the fact that the only regret of his entire childhood, he later affirms to be those two years wasted in learning a trade, which might better have been given to his education. This too, from a man who honored labor all his life by example as well as by precept, proves how keen must have been his hunger to know the world of science and art. Securing a release by purchase of the remaining time of his apprenticeship, he attended the Manual Labor Academy of Whitestown, New York. Here he studied Analytical Geometry, Differential and Integral Calculus, Applied Geometry, Astronomy, Botany, Physics, Geology and Chemistry.

Here too, he tells us, his dream of duty and obligation of carrying on the farm and business enterprises of his father received its "first death blow." The "second and final blow" was dealt when after a winter of teaching, he returned to the sowing and harvesting, work and planning of the home estate. The vision splendid that now possesses him is that of a teacher, looking toward a period of study in foreign countries, a much more rare occurrence then than now. He transformed the second story of the father's blacksmith shop into a school, called the Jordan Bank Academy. The school prospered. He managed the estate, studied the problems and means of successful farming, and made a fair competence by his industry and thrift. In August 1853, having the property in his own right he sold it for twenty-eight hundred dollars, and with some misgivings on his own part and with mingled wonder and fear on the part of relatives and friends, he prepared for a period of six years of study and investigation in Germany, France, and England.

On September 7th, 1853, Pugh embarked on a sailing vessel, the George Canning, Captain Jacobs, bound for Hamburg; the entire voyage lasting nearly a month.

He spent one year and a half at Leipzig studying chemistry, geology, mineralogy, botany and microscopy under Erdman, Newman and others. He was advised to take only such baggage as could be carried in a carpet bag but he arrived in Leipzig with a box of minerals, one hundred pounds; pressed flowers, sixty pounds; a chest of books and a trunk of clothes. The minerals and flowers he proposed to use for purposes of sale and exchange. He detailed his difficulties with transportation and customs officials, and of his search for rooming quarters in the city. He described his large room with two chairs, sofa, book-desk and tables. "In America such a room would cost $8 to $10 a month, yet here the owner asked me only $3 per month and into the bargain they bring me my meals, and keep it swept out and in order." He portrays vividly the work of the University, deprecated the beer-drinking, and loafing habits of many of its students, including Americans, rejoiced in a friendship with Johnson who later made "crops grow" at Yale and at the Connecticut Experiment Station.

He studied one year at Gottingen, wherein he says the names of Woehler, Weber, Derichlet, Hausmann and kindred spirits among its professors are sufficient to explain its advantages without entering into detail upon them.

Here he did two things not anticipated when he went to Gottingen, first, giving more attention to Mathematics, and second, the attainment of the Doctorate. Of the former he wrote, "the importance of mathematics becomes more and more apparent as we go deeper into the study of the physical sciences. Mathematics is the great lever by which the facts of nature are thrown around into such order that nature's laws are written on them in terms intelligible to man." An indication of the proficiency Pugh attained, we may infer from a letter written by De Morgan in London to Pugh as follows:

"7 Camden Town, N. W.
London, England
July 12—1858

My dear Sir:-

I think you will find the accompanying correct. And you will see that your own solution was correct up to the step n=00 h= o enclusive

Yours faithfully,
De Morgan

Last night we wrote down dv instead of dx
Dr. Pugh"

An entry under date of March 14th, 1858 shows another side of his nature: "I have had a jolly time attending all the meetings of the Chemical Society, and some of the Royal Society this winter. We take tea after meetings, Chemical, Royal, and Linnaeus Societies all together. To meet such men as Faraday, Lyell, Graham, Hoffman, etc., etc., is not (small potatoes) by any means."

Lawes and Gilbert wished to retain Pugh, offered inducements both in facilities and means to continue his work. But he finally declined. He summed up his European experiences by saying that with no part was he more pleased than with that on this Anglo Saxon sand heap. He returned with academic honors and with completed work to appear in the Proceedings of the Royal Society of Great Britain. He was thus assured of recognition in scientific circles wherever he went. In 1862, he was elected to membership in the American Philosophical Society.

A born teacher and a trained research man he was, however, again sacrificed to administration. In October 1859, he assumed the Presidency of the Farmers' High School; and his energies were absorbed in bringing order out of chaos; providing for discipline and rules of conduct; organizing courses of study; stimulating public interest and sentiment; beseeching the legislature for aid. Old Main but a torso must be completed; the Federal Land Grant, in a bitter fight held for the Agricultural College against the selfish ambitions and greed of denominational colleges; the newspaper press of the State informed and placated; faculty and trustee problems solved, dissensions and misunderstandings abated; local enemies in friendly guise dealt with, adjustments effected because of the Civil War with its consequent excitement and depletion of student and faculty ranks.

He was President, instructor of a settee of subjects, Director of Chemical Laboratories and Museum, Dean, Publicity Director, Supt. of Grounds and Buildings, Purchasing Agent, Financial Agent, College Steward, Store Keeper, Director of Labor and Recreation, Dean of Graduate Instruction, Long hand College Stenographer though an adept at Shorthand, Responsible and active leader for legislative support and recognition in the Commonwealth, and for the Land Grant Act and other Agricultural interests in Washington.

Small wonder the Philadelphia *Ledger* in an editorial on the Farm School in 1859 asserts that there are not five men in the Commonwealth whose ability would not be taxed by the headship of the Institution. That he was rather too frank to be a successful politician in those days and that he chafed under the delays of the law, we may cite as evidence the following in a letter to Professor Samuel Johnson bearing the date March 13th, 1861: "I am a little blue about it. Blue because all my vacation was wasted with those legislative blockheads; blue because honesty has not availed us in a righteous course, yet with not any less confidence in honesty; and blue because our F.H.S. must cease to go on if we don't get money; and blue because we are not now doing and are too poor to do what will be creditable to us. If our bill is defeated you will hear of it as I am determined that a knowledge of the evil that some devil dodging politicians have done shall live after them, so far as to be known is to be alive."

A carefully prepared address, delivered at Carlisle and later printed, blocked out the needs of Pennsylvania agriculturally. Secondary schools of Agriculture, headed by our own developing Agricultural College are of prime importance. A state chemist and a vision of agricultural statistics are urged; a

National Bureau of Agriculture championed. More significant is his insistent anticipation of agricultural and scientific investigation stations, whose functions he outlined thus: (1) To establish by experiment the facts and principles to be taught; (2) To establish an experimental farm; (3) To install laboratories for analysis; (4) To equip stalls, stables, etc., for experiments on feeding and for determining the comparative value of foods; (5) To issue a paper or publication to put results into the hands of the farming profession. Here are instruction, research and extension; with emphasis, too upon animal nutrition and physiology, as the mansard roof of the agricultural temple. He wrote a concise history of Agricultural Education in Europe, including the Farmers' High School and Agricultural College to 1862. "A report on Organization and facilities for Colleges of Agriculture and Mechanic Arts with special reference to the Agricultural College of Pennsylvania in view of its endowment by the Land Scrip Fund", printed January 6, 1864, is one of the most important of Dr. Pugh's papers. It was supplemented by a masterly statement before the Judiciary Committee, March 3, 1864 in reference to the proposition to deprive the College of its endowment.

Old Main was completed under Dr. Pugh, the legislative campaign for funds in 1861 being long and trying. In 1862, Dr. Pugh recommended the change of title from The Farmers' High School to The Agricultural College of Pennsylvania. We may infer from the opposition in some quarters to the name "College," the real reason that the more distinctive title at that data, State College of Agriculture and Mechanic Arts, was not urged. Despite the war, the school grew in numbers; 142 were enrolled in 1863, and 146 in 1864. Thirty-eight to forty counties of the State were represented. Two graduate students appeared in 1862, and in the following year, the number reached eleven. The graduation theses were upon subjects, with field and laboratory data, in agriculture, geology, botany, and chemistry.

Three laboratories in Chemistry, for which Dr. Pugh contributed five hundred dollars annually from his princely salary of fifteen hundred dollars, were "as well equipped as any in the country at that date." More than all, the work and word of Dr. Pugh were respected in scientific circles, and the institution with which he was identified was known for its pioneer activities in Agricultural and Industrial Education.

Dr. Pugh had tempting opportunities to go to Washington to organize the scientific work of the Department of Agriculture, and he has left in manuscript a most thorough paper in which he plans for the commissioner in charge, then under the Patent Office, the ways and means of making that department what it should be. A second invitation came to him while he was recovering from an accident at his home in Chester County. On Saturday night, June 6th, 1863, Dr. Pugh was returning to Willow Bank when a severe thunder storm arose. The horse he was driving was frightened, and backed the buggy over the bank into the stream, throwing the future Mrs. Pugh and himself under the vehicle. Dr. Pugh managed to extricate himself, raise the buggy and rescue his fiancee who suffered severely from bruises and shock. Dr. Pugh sustained a broken arm, and on account of unskilled surgery was compelled to go to a Philadelphia hospital for treatment. While he was recovering at the home of friends in Chester County, a formal call came to the position of Chief Chemist at Washington. The letter was opened by Professor Wilson, Vice-President of the College and forwarded to Dr. Pugh with a letter urging his acceptance of so promising a position. Dr. Pugh's reply is evidence complete (if we had no other) of a rare devotion to the ideals of duty and a frank surrender of personal ambitions to the task upon which he had set his heart.

Oxford, Chester Co., Pa.
September 18, 1863

Professor Wilson

My dear Sir:

Your letter with enclosed from Paschall Morris came a few days ago. I refused to accept the head of that department when it was offered to me two years ago—because I wanted to devote myself to agl (agricultural) education, in the State Agl. College called or to be called into existence by the Congressional Appropriation. The best way to do this I conceive is to make our own college a model which other Agl. Colleges will adopt. As yet we have done almost nothing worthy of an Agl. College and I never shall think of abandoning our work till we have done something—till we have avoided the one extreme of passing into a literary college as Maryland has done, on the other of becoming a mere farming school as some people would have us. These alternatives are the Scylla and Charybdis upon which meddlesome critics will labor to draw us and which have already ruined Agl. Colleges. Another danger in regard to our college and one that I have felt was serious from the first time I studied its affairs, is that it may be damaged by local influences. This is feared by the friends in this part of the State and it is seized upon by its enemies to show that it is unworthy of state patronage... To combat these influences, and to labor to build up a character for the institution of such kind that local people will no more presume to modify the affairs of the college to suit their prejudices and interests, than the people of New Haven or Cambridge would presume to meddle with the affairs of Yale or Harvard—to do this I am resolved to stay with our College, while God gives me strength to perform my duties there, whatever may be the pecuniary inducements or prospects of honor elsewhere.

It is my duty and my destiny to do so, and I shall seek honors in the path of duty and of destiny rather than at Washington.

I am however trying to get a good man into that place at Washington. It is of vast importance to us that such a man be got there. There must however be some radical changes at Washington before that department fulfills its mission. But I am disposed to let the practical men have their trial there before I do anything very active to mould that department.

I am very sorry to hear of Baker's illness. It seems that Providence has chosen especially to afflict us this year.

Yours sincerely,

E. Pugh.

In 1862, Dr. Pugh proposed to donate $1,000 toward a house for the President, if the college would furnish an additional $2,000. The house was not completed at the time of his death; and his bride with whom he fell in love at first sight four years previously when he was visiting an iron master in Bellefonte to compare methods of smelting iron here and abroad, never occupied the house. They were married February 4, 1864, after an engagement of three years, and in two months separated by the passing of Dr. Pugh. Mrs. Pugh, a woman of culture, refinement and of rare sweetness and purity of soul, kept faithful tryst of the poignant romance so ruthlessly shattered until her own death on July 7, 1921,—fifty-seven years of widowed, worshipful, romantic devotion.

J. B. Lawes of Rothamstead Station, England, wrote Mrs. Pugh, having received by the same post, wedding cards and the news of Dr. Pugh's death: "Although I had my fears that he was taxing his powers too severely, I was watching his course with greatest interest, as I felt certain that if he lived he would be the founder of a great college. I hope some permanent memorial is proposed. I shall be proud to become a contributor in honor of a man whose character and abilities I so greatly admired." *That memorial remains to be erected; somewhere in the Commonwealth there should be the will and consecrated means to give it fitting form and substance.*

CHAPTER 4

Preparing the Plant: Early Scenes and Bucolics

"We must combine the cultivated intellect and social amenities of mental refinement with the strong practical usefulness and sound virtues of the agriculturist. If these be not thus wedded, (then as now the fact will remain) that the great agricultural body—have not the power and influence which they ought to have for the proper balance and benefit of society."

Frederick Watts

The farm is described by the Committee on Location of The Farm School as comparatively new, having been cleared within a few years, while the grass growing upon it shows the fertility of the soil. It is a "fine quality of limestone sufficiently rolling in its surface, all cleared and fenced but about thirty acres of each farm: there is no stream of water upon the surface of either but water is easily obtainable by digging." The report of 1859 affirms, "about one-half of the corn ground this year, in all fifty-five acres, was of the rough belt never grubbed or cleared of stone. Much labor was necessarily expended... The ground for corn next year comprises the remainder of the stony belt, and the worst of it." Some practical difficulties may be gleaned from the order book of W. G. Waring to a nursery in Philadelphia under date of April 14th, 1859:

"12 light onion hoes, best quality strong
12 best strong steel hoes for general hoeing *
12 digging forks, steel tines, well ironed

I am induced to trouble you with the items marked * through out finding it impossible to get tools that will stand usage in our soil unless selected by some one who *knows*."

Progress is reported in the first catalogue, that of 1859: "The farm being in a very unimproved condition, has since been thoroughly grubbed and plowed, and in the intervals of the ordinary farm duties over three thousand two horse wagon loads of stone have been removed from it, and put in proper places for making turnpikes, and stone fences, and leveling up irregularities in the surface." The following year the prospect widens and cause and effect are brought together: "New land has been to clear and break up, rocks to blast, stones to pick, nearly all of which has been done by students."

The Board moved with commendable zeal in preparing for the work of the institution. At the third meeting, with ten members present, and with Governor Pollock presiding, a committee alternately called Building and Business Committee was selected, to "make preparations for buildings and for other purposes." This committee consisted of Watts, McAllister, and Miles. At the fifth meeting of the Board, January 4th, 1856, plans for buildings were considered. The plan of barn by Frederick Watts and of College Building by H. N. McAllister were approved, and the Building Committee instructed to invite proposals and to proceed with construction. An appeal for support to the Legislature was authorized, and a committee consisting of McAllister, Hiester, and Walker drew up a Memorial setting forth the needs of the Institution. Additional actions were taken, appointing W. G. Waring, Superintendent to lay out grounds, aid in location of buildings, plant shrubbery, etc. The appointment of a Treasurer, Edward C. Humes of Bellefonte and the re-election of Frederick Watts as President of the Board completed the organization.

The Building Committee contracted for the erection of the necessary plant on May 12th, 1856 to Turner and Natcher for the sum of fifty-five thousand dollars. A convenient farm-house, a large barn, corn cribs, wagon sheds, and other necessary outbuildings were completed late in the year 1856. The College building was also under construction. "A party of brick makers and excavators commenced work on the 24th of June and the first stones were laid in the Foundations on the 18th of August." The Report of 1857 reveals that the "walls of the west wing are up three storeys and are plainly but very substantially built of superior, gray lime stone. They are four feet thick at the base, and are founded entirely on solid rock. This wing will contain a complete suite of rooms on the first and second floors for a private residence with front and back separate entry halls; four recitation rooms on the first floor, 18x17; two rooms on the first and second floor 27x17; one society hall on the third floor, 37x19; sixty-nine chambers on the different floors, (each supplied with warm air by a separate flue,) 17x9; five store rooms with roomy passages, 9x5." Work was continued during the Winter and the hope indulged of having the west wing completed and ready for occupancy in November 1858.

These hopes were not to be realized, the lack of funds; the shrinking of subscriptions; the delay in getting farm and grounds in shape for instructional purposes, the panic of 1857, all contributed to make progress slow. It had become clear that the Contractors could not under the changed conditions complete the structure. They finally abandoned work on July 7th, 1858, and the Building Committee took charge with instructions to complete the "west wing and curtain." Mr. C. B. Callihan "an architect of long experience and great professional ability, who takes unbounded pride and satisfaction in perfecting the great structure entrusted to his skill and fidelity" directed the operations. The torso as a result calls out enthusiastic praise as "all visitors unite in pronouncing the whole situation and the rooms now finished, in the highest degree sound, enduring, chaste, grand, and *finished*. Economy and propriety have governed the design, and there is nothing of pretentious ornamentation to be seen; yet nothing is wanting to satisfy the severe eye of architectural taste."

The kitchens, dining room, and store rooms (or as they were scholastically termed the "culinary department") were planned for the central part of the building. Since this was not completed, a "large temporary wooden building at the rear (literally constructor's shed) is being cleaned and fitted up for present culinary and victualing uses." A cistern, called euphoniously "a soft water reservoir" is located in the rear of the building. It will supply at least ten barrels per day all the year round and, when necessary, it may be supplemented from a well, "Inexhaustible in the dryest weather."

Thus one third of Old Main was completed under the most serious difficulties and with fears, tacit and expressed, that the project might fail at any time. Only the self-sacrifice and devotion of the Building Committee, their faith in the inherent value and necessity of the cause kept the institution alive. A description of this completed west wing and curtain, the real genuine "Old Main", from the second annual report is herewith incorporated: "The wing is 42 feet front by 82 deep; and the curtain 48 front by 52 deep; height 6 stories; basement 14 feet clear; ... containing 63 chambers 9x17; five class rooms 20x20; a dining room and lecture room each 20x40; large corridors and roomy halls affording a passage to all the rooms in the building; closets in all the dormitories or chambers; a complete private residence, with separate halls and entrances; abundance of cellarage, well aired and equable in temperature and in hydrometric conditions at all seasons. The whole will be supplied with warm and cold water, soft and hard; sewerage; ventilation for summer and winter in all the rooms, temperature arranged by a separate flue for each room starting in the basement story and built in corridor or brick walls, thus keeping the heat in the center of the building. Five furnaces are now used in heating, located in the basement story—three in the wing, two in the curtain—so constructed as to give an equal portion of rooms to heat... Who desires to be comfortable could not fail in being pleased with the pure balmy air furnished to the different apartments."

The vision and prospect unfolds generously: the "Main building when surrounded with the intended arboretum in full growth, with the fountains of water and avenues, its great elevation and its whole appearance at once graceful, magnificent and permanent will distinguish it among the many great edifices of the State."

Work on the farm went on apace although up to the 27th of July, 1857 "wholly with hired teams and implements, and their concomitant disadvantages. The four mules and two horses, now the property of the institution are all young, very gentle and docile, strong, healthy, handsome and well trained. The arrival of these animals was quite an era and afforded great impetus and encouragement to the labor." These first enrollments preceding even students or professors deserve enumeration. The "Entrance Conditions" might constitute a basis for a personnel or aptitude test upon human material even today. The horses are Charley and Lucy, inventoried at one hundred and fifty each; two mules, Tom and Coaly, one hundred and ninety each; and two, Perry and Beck, one hundred and sixty each. Among the recommendations is that of the erection of hog pens early in the season. "If we had suitable pens, we should have respectable tenants placed in some of them by the generosity of individuals who have offered to contribute specimens of favorite breeds."

Progress is indicated, also, by the fact that two important public roads have lately been laid out, from the south and northwest, converging at the farm. Petitions for a mail route passing the farm are also noted. As the present "nearest post-office (Boalsburg) is five miles distant, it is hoped this convenience will soon be obtained."

Experiments are described under the headings; Ground for rutabagas and buckwheat, apply various fertilizers; sugar cane, cutting, pressing, boiling and experimenting; trying means of arresting insects. The year 1858 lists one hundred and ninety-six different experimental trials, each numbered and registered. That these were busy years, let but the record of 1857 prove: seventy-five acres prepared, grubbed and sprouted for corn; forty-three thousand nursery plants, sixteen thousand plants of over one hundred different sorts, six hundred apple trees, four hundred peach trees, two hundred plum, apricot and nectarines, two hundred and fifty pear, two hundred cherry, fifteen hundred grape vines, sixty avenue maples, and five hundred pine, spruce and fir are set out.

Under the stimulus of the support which the Legislature of 1857 gave, a sort of house warming and home coming was held at the Farm School on September 2nd, 1857. The Act, approved May 20th, 1857, appropriated twenty-five thousand dollars, absolutely, and a like amount upon the condition that an equal sum should be raised by private subscription. The Trustees, and the Delegates (commissioned by Act of Incorporation to elect the governing board) present from twenty counties met at the Farm School. Joined by distinguished guests, friends, and enemies of the new movement, the community was sorely taxed to provide "chariots and horses" sufficiently dignified for so large a company. But if transportation lagged, not so the collation. After the Election of Trustees, we read, "a collation was served by the Ladies of the neighborhood." No part of the College (as Old Main was then called) was complete enough to use, so the massive barn floor was utilized. Accompanied doubtless by the strains, bucolic and seraphic of a barnyard orchestra, a dinner was served to the Board and about two hundred visitors and friends. The feast was spread, "laid out on a table eighty-six feet long, arched over with foliage, tastefully decorated with flowers, fruits, and garlands, and ladened with the best "Substantials" and desserts that the accomplished and indefatigable troop of lady friends of the Institution could possibly spread before their guests."

The table cleared figuratively and literally the Hon. James T. Hale spoke briefly, before calling upon Judge Watts. The President of the Board responded in a speech which is worthy of preservation and acclaim among the great addresses of all time. It should be known as the Barn floor speech of 1857, and is a simple though masterly statement of the new education. After affirming that influence depends not upon calling or profession but upon education, he continues:

"There is stimulus in this idea. It shows us how essentially important it is in a State where Agricultural pursuits prevail and constitute the broad basis of the wealth of that State, that agriculturists should have an education suited for themselves and equal in power to their own want, and the nation's want...

"We must combine the cultivated intelligence and social amenities of mental refinement with the strong practical usefulness and sound virtues of the agriculturist, who, giving the sweat of his brow, receives from Providence such bounties as are now stored around us in this building, and spread upon these tables, the daily support of all human life; and who dispenses them to all other classes... If these be not thus wedded, this great agricultural State of Pennsylvania must remain as now, with the balance of influence and power in the hands of comparatively few, for I may be allowed to repeat,—feeling no desire but to contribute to the security of the future prosperity of our glorious commonwealth—that the great body of citizens, that the great agricultural body, have not power and influence which they ought to have, for the proper balance and benefit of society. Something must be done. How shall we increase their power? The remark of my friend answers the question. 'Education will impart influence.' But it must be such education as will lead to the desired end... Science, art, and labor must be combined...

"Now the institution we are striving to establish at the earliest possible period is intended to supply this great social, political, moral and economic want, and while it improves the agricultural mind, and trains the hands, it will do both at less expense than the purely literary training can be obtained for. Thus, while reducing cost very greatly, it will educate better, and fit for every business or relation of practical life... We have started—there must now be for us no such word as 'fail'. Our Legislature has done much to aid us—we have much to do ourselves. Let us ask ourselves, each one of us, how much do we owe to society, and especially to the great class that forms its basis. Probably no assemblage of men of various pursuits combining so much acute intelligence as the one here met could be convened for any other object. And I believe myself justified in saying that our object meets the unanimous and warm approval of every one present. If then it meets our views, if our motives are right, how much ought we to do? Let every man seriously consider how much he owes the world, his fellow men, and posterity, and answer by the exertion of his influence, taking care to do, what he finds to do, with all his might. Let men dampen with faint praise, or make no exertion with pen, or tongue, or purse, or speak evil of the cause or of its advocates, and with downward grade in their favor, they may counterbalance the efforts of those who strive to push upward and onward this car...

"We must obtain the twenty-five thousand dollars by individual contribution, and I say for myself, only because I am urged to say it now, that I will be one of ten, to give a thousand dollars each, toward making up that amount."

Vigorous applause followed, and generous responses presaged the raising of the sum needed to meet the conditions of the Act of 1857. In the midst of general good feeling and expressions of good will, the proceedings were "interrupted by a call of 'Stage for Spruce Creek' and after a hasty adjournment, and a general discharge of kind wishes and farewell expressions, one of the most intelligent, philanthropic, liberal, and important conventions by which Pennsylvania was ever represented from Erie to Bucks, was dissolved."

At the meeting of the Board of June 16th, 1858, the purchase of the additional two hundred acres of land, upon which rent was paid and an option held, was authorized. The apparent embarrassment of the contractor was discussed. Bills were over due, liens upon building for materials and labor were threatening. A renewed campaign for subscriptions was determined upon. An Address to the People of Pennsylvania was issued, setting forth facts as well as needs, and signed by every member of the Board. An agent to solicit subscriptions, and members of the Board, also, prepared to make personal appeals for aid in their respective districts and among the friends of education. Nothing daunted, the first admission requirements were drawn up. Pupils must have attained the age of sixteen; tuition, boarding, fuel, light, books, etc., were fixed at one hundred dollars per session, commencing in February and ending in December. One hundred pupils were to be admitted on recommendation of the respective County Agricultural Societies, "apportioned among the counties according to the number of taxable inhabitants." No pupil was to be enrolled without good moral character, and qualified, moreover, by elementary branches taught in the Public Schools of the State.

At the fourteenth meeting of the Board, held on December 8th, 1858, with Governor Packer present, the Business Committee was given power "to employ Professors and Teachers, secure necessary furniture for the rooms of students", and in general to make all arrangements "to put the school in operation by the 16th day of February 1859." Prospective subjects to be taught covered almost university scope, from mathematics to malpractice, from the sciences of production to the principles of distributing and marketing, from agricultural architecture and accounts to agricultural genetics and experimentation.

It was evidently easier to map out a program than it was to furnish the instruction, even when the expansive and convertible "chairs" are taken into consideration. Subjects and relative positions in these benches of science change in succeeding catalogues, doubtless as the omniscience of one professor grows and the limitations of another sprouts. In one case, literature and science change chairs, and although not intended as a reflection upon the occupant or a cause for libel, the former is starred and a footnote reads: "Recently resigned; the position will be filled by a competent person next session."

There can be no doubt however, but that the institution was of collegiate grade from the beginning. Comparative study of curricula, the emphasis upon the sciences and the provision for laboratory work, the academic training and outlook of that first faculty, Pugh, Wilson, Waring, Whitman, Baird and Allison, all bear positive testimony. Confessedly the Farmer's High School was used to ensure the undivided and enthusiastic support of classes wherein lingering prejudices against "college" training might be found, and also to placate the dogmatism of others which affirmed education impossible outside the learned professions. A few brief quotations of contemporary issue will serve to reinforce these viewpoints. Judge Watts wrote in 1857; "Provision will be made for ample and extensive mathematical training and engineering practice, and all the branches of natural science will be fully illustrated and taught. Moral and civil science, and all the arts of practical life, excluding nothing but what is exclusively literary as the acquisition of the dead and foreign languages. Thus, while reducing cost very greatly, it will educate better and fit for every business relation of life." More significantly, the first catalogue (1859) states the object of the institution "to afford a system of instruction as extensive and thorough as that of the usual course of our best colleges, to emphasize scientific instruction, and to develop to the fullest extent possible those departments of all science which have a practical or theoretical bearing upon agriculture and agricultural interest." Dr. Pugh, writing in 1862, says: "The fundamental idea of the Agricultural College is to associate a high degree of intelligence with the practice of agriculture, and the industrial arts and to seek to make use of this intelligence in developing the agricultural and industrial resources of the country, and protecting its interests."

There is no equivocation here, the institution was an Industrial College, an experiment of democracy in self-education. Standards were set high, and standards were maintained at all cost. A letter from Dr. Pugh to Trustee McAllister is redolent of devotion and interest in academic aims and ideals. The letter is written from Altoona, April 9th, 1860. "You remark that what you say in regard to economy also, would apply to the chemical department. I shall make no expenditures that I would not rather make at my own expense than not make at all. I will not sacrifice my chances of success in developing a course of chemical instruction, such as I think we ought to have for want of apparatus, though it take every dollar of my salary and more to do it. It would be very bad economy, to say nothing of the interests of the school to do so, and I will *not do it*. I desire to order nothing at present but such as will be sold at cost to the students. Each one must have from 5 to 10 dollars worth which will make a pretty good bill for 70 students. My course of instruction with them will be an experiment. I wish to do everything possible to make it succeed, and I am confident that it will. But if it does not, I shall be willing and ready to see anyone else attempt it in my stead as I have no faith in an institution without it."

The first graduating class, entering with fifty-five members, was reduced by academic and other casualties to seventeen. Eleven, only, survived the final tests and took the degree of Bachelor of Scientific Agriculture in 1861. Both in training and in graduation theses, these men show the impress of Dr. Pugh's scientific genius, and they expressed by word and deed in after life their undying regard for him. Of this class, Dr. Pugh wrote in 1862: "This was also the first class that graduated at an Agricultural College in the United States, and they graduated upon a higher scientific education standard than is required at any other Agricultural College in the world." Whether in the last analysis, literally true or not, there is sufficient honor in the first class to justify a call of the roll:

> James Miles, Jr., Erie County
> A. C. Church, Luzerne County
> J. W. Eckman, Lebanon County
> Samuel Holliday, Erie County
> E. P. McCormick, Clinton County
> M. S. Lytle, Huntingdon County
> John N. Banks, Juniata County
> J. D. Isett, Huntingdon County
> L. C. Troutman, Philadelphia
> C. Alfred Smith, Berks County
> C. E. Troutman, Philadelphia

A feature of the Farm School contemplated by the founders and held with astonishing tenacity during later years was the "Manual Labor Fetish." The first circulars and Memorials issued by Trustees forecast it and the first catalogue announces: "All students will be required to perform every description of labor necessary at the Institution whether on the farm, in the shops, or at and about the college buildings; and three hours of active labor may be required each day but no more unless some special emergency arises." It was put on the high plane of honoring equally all kinds of labor and "excellence therein will constitute a ground of merit, equally with proficiency in other branches of study and practice." What a variety, too, in labor details: Putting handles in brushes and hoes, grafting, hauling water, picking and hauling stones, mangling, ringing bells and tending lamps, assisting the baker, sweeping halls, turning washing machines, planting beans, setting out hedge, running errands, dusting and tending office, disbudding trees, making crock lids and jockey sticks, hoeing and cultivating, "raising potatoes", paring apples and potatoes, etc., etc. How popular must have been such details as carrying mail, distributing mail, repairing Prayer Books. What possibilities in academic statistics in such entries as "making the labor roll", and "tending to visitors", the Blue Keys of the sixties. What vocational bliss in hauling coal from Snow Shoe or Bellefonte (although this detail was not ordinarily entrusted to mere unchaperoned students) and how saturated with envy must have been the atmosphere when the mule teams fared forth as the announcement reaches the College that a shipment of coal has been made by the Baltimore Coal Company of Wilkesbarre to the port of Bellefonte on boats, "Wide Awake", "Gas Kas Kia", or "Anna Eliza".

It should in justice be noted, however, that the manual labor idea while abstractly defensible on grounds of the inherent value and dignity of toil was practically prompted as well. It served the needs of the institution itself in construction, repair, and in running the farms. It familiarized the student with actual conditions. It aided in satisfying the demand for the practical on the part of the constituency. It helped to reduce the students' expenses, and in a by no means unimportant way furnished physical exercise and vicarious expression for pent up energies.

There is abundant evidence, also, not only in the early plans but in their fruition, under Dr. Pugh, that the laboratory idea was the really dominating one in the manual labor complex. The translation of a labor detail into a practicum and a practicum into a laboratory problem was in a sense the ever present opportunity and challenge of the real teacher. In an address to the People of Pennsylvania signed by every member of the Board and issued in 1858 are found these words:

"In boyhood there is no stimulus so great, no incentive so powerful, as ambition. Manual labor schools have failed, and always will fail of success where labor is associated with the necessities of poverty, in contrast with the immunities and privileges of wealth; where one class labor because their parents are poor, and another class do not labor, because their parents are rich. To ensure success, all must start together on terms of perfect equality, with no standard but skill in labor, and attainments in learning to elevate or degrade. The boy must be made to feel that he is the architect of his own fame, as it is well that he should be of his own fortune—a lesson which lies at the very foundation of success throughout the whole voyage of life. An actual distaste for manual labor; the low repute in which it is held; habits of idleness from this cause, dissipation arising from the lack of excitement, ignorance of the applications of science to the business of life; are among the evils of our present system of collegiate education—evils which this Institution proposes greatly to lessen, if not to remove. The education is to be practical as well as scientific. It is designed to make business men. How many students pass through the whole routine of a collegiate course acquiring little else than abstract ideas. Knowledge—if it deserve the name—the use of which in its application to the every day wants of life, they never learn. From the study of the philosophy of the mechanical powers, we propose to lead the class for illustration, to their actual application in the various operations of the farm; from their recitations in Geology, not only to a carefully arranged cabinet, but to the actual collecting of the numerous specimens with which the varied strata in the vicinity of the Farmers' High School abound; from the lessons in Botany, to the cultivated fields, the nursery, and the botanical garden; through the fertile valleys to the neighboring forests and mountain ranges; and even in their rambles for pleasure through the arboretum, we would introduce them to an actual personal and practical knowledge of every tree which this climate can be made to produce. Such acquaintance with the productions of Nature will make them feel, wherever on the earth's surface their lot may be cast, not as among strangers, but amid the friends of their youth."

Before proceeding with the story of the completion of Old Main, we turn to some of the lighter contemporary sources, to letters, reports of visitations, reminiscences, etc., in restoring a picture of these early scenes and struggles, the primitive bucolic days of students, school, farm and community.

We must picture to ourselves the opening of the College, The Farmers' High School on February 16th, 1859 with sixty-nine students present, a faculty of five teachers, one-third of the College Building completed. In addition, a barn, farm residence and other out-buildings were placed about where the Library now stands. The village adjoining the college fields contained the magnificent total of three buildings. Add to the picture, the constructor's barracks, plain board and rough structures to the rear of the west wing, used as kitchen and dining hall wherein as C. Alfred Smith with slight exaggeration, doubtless, says, "We shared our food with swarming flies in summer, and hunted for warm fragments amid the snow drifts in winter." The only food served, so it seemed in the lapse of years to some of these pioneers, was doughy, underbaked bread, molasses, and rhubarb pies, while to others it was an identical roast beef, with changes on the menu, a matter of linguistic alterations only.

The grounds surrounding the building were strewn with stone, sand, brick, frames, and other building material for the incomplete structure. Picture a ride of five hours on a raw February day from Spruce Creek by stage to the Farm School by way of Pine Grove Mills; or from Lewistown by way of

Bellefonte, again by stage. Local color issues from newspaper items of the time. On September 10th, 1858, the *Central Press* of Bellefonte announces:

"New Stage Line. From Bellefonte to Pine Grove. By way of the Farmers' High School. The subscribers respectfully inform the public that they have placed a two-horse coach on this route and will carry passengers to and from the Farmers' High School, Pine Grove and all intermediate points at cheap rates. This stage will be run three times a week, leaving Bellefonte, Mondays, Wednesdays and Fridays. A comfortable coach and careful driver will be provided, and render the traveller comfortable.

R. D. Cummings

Jas. Dunlap"

On July 1st, 1859, a daily stage is announced, Spruce Creek and Farmers' High School "to accommodate the increased travel in that region". At this date these trunk line facilities were properly launched, "leaving Spruce Creek at 9 A. M. and arrive at the Farm School at 2 P. M. the same day." There was no railroad in the county, the ore road to Scotia was under construction, turnpikes and canals were the means of transportation, horses and mules the sources of power. Again, see the west wing without entrance steps, only a cleated gangway plank for entrance, which in the absence of janitorial force must be navigated, bag and baggage, by even the transplanted, sophisticated city lad. The dark and dingy halls were illumed by lard oil lamps and students studied by the light of a single candle. We must see stools taking the place of dining chairs, an orderly march to meals following assembly in chapel and the ringing of the college bell, a hand bell. Variety added its touch to routine in that "laundry bags were brought to Monday noon roll call and deposited in the corridor." The rising bell sounded at six, the day well filled with study and recitation, together with three hours of labor detail on the farm, in the gardens or about the buildings.

Picture all this and more (luxuries only have been enumerated), the least that can be said is that the sixty-nine students enrolled on that opening day must have been desperately in earnest about education. They embodied in very truth the mental state of two prospective students who wrote to President Pugh, "our very souls (excuse the term) yearn after a scientific and practical knowledge of agriculture."

Vacations were strangely supposed to interfere with work, so the college session ran from February to December without a break. During the first year, the students petitioned for a vacation of two weeks over the fourth of July. Dr. Pugh writes: "If we could be positively certain about them all coming back with punctuality at the end of two weeks, there would be no serious objection to a vacation, but here is the difficulty." The boys, as usual in such cases, got their vacation and are very enthusiastic over it as early as June 22nd. The following year, vacations were granted by classes at different times and on request of parent or guardian; the faculty instructed "to substitute such relaxation for others as could be provided." Excursions, geological, hunting and camping trips were organized. These were continued in various forms for a decade, thereafter military camps were featured. Supt. Waring wrote Trustee McAllister on July 25th, 1859, "I am alone, trying to get the accounts posted up, but much interrupted by visitors and inspections, etc. Professor Whitman is at the Bear Meadows with nearly 25 or 30 students who have not gone home."

The right of petition was expressed by the students "on the subject of forming a musical band." The Board responded with a rhythmical diplomacy that must have amused if not chagrined the petitioners: "Whilst the Board approves the idea of the young men as to their musical band, it does not require any other action on their part than the expression of their individual hopes that they may be successful in their efforts." The formation of Literary Societies, the Washington Agricultural Literary Society, The Cresson in 1859 met a less ingenuous and more encouraging response. Two hundred and fifty dollars was voted to each for the purchase of books with which to commence the formation of libraries.

Letters also may aid us in visualizing the experiences of those early days. C. Alfred Smith describes his arrival at the College, "on a farm wagon without springs, my trunk for a seat, Spruce Creek to Farm School, twenty-two miles with dinner at Pine Grove." C. C. Lobinger says: "We viewed the landscape of lime stone rocks alone. We wore out our finger nails picking rocks on the farm, and the college building was almost surrounded by rocks." J. S. Read, after the flight of years sends "special greetings to the one who will own up to tying the black snake on the door knob of the Professor Logic, whom we called Nehemiah." M. S. Lytle tells us of "Jakey" and "Tommy" as professional but not disrespectful epithets for the somewhat garrulous Whitman and the supra dignified Baker. Pranks, student escapes range from "liquor parties," class room disturbances, "borrowing" Professor Wilson's Thanksgiving Turkey or making merry with some predestinated ear marked refreshments, raiding nearby orchards; putting the "bit brown mule, Ned," in chapel, tying teachers in and out of their rooms, to even an occasional "pugilistic encounter twixt one another or with a hapless novice on the teaching force."

Araspus A. C. A. (Azen, Cotis, Athos) Jones details his experiences in a first person journalese:

> "I arrived at the College in 1862 on a cold day in March, sometime in the afternoon, staging it from Spruce Creek and coming from St. Louis, Mo. I was greeted by some epithets from the upper windows that I had never heard before, such as 'Fresh Fish,' and other expressions that were equally as appropriate, I did not know what to make of this, but I thought it was wisdom to keep still. I was shown to Dr. Pugh's room and I do not know how wisely I answered some of his questions, but he saw fit to assign me to the Sophomore class. I was also the victim of his wisdom when I remarked before going out of his room about the beauty of the scenery from his window and he replied, 'Students do not go to College to look out of the window but to study,' and he rewarded me by giving me the poorest room on the second floor, as far as outlook was concerned."

> "I do not remember much of our school recitations, although I managed in some way or another to recite so favorably as to get first class marks. This came about by steady application and memorizing which I have afterwards come to believe is the poorest

recommendation that a student can have. What a College should give, is to learn how to study and think, and not how to make a perfect recitation.

"Professor Whitman, as I remember him liked to talk on Botany and was not very critical in recitation. Prof. Baker on Mathematics did not push us hard and was easily satisfied, but Prof. Wilson in English was the grandest of all and asked questions in such a way that the answer was 'yes' or 'no' and he gave hints as to which it should be, unless you gave no consideration to his talk at all. He was very religious and generous in his judgment of others. I have the kindest remembrance of him. The Doctor [Dr. Pugh], however, was entirely different; he knew so much that a book was wholly unnecessary to teach from and expected answers to his questions that had some intimation that you knew something of the subject we was questioning you upon. I think the Doctor was the most convincing man that I ever met and he could make you believe his conclusions were right at the time even if you felt like cowhiding yourself afterwards for thinking so. Whether rightly or wrongly, Doctor Pugh thought I knew something and he urged me to take a course at some European College. I did not agree with him. I felt his loss very much and believe the College at his death lost its most worthy advocate.

"If you can recall, we had chapel after supper and the exercises consisted of reading the Bible, prayer, and orations by the students, arranged by classes in alphabetical order for each class. At one period of our college life when our class time came to orate some number of it conceived the idea that each member should speak the same piece and the one chosen by "Excelsior." It was the Doctor's time to conduct the exercises and I think only two members spoke before the orders of the day changed."

Tellico Johnson thus enlivens and adorns the tale:

"In the spring of 1863, the writer left his home in Buffalo, N. Y., and journeyed by rail to Lock Haven, thence by stage, over the most dreadful roads, to Bellefonte and thence by hired rig to College, over *very* bad roads. ... I was assigned to the farm detail, and my first job was picking up stones in a field N. W. from the main building. Oh! those awful stones, sharp edges, sharp corners, ragged as cinders, and millions of them. I labored for weeks at that job and it seemed as if there were more stones in the field at the end than at the beginning. ... Our dining room was a board shanty... and the students sat at long tables extending the length of the dining room, with a Professor at the head of each. We had grace at each meal and I sat at a table presided over by Prof. Wilson. During grace I peeked, and saw Prof. Wilson with wide open eyes, looking at me and saying grace as usual. I ducked down and after dinner I asked a student why he kept his eyes open. He told me Prof. Wilson used to close his eyes during grace, but a rough fellow threw a pot of butter at him, hitting him in the face, and he never said grace after that with closed eyes. Prof. Wilson was a fine, old school gentleman and was liked by all the students. No one dared throw butter at Dr. Pugh. His was a most commanding figure and presence. I have never seen a stronger man, in fact he was almost a giant. I have seen him take a barrel of oil by the chines and put it into a wagon. Very tall, with immense chest and Samson build, piercing eyes, commanding voice, he was an ideal leader.

He was undoubtedly a very learned man, but I did not care for him as a *teacher*. He knew so much about chemistry, that the ordinary minds could not absorb, at once, what he told them and he was impatient with us stupid fellows." "I like Dr. Pugh very much; although a strict disciplinarian he was a just man and played no favorites. He did his duty and expected every one else to do theirs, and woe unto you if you failed. He laid down his life in his devotion to the college and he deserves the greatest honor for his scholarship and brave struggle against great odds."

"There was a deep hole at the North end of the building, where the stone for the building was quarried and one of our jobs was to dump stone and rubbish into it. We worked three years at that hole and it seems to me it was as big as ever when I left. The campus was covered with piles of stone and earth and there were no trees on it. It was gradually cleared of the stone piles and rubbish, the worst holes filled up, and the ground leveled somewhat, and some of the Philadelphia boys, Stokes, Lex, Newhall and others played a little cricket on it. There were no sports, so to speak, no baseball, no football, at that time, as the energies of the students were spent in their studies and the three hours daily labor. Back of the College, near the woods, were some rings and parallel bars and that was the only gymnasium equipment on the place. Gathering specimens of flowers and plants was much encouraged, and Saturday afternoons were devoted by many of us, to tramps all over the valleys and mountains, searching for new or rare flowers and plants. Trips to the 'Bear Meadows' were arranged so as to secure Pitcher Plants in bloom and some of us took long tramps to Snow Shoe, Rattlesnake Tavern, and other places, in fact covered the neighborhood in search for specimens."

No records of Faculty Meetings have been preserved prior to 1864. The explanation may be, as Mr. John I. Thompson affirmed in the fact that in his time a misdemeanor was taken care of immediately. A few words from the Professor especially interested in the case spoken to the President ended the affair. A favorite punishment, particularly for absence from classes, was sending the offender away from the table with the penalty of losing his meal. The command was given thus: "Mr. Jones was absent from his 10:30 class in Algebra. He will leave the table." The command had to be promptly obeyed, else the whole effect of discipline was nullified.

Rules and regulations were issued in 1859, and they bear the title of "College Rules and Regulations for the Farmers' High School of Pennsylvania." Dr. Pugh wrote that he tried the rule of no rules in his academic in Chester County, depending upon all to do the right and proper things. He concluded that rules aid in pointing out the right and in strengthening the impulses to do it. In this set of rules, the student is approached "as a gentleman," and is pledged treatment "as a friend." Chapel assemblies served as means of roll call and preceded "an orderly march to meals." They served to check up labor details as well as occasions of rhetorical and devotional exercises. Rooms and persons were to be in order for inspection; punctuality observed in recitations, study hours, and periods of detail. "At the ringing of the bell for retiring, each student is required to extinguish his light and retire for the night." Sunday observance is somewhat meticulously enforced, excluding "boisterous noise or disturbance," but also a "visit to each other's rooms," and attendance required at "the regular devotional exercises of the chapel." Prohibitions include intoxicating liquors; playing at any game of chance or keeping cards about the College; possessing fire arms (except as deposited with Professor Whitman), or keys to any apartments but one's own. Peculiarly on the index were wanton damage to property, unkind treatment of animals, and entering into a conspiracy to shield offenders by withholding information.

The order of exercises and plan of study reproduced show scant opportunity for idle hands or minds. Justice moreover is tempered with mercy in that, fourth class and elementary scholars are assigned to "recreation," instead of work or chemistry in that sleep engendering hour of six to seven in the morning.

Editorials and Committee visitations to the Farm School furnish addition information and criticism. Under date of June 2nd, 1859, the first year of the institution about half over, the following account appeared in the Centre County *Press*:

"The principal of the institution, Mr. Waring, and his assistant Mr. Gilliland, had the kindness to show us over the most attractive parts of the farm, which contains 400 acres, all in one field... The different kinds of trees, shrubs, etc., are all planted in families. Mr. Waring pointed out to us 60 different kinds of willow trees; and this novelty will be found among all the plants or trees and shrubbery on the farm; some to the number of 10, 20, 60, 100 and perhaps 200 different kinds. Mr. Waring also drew our attention to the wheat field which contains 100 different kinds of wheat—what a feast this presents for the eyes of our farmers. This will also be found to be the case with every other kind of seeds and grains. These seeds are brought from all parts of the world, for the sake of experimenting, so that farmers may learn which kind is the best suited to our soil, and which are the most productive. We were next conducted through the barn and workshops... We then visited the science building; of which only about one-third is completed, it is five stories high, built of stone, and already makes a very impressing appearance. We were conducted through the postoffice, library and reading-room. The latter contains newspapers from all sections of the state for the benefit of the students. We then got to the room containing the philosophical apparatus which is complete and the most splendid we ever saw... The Institution numbers 103 students, and a more contented and happy looking set we never saw, and we felt as though we could always be among them. Students are required to labor on the farm 3 hours each day, which they do in classes; while there one set were engaged in planting beans; another at harrowing; others plowing, etc., and Mr. Waring assured us that they are always willing to perform the labor assigned them, and do it cheerfully. This speaks well for them, and is a promising omen for the Institution."

The Report of a Committee from the Chester County Agricultural Society in 1861 is somewhat less roseate, and also more informative if we read between the lines:

"No class of men requires more scientific knowledge to enable them to thoroughly understand and appreciate the value of the various operations they have to perform or should perform, than do farmers. Notwithstanding your Committee are aware of all these things, they have some doubts of the success, general utility and practical benefit of the Institution to the common farmer; and yet if the various experiments instituted by the professors to test the benefits of the various fertilizers, be carefully carried on and the results published, it will be a great advantage to farmers generally," after noting that a number of students "keep excellent private gardens in addition to the duties required of them by the Institution," the report continues:

"We found the wheat field carefully measured and staked off in strips, upon which some dozen or more different substances called by some, fertilizer, had been sown and cross sown to test the affect of each, singly and in combination, which experiments are to be carried on for several years so as to embrace several different seasons and to afford all an opportunity or time to perform their action in the soil. The grain is to be threshed and cleaned separately and a fair account of the result kept for publication. In this way we think the institution may and will benefit the farmer. Had some of us known the exact value of the several kinds of fertilizers kept in our markets for sale, year ago; we might ere this have saved much more than our share of the cost of the institution."

"Your Committee did not find the interior of the building in as clean and neat order, not the nursery near so well worked and cleaned as they expected, and thought they should be; and so expressed ourselves to the professors, who excused themselves by pleading that in the unfinished condition of their building and the consequent disarrangement of the whole original design; not having proper persons to attend to the different duties not means of carrying out these plans as they wish or expect to, when they get the establishment finished and the whole thing in proper operation." Barring split infinitives and the complications of qualifying discourse, the report finds:

"One very serious objection, in our opinion to the Farm School property is that there is no water on it and none within near a mile except in the wells and cisterns; but as it is, neighbor like they don't mind it much. Very few springs are to be found in those valleys... Your Committee found much of the pigeon and chick-weed growing in the wheat fields and in some instances destroys nearly the whole crop. The pigeon weed particularly is much complained of and is very prevalent on the school farm."

While this Committee saw and chronicled "weeds," the Northumberland County Committee, J. F. Wolfinger, Chairman, a year later sang of flowers and fruits. They have left us in manuscript an account of the botanical garden, a part of whose form and comeliness has resisted the changes and ravages of three score and ten years. "The botanic garden is a very pretty spot—very neatly laid out into beds and walks, and adorned with many choice flower-bearing trees, shrubs, plants and vines... Connected with this botanic garden, there is a beautiful green-house or conservatory under glass, of rare and tender plants from California, China, Japan and Australia, and other foreign lands. Ladies, who visit the College, will always, especially in the summer season, find this a very pleasant and attractive spot—one that will please the eye, and give them enlarged views of the botanical kingdom. And the botanical, entomological, mineralogical, and conchological specimens and curiosities, in the possession of J. S. Whitman, the professor of botany, will be very interesting and suggestive of thought to all such persons as admire the wondrous works of our great and adorable Creator."

The college, so provincial, so bucolic might have lingered on a few years, with its unfinished buildings, and the severe handicaps of uniquely primitive conditions. The inventory of 1860 merits reproduction as a bald and true outline of its various possessions with which to meet the volume of criticisms poured forth, and to bear the even more treacherous mead of praise.

The Farm

This embraces 400 acres of land—with the exception of a small portion, reserved for a park, has been broken up, and the principal part of the stones picked off it; the stumps have been grubbed up, fences built, and hedges and orchards planted, so as to bring it into good condition for future cropping, and thus very materially enhance its value.

Farm Buildings

1st. An excellent double-decked barn 59 by 75 feet, and constructed upon the most approved plan, with wagon shed, corn crib, water cisterns, etc.

2nd. A large hog pen, with a granary over it 22 by 83 feet, including also a place for butchering.

3rd. A blacksmith shop, 20 by 28 feet, with all the appliances for doing smith work.

4th. A carpenter shop and tool house, 16 by 44 feet.

5th. Wash house. This building is 16 by 40 feet, situated near the barn, and is fitted up for washing students' clothes.

Dwelling Houses

One frame house, 28 by 28 feet, now occupied by the carpenter and superintendent of the college buildings.

College Buildings

These with few exceptions remain as they were when abandoned for want of funds in 1859. Mason work of entire basement is up and one-third of remaining five stories carried up and completed.

Temporary buildings for kitchen and dining hall are in use but poorly adapted thereto.

Nursery

"A large assortment of choice plants ready for sale at the proper season" which added "to the furniture and scientific collections in the college, and the stock and implements on the farm and garden, we will have the sum total of material belonging to the Institution."

Estimated Value

The following Estimate has been made of the value of the property belonging to the Institution:

400 Acres of Land, at $75—	$30,000.00
Nursery stock,—	$3,500.00
Barn, corn crib, sheds, etc. (original cost),—	$7,800.00
Hog pen and granaries, —	$1,000.00
Dwelling house and stable near smith shop—	$950.00
Dwelling house near college buildings—	$1,500.00
Tool house and carpenter shop,—	$400.00
Wash house and cistern,—	$450.00
Farm and garden tools, wagons, etc., etc.,—	$1,000.00
Stock for butchering—	$600.00
8 milch cows, at $25—	$200.00
8 Mules, —	$1,200.00
2 Horses,—	$120.00
60 Acres wheat in ground, at $9 per acre,—	$540.00
5 Acres rye in ground at $9 per acre—	$35.00
Chemical apparatus,—	$1,250.00
Philosophical apparatus,—	$1,000.00
Maps, charts, etc.—	$500.00
Libraries,—	$1,000.00
College buildings,—	$57,500.00
Furniture,—	$3,500.00
Material on hand to complete building,—	$14,000.00
	$128,145.00

The completion of the college building was now the herculean task upon which all interests centered. Every effort had been made by voluntary subscriptions to secure funds. Trustee McAllister during the years 1857 to 1860 personally carried the campaign of subscription and collection into ten counties. Dr. Pugh labored under no illusions, either as to what had been accomplished or what was yet to be done. Even though war threaten and destruction rage, this experiment in industrial education must not be allowed to fail. In his report to the Board at the close of the second academic year, Dr. Pugh reviewed the work of the institution; income and expenditures; results achieved on farm, in the nursery, and in the class room. The manual labor plan has so far succeeded "even in our present unorganized state" that "those who are efficient in class, are generally most reliable at work and the converse." The fact is urged that thirty-eight counties of the State are represented, and that many applications were received from other States which because of the instructions of the Trustees had to be refused admission. "We have not advertised more fully because the school has been filled without doing so, and because it has been advisable to get our buildings completed before we make special effort to have all the counties represented."

The report closes with an appeal for immediate actions:

> "Some persons who have felt interested in the Farm School, have fallen into the very great mistake of supposing that the Trustees commenced operations here upon too large a scale. It is said that they should have constructed a building that would have been complete for 100 students, rather than have commenced with one for 400 students, which they have not been able thus far to complete. It requires but little experience, with the working of an Institution like this, to perceive the fallacy of the above objection to the plan that has been adopted. A school like this can only succeed as a large school. It can only be completely organized as a large school, and without complete organization it cannot prosper. A small Agricultural School, complete in itself, would go down as a result of its inefficiency. A grand idea would be made to appear impracticable, because attempted upon too diminutive a scale.

"If we fail in the present unfinished state of our College Buildings, (as we must if they are not finished), it will be obvious to every one, who is acquainted with our circumstances, that our failure is the result of our not having received that pecuniary support which was absolutely necessary to bring fairly our Agricultural School into existence. Our experiment would fail because the conditions upon which its friends had predicted its success had never been supplied; while the question of success with the conditions supplied would still be left open for another attempt. But since a small Agricultural College, with our rates of admission, could not live, however well started, the inevitable consequence of an attempt upon such a scale would be, not only a failure in the act itself, but a loss of confidence in the principle involved in Agricultural Institutions such as would discourage the idea of a farther attempt to establish one.

"It cannot live long as it has been living. The friends of Agricultural education everywhere in the State should know that about $120,000 have already been expended here, and that $50,000 are wanted to make the material for which this sum has been spent, available for the purposes it has been expended. It cannot be too distinctly understood, that without an additional expenditure of $50,000, the $120,000 already spent must become a total loss. Our buildings must be completed speedily, or our school must cease to exist. I can see no middle ground between these alternatives."

The Board on December 5th, 1860 ordered the Report of Dr. Pugh printed for circulation, and took steps to secure from the Legislature the sum of fifty thousand dollars deemed sufficient to complete the building. At the next meeting of the Board, a Committee consisting of Pugh, McAllister and Watts was appointed to make any necessary modifications in plans, and to proceed with construction so as to have the building under roof before the first of November next. By Act of April 18th, 1861, the sum of forty-nine thousand nine hundred dollars was appropriated. Opposition was registered on the score that it was a school for special classes; that no one will be benefitted by the school's continuance. The condition of the State Treasury was cited, and petitions were presented remonstrating against further appropriations unless applied to the creditors of former contractors. Representative Butler refused to vote and gave as the reason that he "could give his assent, only, if buildings and grounds are owned by the State." The bill passed the House by a vote of 57 to 31.

In the Senate, the vote on the measure stood 18 to 12. It found an earnest supporter in Senator Ketcham who reviewed what other states were doing, and emphasized the fact that we legislate for other interests, commercial, mining, manufacturing, for everything else but the farming interest. Senator McClure, also, heartily championed the measure, affirming: "I regard it as the most necessary of all the appropriations we have made. After the actual necessities of government have been met, I shall vote against every other appropriation proposed in this body, if such action be necessary to secure this amount to the Farmer's High School."

A contract was entered into with George W. Tate of Bellefonte to complete the building under original plans for the sum of forty-one thousand five hundred dollars, the structure to be complete in every detail on December 1st, 1862. The war with increased difficulties in securing labor, the mounting costs of materials, etc., again made the terms of the contract impossible of fulfillment. However in December 1863, the building was completed, "a stately and substantial edifice constructed of a silicious magnesian limestone," "for commodiousness, completeness of detail, and stability of construction not equaled by the building of any Agricultural College in the world." Had it not been for a movement on the part of the Federal Government for endowing and organizing these new educational endeavors, it is still problematic, if the Farmer's High School of Pennsylvania, together with pioneer institutions in other States, would have survived.

This movement must now engage our attention.

CHAPTER 5

The Refounding of the College by the Nation and Commonwealth

"The Land-Grant Act is probably the most important single specific enactment ever made in the interest of education."

L. H. Bailey, Cyclopaedia of American Agriculture, Vol. IV.

"These institutions represent the genius of American Democracy, embodying Washington's ideas of national aid and control; Jefferson's physiocratic theory of the fundamental importance of agriculture; Franklin's plan for vocational training; and Lincoln's plea for the education of labor."

Yale Chronicles of America, Vol. 33.

"At least one college where the leading object shall be, without excluding other scientific and classical studies, and including military tactics, to teach such branches of learning as related to agriculture and the mechanic arts, in such manner as the Legislatures of the States may respectively prescribe, in order to promote the liberal and practical education of the industrial classes in the several pursuits and professions of life."

Federal Enactment, July 2nd, 1862.

"The same is hereby accepted by the State of Pennsylvania, with all its provisions and conditions, and the faith of the State is hereby pledged to carry the same into effect."

Statutes of Pennsylvania, April 1st, 1863.

Would these beginnings in industrial education in Michigan, Pennsylvania and Maryland have failed temporarily like those of other States had not the larger movement of a national system of schools worked itself out? An interesting academic question perhaps, but difficult to answer. We may affirm of Pennsylvania that such larger prospect was on the horison of the founders and friends of the Farm School, and that they bore an effective part in realizing it at Washington. Dr. Pugh wrote on January 6th, 1864: "The friends of the Agricultural College of Pennsylvania secured the passage of the Land Grant bill by Congress. A member of their Board of Trustees (then as now a prominent member of Congress) devoted almost an entire session in Congress[5] to its passage, and other friends of the college visited Washington several times for the same purpose. Without their aid the bill would not have passed." Still more explicitly, Dr. Pugh adds: "It was part of the plan of the friends of this College, when asking the Legislature to appropriate money to put up its large buildings, to secure an endowment from this source, and to this end they were at the same time laboring in Congress for the passage of the Land Grant bill. In view of their being confident of securing an endowment from this source, they promised the Legislature, when asking for money to complete the College buildings, not to ask the State for an endowment." In a

---

[5] James T. Hale- 36th-38th Congress. General James A. Beaver says of him: He was one of the loveliest characters I have ever known; not only a man of great ability but a diplomat as well. In Congress, he was the devoted champion of the land grant act and efficiently aided Mr. Morrill, of Vermont, in securing its passage... and in the times of stress and strain in the Legislature, he would be called to Harrisburg to assist in the passage of the measures affecting the welfare of the College. His presence nearly always led to a change in the atmosphere, and the correspondence...shows how much he contributed to the passage of the Acts which were essential to the welfare of the institution and prevented those which were detrimental. His connection with the college and the service which he rendered to it can hardly be appreciated by this generation. They ought to be appropriately recognized in Memorial Hall.

statement to the Judiciary Committee on the attempt to deprive the college of the benefits of the Federal Act under the date of March 3rd, 1864, we read: "They (Trustees and friends of the College) were astounded when they found the claims set up for this fund which are now before your honorable body, claims which would utterly defeat the object for which they asked the grant from Congress and for which Congress gave it."

We have previously mentioned the testimony of Dr. Pugh as to the early interest of Trustee Watts in industrial schools, twenty years prior to its agitation in Pennsylvania. We have, also, explicit statements of Judge Watts to the Legislature under date of February 24th, 1865, against the injustice of repeal because "the labors of the Trustees of the Agricultural College of Pennsylvania were steadily and persistently directed to the procurement of this very endowment fund at the same time they were engaged in the erection of the college buildings; and the institution never would have had existence, but from the confident expectation of a liberal endowment arising from the proceeds of the public lands." A year later, February 8th, 1866, Judge Watts adds: "The Board of Trustees looked upon this Act of Congress as almost the work of their own hands—as an endowment of their own institution; and not doubting for a moment but that our Legislature would so consider it, the Board set about to complete the building, a part of which only, capable of accommodating one hundred students, had at this time been built."

The grants of land to the states and to public enterprises was no new thing. But that such grants should be confined to causes which benefited all alike was not so well recognized. As early as 1803, Andrew Gregg, a member of Congress from Pennsylvania, opposed the Act of admission of Ohio with the attendant grant of public lands for roads and schools, on the ground that he has always been accustomed to consider the lands of the United States as common property. With what justice, he argued, can we then put out lands into this common fund or lay hold of any portion of these lands and apply them to the use and benefit of the people in one part of the country, to the entire exclusion of the rest as is contemplated by this bill. What authority, he asks, have we to give to the people of Ohio, land equal to a thirty-sixth part of their whole State; or to expend on the improvement of their roads, three percent of all money arising from the sale of public lands in that country. In reply to advocates of the bill, he concludes: "It is an absolute grant of a common property to the exclusive benefit of a few."

The violation of this principle, which was indeed the rule and not the exception, had brought all land grants under suspicion, and when the agitation started in various quarters for a national system of land-grant institutions, it met the prejudices which a reckless, wasteful policy for private gain had engendered. "Vote yourself a farm" was not amplified by the enemies of the new movement, into "vote yourself an education with your farm."

It is true that the slogan something must be done for the farmer, for the industrial worker, was used effectively. But the object in the mind of Representative Morrill was not to secure resources, merely; but rather to build a type of citizenship by a new kind of training. "Let us have such Colleges as may rightly claim the authority of teachers to announce facts and fixed laws, and to scatter broadcast that knowledge which will prove useful in building up a great nation great in its resources of wealth and power, but greatest of all in the aggregate of its intelligence and virtue." Now familiarly the argument runs as we recall the sentiments of the founders of The Pennsylvania State College as the Farmer's High School: "The farmer and the mechanic requires special schools and appropriate literature quite as much as any one of the so-called learned professions. The practical sciences are nowhere else called into such repeated and constant requisition." Yet more significant and prophetic, Mr. Morrill, continues: "It is plainly an indication that education is taking a step in advance when public sentiment begins to demand that the faculties of young men shall be trained with some reference to the vocation which they are to be devoted throughout life." It was this "public sentiment" working in the several States and issuing in definite institutions in some cases, that crystallized in the mind of Mr. Morrill and led to the legislation that bears his name. The claim that Professor J. B. Turner of Illinois was the originator of the Land-grant Act, and that he placed the enactment of the same into the hands of the Representative of Vermont, even if supported by unquestionable documentary evidence, which it is not, would prove too much.[6] The claims of pioneers and prophets from Michigan, Pennsylvania, Maryland, New York, Ohio, Tennessee, and a dozen others might be cited. All of which serves to prove that it was not an "idea" that originated in an individual mind so much as that it was a social movement, a common consciousness of a new and impelling need. The significant letter of Senator Morrill to President George W. Atherton under date of February 5th, 1894, so specifically and generously attributes the origin of the idea to environment and conditions, that I quote:

> "My service began in the House of Representatives in 1855. I soon noticed (first) that large grants of land were made for education as well as for other purposes, and that the older States were receiving little benefit from this large common property. Second, that the average product of wheat per acre in the Northern and Eastern States was rapidly diminishing while in England under more scientific culture, it was doing far better. Some institutions of a high grade in agriculture and the mechanic arts, I knew had been established in Europe. Third, the liberal education then offered at our colleges appeared almost exclusively for the instruction of the professional classes, or for ministers, lawyers, and doctors, while a far larger number, engaged in production and industrial employments, would be greatly benefited by appropriate higher education. Few of then existing colleges surrendered much time to practical sciences, which deserved greater prominence, and offer a larger field to liberal education.

> "My first bill, under such considerations, was introduced, and passed both houses in 1856. I do not remember any assistance prior to its introduction. After that Colonel Wilder of Massachusetts, Mr. Brown, President of the Peoples' College, New York, and others,

---

[6] A summary of the evidence may be found in "The Life and Public Services of Justin Smith Morrill by William Belmont Parker, pp. 259 ff. confirmatory, if not conclusive evidence that the honor of Father of the Land Grant Colleges belongs rightly to Mr. Morrill as the result of the thorough study of Federal Aid to Vocational Education by J. L. Kandel under the auspices of the Carnegie Foundation. Bulletin, Number Ten.

encouraged members of Congress in its support. My own speech was about all it had in its favor, but there was talk as well as a report of a Committee against it. Cobb of Alabama, and Spinner (?) of New York were opposed to it. In the Senate it had the earnest support of Senators Wade, Crittenden, and Pearce. It was vetoed by Buchanan, who suggested that he might have approved a bill providing for a professor of agriculture in some college in each State. Of course I had then to wait for a change of administration, and in 1862 again pushed through the bill amended so as to endow the colleges with more land. The value of the land grant to colleges was considerably diminished by the large amount of railroad grants and bounty lands competing in the market at that time. There was never any doubt about the approval of President Lincoln. Buchanan left Washington at once after March 4, 1861."

The following historic letter from Professor Turner to Dr. Pugh while it seems to emphasize the aid of Illinois to such a program of education contains no reference to the yet unsuccessful attempts to secure federal legislation and support. Nor is any shadow of a claim made for his own part in Morrill legislation by initiation at Washington. Nor, again, do his strictures on the type of training to be afforded by these institutions evince a grasp of principles such as the land grant legislation contemplated, nor such as President Pugh had already put into successful operation at The Farmers' High School of Pennsylvania. The letter is particularly important for its reaction upon our own early program of study and work. I copy it, unique in spelling, punctuation, and as written:

Jacksonville, Ill.
Nov. 20, 1861

Hon. Evan Pugh
Pres. Farm School etc

Dear Sir

Yours of Nov 4 is at hand: and I send you by this mail our League report which is as I suppose the document to which Mr. Foster refers—or at least the principle one—We began the agitation for farm schools in this State about twelve or fourteen years since: when the whole Union was a dead calm, on that most important and most interesting subject: We ultimately formed a league for the purpose: and after many years of incessant labor and struggle had the pleasure of seeing our ideas of the subject become popular over the whole Union, with varied attempts to realize them, as well as in our own State —

I believe the State of Illinois, both before the people and by legislative act, was the first State on the continent, to move toward any *general endowment* of such a scheme of education though perhaps not the first to attempt local and private enterprises: an outline of all which you will find in the report of the league herewith mailed.

I have looked over your catalogue with great pleasure in the evidence which it presents of your practical success, and of the soundness of your general views: It is true that an agricultural school cannot ever succeed on a *small scale,* in the very nature of things: Whether in this country any one can at present succeed, without the constant patronage and annual endowments and grants of the states in which they are located, is to say the least doubtful: No other system of education what ever has been self sustaining; and why should we expect this to be, alone of all others? But it will in the end like all other good systems amply repay all the cost it makes, either to the state or to individuals. I think the plan of only a *short six months term* for the winter, when the farmers can best spare their sons, with, a return home to labor on the farm in summer, (or at the institution,) is a better plan than the old Manual Labor plan, of alternate hourly work and study through the years:

> 1 Study can thus be safely driven for the six coolest months of the year almost exclusively:

2 The cost of board is far less.

3 The pupil can work to advantage, six months and apply his knowledge and observe facts, as well off from the Institutes farm as on it: and thus earn enough to support him the other six months at the Institute.

4 The plan opens the institute to a *much larger class* and gives a more undivided and uninterrupted time for both work and study in their turn, with equal safety to health, less cost, and greater chance of proficiency in knowledge

Yours truly

J B Turner

Justin Smith Morrill, the real founder of the system of Peoples' Colleges, the State Colleges and Universities was born in Strafford, Vermont, April 14th, 1810. His father and grandfather were blacksmiths and iron makers. His own education in schools ended when he was fourteen years of age, but his career shows him to have been a learner through an entire life time. Although Morrill speaks with pride of the "family escutcheon" as the blacksmith's hammer, and although he hails himself repeatedly as of the "plain people," his family was one of distinguished English extraction. His forebears, too, had honorable records in the Revolutionary War, and in the War of 1812. He engaged in business in his native town, later ventured a large general store in Portland, Maine. In 1830, he returned to Strafford, formed a business partnership and promoted a large and varied enterprise, "an anticipation in miniature of the great department stores of today." He read books from the circulating library, and through the help of friends and the activities of the lyceum, he became acquainted with the best literature. Through an attorney in Portland, he had been introduced to Blackstone's Commentaries and to the law.

His taste and personality developed as his business ventures prospered. By 1848, he had acquired a sufficient sum to withdraw from business entirely. He had as he said a love for agriculture, and for peaceful pursuits of rural life. Although but thirty-eight years of age, he "settled down to the quiet life of tilling a small farm, rearing a few sheep, improving his orchard, growing his flowers, and browsing in the library which it gave him so much pleasure to gather and increase."

But the future proved itself vastly different. He was elected to Congress in 1855, and for twelve successive years was a member of the House of Representatives. In 1867, he was transferred to the Senate, where he served continuously for thirty-two years. Tariff acts; Revenue and Finance Measures; Public Buildings and Monuments; the completion of the Washington Monument; the Library of Congress; but perhaps the great of all The Land Grant College Acts, are some of the achievements of his unique legislative career.

In the first session of the thirty-fifth Congress, December 17th, 1857, Representative Morrill of Vermont, introduced the Land-Grant Act. It is interesting to read the entry as it stands on the Records of the *Congressional Globe*: "I ask leave to introduce a bill donating public lands to the several States and Territories which may provide Colleges for the benefit of agriculture and the mechanic arts." In the course of the debate on Committee reference, he adds, "where a liberal education for those engaged in the industrial pursuits and professions of life may be obtained." Mr. Morrill wished to have the measure referred, not to the Committee on Public Lands which he rightly forecasted was somewhat hostile, but to the Committee on Agriculture of which he himself was a member. After much discussion, the bill was committed to the former body. Representative Cobb of Alabama, chairman of the Committee, a vigorous opponent of the grant to the States but not to the educational object of the grant itself, admitted that the chief objection arose because of accusations brought against the Committee during the last administration. Himself a member of that Committee, he was doubly sensitive to the charge that "the Committee did more business and committed more high-handed plunder (I use that word) during the last session of Congress than any Committee of the House ever did before."

While denying the charges, he continued, "the committee have this session determined to husband the public lands." He adds naively that if he dared do the unparliamentary thing, he would confess that "only two members of the Committee favored the minority or affirmative report."

Other objections were pressed. The bill proposes the "inauguration of a new system, the result of which no man can forsee. Certain it is that the result will not be a good one." The object is worthy, but the means of obtaining it are not so. The spectre of States Rights stalks into the argument; the general government was not formed to support local institutions. It has not the power, and if it had, its exercise would be unwise. Representative Cobb argues the proposition that the voting of lands without pecuniary compensation is an abuse of power, of doubtful constitutionality. He justifies his vote and that of others on immense grants to railroads as not consistent with this principle since such grants increase the value of lands. The argumentum ad hominem is fasted upon him by his own vote for land grants to found asylums for the insane. He frankly admits, he was in error, an error of judgment in the face of a strong sentimental appeal, and he seeks absolution from his colleagues for his unwise and unconstitutional lapse.

Still other objections poured forth from the inequality of distribution; the new states with large tracts of public lands within their borders would not be willing to share their bounties with states having no such lands. There was genuine fear, too, that the locating of lands in one state by the citizens of another, would lead to serious complications. Large tracts would fall into the hands of non-resident speculators; and held for profit would retard the growth and development of the West. Finally the unworthy objection is raised that the measure would necessitate taxation by the various states to erect the buildings. While it is clear that New York, Michigan (and Representative Cobb might have added Pennsylvania and Maryland) have colleges built, in other States, the burden of taxation renders it in view of all its features, "one of the most monstrous, iniquitous and dangerous measures which had ever been submitted to Congress."

In the Senate, the bill met with yet stronger opposition. To Senator Clay's standard rallied such influential leaders as Pugh of Ohio, Mason of Virginia, Davis of Mississippi, Rice of Minnesota, Jones of Iowa. The educational features of the bill were relatively ignored in the Senate debate. While the tactics of the negative in emphasizing constitutional points brought the Southern Senators and their Northern conferees together; the result was equally to concentrate and consolidate the affirmative support among the Northerners. The unique position was advanced by Senator Rice, that the best way to establish agricultural colleges was to give to each man a college of his own, one hundred and sixty acres of land, where he and his children can learn how to make the earn fruitful and yield abundantly. He adds, "but do not give lands to the states to enable them to educate the sons of the wealthy at the expense of the public. We want no fancy farmers; we want no fancy mechanics; but we do want homes for the working artisans and the cultivators of the soil." Delays in consideration and even recommittal to Committee kept final action from being taken in the Senate until February 7th, 1859, when an amended measure was passed by a vote of twenty-five to twenty-two. This Senate bill as amended was agreed to by the House on February 16th, 1859.

The prestige, wisdom, and parliamentary skill of Representative Morrill had brought a much earlier decision in the House. Nearly a year before the Senate reached a vote, on April 22nd, 1858, the House passed the Morrill Act but by the close vote of one hundred five to one hundred. The arsenal of arguments was prepared by Representative Morrill himself, who anticipated nearly all the objections raised in both branches of Congress, as well as in the veto message of President Buchanan. In a deliberate, carefully prepared, and significantly prophetic speech, he constructed a positive case for the wisdom of the people in establishing a national system of education through the agencies of the several states.

Mr. Morrill reviewed the veritable new array of interest in agriculture and mechanic arts as evidenced by societies, organizations, petitions from every source, and memorials from State Legislatures. He affirmed that he was not greatly impressed nor concerned with the constitutional arguments in the case. The facts are that the Federal Government has done much for the army and navy; has given grants of land to railroads; guaranteed literary protection by copyright, and patents to inventors. Bounties have been extended to seamen and educational grants made in the new states. Commerce has been gladly aided when it "comes to our doors, gay in its attire and lavish in its promises, we hand out and deliver at once our gold... but all direct encouragement to agriculture has been rigidly withheld." He illustrated the necessity of Federal aid by the example of foreign nations, and the greater populations their resources support. Our mineral wealth and resources call loudly for development and conservation—that includes instruction and americanization of the workers. Mechanics are the "right arm to do the handwork of the nation. Let us furnish the means for that arm to acquire culture, skill, and efficiency. We educate for war, why not for peace." There is no conflict with literary colleges; and in a homely illustration, he affirms that the literary colleges need have no more jealously of agricultural colleges than a porcelain manufactory would have of an iron foundry.

Experimentation is demanded by the problems arising in connection with soils, fertilizers, grain, stock-breeding, diseases of plants, fruits, and animals. All ages have recognized the importance of agriculture and foreign, nations have established schools. There is abundant precedent for the dedication of public lands for educational purposes. To June 30th, 1857, over sixty-seven million acres of land have been set aside from schools and universities in different states and territories. The Fathers of the Republic sanctioned such uses of public lands as a right of the sovereign people through its Congress. "This measure is but an extension of the same principle over a wider field—wider in its application but not wider in amount, for the number of acres now proposed (20,000 acres to each State for each Representative and Senator from that State) is scarcely larger than have been donated to individual States."

Line upon line, precept upon precept, Mr. Morrill continues:

> "Pass the measure and we shall have done:
> Something to enable the farmer to raise two blades of grass instead of one;
> Something for every owner of land;
> Something for all who deserve to own land;
> Something for cheap scientific education;

Something for every man who loves intelligence and not ignorance;

Something to induce a father's sons and daughters to settle and cluster around the old homestead;

Something to remove the last vestige of pauperism from our land;

Something for peace, good order, and a better support of Christian Churches and Common Schools;

Something to enable sterile railroads to pay dividends;

Something to enable the people to bear the enormous expenditures of the national government;

Something to check the passion of individuals, and of the nation, for indefinite territorial expansion and ultimate decrepitude;

Something to prevent the dispersion of our population, and to concentrate it around the best lands of our country—places hallowed by church spires, and mellowed by all the influences of time—where the consumer will be placed at the door of the producer and thereby

Something to obtain higher prices for all sorts of agricultural productions; and

Something to increase the loveliness of the American landscape. Scientific culture is the sure precursor of order and beauty. Our esthetic Diedrich Knickerbockers, who have no land, will have a fairer opportunity to become great admirers of land that belongs to others."

Mr. Morrill closed his appeal by effectively quoting the latest report of the land office showing 1,088,792,498 acres to be disposed of. While with the bill passed, there would still remain 1,083,000,000 acres.

The Morrill Act was vetoed by President Buchanan, February 24th, 1859, on the following six counts:

1. It is not financially expedient at this time
2. The functions of the Federal and State Governments must be kept distinct
3. The measure would operate injuriously to new states

4. There is no power in the Federal Government to enforce or secure the state's fulfillment of the contract gift

5. The institutions, if established, would interfere with existing colleges in which agriculture is taught and in which it ought to be taught

6. The President doubts the power of Congress under the Constitution to donate lands.

Efforts were made to forestall the veto. The Board of Trustees of the Farmers' High School of Pennsylvania adjourned and in a body went to Washington to plead for justice at the hands of a fellow citizen of the Commonwealth. Keen regret was felt over the action of the President. Dr. Pugh wrote: "I noted while a student in Germany with shame that a countryman of mine vetoed this beneficent act." Mr. Morrill with self-control but with evident deep emotion replied to the veto message, and called for the passage of the bill over the veto. It failed to secure the required two-thirds, however; and until a change of administration, Mr. Morrill or his friends made no further attempt. The President had lost an opportunity to placate fate in the interests of a sure bid for a just name and fame. Mr. Morrill's estimate of the veto deserves reading for its insight into the spirit of the man but also for its devastating judgment of monetary power linked with party ignorance and political prejudice. "The measure was not introduced as a party measure, nor was it advocated as a party measure. It has received the cordial support of members of both sides of this House. It fought its way on its own merits... The telegraphic news of this veto will start a tear from the eyes of more than one manly boy whose ambition will now be nipped in the bud. Our great object was to arrest the degenerate and downward system of agriculture by which American soil is rapidly obtaining the rank of the poorest and least productive on the globe and to give to farmers and mechanics that prestige and standing in life which liberal culture and the recognition of the Government might afford. To all this the President turns a deaf ear... in my judgment the President has committed, if not a crime, at least a blunder."

When the thirty-seventh Congress convened Mr. Lincoln was President and the atmosphere both in the North and in the South was electric. Coming events which were already casting their ominous shadows might well have deterred Mr. Morrill from pursuing his vision and task. The Civil War had begun—surely the times demanded undivided surrender to the crisis at hand. But Mr. Morrill's sight and faith penetrated the depths of despair, to find the conviction that the Union must and will endure; that its greatest problem is not and will not be war, but the reconstruction of peace, the rebuilding of the national life. In this task, education of the kind he advocated, colleges and universities of the kind he would establish must play the major role. Such training, such institutions must be provided and developed even in the midst of the darkness and destruction, the chaos and disorganization of war.

Mr. Morrill re-introduced his bill in the House of Representatives on December 16th, 1861. With a negative recommendation it was brought out of committee on May 29th, 1862. In the Senate, members from the seceding states being absent, the bill was favorably reported by Committee. It passed the Senate June 10th, 1862. The vote was recorded, thirty-two to seven, the negative votes issuing from the states of Wisconsin, Iowa, Kansas, Delaware, and Minnesota. The House (whose Committee action has been variously interpreted and misinterpreted was really based upon the exigencies of war) was brought to support the action of the Senate. On June 17th, 1862, by a vote of ninety to twenty-five, the measure passed. This was the most decisive majority the bill ever received in the House. Promptly on July 2nd, 1862, President Lincoln, the friend of education, of labor, of the artisan and of the farmers approved the bill. So long as the Republic endures, these institutions, State Colleges and Universities will be monuments to the genius of democracy in Abraham Lincoln, carrying into future generations emancipation of mind and hand from ignorance and slavery.

The second Morrill Act differed from the original by an increase in apportionment of land or scrip to thirty thousand acres for each Senator and Representative in Congress. Military Training was specifically included, and a more effective plan of supervision worked out, without, however limiting the initiative and regulation of the several states. Various misconceptions and misunderstandings were engendered during the consideration of the measure, some of which still persist in critical discussion and attacks. The ghost of federal control at the expense of the freedom of the state nurtured a fear, then as now, that obscured the real questions of merit. The interminable discussions of lands and scrip, the interests of the farming class eclipsed the broader purposes and ideals of these so-called Agricultural Colleges. A convenient or accidental label of a filing official, a short-circuited epithet fastened on the measure a class or early "Farm bloc" interpretation, which enlightened agricultural education has long since abandoned, if indeed it was ever seriously held by any one. Democracy is not advanced by classing opportunities so as to force and enforce a vocational caste, merely; but by massing opportunity so as to provide full play for individual aptitudes. The means so to develop them must also be present in their larger social perspectives. The man and the citizen must be included in the training of the artizan or farmer, the engineer or chemist.

The oft-repeated strictures that Mr. Morrill had no conception of the kind of training or sort of institutions he was promoting; that no well-defined subject matter, method or equipment was available; that, in still more modern phraseology, no general policy, no project or objective was in the minds of the Peoples Colleges or National Schools, constitutes a veritable boomerang when it is realized that the very genius of these institutions, the services they are rendering, are owing to their flexibility and adaptability to the various conditions, needs, opportunities, and responses of the individual states. A perpetual fund, so reads the enactment, is to be held inviolable by each state which accepts the Act, "to the endowment, support, and maintenance of at least one College, where the leading object shall be, without excluding other scientific and classical studies, and including military tactics, to teach such branches of learning as are related to agriculture and the mechanic arts in such manner as the Legislatures of the States may respectively prescribe, in order to promote the liberal and practical education of the industrial classes in the several pursuits and professions of life." Here are both sailing orders and port aims, the voyage is the test of democracy, the people themselves, in the diverse and individual commonwealths.

In faded ink on the records of the Board of Trustees, meeting in the college building, September 2nd, 1862, the following action may be read:

"Whereas by an Act of the Congress of the United States passed at its last session entitled, An Act donating Public Lands to the several States and Territories which may provide Colleges for the benefit of Agriculture and the Mechanic Arts requires the action of the Legislature of Pennsylvania at its next session that our institution may derive the benefits, therefrom, to which it may be entitled, Therefore

"That the same be referred to a Committee whose duty it shall be to procure the action of the next legislature on the subject." The Committee consisted of Messers. Watts, Hiester, and McAllister, but upon the request of Mr. McAllister the name of Judge Hale was substituted for his own.

The Committee proceeded with its commission and on January 20th, 1863 an act was presented in the House by Representative J. P. Rhoades of Cumberland County. It was referred to the Committee on Judiciary General and on February 4th, 1863 was reported back to the House. The Act recited the "high regard for the agricultural interests of the State" by the Legislature as evidenced by the "establishment of the Agricultural College of Pennsylvania, and by making liberal appropriations thereto." Therefore in the five sections of the Act, the Commonwealth accepted the Federal Grant; provided for the disposition of the Land Scrip; authorized a Board of Commissioners consisting of the Governor, Auditor General, and the Surveyor General to act with power in sale of scrip and in the investment of proceeds. Section four provided for payment, until otherwise ordered by the Legislature of Pennsylvania, the Annual interest accruing, to the Agricultural College of Pennsylvania for the endowment, support, and maintenance of said institution, which College is now in full and successful operation, and where the leading object is, without excluding other scientific and classical studies and including military tactics, to teach such branches of learning as are related to agriculture and the mechanic arts. The last Section, five, required a report to the Legislature on or before the first day of February of each year of the receipts and expenditures. Various amendments were made to the measure as originally presented. The Surveyor General was substituted for "land office and Secretary of land office." A Senate amendment was accepted by the House prohibiting investments "in any other stocks than those of the United States or of the Commonwealth." Consequent upon the claims that the income would be large for one college, at the suggestion of the Speaker of the House, unanimous consent was secured to insert in Section four that "until otherwise ordered by the Legislature of Pennsylvania."

The beginnings of opposition tactics appear in the attempt to postpone action, defeated by a vote of thirty-one to fifty-eight. More significantly, Mr. Pershing of Cambria proposes the addition to section four, "and such other Agricultural College or Colleges in equal proportions as may hereafter be incorporated." Mr. Pershing, also, advocated the use of part of the proceeds for asylums for disabled soldiers, or for the common schools. Mr. Vincent countered rightly that there was nothing in the act to prevent division of the fund later. However, he urged immediate action on the bill, since the value of the lands was decreasing, the best lands to be located were being taken. The Act, he insisted, should have been passed a year ago as in the case of States in which lands lie, where special sessions of legislatures were convened. The measure finally passed the House by the decisive majority of eighty-two to nine on February 26th, 1863.

The bill promptly appeared in the Senate, and on March 11th, 1863 was reported from the Committee on Agriculture but with Sections four and five omitted. These were restored, and an action governing the type of investments was voted. Amendments to fix a minimum price per acre for the land scrip, at seventy-five or fifty cents per acre were debated and lost. The most convincing argument seemed to be that any fixation of prices would be a reflection upon the business and executive sense of the Commission itself.

Mr. Johnson of Lycoming argued rightly either accept the grant for one institution already in existence, or else accept it and build from the beginning. He reviewed the history of the Agricultural College, and on the basis of Philadelphia quotations on land scrip as sixty cents per acre, he argued that the income was not too large for any one college. So many misunderstandings and misconceptions of the terms of the Land Grant came out in debate that it is distinctly worth while to quote from the speech in the Senate of Mr. Johnson. After a clear and concise statement on the conditions of the Federal

Act, he continued: "Now, Mr. Speaker, those are the conditions under which we may accept this munificent grant under the Act of Congress, and we cannot accept it under any other conditions. And the question arising here is... whether we will pledge to the Congress of the United States our faith, that we will appropriate out of the funds of the Commonwealth, some two or three hundred thousand dollars for the erection of an Agricultural College accompanied with an annual expense thereafter, out of the funds of the Commonwealth for keeping that college in repair, or whether we will avail ourselves of the circumstances in which we find ourselves placed at this time, in reference to the Agricultural College erected in the County of Centre, which is a State Institution, having been erected in part out of funds paid out of the Treasury of the Commonwealth, and in part by the contributions of citizens of this State—an institution which is in every particular just such a one as is contemplated and described in this act of Congress."

This well-high interminable but veiled hypothetical question proved effective, and the bill passed the Senate, and was signed by Governor A. G. Curtin on April 1st, 1863.

The reaction of the Agricultural College may be appreciated by this historic letter of Dr. Pugh to Mr. McAllister written at Harrisburg, Monday, ten and a half P. M. (March 23) 1863: "I hasten to inform you that our bill passed (thanks to the industry and influence of Judge Hale) this evening. It is all right and ready for the Governor's signature, which Judge Hale will secure as soon as he comes home which will I think be tonight or in the morning. I shall try and get Hale to go to Washington and see about securing the Land Warrants that the Scrip may go into the market at once.

"I leave at 2 A.M. to meet the Spruce Creek Stage. I trust it may never be necessary to so wholly neglect my duties at the College for so long a time again, but I think the friends of the College will under the circumstances pardon the neglect."

The dream of Dr. Pugh was not to be realized. The convening of the Legislature in 1864 was marked by the efforts to repeal, to modify, to practically annul the very act itself. This rather bitter struggle, too, was continued through the Sessions of sixty-five, sixty-six, and sixty-seven with intermittent echoes in later years down to 1881. The Act of 1863 carried no funds for the expense of the Commission, although Section three of the Federal Act expressly provided that such payments be made by the States accepting the grant. No time was stated with which the commission should act, and the delay was, also, fostered by certain institutions and interests in the Commonwealth which hoped to share in the benefits of the Federal Law. More important than all, the prosecution of the War detracted from decisive and speedy action by the Commission. When the Legislature met in 1864, there were organized groups favoring a repeal of the Act of Acceptance of the year previous; of division of its bounty to three or more institutions; of using it for the education of orphans of soldiers and sailors of the War; of diverting it to the support of the Common Schools; and even of establishing separate institutions for Agriculture, Mechanic Arts, and Military Science. The discussion served to clarify the aims and purposes of the grant within the body of the Legislature itself, but the picture of "greed" and "cupidity" on the part of certain denominational colleges (on behalf of them at least) does not constitute a pleasing one. The compliment to the lobbying propensities of some of these denominational colleges was bestowed on the floor, in open session, by a protesting solon that there are "more outside borers (if such they may be termed) with reference to it than I ever saw interested in any bill before." The Representative from Blair County affirmed: "Now, Mr. Speaker, I think that the Classical Colleges and their advocates ought to absent themselves from this hall for at least the remainder of this session. We have had them here all the session annoying the Legislature about this land scrip. Yesterday as was supposed they received a quietus, and I trust that we shall not this morning revive their drooping spirits." The Representative from Centre speaks in less guarded tones to Mr. McAllister: "I have been closely watching the movements of the land thieves that infect this capital, but until this morning I have not been able to get any information of importance. Dr. ----- of the ----- arrived here yesterday and has succeeded in getting a meeting of the Committee having the matter in charge. They adjourned this morning without taking any action on the subject but will meet again tomorrow morning. They are likely to report in favor of dividing it into three parts. The

Allegheny College, the Polytechnic are the favored institutions. I feel pretty well satisfied that this bill cannot pass—in the Senate the measure has not met with favor. The Committee there refuse to report any bill. They will however make a strong effort in the House to procure the passage of some bill. If they report a bill I will inform you. Either yourself or Dr. Pugh should come here and assist in preventing its passage."

For thwarting all efforts during 1864 to divide and dissipate the endowment too much emphasis can scarcely be attributed to the work of Dr. Pugh. His "Plan for the Organization of Colleges for Agriculture and the Mechanic Arts with Especial Reference to the Organization of the Agricultural College of Pennsylvania" is a masterly presentation of what he saw clearly, and prophetically realized in the cause of industrial education. Although addressed, as the sub-title indicates to the Board of Trustees of the Agricultural College of Pennsylvania convened at Harrisburg, January 6, 1864, in view of the endowment of this institution by the land scrip fund donated by Congress to the State of Pennsylvania, it had a wide appeal and influence. The correspondence of Dr. Pugh shows that it was widely sought for, and that it had a decisively moulding influence upon the early, inchoate aims and programs of these new institutions throughout the country. In the educational history of the Commonwealth, it in all justice, enforces the comparison with the underlying achievements of the Hon. Thaddeus Stevens. The one was the champion and preserver of our Common School System; the other of its democratic completion and logical development into the State College or University.

It was an illuminating study of the character and resources of existing colleges, budgets, expenditures and balance sheets. The resources required to sustain Agricultural and Industrial Colleges were detailed. The organization, personnel, buildings were set forth, and the inevitable necessity of experiment and research. "The spirit of the present age has been moulded to its present form by the investigations of science... The spirit of the age proclaims the necessity of scientific researches in every department of industrial pursuits, from the peaceful operations of the Agricultural Bureau at Washington, to the death-dealing avengers of treason, now in Charleston Harbor. Our Industrial

Colleges, to meet the demands of the age, must be experimental Institutions, no less than for teaching what is already known, in science... There is scarcely any limit to the amount of means that may be advantageously spent in scientific investigations, in all the experimental sciences." He puts in a plea for scholarships, prizes, etc., for poor but meritorious students, and adds the personal note that during the year and a half in which he was a student in the University of Leipzig, Germany, about three hundred students derived gratuitous aid from the University. "It was from these students, much more than from their wealthy associates, that the succeeding great men of the University were derived." Plan and courses of instruction were set forth under six headings, and an estimate of the probably income of the Land-Grant Fund compared with the outgo demanded of an Industrial College. The whole was eminently practical as well as thorough. A copy was placed in the hands of every member of the Legislature and sent to the newspapers and other moulding forces of public sentiment and thought.

At the close of the report, Dr. Pugh recites that in "some States the representatives of several Literary Colleges with singularly bad taste, made a general rush to the State Legislature to secure a portion of the proceeds of the bill and in a general scramble for a share of the spoils, in some instances, defeated all legislation upon the subject." He concludes by remarking that it is "due to the 23 literary colleges in Pennsylvania to say that they made no effort to obstruct legislation upon the bestowal of the income from the endowment fund, doubtless knowing, as they must have known, that the friends of this College had been mainly instrumental in getting the bill, donating the land, through Congress; and hence *by courtesy*, no less than *by right*, and according to the spirit of the bill were entitled to the fund for the endowment of the State Institution for which they procured it." A melancholy postscript adds that since the above was put into the printer's hands, it appears the tribute was "too hastily expressed." He closes by enumerating a few of the many and obvious reasons why the bill read in places and referred to a Committee, proposing that one-third of the land scrip be assigned to Allegheny College, at Meadville should not be "encouraged," a "claim so unreasonable, so unjust, and which will so effectually tend to defeat the object of the land grant bill, while it must cripple, for many years to come, the cause of Industrial Education in our State."

The amplification of this appended note into "A Statement made by E. Pugh of the Agricultural College of Pennsylvania, at a special meeting of the Judiciary Committee at Harrisburg, convened March 3rd, 1864 in reference to the proposition to deprive this College of its Endowment" is a logical, unanswerable brief for the cause of Industrial Education. President John Martin Thomas has called it an "educational classic." It was forged at white heat in a situation which united, as do all great crises in life, a call for clear thinking with deep feeling. The words flow like sparks from the tempering steel of his active life.

> "What I have said is what I wrote down in moments snatched from days in which I was already overloaded with duties; but I leave the question with you. You are called upon to act in a question of the most momentous interest that ever engaged the attention of legislators in this or any other country. You are called upon to decide whether the future generations of our State shall have for the education of the industrial classes one grand, efficient system of education in our noble Institution which must command the respect of all the friends of education the world over, or whether the means with which such an Institution might be founded are to be dissipated amongst a large number of Institutions, leaving all too poor and inefficient to afford thorough instruction in Industrial Education anywhere in our State. The Industrial Classes and the friends of Industrial Education of the present age, and their more enlightened sons in future generations, will sit in judgment upon your decisions. You will either give to them one Grand Institution like Harvard University, or the world-renowned Educational Institutions of Europe, which will unite all the interests of Industrial Education in our State, or you will transmit to them a number of petty Institutions jealous of each other, who will come up to succeeding Legislatures to exhibit their poverty and dispute with each other about whatever means of support may seem to be within reach of their needy hands.

Whatever you may do, and however weak or illogical may have been my effort to induce you to keep the fund together, the time will come, gentleman, when every word that is now said, and every act that is now committed in reference to this thing will be weighed as precious elements in the history of Industrial Education in this Country."

With so strong a conviction in the righteousness of the cause, he hurls the challenge:

"If any other State Institution should ever arise having stronger claims upon this Fund than the Agricultural College of Pennsylvania, let it have it, not a *part* of it, but all of it. The Agricultural College of Pennsylvania, like the Hebrew mother before Solomon, would rather see her child given undivided to a usurper, and die herself for want of its support, than share with them the mutilated fragments of what could only effect the object of its existence by being undivided... This College, although it has about $200,000 worth of property, also has about $40,000 of debt. The debt is increasing every year, even with its very small number of professors. It cannot fulfill its mission with its present resources. We are constantly receiving questions from all parts of the country which we cannot answer. We are often applied to, to make investigations which we cannot make; and we see scores of subjects associated with the industrial pursuits of life, which need investigations in order to teach properly, but which we cannot investigate because we have not a sufficient number of professors to allow all these things to be done; and yet they all should be done, and we are here today to beg of you, gentleman, to encourage no legislation that will prevent us from obtaining those means by which alone they can be done."

The battle in the Legislature of 1864 for repeal, for division, for diversion into other channels, for holding all funds in the Treasury, etc., was a long and difficult one. In the interests of allaying misunderstandings, the plain legal issues of the Act being repeatedly ignored, the House on motion of the

Representative from this district, reprinted the Act of Congress of July 2nd, 1862. An invitation to the Legislature to visit the College was also sent by the Board of Trustees. The invitation follows:

Carlisle, Feb. 26, 1864

To the Honorable House of Representatives
and the Senate of the Commonwealth of Pennsylvania:

The great interest which has been evinced for the establishment of the Agricultural College of Pennsylvania, suggests that the important features of the Institution should be well understood; its aims and objects, and the character of those who have it in charge; its location, its general fitness to attain success. This information cannot be so well imparted to the people of the State as through their representatives.

It would afford the Board of Trustees and Faculty great satisfaction if the Senate and House of Representatives would appoint an early day to visit the Institution.

I have the honor to be

Very respectfully your obedient servant
Frederick Watts
President, Board of Trustees

The invitation was accepted, a goodly number but without roll call were present. Preparations for the August visit were thus described by Tellico Johnson a student of the Agricultural College: "We had everything put in ship shape, fires in all the furnaces lighted, laboratory stoves and furnaces running full blast, everything in the way of apparatus on display, a big dinner prepared, turkey, ice cream, everything the best and plenty of it. We students enjoyed that dinner; it was most unusual. The members of the Legislature and their wives and the State officials inspected everything and then sat down and ate their fill. Dr. Pugh told me he was afraid the dinner would cost more than the College would get out of it."

The plan of campaign in the Legislature against the Act of April 1863 accepting the Federal Land Grant shaped itself under two measures, one for repeal, followed by a second one for a re-distribution or assignment. Various unorganized attempts to effect these ends were either held in Committee or brought out with negative recommendations. The real battle began on March 30th, when an act to repeal was read in place. Henceforth events moved with almost drastic force to a tragic climax at the College. The Committee on Education reported the bill with repeal of the four sections, authorizing disposition by sale of the Land Scrip, and also its benefits to the College. As amended, only the latter sections were excluded. Mr. Clymer of Berks County argued that the grant was too large for any one college; that the grant of 1863 to the Agricultural College was temporary and provisional. No other institution was ready at that time to comply with the conditions. Therefore, if repealed, the Legislature is free to distribute to three or more institutions. Mr. Lowry of Erie a protagonist for Allegheny College affirmed: "But now she [the Agricultural College] comes swaggering in here and says the whole of its must be hers. Unless she is willing to take a fair proportion of it, I will cast my vote against giving her one dollar of it. If she is a prudent institution she does not need it, if she is an imprudent institution, she does not deserve it."

Mr. Johnson of Lycoming argued against both repeal and division. He emphasized the legal or constitutional point that the repeal would put into jeopardy the right of the Federal Grant to the State. He also stressed the practical objection growing out of the manifest inability of the legislature to agree on the disposition of the remainder. The bill on final passage was carried, by a vote of twenty-three to nine.

The scene shifts to the House. It is referred to the Judiciary Committee on April 22nd; and five days later the House voted, forty-eight to thirty-six to discharge the Committee from further consideration of the Bill. Mr. Smith of Chester defended the Committee, while Mr. Wells of Erie countered that it looked like a "smothering process," and averred a kind of "recklessness of expenditure" about the Centre County College. He criticized Dr. Pugh's estimates of the amounts needed to support a genuine industrial college. Mr. Alexander insisted no action on the bill was needed. Nothing could be gained by legislation at this time, and nothing will be lost by leaving the acceptance act as it stands. He made a strong defense of the college, not as a local or Centre County institution, as insinuated, but as a college of and for the whole Commonwealth. He showed the need of the kind of training provided, and insisted that the animus of the repeal was one merely of throwing the land grant into the arena for open scramble. It is unjust to the college to divide; a species of robbery and of covetousness; a lack of common decency, at least, not to wait until the scrip was sold. If it were too much for one institution, it could then in all wisdom and fairness be divided.

A call for the previous questions was precipitated. Mr. Olmsted came to the rescue of the member from Centre, "who has sat here all the session while others were making their speeches with the volubility of the mistress of a Vienna Fish Market, and when he gets up to make a speech in a reasonable and proper manner, this call of the Previous Question is an act of flagrant injustice." On May 2nd, the bill was again called up. Two members noted the absence of Mr. Alexander at the funeral of President Pugh, and a vote was delayed. Attempts to postpone a vote to a definite date were defeated, but on May 4th (Mr. Alexander having returned, the House proceeded by a vote of forty-five to forty-four to a consideration of Senate Bill, Number 617) Mr. Wells moved amendment to strike out all such parts as authorize the sale of the Land Scrip; and, (contrary to the express conditions of the Federal Act) the State is authorized to locate the lands and hold for sale. These and other proposed amendments to fix a price for sale of Scrip did not meet with favor.

In the midst of debate, Mr. Olmsted pointed out that in order for the House now to pass the bill, a two-thirds vote is necessary, since it is one day before adjournment. Were the bill amended, it would require on the morrow, a majority of two-thirds in both branches of the legislature. Deliberately and dramatically pointing to the fact, the admitted fact, that two-thirds of the members of the House do not favor the bill, he moved indefinite postponement. A call of Ayes and Noes was demanded by Mr. Olmsted and Mr. Alexander, the vote stood, forty-seven to forty-four.

In the interval, while the House was giving consideration to Senate Bill Number 617, another measure was offered in the Senate (Bill 809 read by Mr. Turrell, Committee on Education) on April 14th. This measure fixed as a minimum for sale of Scrip the sum of eighty cents per acre, and prescribed that the fund be divided into six equal portions and "apportioned among the six following Colleges within the State viz Allegheny College at Meadville, Polytechnic College at Philadelphia, Agricultural College in Centre County, Pennsylvania College at Gettysburg, University of Lewisburg in Union County and the Western University at Pittsburgh." The colleges as designated were to pay to the Commissioners of the Commonwealth eighty cents per acre without expense to the State. Such colleges shall have their leading object as stated in the Federal Statutes. "Annual Reports are required and as an equivalent for said appropriations, tuition shall be free to the sons of the citizens of Pennsylvania." Action must be taken by notification to the Governor, within one year, by any of these institutions, otherwise "the fund shall be divided pro rata to such institutions herein named as shall accept the same and give the notice aforesaid."

The other side of this picture of legislative and institutional rivalries was being tragically enacted at the College. This last attempt to throw into utter confusion the whole magnificent opportunity before the State was keenly felt by Dr. Pugh. This blow at Industrial Training came with almost the force of a personal affront, his own sense of justice and fairness was outraged. He was engaged upon a reply to this "nefariously stupid legislation," as it seemed to him; the last act and word of his for the college, when destiny enacted its closing scene. Appended to the draft in his own handwriting, and broken off in the very midst of a sentence the explanatory note follows, written by Mr. C. Alfred Smith, one of his honored students and closest friends: "On Friday morning April 22nd, 1864, Dr. E. Pugh was engaged in his lecture room upon this article, when he was seized with a violent chill, followed by fever. He vacated the lecture room for his bed, and on the 29th of April at 10:15 P. M. died at Willow Bank." We seem justified in affirming, therefore, that it was "the martyrdom" of Dr. Pugh, at the early age of thirty-six years, this devotion to the college that knew no bounds, that constituted the decisive factor in the anomalous struggle—the blood of the martyrs again the seed of victory. For the Session of 1864, at least, all destructive action was thwarted, never again presenting so menacing a prospect.

The poignant interest of this last will and testament calls for its appearance here:

> "A bill entitled etc., etc., a supplement etc., etc., has recently been reported in the senate of the state of Pennsylvania by Mr. Turrell from the Committee on Education which is in the highest degree discreditable alike to the originator of the bill and the Committee which reported it and should it pass the Senate, it would stamp a lasting disgrace upon that body. The effect of the bill is virtually to squander the entire proceeds for all time to come of the magnificent grant of public lands from Congress to this state for the purpose of industrial education. That there should be a few unprincipled politicians and irresponsible demagogues get into our State offices at Harrisburg is not remarkable but that a majority of the Senate should thus agree to sacrifice this magnificent gift is incredible. And if there is not an industrial constituency at home sufficiently intelligent to see the enormity of this legislation and visit a speed rebuke upon the unworthy representatives who cast their votes in favor of this bill, we may well despair of any progress among the industrial classes of our country. But the intelligent agriculturalist, manufacturers, and industrial operatives generally of our State cannot fail to see the enormity of this great fraud which their representatives have perpetrated upon them and they will see hereafter that more worthy men represent them in our own State Legislature.

> "Let us look at this bill.

> "Section 1 requires that none of the land scrip be sold for a less sum than 80 cents per acre. This act prevents a single acre from being sold until New York (now selling above 1,000 acres per day at 75 cents) sells nearly a million acres. That is, the New York sales alone will prevent the sale of any of this scrip before 3 years, and if other States

agree to sell on the same terms with New York or to sell in competition with her, it may be five times this long before an acre of the Pennsylvania scrip can be sold.

"Had the author of this bill by malicious design intended to frustrate the sale of the scrip he could not have done it better than by the first section of his bill.

"Section 2 requires the distribution of the proceeds of the sale of this land equally amongst 6 colleges—five of which are private institutions, as much as any incorporated private institution in the State—and most of them not only private but merely local in the sphere of their operations and sectarian in character. The 6th, The Agricultural College of Pennsylvania is a State institution. Not simply a State Institution in the sense of some Institutions which are called Pennsylvania State Institutions in order to give them a more general character and secure state patronage, but which were originated and are owned by local boards of Trustees. But it is a bona fide State Institution, originating under State Patronage, built by the State, and now owned by the State as truly as are the Legislative halls in which this monstrous act was passed. To place such an institution on the same footing for State patronage as the other 5 institutions would be an enormity only equaled by an attempt to divide in like manner the funds appropriated to sustain the Legislature at Harrisburg. The men who voted to dissipate the Land Grant Fund amongst these private institutions to the utter ruin (for such it would be) of the only State Institution in the State, would be able to see what a monstrous outrage it would be to thus dissipate the fund appropriated to sustain the Legislature because some of the money would come out of their own pockets. We are mistaken, if the Agricultural constituencies of the State don't see equally clearly the manner in which this Legislature attempts to swindle them and the State out of the only means they have of sustaining the only State Institution of the State."

Part III

Drifting and Experiment

1865—1881

CHAPTER 6

Carrying On—President William H. Allen

"Electors of the Trustees, you are the sovereigns of the Agricultural College of Pennsylvania. Over what other institution can you exert such control? And will you suffer this Agricultural College, originated as we have seen by the wants and necessities of the age, and thus far crippled by poverty, to be deprived of the Endowment mainly secured by its founders and absolutely necessary to its success? Deprived of it too by institutions which we have seen, despise industrial colleges and only propose "to teach such branches of learning as relate to Agriculture and mechanic arts" because they love the 'goodly Babylonish garment and the wedge of gold' which they expect the proposition to bring."

Address to their Constituents, the Industrial Classes of Pennsylvania, by a Committee of Electors of the Board of Trustees.
September 6, 1865.

The struggle to wrest the Land Grant from The Agricultural College was continued in the Legislature of 1865 and following years. Bills were introduced to repeal portions of the Act of 1863, and to distribute the proceeds of the Grant among three or more institutions. The "all or none policy" of Dr. Pugh had thus far successfully vanquished the "now or never policy" of division, and the phrase the "lion's share" as due the college was used to convey a growing spirit of compromise. Under the mistaken idea that the grant was made for "educational purposes," petitions were received from Waynesburg College, Westminster College, and for the support of the Medical Department of the University of Pennsylvania. The friends of the favored institutions were particularly insistent in furthering their claims. Senator Graham maintained that the bill to repeal was defeated last year by an unfortunate delay of the vote. The sentiment of the people and two-thirds of the Senate favored repeal. Senator Lowry was "censored by his constituency" for not securing action for Allegheny. So the battle from almost every angle was renewed.

The inherent right of the Agricultural College to the benefits of the Act was defended by Senators Wallace of Clearfield and Hall of Blair. They strenuously opposed division or diversion of the fund. Considerable feeling was shown in the debates. Insinuations against the friends of the College and methods used in pushing its claims were met by counterchanges that the efforts of other institutions to fulfill the conditions of the Act of Congress and to qualify as having for their principal object agriculture and mechanic arts, were "all moonshine, were subterfuges which are gotten up for the purpose of stealing from the State Institution the money to which she is entitled." Senator Wallace was very effective in his claims that a repeal of the act in any form would endanger the validity of the grant itself for the Commonwealth. It was not a grant for general "educational purposes," a "bounty loose for a sort of grab game" (as Senator Wilson of Tioga aptly phrased it), but a specific grant for a specific kind of institution, and for a specific sort of instruction. For this the only college in the State, so qualified is named and designated in the Act of Acceptance.

Sectional interests and sentiments began to be heard. Why not an institution in the eastern part of the State and over in the western part, as well as in the center of the Commonwealth? A vulnerable point (not only here but in all land grant colleges at this time was brought forward by Senator Bingham) mechanic arts was overlooked entirely. Manual training could hardly quality as fulfilling conditions of the Act; and "of all places to study machinery, Centre County" was presumably a derogatory and effective argument, Senator Wallace urged that the Senate rise above merely sectional interests and petty carping over particulars in these terms: "I have no College in my district but I have a desire to see a great State Institution. I confess that if I had the power I would give to this institution every dollar of the fund. I would create there a noble institution, such as Yale, or Harvard, or Princeton. I would create an institution to which we, as Pennsylvanians should look with pride and with pleasure. I would not occupy the position of a partisan, and divide this fund among a dozen small colleges, but I would create one great institution that would carry out in all its meaning and spirit the Act of Congress, and I would there endeavor to educate those who are the bone and sinew of the nation, the pith and germ of the State."

Action in the Senate centered upon the Amendment to the Act of Acceptance sponsored by Senator Clymer of Berks who was an advocate of three great colleges, such as Senator Wallace pictured in glowing terms. The amendment forbade any sale of scrip at less than eighty cents per acre, and provided that one-third of the proceeds be devoted to the endowment of the Agricultural College. "Take one-third now, or you may get none" was the counsel and even threat of the opposition. An attempt to substitute one-half to the Agricultural College instead of one third was defeated by a vote of seventeen to nine.

In the House the friends of the college succeeded in forestalling any change in legislation. This was due largely to the labors of Trustees McAllister and Watts, and to the work of the Representative of Center County, Mr. Alexander. The campaign of education began with some elementary lessons based upon the Act of Congress of 1862; copies of which were again made available. Recalling the fact that more than once in debate, the admission was made that the basic law itself had not even been read; the importance of this move is apparent. Moreover much of the opposition to its bestowal by the Act of Acceptance of 1863 had arisen from ignorance and misconception of the basic Federal Act itself. The Watts Memorial to the Legislature of 1865, together with an address to the Legislature of Ohio by the Governor of that State showing the wisdom of keeping intact the Land-Grant Fund, were effective weapons.

In the session of 1865, a Memorial of the Board was presented to the Legislature showing that the persistent, continued efforts of the other colleges, many of them literary and denominational had a tendency to prevent the sale of the land scrip. It followed that competition with other states had reduced the price far below what might have been realized. It was further pointed out that no provision for expenses in advertising and selling the scrip had been provided. The college had sustained this burden although the Act of Congress clearly provided that all expenses of sale, locations of lands, etc., be met by the state accepting the grant. The indebtedness of the institution, about eighty thousand dollars; was due to the increased costs of labor and materials incident to the War, and to inadequate fees of maintenance. The moral and legal justice of the rights and claims of the college were again urged. A compromise was affected, and the Act of 1866, Supplement to the Act of 1863 was passed by the Legislature. It received the approval of Governor A. G. Curtin on April 11th, 1866. Its provisions were three, payment of commission expenses in sale of scrip, limiting the sale, however, to one-third of the total distributive shares of the land scrip. Authority was given to the Board of Trustees to borrow a sum not exceeding eighty-thousand dollars, at a rate of interest not exceeding sever per cent with which to consolidate and pay all the debts of the institution. The bonds were to mature in ten years, and were secured by a mortgage upon the property as designated in the Act. The interest on this debt constituted a severe drain upon the resources of the Institution until 1875, when under the administration of President Calder, an appropriation was made to cancel the mortgage.

In the session of 1867, the friends of the college took the initiative. The Board had determined to ask for the removal of the restriction on the sale of the scrip, and to seek authority for the purchase of Model or Experimental

Farms. In order to secure as wide a variety of conditions as possible, as well as to enlist all parts of the State in the enterprise it was proposed to use one-tenth of the proceeds, as was provided in the Federal Act, of the total grant for the purchase of three experimental farms. The bill was duly presented, and again vigorous efforts were made in both houses to substitute two additional colleges, or to leave the two outlying proposals open, to be filled in later by qualifying institutions. The Senator from Allegheny again insisted that the institution had ignored the provision for mechanic arts, and the one-tenth (if authorized) ought to be used to carry out the Act of Congress in regard to mechanic arts. In the following effective manner Senator Landon of Bradford summarized the case for Agriculture: "The truth is the whole matter of Agriculture from the flower garden to the corn field, from the raising of a guinea-chicken to the forty-four hundred bullocks is a scientific subject. He that follows it scientifically, follows it renumeratively. The reason why many men reach the confines of the poor house is this. They farm with muscle but never with brains." He assigned the comparative failure of the institution to two fallacies, the attempt to educate the student at one hundred dollars per annum, and the manual labor fetish. He thought there were difficulties in management by the State, but found a genuine source of hope in the present effort to institute experiment under diverse conditions, in different localities and with different soils. Both Houses finally passed the measure, and on February 19th, 1867, it became a law. Thus ended the struggle (with the exception of skirmish shots in 1879 and 1881) to settle the Land Grant upon the college; but vastly more important to link the Commonwealth indissolubly with the Federal Government in maintaining and developing its very own public, industrial university for which its "faith" was pledged in 1963.

The records show that the College had made prompt and vigorous efforts to realize upon the land scrip. President Pugh in the moment of victory over the acceptance of the land grant Act proposed immediate action by Representative Hale in Washington to secure the Scrip for the State. But the delay in the acceptance by the Legislature was already working adversely. The spirited and prolonged struggle t o maintain the status quo of the act of acceptance, also, served to delay effective results. For these and other adverse factors, the Board of Trustees could not reasonably be held responsible. On June 15th, 1864, a committee of the Board, consisting of Messers. Kaine, McAllister, and Watts was appointed: "to procure such disposition to be made of the land scrip donation by Congress and the State legislature to the Agricultural College of Pennsylvania as shall make the same immediately available to meet the necessities of the Institution." The Board of Commissioners, consisting of the Governor, the Auditor General, and the Surveyor General, held their first meeting in Harrisburg, on July 14th, 1864. They resolved that it is expedient immediately to dispose of the Land Scrip. They formulated rules of procedure, and empowered the Surveyor General to appoint an Agent to arrange for the sale of scrip. This was the first meeting of the Commission, although more than a year had elapsed since the Act of Acceptance was approved. Again the delay cannot be justly charged to the Commission or to the Board of Trustees. The uncertainties of legislative action and the prosecution of the War must bear the blame.

At an adjourned meeting of the Commission on August 2nd, 1864, Dr. William H. Allen, President Elect of The Agricultural College was appointed Agent for the Commission. A circular was issued inviting bids, the same to be opened in the presence of the Commissioners on December 1st, 1864. At an adjourned meeting held four days later, the first allotments were made. It was agreed that minimum bid for scrip to be allotted should be eighty-five cents per acre. Only one hundred and forty-eight pieces were disposed of up to July 11th, 1866, when a wide advertising campaign was begun. Attempts were made by President Allen and by the Surveyor General to interest capitalists and bankers in large purchases. Although the minimum was lowered by the Commission to seventy-five cents per acre at a meeting held May 5th, 1865, the general air of uncertainty in the legislature, and the actual limitation of one-third placed upon the sales by the Act of 1866, caused investors, prospectors and speculators to be over-cautious. The Act of 1867 was promptly followed by an invitation for bids upon the remaining scrip of five hundred and twenty thousand acres. On April 10th, 1867, the scrip was awarded at prices ranging from fifty-five cents to one dollar per acre; the allotments ranging from one hundred and sixty to nearly three hundred thousand acres. Bids as low as ten cents per acre were received, while three bids for the entire amount were received, 54 5/8, 54 45/100 and 54 53/100 per acre.

An official statement issued by the Commissioners, August 28th, 1867 shows the total proceeds and the way in which the one-tenth was set apart for the purchase of experimental farms:

Cash received for 716,000 acres:	$403,986.80
Investments with Premiums:	$395,300.30
Cash on hand:	$8,686.50
64,000 acres awarded at 55 cents:	$35,200.00
Amount held for Experimental Farms:	$43,886.50
Added to investments:	$395,300.30
Total realized from sale of Land Scrip:	$439,186.80

Much has been said of the amount thus realized from the munificent grant of the Federal Government. The action of the Board of Trustees has been subject to comment for urging the sale of the scrip, instead of locating it and holding same for increased values. Most of such criticism was and is based on misapprehension of conditions. Ten States, only, had lands within their borders subject to entry; while twenty-seven states were Scrip States. The scrip had first to be sold, before it was subject to location; and the profit, therefore, would accrue only to parties of the second part. If Pennsylvania had had a benefactor such as was Ezra Cornell, who purchased the scrip for New York, located it, paid all expenses, and reserved for Cornell University all profits, this Commonwealth would have a much larger endowment. Some members of the Legislature and other citizens of the State, were alive to the possibilities of this enhancement in values. Attempts were made by the Board of Trustees to seek out friends of the College to render this service. But bricks could not be made without straw, the burdens and needs of the time called for an immediate utilization of resources. As a matter of fact, at least nine states realized a lower average per acre on their apportionment, than did Pennsylvania. The figures range from forty-one and a half cents to five dollars and sixty-two cents; with some of the Western States having still valuable, income producing lands as part of their endowments. Subsequent legislation, too, enhanced values by removing restrictions on the location of scrip. It must be pointed out, also, that the tardy authorization for the disposal of the grant in Pennsylvania, led to further competition with the Southern States, qualifying at the close of the War.

A committee of the National House of Representatives made a report upon the whole subject of the land grant sales, and of the way in which they were handled by several states. This report of 1875 of the Committee on Education and Labor by James Monroe of Ohio as Chairman affirmed that in a large majority of the States the land fund was conscientiously and judiciously managed. "This result is gratifying to the friends of education, is creditable to the States which accepted the trust, and reflects credit upon the Government which bestowed it." More significant than this, the report continued, "It must be added that the reports sent from these colleges reveal, in many cases a certain fresh interest, a spirit of youth, a new enthusiasm, which when intelligent and enduring, is one of the best prophecies of success! Strong evidence is afforded of the power of these institutions to establish sympathetic relations between themselves and the communities in which they are placed, in the fact that they have already received in appropriations from States and in donations from towns, counties, and private individuals an amount almost equal to the bounty of the Government."

These statements constitute an eminently fair appraisal of the case for Pennsylvania. The part that the second President of the College took in it has been suggested. We turn now to an account of his brief administration and to the conditions which led to his retirement. At a meeting of the Board held June 15th, 1864, formal announcement of the death of President Pugh was made, and Resolutions of respect were adopted. Professor William H. Allen was elected President to take effect at the Commencement of the next college year, February, 1865. He was in the meantime to have general supervision of the College. This we have seen was in the interests of the disposition of the land scrip, and in other legislative interests of the college.

Dr. Allen was born near Augusta, Maine, March 27th, 1808. He prepared for Bowdoin College, teaching school and working during vacations to meet his expenses. He graduated in 1833. He had an ambition for a career in the law; his friends urged the ministry; he chose teaching. He taught Greek and Latin at the Oneida Conference Seminary, at Cazenovia, New York for three years. In 1836 he took charge of the Augusta High School. In a year he was called to the Professorship of Chemistry and Natural History at Dickinson College. Ten years later he was transferred to the chair of Mental Philosophy and English Literature. He also served one year as President, after the death of Dr. Robert Emory in 1848. On the first day of January 1850, he was inaugurated as President of Girard College. He served for twelve years, the institution gaining in numbers and in prestige. A policy of retrenchment in expenses and salaries entered upon by the Board of Control, was interpreted by him as a reflection upon his administration of the affairs of the institution. This subversion of his ideals of scholarship and public service led him to tender his resignation. He returned to his rural home on the banks of the Delaware, near Philadelphia, his work closing at Girard, in its first phase, on January 1st, 1863.

As President of the Agricultural College of Pennsylvania, he served two years. The important work which he accomplished in the furtherance of the financial prospects led to radical proposals in internal administration, and in the direction of public activities. That he was a party to all these changes is evident, but it is equally apparent that he was not a partizan. This gave him that agreeable opportunity to relinquish the post, and again seek retirement. Professor Thomas R. Baker, a member of the faculty at that time, writes: "Dr. Allen and especially his wife, seemed dissatisfied with their life at the college, apparently regretting that they had moved there." Conditions were primitive, indeed, for one who was accustomed to an urban environment. To this must be added, a rather vigorous campaign of innovation, inspired by Professor John Fraser (who became his successor), added to the inherent difficulties of adjustment. The future held for him again, a very brief retirement. On September 11th, 1867, he was re-elected President of Girard College, serving for a term of fifteen years, until his death on August 29th, 1882.

Public honor and acclaim were his in due measure. Union College conferred upon him the degree of Doctor of Laws. He was President of the American Bible Society for eight years, and an earnest advocate of religious education as over against sectarianism. As President of Girard, he prepared a Manual of Public Devotion, Prayers and Scripture Readings for Chapel Services, which admirably met the somewhat unusual conditions obtaining there. He lectured throughout the country on a wide range of subjects. Peace, Temperance, the Bible, Labor, Public Welfare, Economic Conditions, and Farm Life were some of his varying themes. An address on Men and Money, delivered on many occasions, and a Phi Beta Kappa discourse on Our Country's Mission in History, are indicative of both his versatility and of the times.

In the history of our own college, it is, however, the personal qualities and influences of Dr. Allen that are most cherished. He was described by one of the students, "as a fine looking old gentleman, with independent means, very fond of chess. He had an occult way of finding out the makers of mischief and a telepathic intuition of a coming student brawl. This, on occasion, led to the expulsion of several students for bringing whiskey into the college building." In defense, if not in extenuation, Mr. Johnson adds, "we were a nice peace loving community, full of fun and life into which Dr. Allen brought the breath of real culture, of sweetness and light, by his friendly contacts and public address."

No unusual acumen is needed to sense difficulties in enforcement and possible official friction in prescribed and supervised study periods for young men of Agricultural College age; of "Lights out at ten o'clock" and to ensure compliance the different stories of the building were assigned to different professors; of Bible Classes at nine o'clock on Sunday morning, and preaching services at three; of depositing fire-arms with Professor Whitman (what a collection he must have had); of reports made to parents and guardians; of the solemn duty imposed upon the President of examining all Literary Society performances before their delivery. The increase in fees to two hundred dollars a year, and the organization of military instruction and drill were not of a nature to foster the bestowal of bouquets. Yet with what courtly dignity and grace did the students take leave of President Allen. It is a genuine expression of academic life and with all its Chesterfieldian spirit and Johnsonesque style.

***

Pennsylvania Agricultural College, November 26, 1866.
Dr. Wm. H. Allen,

President of Faculty,

Dear Sir: It is due alike to you and our own feelings that, before parting with one so highly esteemed as a president, teacher and gentleman, we should tender this memento and testimonial and our sense of obligation for the uniform kindness and administrative ability which so eminently fitted you for the responsibilities imposed upon you in your association with the Institution.

Permit us to express our deepest regret in thus being separated from one whose superiority of mind, has already placed him among the foremost in the classic field and whose personal worth has won for him the love and veneration of all who have been placed under his collegiate guardianship. Be assured, dear sir, that in retiring from this Institution you carry with you the personal esteem of every student of the College; and that you leave behind you a souvenir of priceless value, which will be cherished and venerated throughout our lives.

With heartfelt thanks for your past acts of favor and kindness, and with the earnest hope that you may live long to enjoy the fruits of your labors, we bid you an affectionate adieu! While in sincerity of soul we would add:

"Fare thee well! and if forever,
Still forever—fare thee well!"

Respectfully, your Students,

D. H. Barrick, Eugene McMurtrie, J. W. Butler, Howard Phillips, Geo. G. Roberts, W. S. Black, T. H. Boardman, John F. Bulwinkle, F. J. Bechtel, Cyrus Gordon, H. Hughs, George Evans, Wm. T. Boardman, Henry C. Moore, George Blackstone, Wm. C. Holahan, Lewis Wayne, A. B. Loomis, Wm. E. Judson, Benj. F. Kemp, E. Biddle, Hugh Hamilton, W. T. Scott, Adolphe E. Verdereau, Joseph E. Wright, A. A. Breneman, Anthon B. Cram, G. Hiester, Daniel Cessna, Thomas L. Kelton, J. C. Blickensderffer, J. W. Eldred, John C. Kelton, J. Q. Crouch, R. L. Woodward, C. B. Andres, Jr., Robert L. Stanton, Thomas Leabroo, E. S. Dubbs, L. M. Ebert, C. E. Hadley, C. A. Evans, Edwin B. Longnecker, G. B. Rock, Horace Whiteman, Jos. B. Stavely, E. M. Austin, A. M. Chalfant, Wm. A. Buckhout, W. M. Stackhouse, George Bechtel,

***

President Allen replied as follows:

My Young Friends: I thank you with a full heart for the kind sentiments which you have so well expressed. Among the rewards of a teacher of youth, there are none more precious than the affectionate regard and remembrance of those who have been under his charge: and I shall retire from this College with the pleasing assurance that wherever I may meet any one of you in future life, I shall grasp the warm hand of a friend. You have been indulgent to my short-comings and errors, and never under any circumstances, have I have received from you anything but kindness, courtesy and respect.

These manifestations of good feeling on your part, have been flowers in a pathway which has been somewhat rugged and beset with difficulties.

In taking leave of this College, I do not feel that I am escaping form a sinking ship; I am rather surrendering the helm of a remodeled and well-rigged Argosy, to a resolute pilot and a new crew. May her voyage be safe and prosperous.

Having been taken by so sudden a surprise, I am totally unprepared to speak to the several points of your address as they deserve. You will accept the emotions of an overflowing heart, which I find no adequate words to express. But be assured, young gentlemen, that I highly appreciate every sentiment which your address contains, and cordially reciprocate every kindly feeling which your generous, and perhaps too partial friendship has prompted you to offer.

In retirement to private life, which I earnestly desire, and which advancing years admonish me to seek, I shall preserve this testimonial as a precious memento; and when I pass from earth, shall leave it as a legacy to my children.

And now gentlemen, again thanking you for this proof of your esteem and love, I bid you affectionate adieu.

"Farewell! a word that must be, and hath been;
A sound that makes us linger, -yet, farewell!"

CHAPTER 7

Reorganization and Deorganization

"That for reasons which it is not the purpose of these resolutions to specify, the Agricultural College under the educational policy hitherto pursued, has failed, and in the judgement of the Faculty cannot but fail, to satisfy the expectations of the friends of enlightened practical education."

To the Faculty by Professor John Fraser,
May 7th, 1866.

"Here then for the present our anchor is cast—but which, let it be hoped, may prove to have been a wisely ordered voyage of trial and adaptation for a last and crowning labor.—As such it is accepted: The task being understood to be that of so uniting, in due order and proportions, manual, intellectual and moral training, as to send forth into and for the work of life, good, learned, industrious and useful men; and also thereby to prove that respectability, as it is called, is not owing to calling, but to culture.—And, finally, the dignity and value of knowledge are to be made as apparent in the right process of planting a tree or housing a crop, as in the correct translation of a Latin sentence or the true solution of a problem in Geometry."

President Thomas H. Burrowes, 1869.

To 1866 but one course of study was offered, a course in Agriculture. The aim of this Miltonian training, however, was to furnish the student with a "thorough scientific and practical knowledge of all the ordinary subjects and things to which his duty or pecuniary pleasure may call his attention through life, and thus, as far as possible, fit him for intelligent, efficient and manly action, in whatever sphere of influence he may be called to labor." The acceptance of the Land Grant Act had placed wider responsibilities and opportunities upon the institution; amply sensed and developed by Dr. Pugh in his Plan of Organization. The struggle to hold the Grant claimed all the attention, and the tardy realization of any income from endowment rendered expansion impossible either on the part of Presidents Pugh or Allen. Moreover a considerable element in the Board, and also influential individuals and organizations in the State, looked upon the College as exclusively engaged in furthering Agriculture and agricultural education, as indeed its very name implied.

In 1865, a vigorous teacher was added to the staff in the person of John Fraser, Professor of Mathematics and Astronomy, and Lecturer on Tactics. Professor Fraser born in Cromarty, Scotland in 1823; educated at the University of Aberdeen; taking the Huttonian Prize for proficiency in mathematics. As a teacher, he emigrated to Bermuda, and later became a tutor in a private school in New York. He became involved in debt, and was even compelled to pawn his library which was large and varied. Connellsville, Pennsylvania next finds him, engaged as a private tutor. Here he had the good fortune to make the acquaintance of the Reverend James Black, which led to his election as Professor of Mathematics at Jefferson College in February 1855. Here he taught seven years, enlisting in the volunteer Army at the close of the college year of 1862. His promotion was rapid; Captain, Lieutenant Colonel, and Colonel of the 140th Pennsylvania Volunteers; and finally Pvt. Brigadier-General in the Second Army Corps. He was captured while reconnoitering and taken to Libby prison. He helped to maintain "cheerfulness and courage" by delivering "courses of lectures, notably on the Plays of Shakespeare, trusting to his remarkable memory; and in many other ways alleviating the condition of a captivity the influence of which was as demoralizing as it was disheartening." He was mustered out of the Army on May 31st, 1865.

Of his teaching at Jefferson College, it is affirmed that not only in his own department of mathematics but in all the studies of the curriculum, he proved "an inspiration for the more studious young men. He was equally at home in the classical authors; in philosophy (Kant's Critique of Pure Reason was a favorite subject for reading and discourse); and in the sciences, in which he also lectured under the topic, "The Earth and Man." A pupil of his after forty years experience in teaching the classics, pays this tribute to him: "His classical training was simply superb. He not only knew the great authors, but he loved them. Beyond any man the writer ever met he possessed what might be called a "Greek soul." With such a breadth of interest and enthusiasm, he enlivened and "humanized" his lectures on mathematics, applying the subject so that the most abstruse forms of reasoning challenged the interest and activity of the class; His extensive library was a sort of nine days' wonder when compared with the collection even of the Agricultural College. Such a man was bound to be innovator, a Socratic disturber of academic traditions, and so it proved. He was appointed Professor in 1865; elected to the Presidency September 5, 1866, and resigned March 14, 1868.

He severed his connection in June, 1868, stating as his reason, seemingly, "irreconcilable differences with the Board of Trustees as to scope and policies of the institution."

He was elected Chancellor of the University of Kansas, entering upon his work June 17, 1868.[7] After a noteworthy service of six years, he resigned on account of financial stringency in the affairs of the University" and "To some

---

[7] The Main Building at Lawrence is his monument, erected by bonds issued by the city at his instigation, and later assumed by the State. He married a pupil of his at Lawrence, and an amusing story of his ready wit is current. A skeleton was let down on the platform at Commencement, labeled with the endearing term "Prex." His young wife's anxious concern, if not intuitive solicitude was aroused as she directed the inquiry to Mr. Fraser, what "Prex" meant. He replied in a flash, but sotto voce, "The Faculty."

extent the result internal strife due to his lack of powers of controlling men and harmonizing discordant interests." He was State Superintendent of Public Instruction in Kansas for two years; after which he accepted a teaching post in the Western University of Pennsylvania, where he died in 1878. The Board of Trustees of the Pennsylvania State College passed the following resolutions to his memory June 26, 1878:

"That we have heard with profound sorrow of the recent death of General John Fraser, formerly President of this College. His patriotic services during the War of Rebellion, his brilliant talents, great literary and scientific acquirements, and the earnest labors for this institution are gratefully remembered, and will be long cherished, with regret that a life so full of promise should have been so soon closed."

The work of reorganization with which we are concerned was undertaken in installments. A resolution by Professor Fraser was read in the Faculty meeting of May 7, 1866, affirming that it is the sense of this body that "the entire educational policy of the institution has failed and cannot but fail to satisfy the expectations of the enlightened friends of education." It was further resolved that Professor Fraser communicate this action with Mr. H. N. McCallister, the local trustee, as he was called, with the recommendation that the existing policy be reviewed by competent persons so as to bring it into accord with the best of educational experience. Confidence was, also, definitely expressed in President Allen and with his administration of public affairs. But with a touch of naiveness, to say the least, it is "desired to relieve him as recently elected, from the disadvantage of appearing as an innovator." The faculty, thereafter, chooses to sponsor important changes which it is "persuaded his own excellent judgment will pronounce to be absolutely necessary to the success of the institution."

Evidently a drastic re-organization, if not revolution, was pending. The work was entrusted to a committee of the Board of Trustees, President Allen, Messrs. Watts, and McAllister, together with three members of the Faculty, Professors Fraser, Caldwell and Whitman. The "Plan of Re-organization" which was issued as a circular of the College on October 1, 1865, was adopted

The Pennsylvania State College 1853-1932 Interpretation and Record

by the Board and submitted for approval, also, to the Delegates from the various counties to elect Trustees, which met September 5th, 1865. This action seemed prompted by the lack of complete confidence, and unanimity of the Board as to the wisdom of the impending changes. It served, also, as a wall of defense when the Board was forced by financial embarrassment to nullify speedily and unceremoniously its own action; placing the blame, if any, squarely upon the Executives and Faculty, who promoted these radical proposals, and upon the electors who gave their endorsement.

The modifications were as follows: The Labor Rule shall cease to be enforced. It is described as "having proved uniformly injurious to the financial and educational interests of the College." In its place, serviceable labor to diminish the expenses on the part of the student will be provided at the discretion of the President. A four years' training course in military science and art will provide for the physical needs of the College Department. While in deference to their immaturity, "the students of the Preparatory Department will be exercised one hour daily in a gymnasium which will be provided for their use." The college year was divided into two terms of twenty weeks each, commencement occurring in June instead of December as was the case previously. The scheme of instruction provided for three separate courses, a General Science Course, a Course in Agriculture, and a Course in Literature. They were to lead, respectively, to the degrees of Bachelor of Science, Bachelor of Scientific Agriculture, and Bachelor of Arts. Fees were raised to one hundred and thirty dollars per term. The Entrance Conditions definitely required examinations in Arithmetic, Algebra through simple equations, English Grammar, United States History, Elementary Science, and Political and Physical Geography. The privilege of rooming and boarding near the College, with consent of the parents and approval of the President, was announced, a distinct step from the boarding school, manual labor plan under which the institution was working. However, "accommodation cannot be procured in the neighborhood for more than thirty students, at present."

The resignation of Dr. Allen on September 5, 1868, and the elevation of Professor Fraser to the Presidency on the same date led to a more complete "re-organization" as a school of science and practice. All the contracts were terminated by the Board of Trustees at the close of the year 1866, President Fraser was to have a free hand. On November 1, he recommended additional courses in Mechanical and Civil Engineering, leading to the degree of Civil Engineer; and in Metallurgy, Mineralogy and Mining, leading to the degree of Mining Engineer. A parallel course of laboratory and of systematic field practice, in connection with each of the sciences, was adopted. This was called "Practicum" and appeared first in the catalogue for 1867-68. The term itself has continued, a distinctive, if not unique possession of the College. A faculty of twenty-three is proposed to effect these changes; the Board while approving, nevertheless limited the expenditures to the income derived from a student body of seventy.

President Fraser brought together a strong faculty, outlined the courses, even though some major appointments were manned in blank. Laudable but over-generous, it seems, students of high standing in the last two years of their College Course are given the "Honorary privilege of pursuing a resident graduate course of two years, free of all charges for Tuition, Boarding, Room-Rent, washing and Fuel." "An Agricultural Journal" was also announced. It was to be edited by the faculty; and its materialization reached the stage of affixing signatures to a contract for publication. The net results are, no suit for breach of contract was ever entered, and no copy was ever issued. The Board was assured that as a result of these new agencies, actual and prospective, a marked increase in the student body would result. But the reverse proved true. In 1866 there were one hundred and fourteen enrolled. In May, two years later, when the Trustees acted to "deorganize", the College had but thirty students.

It is fairly evident that the criticism of the College in the Legislature during the seasons of 1865, 1866 and 1867 in not providing for mechanic arts and engineering was part of the causal stimulus that led to a thorough plan of re-organization. In 1867, Senator Bingham challenges anyone to point out any one thing in the College making provision for mechanic arts. "Its situation is almost out of sight of a blacksmith shop; I had almost said it commanded a view, but of all places, it is least adapted to giving instruction in the mechanic arts." Goaded by replies in defense of the College, its program, and its plans for the future, he reads from the catalogue the roll of Professors, Mathematics; Chemistry; Zoology; Agriculture; Latin, Greek and English Literature; Book-keeping, Lecturer in Veterinary; one instructor in Military Tactics; and a Professor of Vocal Music. "Vocal music," he repeats, "perhaps that is a mechanical department." Unfair, ill-advised, ill-informed criticism, it may have been, it yet merits attention as the justification for efforts (too early to be wholly successful here or elsewhere) to re-organize the work of the College. It furnishes, also, the explanation for the rather optimistic claims of the College in 1868-69, when the much reduced program was imminent, the catalogue announces enthusiastically: "In addition to the ample theoretical and practical knowledge imparted in the recitations and practicums of this course, the student enjoys the great advantage of studying under the guidance of his instructors, the mechanical principles involved in the structure and operation of the following Works, which are located in the vicinity of the College, viz: The Oak Hall Woolen Factory, The Bellefonte Water Works, Gas Works, Class Works, Steam Planning Mills, Steam Flouring Mills, Smelting Furnaces, Forges, Foundries, and Steel Fire Works, The Snow Shoe Coal Mines and numerous other works which are in successful operation, in the thriving industrial region in the midst of which the College is situated."

The Act of 1867 assuring the entire land grant fund to the College was also valid stimulus to this broadening of the work of the College.

Regular semi-annual payments were not received until 1868, the income from this source being but eleven-hundred-seventy-six dollars in 1866 and six thousand two-hundred-ninety-three dollars and ninety five cents in 1867. In the meantime the appropriations to the experimental farms, the interest on the mortgaged debt authorized by the Act of 1866, and the severely marked decrease in the student fees led to serious deficits in those years. In the last mentioned item of income, the amount received in 1869 was nearly thirteen thousand dollars less than that of 1866. Sensing the censure of "irreconcilable differences" at hand, the President asked to be relieved from financial affairs to give all his attention to the "Educational Department" as it was called. A Business Manager was provided, and the duties added to those of Executive Manager of the Farms under John Hamilton.

The verdict, therefore, upon the work of General Fraser must be that he was too far in advance of his budget. He knew more about men than money, and prized them correspondingly higher. Such men as J. T. Rothrock, Henry James Clark, George C. Caldwell, Francis Fowler, John Phin, A. A. Breneman, Albert A. Tuttle, all had able careers and would have graced any faculty center anywhere. But particularly, the work of James Y. McKee, Professor and administrator from 1867 to his death in 1892, four times acting as President during executive changes, a teacher of the old school who taught the best things of life outside of as well as in the class room, and John Hamilton instructor, farm executive, business manager, treasurer of the College, publicist and organizer of Agricultural interests both as Secretary of Agriculture for Pennsylvania and as Director of Farmers' Institutes in the Bureau of Agriculture in Washington, benefactor of the College to have initiated the work of men like these, assures genuine distinction to the Administration of President John Fraser in the annals of the College.

De-organization began with the following resolutions of the Board of Trustees, May 27th, 1868. Whereas the plan of instruction adopted by the Board of Trustees upon the recommendation of the Faculty, two years ago, has failed to attract students as anticipated and has proved too expensive to justify its longer continuance, in view of the fact that the duty of establishing, conducting and maintaining, in connection with the College, three experimental farms has devolved upon the Board, therefore: Resolved – That the Board of Instruction be and is hereby reduced to a faculty consisting of a President and three regular professors, with such assistants and tutors, as it shall, from time to time, be found necessary and profitable to employ. Resolved – That, for the present, the Faculty shall be composed of James Y. McKee, Henry James Clark, J. T. Rothrock, and A. P. S. Stuart, of whom James Y. McKee is hereby designated as Vice-President of the Institution.

Resolved that titles, special studies to be taught by each and matter for public information be committed to Professor Fraser and McKee; to report to a committee of the Board, Messers. Watts and McAllister for approval."

At the October meeting of the Board, the chief problem remained for consideration; "how to fill the College with students." Governor Geary was present; and Dr. Thomas Burrowes formerly Superintendent of Common Schools of the Commonwealth was called in consultation. He made definite recommendations concerning the course in Agriculture; practice must become more prominent, science less so, and expenses must be reduced. A President should be secured who has administrative ability as well as scientific and literary attainments. He inspired hope in the Board, his services to education through long years of experience, gave a touch of authority to his words. He was offered and accepted (all conditions finally ratified at the meeting of the Board in December) the post of President "with full authority to so modify courses, select faculty, direct the affairs of the farms, the finances, as to restore confidence of the public in the Institution."

The administration of Dr. Burrowes was so personal, de-sytematized, yet so important and crucial, that the facts of his life assume a peculiar interest. He was born at Strasburg, Lancaster County, November 16th, 1805. His parents were natives of Ireland, emigrating to Delaware in 1784, and thence removing to Pennsylvania in 1787. When he was five years of age, the family went to Ireland to take possession of the ancestral property, remaining there for seven years. His education was furthered privately. In the home he learned lessons of industry, thrift, and self-dependence. From the age of nine to twelve, he was under the tutelage of a clergyman of the Church of England, a kinsman of his mother.

His family returned to the New York in 1817, settled in Quebec, where for five years, Burrowes attended English and Classical Schools. However, again, the family returned to Ireland and for a stay of three years. Throughout his period, Burrowes was under the private instruction of a Presbyterian Divine, who as a Scholar of Trinity College, gave him the advantages of the institution; though the uncertainty about the length of his stay did not permit of regular enrollment. The estate in Ireland was finally disposed of, and the family returned to Strasburg.

In the choice of a profession, he read law for two and a half years in the office of Amos Ellmaker of Lancaster, entered the Yale Law School in 1828.

But as usual with the breadth of interest which had characterized his training thus far, he became engrossed in the scientific lectures of Silliman and Onstead. The following year he was admitted to the Bar, became interested in politics, and was a member of the House of Representatives in 1831 and 1832. He took an active part in the campaign of Governor Joseph Ritner, and received as he himself says, "on political grounds alone" the appointment of Secretary of the Commonwealth. The educational duties of the post were secondary in the minds of his predecessors, and he found an accumulation of material calling for a clearing of the docket. A bushel basket full of letters, unanswered, was dumped on his desk within two weeks of his assuming office. It was his first contact with education in an administrative way, and writing editorially of his experiences, he says: "There were questions of every school hue, kind, and scope – involving difficulty as to the location of school houses, the assessment and collection of taxes, the qualification of teachers, the selection of branches of study and school books, the use of the Scriptures, instruction in catechism, modes of government, kinds of punishment, opposition to the system, etc., etc. And these, too, addressed to one who knew about as much of the details of school affairs as he did of the local geography of the moon." His own modest fears were shared by the friends of education who weighed the results of "a prentice hand" of but thirty years of age. But as Wickersham says: "Never were men more agreeably disappointed. During the three years he remained in office, he pressed forward this work with so much ability and zeal, and with such a measure of success that his name well deserves to be ranked among the chief benefactors of free schools."

The School Law of 1834 was inadequate and practically inoperative. He directed his attention to changes and remedies in his Reports of 1835 and 1836, resulting in the Common School Law of the latter date. He advocated a "System" of schools, from Common to University. His plans for Secondary Common Schools, and Model Schools for Teachers waited years for realization. The fatalities of politics and change of administration sent him into retirement. The voice of the people could not be "treated just as though it had not been expressed" and he left the Senate Chamber through an open window to seven years of professional farming.

In 1845, he resumed the practice of law, reviving his interest in education. He published papers urging among other reforms, the appointment of County Superintendents. He served many years on the School Board of Lancaster, and also as Mayor of the city.

Burrowes was President of the Convention that organized the State Teachers Association of 1852, and an active promoter of its work for the profession, and for its legislative plans.

He established the Pennsylvania School Journal in 1852, and continued for eighteen years as its editor. He also issued the State Book of Pennsylvania in 1847, and an elaborate treatment of School Architecture of Pennsylvania in 1852. He wrote the Normal School Law of 1857, the subject of adequate preparation of teachers in the Common Schools, long having had place in his thought. He served as Superintendent of Schools a second time (and by election, not political accident) from 1860 to 1863; the term characterized by improved methods of supervision and report. He also issued a Digest of School Laws and Decisions, and fathered a bill for District School Libraries.

His last constructive task before taking up the work of the Agricultural College was connected with legislation and organization of the Soldiers' Orphans Schools of Pennsylvania. A large donation was made by the Pennsylvania Railroad Company for such schools, and the interest of Dr. J. P. Wickersham as Superintendent of Public Instruction was secured. He drafted a bill, which was in part utilized by Dr. Burrowes as the measure before the Legislature in 1864. In short, it was largely due to the personal interest of Governor Curtin and the persistent labors of Dr. Burrowes that justice was won for these schools. It will be recalled that it was a fond illusion of certain factions of the Legislature to use part or all of the National Land Grant for support of these schools, thus obviating additional taxation. Thus was Dr. Burrowes fitted by his many sided activities as lawyer, legislator, publicist, writer, farmer, editor, educational executive, and institutional manager for the task of College President, to which he dedicated the final enthusiasm of his life.

"To better accord with the needs of labor on the farm," Dr. Burrowes re-established the College year, February to December, Manual labor is again a condition sine qua non of discipleship, although he writes suggestively of his difficulties respecting it. "The chief hindrance encountered has been want of confidence naturally resulting from the failure of the Institution by a departure from its proper work," which he describes as "the delicate but vital operation of regularly combining intellectual culture and manual labor." In his own mind, however, there is no uncertainty: "Here when we say labor, we mean labor. We mean that the working of the farm is done by the students in the regular intervals of literary and scientific studies --- and further when our number of students shall be doubled, as it is expected to be next year, and quadrupled as it probably will be the year after that; that it should be worked liked a garden, and made, as it should be a model to the State in intelligent, practical agriculture." Gradually installed, he insists, manual labor is a pleasant relief from the ennui of study, reading, and play, and the support of the Faculty both in theory and in the field, will work miracles in transforming the physical surroundings. During the week of May 25th, 1869, all studies were suspended. Farm buildings were moved to more convenient places; corn cribs, shelters, etc., were erected by the "mechanic and lads" with only the expense of a "few spikes and nails." One professor was away to be married, and two other accompanied him as groomsmen; what more natural than: "I took the opportunity to get up the outdoor work."

At this time and in later years, 1870 and 1871, the bell for rising in Winter was run at six A. M., and in the summer at five. It calls for no strain upon the imagination to describe the other than "home feeling" that would follow such regimen today. Yet there is a silver lining to the clouds, let Dr. Burrowes reveal it. "The month of early flowers and the first fruits of the garden, has passed quietly but pleasantly. Much cleaning up around the buildings has been done, and the lads have been astonished at the change effected by an odd day devoted to improving roads and paths, removing rubbish, trimming trees and extirpating weeds. From this more than any other cause, a love for the school and a degree of home feeling seems to be springing up. Strawberries, too, on the table almost daily, and in quantity to satisfy the boyish appetite; cherries without stint and in great variety, with an occasional treat of ice-cream have served not only to please the palate, but to show that the garden was not worked or the ice house filled for nothing."

The prospect widens, more enticing as it grows: "In agricultural matters another part of our operations is rapidly attracting attention and becoming important. An hundred acres of the farm have been laid off, are being furnished with separate house, barn, etc., and devoted to experiments in practical agriculture, as the "Central Model and Experimental Farm." The whole will be worked in such manner, when all the necessary arrangements shall have been completed, that, without reference to cost, the best results shall be produced that can be taken out of good soil by abundant, careful, and skillful labor. Of this farm, twenty-five acres have been devoted to experiments in the grains and grasses and in potatoes, under all the various conditions as to the preparation of the ground, effect of lime, etc. Our students being to take a lively interest in this Experimental farm, which, though not worked by themselves, is our next neighbor, and often visited.

Another matter of interest is the new turnpike to be constructed, certainly, this season, from the College gate to the end of Nittany mountain – about three miles – and which will give us a continuous turnpike to Bellefonte. This the more attracts attention as it is engineered by our Professor of Civil Engineering, with a corps of assistants from the students; the survey being actually in progress.

Admission requirements were simplified, so that while scholastic conditions counted less, "Age, Height, Weight (both without boots), Shoulder measure, Intended Profession, and Religion" counted more. Courses of study were de-centralized, practically reduced to one, but with the aim to turn out well educated farmers at the end of three years, skillful engineers, surveyors, and scientific mechanics in four years, and full Bachelors of Arts at the end of five years. An offer is made to the teachers of the State of instruction in the sciences, but the project of a Normal School in connection with the Agricultural School has no siren call and meets a rebuff. "Let us have faith in our destiny and duty here. We shall succeed and within two years of this time the clouds now over us will be thought of in wonder that they ever

inspired any doubts or fears; in one year we shall all feel certain of success ---
Excuse a warmth of expression I do not often indulge in, but I am sensitive to
anything that looks like a want of faith in this noble institution and the
success of the great cause it upholds." Echoes of this faith, so freely expressed,
came in letters and endorsements from all parts of the State. An example will
suffice. Ex-Superintendent Waring wrote: "The institution is on the true
track again and I have great hopes now for its usefulness and greatness, and
have great confidence in the prudent patience and agricultural sympathy --- so
to speak, of the veteran, Dr. Burrowes."

Despite fervid anticipations of increased enrollment Dr. Burrowes was
compelled to record that on March 1st, 1870: "Number of students is yet only
thirty-five, with two old ones and six new ones to come in—that is—if they
do come." Still he could delight in chronicling: "What do you think? A
number of farmers have come to the Agricultural College Farm for seed wheat
– I like this." or writing to Trustee McAllister: "I expect to show you a
comfortable barn yard next week, and if the weather holds, a good road to the
College gates." Nothing was too small to be done to win friends for the
institution, and while he made a tour of the State in its interests, and carried a
campaign of advertising to all parts of the Commonwealth, it was not beneath
his dignity to send some "sausage and spare-ribs for the Bellefonte editors with
a short account of our late killing of Chester Whites." This may, also, on the
principle of vicarious enjoyment, recompense the good citizens of that
Borough for the loan of a surveyors level to lay out plots and roads on the farm
and route the turnpike to the College gate.

Small wonder that Dr. Burrowes should have planned the extension of
this good feeling to the Commonwealth at large. On June 16th, 1869, he
proposed a Harvest Home Reception, to Judge Watts, who heartily agreed. By
way of explanation of his plans, he says: "This institution makes no parade of
the long list of 'ologies, 'onomies and 'ographies which graces some catalogues;
neither does it boast of any incredible number of professors actual, expected,
special, honorary and occasional, but with a sufficient number of competent
instructors, all of whom are capable of their respective departments and
citizens of the State, it undertakes to give sound instruction in every branch of

literature, science and practical art pertaining to its class, which any father may desire for his son, and which that son may come prepared to receive. Beyond this no promise is made. This shall be fulfilled. Not many of the citizens of the State know of the existence of this Institution, and very few are aware of the large capacity and adaptedness to meet the great educational want of the day – that of imparting thorough knowledge in all useful branches practically as well as theoretically. The Trustees and officers, feeling the effect of this general want of information and appreciation, have decided to write and even challenge inspection of the institution on the part of the public." It was to partake, also, of the nature of a reunion of old graduates, parents of present and prospective students, and editors of papers. "Plain fare and clean beds will be provided without charge, and every effort made to render the visit agreeable." Entertainment for the students consisted of the regular schedule of examinations. For the elect, there were exhibitions of the farm and nursery, trials of movers, reapers, and plows. For the general public there were lectures on the marvels of science. On two nights of the week, the college building was illuminated (a correspondent of the Bethlehem *Times* tells us fifteen hundred candles were required) and "Sweet music was contributed by a brass band of Pine Grove, a pleasant village some four miles off."

The first of these gala, festive weeks found "fewer friends accepting the invitation than could have been wished." The next year, however, the take is otherwise. Two thousand were present on Thursday, the big day. Provisions and seats had been provided for five hundred, but alas, filled by early participants, "neither invited nor provided for," the loaves and fishes were made to suffice for a thousand fed, leaving many and important unsupplied. Dr. Burrowes undaunted, immediately planned for the following year. Tickets were issued for "full" as well as "partial participation," and thus rendered assurance doubly sure that the gates should not be crashed but that invited guests from a distance, members of the Press, should have adequate entertainment.

Genuine interest of the alumni, the really first adequate interest, was an outgrowth of the Harvest Home Week. The class of '66 celebrated its triennial in 1869, and held a House Party in "Old Main," with refreshments at ten o'clock, dancing to twelve. "The Class birthday cake was furnished by the accomplished daughter of President Burrowes." The gay revelers were accommodated in the College Building, and "in the morning took their departure in carriages and in a happy frame of mind." In 1870, at the second Home Coming the Alumni Association was organized, and six years later, secured representation upon the Board of Trustees. A first-hand description of this momentous occasion, fortunately is available:

"The promised 'Harvest Home' occurred in the last week of July, which was also the last of the Spring Term, and was all that could be expected, 'and more too.' On Tuesday our friends and the agents of reaping and mowing machines began to arrive, and on the evening of that day a most valuable and interesting lecture with illustrative experiments on Chemistry was given by Professor Breneman, to a full hall. On Wednesday the trial of mowing machines took place on the Experimental Farm, seven machines being entered, and all operated in mowing heavy and difficult grass to the satisfaction of the crowd present, and the committee having charge of the trial. In the evening three students of the old scientific class (Messers. A. B. Cramm of Michigan; F. W. Forman of Maryland; and W. W. Galbraith, of Cumberland County, Pennsylvania) were graduated and received diplomas, as Bachelors of Science, after a brief address by the President; the remainder of the evening being devoted to the reception of the friends of the graduating class and of the strangers present, at the residence of the President. On Thursday, the great trial of Reapers took place, in the large oats field on the College Farm—eight machines contending for the award of the Committee, and a crowd not less than two thousand persons from various parts of the State witnessing the trial—The evening of Thursday was devoted to an entertainment of their friends by the Alumni of the Institutions, who, during that day, had formed a permanent Alumni Society, which will hereafter hold its annual meeting during the Thursday of the 'Harvest Home' week. The enjoyment of the members present, and that of their very large number of invited guests seemed to be as perfect as is usual on such occasions; and all left precisely at 12 o'clock (midnight) apparently pleased with themselves and each other. The College Building was fully illuminated during two evening of the week, and made a splendid show both from the College grounds and the distant hills. On the whole, the result is that the Harvest Home has become a fixed fact in the College life, and regulated and extended as it may and will be, promises not only much pleasure to ourselves and friends, but to be one of the best methods of making known the condition and purposes of the institution."[8]

A plethora of opportunities and duties was bequeathed to Dr. Burrowes and to his Faculty in the purchase of three farms under the Act of 1867, previously mentioned. The Central Farm was deeded in Trust by the College for the sum of eight thousand dollars. The Eastern Farm located in Chester County was purchased at the cost of seventeen thousand five hundred dollars. The Western Farm in Indiana County was purchased at a cost of eighteen thousand three hundred sixty eight dollars and fifty cents. These farms were to serve as models and as experimental stations, to be in charge of the Professor of Agriculture. It fell to the lot of Dr. Burrowes to inaugurate programs and methods of work. Local contributions were made in order to secure these coveted locations; money was subscribed for stocking the farms. With these contributions grew a demand for local supervision. Jealousies and rivalries were thus engendered, opposition developed to means used as well as ends, unjust criticisms were bandied about; the College, itself, suffered gravely thereby. Manifestly it was a difficult and costly undertaking to provide proper supervision, at such widely separated points, and the farms (with the exception of the Central Farm) became in a short time models to avoid rather than object lessons to be followed.

In 1869, a series of experiments, elaborate and definite, was drawn up and printed by a Committee of the Board of Trustees. This series was to be zealously followed at the three farms for five years. The Committee consisted of J. Lacey Darlington, A. Boyd Hamilton, Jas. P. Carter, H. N. McAllister, Harry White, Thomas H. Burrowes, and Frederick Watts. Criticisms and difficulties speedily arose relative to the purpose and value of the experiments themselves. It was affirmed that the differences in the Eastern and Western

---

[8] Pennsylvania School Journal. -- October 1870

portions of the State from the Central part would render the results wholly uncertain. Local Committees, official and unofficial, donors and Clubs found objections to any form of centralized control. The Eastern Farm had already started lines of investigation adapted to the particular needs, problems and conditions of the constituency, and therefore, did not fall readily or faithfully into line with the project method of Dr. Burrowes, so concisely, if not pedantically phrased by him. "When the Board prescribes the *essentials of what is to be done* and the Professor of Agriculture instructs *how it is to be done*, the Superintendent has only *to see that it is done in the manner directed.*" In short, the attempt of scientific and experimental skill to discover new ways and means, to work patiently for results was met (and naturally) by a supervision and practical experience were like oil and water, they would not mingle. The result is a curious tale, continued with both humor and pathos until 1887 at least. President Atherton's cogent plea for the sale of the two farms and the beginnings of scientific experiment in Agriculture, as we shall later detail, closed the old story, healed the old wounds of battle.

Student activities were present in some of their characteristic forms under Dr. Burrowes. If they were less colorful and hectic than now, they certainly did not lack a genuine utility. Activities of those days were primarily, practivities. Little recreation may be apparent in "details of never more than eight lads at once, working time, only eight hours each day for five days in the week and with a draft force of only nine light mules "putting the arable portion of a farm of two hundred and fifty acres, including the garden, in as productive cultivation as any farm in the State. Grading roads and barnyard, erecting fences and building a turnpike do not savor of play. Nor do the "valuable lessons in mechanics and farm management in the carpenter and blacksmith shop, including making repairs and horse-shoeing, and making several new farm implements, and all the glazing and lock mending." Yet the "excellent effect upon the health, growth, and physical development of the students of these light but regular labors" is set forth glowingly. As a concession, perchance, to human perversity: "With it all baseball and football received a due share of attention at leisure hours." The lads (Burrowes' favorite term) exercised vocally, also, and he speaks with pride of Professor

Burgan's choir "quite noted for its good psalmody."

Among the student traditions of earlier days which President Burrowes heartily entered into were the hunting, camping and fishing expeditions which served to break the monotony of school life, or gild with radiance an enforced or homeless vacation. He has left a graphic description of one of these. Physical development, social contacts, self-government and self-control are the major features, the background of a gastronomic galaxy bequeathed to posterity, called the "Allegheny Stew."

"In November, 1869, twenty students, the President, one Professor and the Master Mechanic (who is also an old hunter) left on a four days camping and deer hunting trip. A two mule wagon was requisitioned and with food and baggage left the College at noon on Tuesday, in the midst of a flurry of snow; and crossing the valley to the north and Muncy Mountain some eight miles, passed over Bald Eagle Valley; and about six o'clock, P. M. and seven miles beyond, encamped on the top of the Allegheny, having made about fifteen miles. Next morning the camp was moved four miles to the east and on the north slope of the main mountain, and there remained till Thursday morning. Like many other enterprises commenced under a cloud, ours had the advantage of the saying, 'when the world is at its worst, it must mend'; for after the first day and until the last, the weather was just what we wished— clear, cool and bracing; and everything went and behaved right but the deer, which were so shy that none were obtained, though several were seen. Of smaller game, however, and plenty of exercise, good fun and fine appetites, there was no lack. And after a splashing march through constant rain, and over or rather through deep mud, we got home about three o'clock in the afternoon of Saturday—tired, wet and dirty, but without a single accident or even a cold to tell, next week of the excursion. The only drawback was the reception given to the excursionists by the stay-at-home party. However, if they would only have seen how villainously ill their short mocking faces comported with their hypocritical expressions of regret at our want of success, they would have realized how little they had the advantage over us in the way of being nice to look at."

This was an educational as well as a hunting expedition and "imparted three lessons:

1. That the Excursion itself was a good thing and ought to be repeated. It stretched the legs, opened the lungs, widened the local horizon, shook all the members closer together—teachers and pupils—and made each known to the other in phases of character not otherwise obtainable,—whether as to temper, endurance, readiness in expedient, or capacity of—appetite.

2. Some few defects in the preparatory arrangements and the management of the expedition and camp came to light, and afforded hints that will cause the excursion next year to be prepared for better, and conducted with greater ease and comfort, and probably with more success in the main purpose.

3. The discovery and mode of making what is henceforth and forever to be called, known and taken as

The Allegheny Stew[9]

"Take (along) one old-fashioned iron pot with handle. Swing the same over a good fire. Then put in the following order and at proper intervals:

Eight quarts of water.
Six medium sized turnips, pared and cut small.
Three pheasants cut into the usual portions.
Six squirrels.
Twelve partridges, wood-cock or other small game, cut into quarters or less.
Two pounds of cold roast beef, cut small
Two pounds of the fat end of ham, or of good bacon cut small.
Four middle sized onions cut small.
Add butter, pepper and salt to taste.

Just before dishing add a dozen of large cold boiled potatoes, cut small. When these are heated but before they become mashed, dish. Note: If venison

---

[9] Here is an anticipation of Professor Green's Nature Study camp and a delectable and palatable substitute for the "fried rattlesnake" of Professor Ferguson's much heralded menu of foresters.

be on hand, it is supposed that its substitution for cold roast beef would be an improvement; also the addition of a couple dozen mushrooms, if on hand; and if cold potatoes be absent, the raw tubers pared, cut small and put in long enough to boil and not mash will answer. If gunner ever tasted anything better than this in the woods, we would like to have share of it. It was good enough for our mess;—so good that nothing was left of it but the memory of a first-rate stew,—hot, savory and satisfying."

The academico-hunting expedition of 1870 indirectly caused the death of Dr. Burrowes. He suffered from cold and exposure, owing to unusually heavy snows, and on February 25th, 1871, died at the College. Vice-President McKee called a special meeting of the Faculty and arrangements were made for the funeral. A fitting service was held at the President's house on Tuesday, February 28th at 10 A. M. The cortege started for Bellefonte at 12 noon, "faculty, students and employees attended the memorial services and accompanied the remains to the depot." Dr. Burrowes was buried in St. James Churchyard at Lancaster; a noble Roman tomb was erected by friends in 1895, a worthy memorial participated in by contributions from all parts of the country. Of the inscriptions, one may be quoted: "He gave his best; His giving was princely; his work has been grandly cumulative, and will be so through the ages. To no man now living does Pennsylvania owe so great a debt of gratitude."

Professor John Hamilton who served with Dr. Burrowes at the Agricultural College and who was competently aware of the services Dr. Burrowes rendered to the College thus spoke in 1896. The occasion was the presentation of a portrait of President Burrowes to the College:

"He came to this College in the darkest period of its history. The number of students had dwindled to a handful. Public confidence had been withdrawn. The institution had become involved in debt, and the Trustees just before his election to the position of President, had seriously considered the propriety of surrendering their trust to the authorities of the Commonwealth, and of confessing that the scheme which they had undertaken for providing practical instruction for the youth of the

Commonwealth had failed. President Burrowes brought with him the trust of the public, because his had been an educational career that was widely known in Pennsylvania, both in itself and for the success that had attended it. And although he was not in the 65th year of his age, his enthusiasm and natural vigor seemed just as great as it had been years before. His presence re-established public confidence, the number of students attracted by his reputation very greatly increased, the course of study was reformed, and the institution was put into practicable working condition. During his administration, the experimental farm at the State College was founded and put into operation."

He gave personal attention to the interests of Agriculture, and also, had direction, in connection to the interests of Agriculture, and also, had direction, in connection with the Hon. H. N. McAllister, of Bellefonte, of the three experimental farms belonging to the College. There can be no doubt of our indebtedness to Dr. Burrowes for most of this that we enjoy today, for if he had not assumed control at the period at which he did, in all probability the College would have ceased to exist, and the experiment of industrial education, in so far as it was undertaken under the management of the Board of Trustees would have been a failure."

CHAPTER 8

The Classical Age: The Pennsylvania State College

"The change of name was needful, because the old name not only failed to express the breadth of purpose contemplated by the laws, under which the College received its endowment, but also misled many persons as to its real character. In many instances, students were prevented from entering, being under the impression that the College was designed for those alone who intended to be farmers. Under the change of name no change has been made in the courses of study or in the practical work of the institution."

President James Calder.

"It was felt that the important trust committed to the Board would not be fully administered while one-half of the youth of our State were denied its advantages... Therefore, ladies are now admitted to the same courses of study, are subject to the same general rules, and on the completion of their studies, receive the same certificates and degrees."

Catalogue of 1871

With the death of President Burrowes and the accession of Dr. James Calder, the last stages of the tentative, experimental period were entered upon. The Farmers' High School stressed a practical training mainly for the Agricultural classes, and its success under Dr. Pugh was signal at home and important abroad. His vision was true, moreover, of a broader industrial training which the acceptance of the Land Grant made imperative on the part of the Commonwealth and of the College. Had he lived to carry out his plans, with the changes which the years brought forth, it cannot be doubted, but that the shifting, drifting, experimental period would have been largely avoided. Five changes of administration in the course of eighteen years did not make for the continuity or stability needed in growing that delicate plant, an educational institution. Dr. Allen's significance lay in his endeavors to hold the Land Grant for the College and by its sale to realize an income. He followed conservatively the line which the very title of the institution embodied, and at the very time when its national organization was demanding expansion. General Fraser realized the broader obligations of the College, and flushed with the prospects of increased income by the Acts of '66 and of '67, he championed the Arts, Mechanic Arts, and Engineering. With a mill-stone of debt; exasperating delay in realizing on the endowment; with the abandonment of manual labor, the increase of student fees, and the decrease in numbers; with a decided advance in scholastic requirements and in teaching staff; with an over ambitious program of courses; with doubt and even dismay settling like a pall over some of the most undaunted of the Board of Trustees; the institution seemed headed for dark days. Dr. Burrowes' experiment is best described as a salvaging process; and earnest honest endeavor to inspire life and hope in what in many quarters was termed a lost cause.

With President Calder, the Classical period begins, the College loses much of its protective coloring of industrialism, becoming more and more like the average college of the day, a literary and classical school preparing for the learned professions. The main distinguishing features were to be found in military training, and in an emasculated manual labor feature, which was neither manual nor labor. In numbers the college grew, largely due to an emphasis upon the Preparatory department, the admission of women, and the enrollment of day pupils in music, art, etc. The largest numerical attendance up to 1887 was registered in 1878-79, a total of one hundred and sixty-two; one hundred and thirteen men and forty-nine women. However only a sixty-four of the number were in the four year courses. At least half of these were from the immediate region.

By the way of extenuation, it should be noted, also, that these diverse ideas of the mission of the College had their exponents in the Board of Trustees, formed parties and partizans within the ranks of the Faculty. A farm bloc resisted any departure from what was narrowly conceived to be the primary purposes which bought the institution into existence. The advocates of a broader industrialism had scarcely an alphabet of methods available with which to build up language. "The classical advocates had possession of the field and yielded a point only here and there, when the curriculum was to be modified." Not alone is this true of The Pennsylvania State College, every Land Grant College had its Middle Ages, its struggle to defend itself, to conciliate conflicting claims, to meet criticism of a well-high bewildering sort. "Fortunately," affirms Professor Buckhout, "the most serious effect was but temporary, and it is correct to say that at no time were the fundamental principles of industrial education lost sight of or even obscured."

James Calder, the fifth president, was a native of Pennsylvania, born at Harrisburg on February 15, 1826. He was educated in the Public Schools, attended Partridges' Military Institute and Harrisburg Academy. He graduated from Wesleyan University in 1849, entering the ministry in the Philadelphia Conference of the Methodist Episcopal Church. He served as a Missionary at Foo-Chow, China from 1851 to 1854. With changed views on Church polity, he returned to the United States, engaging for five years in pastoral and editorial work under the auspices of the Church of God. In 1869, he was elected President of Hillsdale College, from which position he was called in 1871 to the Presidency of the Agricultural College of Pennsylvania. Upon his retirement in 1880, he moved to Harrisburg. He continued an active interest in Agriculture, and was Lecturer of the State Grange, an Assistant Editor of the *Farmers' Friend*. Hillsdale College conferred upon him in 1866, the degrees of Doctor of Divinity. His was a prominent family in the civic and financial affairs of Harrisburg. His administration of the College is marked by measures tending to give greater publicity, as well as more closely affiliating it with the popular, current types of education. He died on November 22nd, 1893.

The work of this period, 1871 to 1880, the longest term in the Presidency to that time, may be advantageously reviewed under general and special changes.

Of the former, the earliest is the admission of women. The "feminine touch" was represented from 1859 to 1863 by Mrs. Elizabeth Hunter and her two daughters who were in charge of the culinary department and superintended the college parlors. Professor Whitman's daughter, Minerva, has sprung into acclaim in some quarters as the first woman student, but the records seem to indicate that her draughts at the springs of learning were limited to private tutelage and chaperonage of her father's botanical quarters. Mrs. Ann Condill came with the family of President Allen but remained as Matron and Nurse. She is most fondly remembered by the students; and A. A. Breneman pays warm tribute to her motherly care and patient zeal, "An institution in herself." From these beginnings the transition is easy to Preceptress, Lady Principal, and Dean.

Two women, the Misses Ellen Cross and Rebecca Ewing, applied to the Faculty for admission as day students. A special meeting was called June 19th, 1871. After "discussing the question pretty fully," the request was granted subject to the decision of the Board of Trustees. On September 5th, 1871, the Board "authorized and empowered the President and Faculty to open the doors of the College to male and female on the same conditions precisely, under such regulation as they deem expedient." The number of women students increased from six in 1871 to forty-nine in 1879, a number not exceeded in the following thirty years. Dr. Calder never doubted the success of the experiment, and the courage to carry it out under the primitive, if not crude, conditions, reflects credit upon the pioneering spirit of all concerned. Music, art, modern languages, the classics and literature received an impetus, even though the ranks of Agriculture and Mechanic Arts were not augmented.

Women students were housed in the top floors of the Western Wing of the College Building and many perplexing problems besides these of curricula forced themselves upon the Faculty. Whether as a cause or effect, telegraphy was offered as a subject of study, and the relaying of messages via the spouting was expressly prohibited. Upon the index also were campus meetings, clandestine or otherwise, major feats in 1871. The rules expressly forbade: "To walk or ride with students of the opposite sex or to meet such students in the parlor, or any other place, except by special permission of the President and the Preceptress."

Two legislative enactments had marked influence upon the College. The surveyor General joined in a recommendation that as an act of tardy justice the Land Grant Fund be consolidated, by the addition of eighty-nine thousand seven hundred and nine dollars and fifty cents, into a single bond for five hundred thousand dollars. The bond was to be held by the State, to run fifty years and to bear interest at six percent. The entire income as it accrues was to be paid by the College. Here was expressed both confidence in the present and permanency for the future, and the Board voted its "thanks to Colonel Frances Jordan, the Hon. A. Boyd Hamilton who with the efficient co-operation of President Calder secured the necessary legislation." A celebration by the student body was featured, and a public meeting held in the chapel, consisting of the reading of the Bill and remarks by the President, preceded by declamations, followed by essay, oration and Paper, with music interspersed under the romantic titles, Let the Angels in, and When Sue and I went Skating.

The payment of the mortgage authorized by the Act of the 1866 was brought about by legislature enactment in 1878. The interest on eighty thousand dollars at seven percent was a heavy drain upon the income of the institution. The model farms were clamoring for more and more of the endowment income. A movement was begun in 1869 to compel the Trustees to pay not less than one sixth of the entire land grant income to each farm. The bill never succeeded in the legislature, but it led one of the members to voice opposition to the College in these choice words: "This is our *dear* Agricultural College, If there is anything like a sell or decided humbug within our borders, it is the Agricultural College of Pennsylvania." The bonds matured in 1876, but efforts were futile to secure the appropriation to liquidate. A crisis was imminent, and it was frequently and openly asserted that without aid "the plant would be sold out by the sheriff." A bill was finally approved by the legislature for cancelling the bonds in 1878. The vote was without a dissenting voice in the Senate, and the record in the House was one hundred and four to twenty seven. An irritating amendment was added to reduce all salaries above fifteen hundred dollars, fifteen per cent, and between eight hundred and fifteen hundred dollars, ten per cent. Sympathy for the faculty, in no wise dampened the celebration by the students over what was essentially a victory. The College bell was rung and the building illuminated so as to rival the brilliancy of our modern white ways.

In 1873, General James A. Beaver came into actual official relations with the College. He succeeded H. N. McAllister on the Board, serving in various capacities until his death in 1914. During the early days of the College, as student and law partner of Mr. McAllister, he was concerned with supplies, pay rolls, building operations, etc. In a peculiar and vital sense, the College became identified with General Beaver, and to it he gave the choicest, most devoted, most self-sacrificing energies of a busy fruitful life as a lawyer, soldier, governor, publicist, and judge. Whether explicitly stated, or not, the heroic figure, enthusiasm, and energy of the General illuminates every page of College history from 1873 to his death in 1914.

Among other things to be chronicled, the change in College government merits attention. An Executive Committee was formed, January 13th, 1874, to represent the Board in the immediate affairs of the College, but responsible in all particulars to the direction and approval of the Board. A budget was first instituted, a sinking fund provided to cover debt, and an apportionment of funds to the several departments to insure proportionate growth.

A major change was made in the constitution of the Board of Trustees, by the amendment to the charter by the Court of Common Pleas of Centre County in 1875. The number of the Board was increased from thirteen to twenty-three; and Engineering and Mechanical Societies were given representation as electors of Trustees, as previously those of Agriculture. Alumni representation was also provided, and four additional ex-officio Trustees, the Secretary of Internal Affairs, the Adjutant General, the Superintendent of Public Instruction and the President of Franklin Institute.

A major development involving the title of the College is yet more important. On September 23rd, 1873, Judge Hiester moved that General Beaver be appointed a Committee to apply to the Court of Centre County for amendment to the charter to alter the name of the Institution to "Pennsylvania State College," so the record reads. The decree of the Court of Common Pleas was handed down on January 26th, 1874, declaring "that the name of the said 'Agricultural College of Pennsylvania' is changed to that of 'The Pennsylvania State College,' by which name it shall henceforth be known and designated." Back of the formal record was a web of conflicting aims, achievements, hopes, and emotions calling for mutual adjustment and evaluation. President Calder stated the case for the College in his Report for 1873 as follows: "Partly because of our name, but perhaps chiefly because of the opening of the Institution originally as the "Farmers High School," the impression has prevailed that our work was solely that of educating farmers. Hence, it was expected that the instruction imparted should have this single object in view, and should be limited in extent; and especially was it demanded that every graduate should forthwith engage in agricultural pursuits. Our several extensive courses of studies, and the fact that our students on leaving us became civil engineers, chemists, manufacturers and lawyers, as well as farmers and gardeners, led many persons to declare that we were abusing our trust, and that the College was a failure and an imposition on the public. At length it is becoming to be understood that by the Enactments of Congress and our State Legislature we are to be as much a mechanical College as an agricultural one, and that at the same time we are not to exclude the other scientific and classical studies and must include military tactics."

The choice of a more accurate and significant title for the College was stimulated, also, by the chartering of an institution called the Mechanics High School by the Legislature of 1873. The avowed purpose of the institution was that of "furnishing skilled foremen for our Pennsylvania workshops." Here was not only a possible rival in the field of industrial training but a probable competitor or claimant for a portion of the Land Grant proceeds. By authority of the Trustees, President Calder addressed a letter to the Secretary of the Board of Mechanics High School in which he sets forth that "the fourteen years which have passed since our doors were first opened have taught us many valuable lessons, and that the State's benevolent citizens will act prudently if they hesitate to inaugurate a very similar experiment in a new locality, and by unexperienced though otherwise competent agents." Positively the case is this: "Here, on the premises occupied by the Agricultural College, the State, not certain individuals or even the Board of Trustees owns an institution which cost a million dollars. This institution was designated by Congress to do the excellent work which you now have in contemplation. Its managers are more than merely willing to do that work." Dr. Calder further anticipates the objection which may be made to the inappropriateness of our present name by detailing the steps already taken to alter the name of the College. He continues: "Why not, then, have all needful changes made in its name, in its board of trustees, and in its buildings, with the required additions to its faculty and courses of study; and then at once enable the College to do that part of its work which has so long been deferred, avoid the multiplying of institutions which can claim government aid, and escape the expenditure of at least half a million dollars? As a board, we unhesitatingly declare our willingness to co-operate with you in such a movement."

We may accept as a valid estimate of all these general changes, that arrived at by President Calder and the Faculty in 1877, "such as bring the College somewhat nearer in character to the ordinary collegiate institutions of the State and country; but that these changes, while removing evils which experience made manifest, still faithfully keep in view the chief purpose of the founders of the institution, and maintain its distinctive method of imparting instruction *practically* as well as theoretically."[10]

Under the rubric of special changes during the period under discussion,

---

[10] Industries and Institutions of Center County, Pennsylvania, containing a sketch of The Pennsylvania State College prepared by members of the present Faculty under the Supervision of President Calder. Pages 82-122, Bellefonte, 1877.

the beginnings of campus and town are noteworthy. The action of the Trustees on September 4th, 1872 in setting back the farm fence fourteen feet, the property owners on the south side of the township doing likewise led to the dedication of "College Street" as it is called in the records of the Board of Trustees. On the College side, Dr. Calder reports the planting "of many trees in the campus and a fine row of them has been set out along four front upon College Avenue." The "barn-yard" graded and drained, over which Dr. Burrowes enthused in description to the Trustees, is carried over to the "College Yard." Finally when "pale fences, hedge rows, the nursery, the stone quarry, the potato fields and the old rail fences are removed, the 'Campus' begins to emerge."

In the report of 1873, Dr. Calder wrote: "The new approach to main building, entering the campus at the engine house, has been completed, the road-way being well macadamized and the boarders lined with trees. An alumnus of 1875 grows eloquent over the enlarging prospect: "On the southern end of the campus, at the unique looking ground-keepers lodge, begins a wide avenue, lined on either side with maples, which winds up through the broad, handsome grounds to the summit of the College Hill. Standing on the old familiar steps of the main entrance, as he looked around him, he notices that the campus is more beautiful than ever. Rows of neatly trimmed hedges skirt the lanes and avenues in all directions. Immediately in front is an elliptical area, a dozen or more rods in length, enclosed by a beautiful hedge, and in the center, a rustic fountain sends heavenward its crystal stream. Landscape gardening has been the hobby of somebody hereabouts and his models are the admiration of scores of ladies and gentlemen strolling through the numberless inter-winding walks."

These hedges of antediluvian landscaping were almost entirely removed from front campus before 1879 and replaced by "handsome rows of trees" and trees in groups and series. As late as 1877, however, potatoes were "raised" on a part of this frontage. A fence was authorized in June 1875 "in front of the College Farm, from the road separating it from the model farm to the Hotel," the advent of the "Board Fence," the "turnstile," and those striped and streaked gates. Periodically whitewashed and semi-periodically replaced because of the inexorable demands of material for bon-fires, they served until 1897 to delimit town and gown. The board fence gave way, but not for long, to one of plain wires, which the Free Lance complimented as "somewhat of an improvement over the old."

An official in charge of campus was recognized in 1877 when Professor C. Alfred Smith received the help of Johnny Carrigan, and with the mule, cart and twenty-five dollars for lawn mowers began the more intimate work of campus landscaping. A tribute is due this over-worked Professor for his voluntary labor in supervision, and to his "sainted" Irish helper who wrought for many years in making the rough, smooth; and the crooked, straight.

The delicate but vital operation regularly combining intellectual culture with manual labor to which Burrowes gave such explicit care, again began to be irksome. In 1871, it was announced that no farm or household work would be required after the Sophomore year. An increasing assignment of "enforced labor" as a method of discipline and punishment brought it yet more into disfavor. A system of Demerits was in use, and the clearing house functions of rather complicated records of academic book-keeping were loaded upon the manual labor plan. Definite agitation by both faculty and students in 1874 and 1875 met with re-affirmation of the principle of Labor by the Trustees. A formal paper, signed by forty-six students, cited the fact that men were leaving the institution because of the requirement. They petitioned to be permitted "to work in such lines, only, as will best promote their field of study, and combine useful practice with theory." The Board informed the students that the petition was "pleasantly received"; and that they "recognize the right of petition and hope that it will always be exercised in the spirit of this one." The principle contended for was modified to require only so much labor as shall best carry out the design of the Institution. The Charter of 1855 had prescribed that students shall "perform all the labor necessary in the cultivation of the farm, and shall thus be instructed and taught." It was accordingly so modified, in an amendment decreed by the Court of Common Pleas in and for the County of Centre, November 22nd, 1875, as to require the students of the said institution to perform so much as shall from time to time be prescribed by the Board of Trustees, and shall best carry out the design of the industrial classes in the several pursuits and professions of life." Appended to the reply of the Trustees was the proviso: "It being however the sense of the Board that the Labor requirement as hitherto be adhered to in some one department as best for the health and physical development of the student." This brought considerable odium upon the department concerned.

Increased friction in carrying it out under the aegis of the Military Department led to a joint petition with the faculty for the establishment of a complete system of Practicums and for all subjects alike. A conference with the Board resulted in approval and in 1876 a schedule of practicums for all subjects went into effect. Sums in the budget were set aside for these extensions of the laboratory into every branch of the curriculum. For women students, plain sewing, dressmaking, starching and ironing, and fancy needle work alternated with the lighter arts of husbandry in garden, vineyard and orchard. "As rapidly as it could be worked out, Ladies will take science instead of Agriculture; aesthetics instead of surveying; modern language instead of tactics." Miss Anna M. Cooper, Lady Principal, was sent by the Board in 1879 to New York City, her expenses for tuition, etc., provided by the college, "for instruction relative to her Practicums." The compass and chain served a wide purpose, while the college carpenter and blacksmith shops did yeoman duty as apprenticeship aids in the fundamental forms of Mechanic Arts, telegraphy was taught and instanced as one step in making the college of benefit to the industrial classes. "A set of instruments and appliances, therefore, are the gift of William Calder, Esq., of Harrisburg." Trips were also made to iron foundries and other industrial plants from 1871, thus even in the Classical Period holding true to its practical genius. Professor Pattee writing of our College traditions affirms of manual labor: "The tradition of those days still lives; Penn State has never been a kid glove college; it has stood for the dignity of work; it prepares for all the various pursuits and professions of life."

To the nucleus of the faculty, Professors McKee, Hamilton, Rothrock and Breneman, there were significant accessions during President Calder's term. At the opening of the period in 1871, W. A. Buckhout and W. C. Patterson began services which grew in breadth and in depth with the years, some estimate of which will later appear in these pages. A. Alfred Smith,

Charles F. Reeves and J. F. Downey, alumni of the College; Col. Arthur Grabowski and E. T. Burgan gave devoted toil. In 1879 physics and chemistry were separated as department units, and I. Thornton Osmond was appointed to the Chair of Physics, thus inaugurating the longest term of service in the history of the College, and (in 1932) a still honored one as Professor Emeritus.

Three courses of study were adopted in 1871, supplanting Burrowes, "three durations of instruction," Agriculture, Scientific and Classical. These remained practically unchanged for a decade, except for increased emphasis upon certain practicums and upon military training. "Here, Farming is not an ad captandum branch in the catalogue, but a regular and productive pursuit of the student" was repeated year after year. Graduates of the College averaged nine annually, but the majority of these were in the "ad captandum" fields of Latin and Greek roots, general science, and literature. Instruction in English Composition as a practicum was stressed, and public orations, essays, and declamations were exacted of all students. Commencement parts were taken by the classes, and were dominantly general and literary, the scientific note reappearing about 1885. Prizes for both conduct and scholarship were awarded, and honors conferred from 1873. The type of program is indicated in a letter from President Calder to Trustee McAllister, December 12th, 1871: "I trust you will be with us on Thursday evening, at our Commencement exercises. The occasion promises to be an interesting one. The students under the leadership of the Junior Class, have trimmed the Chapel very tastefully; we will have good music of home production; Miss Butterfield, our Preceptress, will read an original production on "Christian Womanhood," and several undergraduates will favor us with original or selected declamations."

The Kaine Oratorical Prize, later known as the Junior Oratorical Contest, was established in 1872. It was supported by Daniel Kaine and later by Thomas Barlow, members of the Board. The fiftieth anniversary contest was celebrated in 1922, at which Judge Ellis L. Orvis, the oldest living winner of the Prize presided. The roll of honor is the roll call, too, of some of the most prominent and successful alumni. The connection of this prize with the rivalries and interests of the two Literary Societies was brought out by Judge Orvis in a description of the first contests: "When Mr. Burkholder of the

Cresson Society was announced as winner, a great storm of cheering broke loose, such as one hears today when the winning touchdown is made in a football game—I was fortunate enough to be the winner of the third contest, and the enthusiastic members of the Washington Society carried me from the room on their shoulders."

To be in conformity with the majority of Colleges, the College year was again re-arranged so as to close in July, beginning in 1872. Three years later, the two sessions became three. A new class spirit is shown by a special recognition of Class Day at the Commencement of 1874. A Class Tree and Ivy are planted, a Class Song is written, five two-minute speeches pronounced, Class History and Prophecy follow in traditional order, closing with the smoking of a "Pipe of Peace." Social and dramatic activities receive some emphasis, and under Miss Julia C. Dent, Lady Preceptress, monthly receptions were scheduled by Class groups, Seniors and Freshmen; Juniors and Sophomores, and finally A Preparatory. These socials extended "from 8 p.m. to not beyond 9:30." Guests are limited in their promenades to College Parlor and the President's Office, and the hall so far as visible from the front door. Chapel was a movable feast from 5:45 a.m., as an inheritance from the vigorous regimen of Dr. Burrowes, to 12 noon; and finally, in 1878, to 8 a.m. Sunday services, which had uniformly been held at 3 p.m., were on petition of the students in 1880 fixed at 10:30 in the morning, but this arrangement was not permanent until 1893, the exigencies and conveniences of a group of local "chaplains" were consulted. Harvest Home was greatly simplified, becoming a sort of field day for trial of implements, in which students enthusiastically vied with the visiting agriculturists and machinists. The Cresson Annual and the Photosphere appear in print to boast of the achievements of the respective literary societies. A Young Men's Christian Association was also established, appearing first in the catalogue for 1876-77. This mention was preceded, however, by what was termed, "A Christian Association" for the years 1874-75 and 1875-76.

Alterations in heating and sanitation were effected at the beginning and end of this period. These made possible the removal of ill-looking structures to the rear of the building, and the yet more ill-favored though famous adjuncts, the "towers" of "Old Main." Dr. Calder found the hot-air furnaces unsatisfactory and expensive. Funds for needed replacements were inadequate, enrollment was reduced so that parts of the building were not used. By vote of the Board of Trustees, stoves were substituted, and the care of fires, and fees for coal for one stove were added to the students' incidentals. There is a certain sense of compensation, however, in the picture of the "Prof" with a Greek or Mathematics Text in one hand, while the other wields shovel and poker upon the recalcitrant fire; the student meanwhile marshalling his forces, and with added information rides to a successful issue. This gives point too, to such regulations, as students are expected to be very careful of their fires; cutting kindling in the building and sweeping from the rooms into the halls are forbidden; all sweepings and ashes must be carried down stairs and emptied upon the ash pile. In 1879, after an adequate supply of water had been provided from an artesian well at the upper gates (the Allen Street entrance), a steam heating plant was placed in the basement of the College Building. A large storage reservoir, sixty feet long, twenty feet wide and sixteen feet in depth, holding one hundred and twenty thousand gallons was built on the Southern part of what is now New Beaver Field. In order to obtain earth with which to cover the reservoir, a large excavation was made in the adjoining grove. This with very little additional labor, Dr. Calder reports "can be prepared as an excellent swimming place for the students." The "additional labor" never materialized, but it became a favorite "ducking pond" of unsavory reputation for disciplining unlucky Freshman and on occasion for yet more ill-starred instructors. It served, also, the more utilitarian uses for filling an unsightly ice-house. The huge reservoir mound, about which fiction and romance have woven their tales, was not removed until 1910.

The College as a compulsory boarding school definitely ceased in 1872, when permission was granted students to board outside. In 1874, Dr. Calder reports to the Trustees, the existence of two successful Clubs. With these Clubs, and in a degree provocative of them came the knowledge of the formation of "Secret" Fraternities. The latter were assumed to be pernicious and by tradition and unwritten consent absolutely forbidden. The rumor, even, of a dance at the Hotel, or the dire emergency that a Fraternity may have a Chapter, sub-rosa, was sufficient warrant for a Faculty meeting, and "all hands on the alert" as professorial detectives to thwart so sinister designs upon the body collegiate. The catalogues from 1874 to 1887 contained express statements forbidding Secret Fraternities or student membership in the same; and during a part of that time, at least, a distinct pledge was enacted of the student before admission to College. The course of the legislation itself, is interesting as a bit of history. On July 18th, 1873, the Faculty voted that the President of the College recommend to the Board "such action on Secret Fraternities as to prevent their future existence in this College." The Trustees on July 23rd instructed the President "to adopt such a course regarding secret societies as will prevent their existence." This action was prefaced by a resolution: "that it is the opinion of this Board that the existence of secret fraternities amongst the students is pernicious, as well as regards the interests of the young men themselves as of the ultimate success of the Institution." Dr. Calder reported as a part of the work of the year 1873, that "the unanimous action of the Trustees of the College, directing the Faculty to suppress certain secret fraternities which had been clandestinely organized, has accomplished its purpose, and the Institution has been happily freed from associations whose existence is uncalled for and whose influence is ordinarily corrupting and mischievous."

The first detail of a regular Army officer was secured in 1877 by the appointment of Lieutenant Walter Howe. The main floor of Old Chapel, the old College Dining Room, was transformed into an armory. A small room in the basement had previously served as headquarters. Military training had been in the hands of some member of the Faculty since 1865. General John Fraser lectured on Tactics, and students returned from the War or on furlough acted as drill masters, among them W. C. Holohan, Tellico Johnson, Albert H. Tuttle. From 1869 to 1875, Instructor John Hamilton and John F. Downey served the Military Department. From 1875-1877, a very elaborate course of training was instituted by Professor Arthur Grabowski, of the Modern Language Department, with all the organization, regulations and ceremonies of a Military Post. An interesting attempt was made through a Chapter of Honor to regard merit, increase discipline, and create a healthy spirit of rivalry in the execution of academic, as well as military duties. The President of the College and the Commandant were presiding officers. There were, also, a Grand Commander, Two Commanders, twelve Knights, twenty-four Esquires. Semi-monthly meetings were held with a ritual of twenty-seven orders, with initiations, promotions, salutes, marches and counter-marches. Badges of Merit were conferred upon the worthy participants in this intricate, human play of chess. Whatever else was accomplished by this riot of ceremonialism, at least it had a part in preparing the Battalion to appear with credit at County Fairs and Patriotic celebrations, or as a crowning even, grace with seventy-two men in line, the inaugural procession of Governor John F. Hantraft on January 18th, 1876.

The College was beginning to enter exhibits of farm products, etc., at State and County Fairs. An "elaborate exhibit which received considerable attention" was prepared for the Centennial Exhibition in Philadelphia. It consisted in part:

1. Of a large and handsomely executed draft of grounds, Buildings and Farm by Professor Downey.
2. Of a fine display of Grasses and Seeds by Professor Hamilton
3. Of an interesting collection of insects, injurious and beneficial by Professor Buckhout.

Plowing matches, and tests of farm machinery under normal field conditions were held, also, upon the grounds of the Eastern Experimental Farm under the auspices of the College and of the Centennial Authorities.

Finally to this period can be traced the beginnings of an institutional or college consciousness. This is shown by increased activity on the part of alumni, also; and led to the representation on the Board. The first Alumni Trustees were Cyrus Gordon, '66; Henry T. Harvey, '62 and James Miles, '61. In 1875, Dr. W. A. Buckhout began the collection of material concerning the graduates of the College, and the first Alumni Record was issued by him in 1880. The Alumni Banquet as it has so long been termed owes its official status to an action of the Board of Trustees of May 11th, 1878, since which time it has served to heighten the tide of friendship and esteem among

Trustees, Faculty, Alumni and the Public for Alma Mater.

While much progress is thus to be noted toward the status of a College, inwardly things were approaching a crisis. Discipline or lack of it was the rock which shattered the fair picture. The artificiality of punishments, even the puerility of some of its forms, fed the flames of discontent. Hazing broke out like a rash, stamping feet and hissing in Chapel, rifling orchards and poultry houses, semi-occasional or otherwise alcoholic lapses are matters of faculty concern. Disturbing hall lights, putting plumbing out of commission, shooting from the building, throwing everything out of the windows except the building itself, such situations demanded more than additional demerits, extra hours for labor, cleaning recitation rooms, sitting on front seats in Chapel, or faculty visitation of rooms. The regulation, "all defacing of walls by marking, posting pictures, driving nails or tacks is forbidden" was a prolific breeder of trouble. "Students wishing nails driven will report to the Janitor who will attend to it" was "Froth" material, had there been such a sheet. Regulations concerning the leaving of grounds or building during study hours except Tuesdays after 4:10 P. M. were too drastic for enforcement on any day. This, too, even though week-ends to Bellefonte on the Beaver State Line were looming on the horizon. As featured by the watchman, Mr. Benjamin Beaver assumes proprietorship on July 1st, 1879. He is "energetic and trustworthy and will accommodate the public with low fares, comfortable coaches and rapid transportation." One regulation at least in this comedy of errors met no over opposition. It savors of athletic favoritism and vicious subsidizing of football before the days of Institutional surveys as "students are forbidden to play ball of any kind, except football, in the front campus." The students complained to the Board of the forms of discipline under twelve counts. A conference between Judge John Orvis, Trustee; with the students and faculty led to the abandonment of the Demerit System, together with punishment at hard labor. But the moment of relaxation is often the time of greatest danger. Dr. Calder seems to have become conscious of weakening grip upon the student body and faculty, and called upon the Board to redefine his position, powers, duties, etc. The solution reached was one of release from local class-room and administrative duties, to visit all parts of the State, with a view to making the

College and its advantages better known to the public. He is delegated to secure increased attendance, and especially to gain the co-operation of manufacturing interests of the Commonwealth by contributions of machinery for the equipment of shops at the College.

There was also growing discontent and dissatisfaction among certain members of the Board of Trustees and of the Faculty that the main purposes of the Institution, Agriculture and Mechanic arts were being obscured. Coming events presaged new efforts "to carry the Institution out of its vortex of idiosyncrasies back into the straight path of duty." Dominating roles in these events will be taken by Professor McKee, Hamilton, Buckhout, Jackson, but particularly by Smith, Osmond and Jordon. The stage is set by the resignation of President Calder on November 5th, 1879. The growing sense of dissatisfaction over the unrealized aims of the College which contributed to his resignation, also led to a series of important investigations which it is the purpose of the next Chapter to resume.

CHAPTER 9

The Period of Investigation

"In conclusion, the result of a most careful and painstaking examination has fully convinced us that the State College is in good faith fulfilling the trusts committed to it by the State, and that much of the misconception respecting it arises from a lack of easily obtained information. We believe it has passed its worst days. Its courses of studies, in the opinion of experts, are well organized; its facilities good, and in some particulars unusually complete; its faculty is composed of competent and many of them highly experienced professors; and whatever mistakes it may have made in the past, the entire spirit and work of the institution, as now organized and administered, are directed to the promotion of industrial education."

Amos H. Mylin, Chairman
Report to the Legislature of 1883 by Committee of same authorized in 1881.

The faculty urged upon the Board of Trustees the need of securing immediately a successor to President Calder whose resignation was accepted January 22nd, 1880. On May 27th, 1880, Joseph Shortlidge, Principal of Maplewood Institute, was recommended by a Committee of the Board and his election followed. President Calder had generously worded his resignation to take effect at the end of the College Year or at such time as his successor be elected. In the embarrassment of riches at the approaching Commencement, the Board, with solemn wisdom decreed: the new President, the retiring President, and the Vice-President shall preside during the exercises at Commencement as the new President may request. The occasion assumed rather unusual proportions, and two members of the Board, A. O. Hiester and Cyrus Gordon were "charged with reporting for the Press the proceedings of Commencement Week."

No formal inaugural ceremonies took place, however, but at the Alumni Banquet, among the numerous speakers, the President-Elect "made a telling speech on the present needs of the College." He urged the "propriety of a new boarding club and spoke with warmth on the construction of a railroad and the establishment of telegraphic communication with the College." An address to the Alumni by Dr. George C. Caldwell of Cornell University on "Invention and Investigation" struck the note of the new spirit in education, but the graduating exercises, consisting of seven orations and essays ranging from "Peter the Great" to "God in History", and from the "Importance of an Early Choice" to the "Vocality of Silence" showed that the Institution was still floating in the stagnant back-waters of pseudo-classical and literary retreats.

At a meeting of the Board, June 30th, 1880, the famous resolution (superfluous in the case of a real executive, and doubly dangerous in the hands of another) was enacted: "Resolved for the best interests of the College and harmony of administration, all members of the Faculty, Business Manager, Superintendents of the College and Experimental Farms and all employees of the aforesaid shall be subject to the orders of the President of the College." Thus with full sail ahead, the College entered upon the shortest, most turbulent period of its history. Candor compels the reflection, however, that viewed in the large, no more blame attaches to President Shortlidge than to the Board itself. Both acted in the best of faith that administrational problems and methods, personal ambitions and external strife would now be resolved— only to find as have other institutions, that both parties were the victims of mistaken judgment. Amid the heat of controversy, charge and counter-charge which ensued, the unprejudiced conclusion of one who lived through this period may be accepted, "The President came at a time in the growth of the College when peculiar and rare talents were needed. One not familiar with the vital purposes of these Land-Grant Colleges could not steer these institutions into public favor." Add to this, the unwise transplanting of a Secondary School atmosphere and scheme of regulations, a rather stern, uncompromising and apparently haughty demeanor in personal relations with the student body, a curious attitude of suspicion toward the major part of the Faculty, you have the factors that led to loss of influence, to lack of co-operation, and finally to open rebellion.

Precipitated by an investigation (of which later) President Shortlidge resigned before the end of the College year, and Vice-President McKee was called upon for the fourth time to carry the burdens of administration, which he did with signal devotion and success. Fifty Senatorial Scholarships were announced, Mechanic Arts (chiefly wood working and drawing) under Mr. John McCormick, a graduate of Ohio State University was begun in the loft of the Engine House; a Farmers' Institute, a course of thirty lectures by professors of the College and others was arranged for January, 1882, and a totally new grouping of courses, two general and four technical, was put into operation. When he turned over the College to President Atherton in July, 1882, for the longest and most important of all periods of the College History, when the Institution had gone through its wilderness wanderings, crossed the Red Seas of Investigation, and traversed the deserts of public criticism, the Board of Trustees formally commended the Faculty for the zeal and efficiency with which they had performed their respective duties and for their hearty co-operation for the common interests, and especially for the "faithful, discreet and efficient labors of Acting-President McKee worthy of the highest commendation of the Board."

Professor Joseph Shortlidge spent his entire life (he died in 1911 at the age of 79) except the one at this College in Secondary Education. In 1862, he bought a large tract of land near Concordville, erected buildings and established a school. In 1870, it was incorporated as Maplewood Institute, and Professor Wickersham wrote of it in 1885 as "well attended and ably conducted". He was a student at Yale in his early life, but owing to ill health did not complete the course. In recognition, however, of his elevation to the Presidency of the College, Yale conferred upon him in 1880 the degree of Master of Arts. His unfortunate connection with the Pennsylvania State College (which he freely admitted was an error of judgment) was not devoid of some achievement. He brought Josiah Jackson as Professor of Mathematics leading to the earliest steps toward a practicum in mechanic arts, and to an impress for many years upon Engineering development at the College, through his worthy sons. Also the appointment of Dr. W.H. Jordan as Professor of Agriculture brought an end to the trifling with purely empirical and haphazard policies regarding the education of the farmer, and the inauguration of scientific methods and experimentation—thus anticipating and incorporating something of the Experimental Station movement. As a resident of the district of the State in which the Eastern Model Farm was located and from which the most persistent criticism arose, it was supposed that Professor Shortlidge would be peculiarly fitted to allay misunderstandings and unjust attacks. But without avail, and in the letters of one "John Plowshare" in the West Chester Local News (and widely copied) both skill and bitterness unite in assailing men, motives and results of the College and its pseudo model farms. Petitions were drawn up by the Eastern Farm Club to be circulated in every county, and to be sent to the Senate and house affirming that neither the College nor the Farms were maintained in the terms and spirit of the Act of 1863, and praying the Legislature to divert the fund from the Pennsylvania State College, to dispose of it by appropriate legislation, that the purposes intended by Congress be more fully complied with and some adequate benefit be derived. That thus not only a class, but the entire community may, at least, indirectly, be profited by the prevention of further waste of so large a sum as is now received by said college.

Forerunners and echoes of these charges came from other sources within the Commonwealth, and the College was entering upon a period of abuse and criticism from which it emerged as the outcome of a series of official investigations, substantially vindicated, its interests well served. Even hostility was better than indifference. In the light of subsequent history, the overt opposition was not owing to any inherent desire to injure the College itself, but arose chiefly from wounded feelings and from dissatisfaction with an experiment in education which did not as yet definitely know what it was about. In relating this part of College History, one could by changing names and incidental details take a chapter from Land-Grant College History in many another State. Conditions were general, not merely local, the lack of an adequate educational program, and undeveloped and as yet only imperfectly mapped out means of industrial training, but especially the superstition that agricultural education without concerted and persistent scientific experiment would work both magic and miracle—these were among the obstacles encountered by these institutions. Here was ample field for investigation to be helpful and criticism to be constructive, but also for violent attack and base calumny. The Pennsylvania State College weathered the storms, therefore, like her sister Colleges in every State in the Union with a more definite consciousness of tasks to be done, methods to be pursued, and with means more and more adequately provided by the joint bounty of Federal and State Government.

A review of the course of these investigations in our own Commonwealth has genuine interest. Mention has been made of the Congressional investigation of these institutions in 1875 and the significant conclusions at which the Committee arrived. This report calling as it did for information, and suggesting as it did the possibilities of closer co-operation with the Federal Government brought to the several States and the institutions themselves, the need of self-criticism, inventory and evaluation of their State Colleges. Thus in 1878 the State Agricultural Society of Pennsylvania suggested changes in the agricultural course in order to render its instruction more effective. The Experimental and Model Farms were constantly under the fire of critics in that they were not experimental, model or even first-rate farms. The advocates of industrial training, in mechanic arts, in mining, etc., were silent neither in the State at large nor in legislative halls in maintaining that the intent of the Land-Grant Act was not being carried out. Generously admitting in most cases that the fault lay not with the Board of Trustees but in meager support by the State herself—yet in time these sporadic criticisms issued in formal and official investigations.

The Grange, which President Calder by example and precept endeavored to enlist in the interests of the College, made a series of reports. In 1878, the institution is commended to the patronage of all classes, and especially the farmers throughout the country. The instruction seems to be of a solid nature; "the female student is prepared for a matron instead of a parlor ornament. The male student is fitted to be a man instead of a fashionable loafer." The Report deems as desirable a supervisory control over the College as far as is consistent with the chartered rights and privileges of others, and a continuance of an annual visitation is recommended. In the Minutes of the Grange held at Greensburg, December 14th, 1880, a series of resolutions urge action on the part of the Board of Trustees. Two of these are important, one calling upon the Trustees "to terminate at once the protracted and inexcusable deficiencies in the Department of Agriculture, and, particularly that henceforth they make that department second to none." A second resolution brands the three so-called experimental farms owned by the College as "unworthy of their name, a reproach to the great agricultural State in which they are located, and as demanding immediate reformation in the purposes, economy and methods of their management." Other resolutions sought extenuating circumstances and ended by pledging the support of the Grange in effecting reforms.

In the meantime, the Legislature of 1879 had, by Joint Resolution approved April 25th, appointed a Committee to investigate the College and Experimental Farms. Charges were made at the time that the real purpose of the "investigation" was to even up political scores between rivals in the county in which the Western Experimental Farm was located. Sufficient incentives, however, existed in the general atmosphere of criticism and attack at the time. President Calder wrote that the College welcomed the investigation, but that manifestly no adequate knowledge of the institution could be arrived at in four hours spent at the College. The more so, as he somewhat naively says to the State Board of Agriculture in session at Harrisburg, since one hour of that time they were engaged in "eating and smoking". We furnished them with eatables, but not with the cigars, as the members of the faculty do not smoke. The committee did not visit a single recitation room, nor look over the experimental farm. The books and treasurer's accounts were available and every opportunity afforded to ask questions. President Calder and Vice-President McKee were but briefly interviewed; supplemented by an evening session in Bellefonte at which Governor Curtin, General Beaver and several of the Board of Trustees gave information and testimony.

The records reveal that the Committee actually held five sessions, May 2 at the College and Bellefonte, May 8 at Harrisburg, May 13 and 14 at Pittsburgh; and again at Harrisburg May 15. The report made to the Legislature on June 5 follows:

"In submitting the evidence, the Committee beg leave to report as the result of their investigation into the affairs of the Pennsylvania State College, that while the evidence does not show actual fraud or disclose corrupt management of funds received by said institution, yet your committee are of the opinion that the testimony does conclusively indicate that the institution has been very badly managed; that its location is a very undesirable one; that the building is entirely unsuited to the purpose for which it was erected; that the agricultural department which was intended to be the leading object of the institution, has never been a success, and that the State has never received and is not now receiving benefits at all commensurate with the amount of money which has been appropriated to said institution by the United States and this State. We also find the Congress of the United States granted to the State seven hundred and eighty thousand acres of land, which by bad management, netted the State only $439,000; the Act of Congress granting this vast amount of land required that the proceeds thereof should be used by the State mainly in the interest of agriculture and mechanic arts; that the interest accruing from this fund, in addition to some $400,000 appropriated by the State Legislature, is used and controlled by the trustees of said agricultural college; that in addition, the trustees aforesaid hold the bond of the State bearing six per cent interest, dated February 2, 1872, calling for $500,000 and falling due fifty years from date, from which the said trustees derive a revenue of $30,000 annually. Your committee find the evidence discloses the further fact that the deeds for all the freehold belongings to said Pennsylvania State College, including the experimental farms, are held by the aforesaid trustees and their successors. Your committee also find that the experimental farms owned by said trustees which were to be conducted solely in the interest of the Agricultural class of the Commonwealth, have utterly failed to accomplish the object intended. This is notably so in the case of the Western Farm, located in Indiana county, which is not now a third class farm, not in as good condition as when purchased. Your committee also find that at the present session of the College but forty-six students are in attendance, many of whom are non-residents of the State, and that there is now in the employ of the College eleven professors, which we deem out of all proportion with the number of students in attendance. Finally, your committee is of the opinion that the trustees have signally failed to carry out the object for which the magnificent land grant was given by the United States, and which was further sought to be accomplished by most liberal appropriations on the part of the State."

A.J. Ackerly, Chairman
J.T. Shoener,
Jacob Provins,
Thomas St. Clair,
Allen Craig.

In connection with the report, Mr. Ackerly for the Committee offered a resolution in the House, if the Senate concur, instructing the State Treasurer to pay no more money to the College, until "it shall be satisfactory shown to this or succeeding Legislatures that said Pennsylvania State College, has fully complied with the requirements of the Act of Congress and of the Legislature nor until the Legislature shall be fully satisfied that the agricultural and mechanical interests of the State are receiving from such college actual benefits which are commensurate with the amount of money expended for its support and maintenance." The House passed the Resolution; it failed in the Senate. The result was that the battle was renewed in the session of 1881, when a bill to support Experiments at the Eastern and Western Farms, together with Green House and Propagating House at the College was pending. The bill was indefinitely postponed, the Ackerly Resolution was re-introduced.

A bill sponsored by Chester County was finally negatived upon Constitutional grounds by the House Committee on Ways and Means because it embodied two subjects, one taking the fund away from the College, the other its redistribution. Senator C.T. Alexander wrote General Beaver under date of March 16, 1881, "A bill in the House appropriating the funds of the College to other institutions is in the hands of a Committee. I am informed that a time will be fixed for hearing the complaints of the Chester malcontents. I will ascertain and inform you of the day. It occurs to me that we should meet them before the Committee. It may become a little unpleasant there, but we can stand it if they can. I will go with you and if it becomes necessary to use harsh language, assign that duty to me for I have lost all patience with these people." But as previously noted, no legislation was effected. The secondary result, however, was an investigation of the College on the part of the Trustees. This was to meet both the criticism engendered from without but also the situation from within which was becoming more and more acute during the academic year 1880-1881.

On January 27, 1881, the Board drew up a series of inquiries and authorized a thorough investigation by a Committee of five, consisting of J. P. Wickersham, Victor E. Piolett, S. W. Starkweather, J. M. Campbell and Cyrus Gordon. The preliminary resolutions cite the failure of the institution to measure up to the standards which its founders intended owing to financial and other embarrassments. Now it is proposed by "personal inspection, consultation with each member of the faculty ... and by every other means within their power to inquire into and ascertain the conditions and needs of the College." In their work the following questions were guidance points:

1. How can the efficiency of the College as a technical institution be increased?

2. How should existing courses of study be remodeled?

3. What additional courses of study should be adopted?

4. Should the classical course of study be abolished?

5. Should the Preparatory Department be abolished, if not, what changes, if any, should be made therein?

6. Has there been any insubordination on the part of any members of the faculty, or other office, to the President's authority?

7. What changes, if any, in its men and methods of work should be made?

The Committee delayed its task, partly owing to the fact that its chairman, Dr. J. P. Wickersham, ceased to be a member of the Board and did not, therefore, serve on the Committee. It was felt, too, that the passage of time might allay certain animosities and secure needed adjustments that would render an investigation more effective. That the faculty welcomed the investigation and realized that delay was adding to the critical nature of the situation is apparent. One of the prominent members of the faculty wrote General Beaver, March 5, 1881: "We have been taught by weeks of waiting, that the work which appears to us of vital import, is regarded by the Committee of the Board as of so trifling a nature as that anytime will do for its accomplishment... After 22 years of experimenting, we are today the laughing stock of the State... As an industrial College we *are* a failure... When the complaint is made that we do so little for agricultural, the reply is that we are no longer exclusively agricultural. Unfortunately we are not anything *in particular*. After 22 years of existence with a fine endowment, The Pennsylvania State College has no distinctly marked policy or line of work... There is an important work for the investigating committee to perform... the institution must be reorganized as to 'Men and Methods' or it must continue to be a failure. Unless the College shall show that it is able to use aright its endowment, the funds ought to go to some other college where they can be made to aid the industrial and agricultural interests of the State. We have at present 15 professors and instructors and but 29 students in College classes; with the existing spirit of adverse criticism throughout the State and the dissatisfaction with the President here, we can scarcely hope for much increase; on the contrary, it would not be surprising in August, if matters continue as at present if the Faculty should outnumber the College students."

A second appeal reached the President of the Board from a member of the Faculty, whose experience elsewhere and whose judgment in work done here warrants a belief in the absence of both "heat" and prejudice. Two indictments are brought, in urging action on the part of the Committee of the Board: "as to organization, first let me say that if the courses of study here are to be commended then nearly every other industrial school of decent character yet established has made great mistakes. We have a Classical course which I should be very sorry to see go from here if the more necessary courses can be provided for. We have an Agricultural course, very incomplete indeed and also poorly arranged. The Scientific course, which by the way is at present rightfully the most popular, is not technical and fits a man for no particular thing. Now, how does this compare with what we find elsewhere? In schools in other States which have no larger income than this, we see a full Agricultural course, courses in at least two Engineering departments, and such other departments as the means of the institution allow. No such thing as Engineering of any sort was ever taught here, so far as I can learn."

And to administrational "inefficiency" and "incapacity", he writes with both feeling and reserve, but advocates action; "either our ideas are right or they are wrong. If they are right we should have a chance to attempt to carry them out. If they are wrong, then men with correct ideas should step into our places. I am certain that until a different working basis is reached this college will not have sympathy, material support, or many students."

Meanwhile the Faculty, also, joined in the task of investigation. A Committee was appointed to revise the courses of study and while as an official body it was ineffective, in its later unofficial personnel and action, it was genuinely important. The chairman in both relations was Professor I. T. Osmond and the story may be best detailed in his own words.[11]

"When the historian comes to the College years 1880-1881 and 1881-1882 he will see that here in an epoch, closing one era and opening another. The College has been fundamentally reorganized.

"The year '80-'81, in the close of the former era, the College has:

1. Nothing whatever in Mechanic Arts and Engineering.

2. Its principal work a Classical Course and next a Scientific Course; Just the usual courses common in small colleges at the time.

3. An Agricultural Course differing from the scientific by only three hours (average) per week in studies and some practicum. Only by this small variation did the College differ from many others in the State.

"The year '81-'82, the opening of the new era, the College has been essentially changed in character. The work is presented in two General Courses, Scientific and Classical, and four Technical Courses, Agriculture, Natural History, Chemistry and Physics, Civil Engineering; also there are Mechanic Arts practicums and increased Agricultural practicums. The College has been distinctly differentiated from the other Colleges of the State, and correlated with the Land Grant Act of Congress of 1862.

"Of this reorganization, Dr. Atherton says in his report for 1892 to the Secretary of the U. S. Department of the Interior, 'In 1881, however, a very important arrangement and enlargement of the courses of study was made by the Faculty and approved by the Trustees, which may be said to mark a distinct epoch in the

---

[11] A letter to the writer, dated October 15, 1913.

educational organization of the College, and one from which may be dated a new era in its growth.'

"I have often thought I would write an account of this epoch, of which I have more intimate knowledge than any other persons, for I made it. I initiated, organized, directed the movement. As much as any one man ever makes a great change in or reforms any organization or institution, I made the reorganization of the Pennsylvania State College in 1881.

"Though a Pennsylvanian, I knew little other than the existence of the State College until I went to Cornell University for Graduate work in Chemistry and Physics, and became acquainted with G. C. Caldwell, Vice-President of State College under Dr. Pugh; and Prof. A. A. Breneman, an alumnus and at one time Assistant Professor in State College. With these, especially with Dr. Caldwell, I had many conversations about the College. Both felt a warm regard for it, but both criticized severely its organization. Thus I became interested in it. And I came to it with the very positive purpose of doing everything I could to effect a fundamental change in the College.

"I discussed the organization of the College with Dr. Calder, President of the College in 1879, but he held that, even if desirable, the making of so great changes was impracticable.

"At the opening of the College year 1880-1881, Joseph Shortlidge began his brief presidency. I soon found out it useless to expect any important change in the College through his initiative or agency. However, I moved the appointment of the committee of the Faculty to revise the courses of study; and, by usage, was designated Chairman. The President appointed, as the other members, Professor Jackson and Campbell. These two took the position that we were only to revise existing courses and it was not in our province to make fundamental changes. So, this committee did nothing—except such trifles as recommending an hour more or less of some subject. Evidently, these two stood with President Shortlidge against any fundamental change. I let this Committee drift along without ever making a final report, and went to work another way.

"I found Professor C. Alfred Smith of the class of 1861 (Professor of Chemistry) heartily in favor of such a reorganization of the College as I sought. At the Christmas vacation, 1880, he went to see Cyrus Gordon, alumni trustee. I prepared and sent with him a brief outline, partly diagrammatic, of a reorganization of the College and a corresponding Faculty. Professor Smith reported that Mr. Gordon was much interested in and approved it. This was encouraging. I had found that Professor Wm. A. Buckhout (Professor of Botany) considered such a change in the College desirable, and though not enthusiastic of success was willing to co-operate with Professor Smith and myself in effecting it. We proceeded to fill out the diagram of organization that I had sent by Professor Smith to Trustee Gordon.

"We soon came to the question whether to retain the Classical Course, though we all wished to keep it if found possible. The question, moreover, involved Professor J. Y. McKee, Vice-President and Professor of Greek, whom we greatly esteemed. I put the matter in which I was engaged and the whole situation plainly before him. He fully approved the general plan, and while he considered that it was very desirable to have a classical course included, he was ready to support the reorganization whether this course could be retained or not. His aid was very welcome and valuable.

"Thus I had, though irregular and without authorization, a good Committee, Smith, Buckhout, McKee. One more came in when Professor W. H. Jordan came to the College about mid-winter. I knew him in Cornell and knew he would be heartily in favor of our work. Our meetings were informal, without designated Chairman or Secretary, at my call. No secrecy was ever enjoined, or the matter ever mentioned, but I believe no others knew about our work.

"Early in April, 1881, there was a called meeting of the Trustees at the College, and President Shortlidge resigned. Mr. Gordon came to me and inquired in what degrees of completeness I then had the plan of reorganization of which I had sent him an outline about the first of the year. I gave him a copy, which he presented to the Trustees, and it was so approved that we were directed to have it in good shape at the regular Trustee meeting in June. At this meeting it was adopted and acting-President McKee, myself, and Prof. Jordan appointed a committee together with the Executive Committee to have charge of publishing and putting in operation this reorganization of the College."

The findings of these Trustees and Faculty surveys were brought together at a meeting of the Board on April 8, 1881. The Committee of the Board reported that it had entered upon its work at the College on April 5, and prosecuted its inquiries, not with as much time and thoroughness as desired but sufficient "to acquaint ourselves reasonably well with the present workings of the Institution and its needs." This "acquaintance" issued in a series of conclusions, confessional, academic, and disciplinary, which may be briefly summarized. The College has not done in the past and is not now doing the work intended by its founders, assigning to financial embarrassment, now largely removed, the principal cause of failure. Dissensions in the Faculty are acknowledged, and as further obstacles, the classics have recently been encouraged so as to encroach upon other lines. The Preparatory department needs reorganizing and it should be separated from the Collegiate department. Provision should be made for schools as "feeders" for the College, and additional inducements, lower fixed charges, facilities for self-boarding, and books stationery, etc., provided at the lowest rates. Horticulture, almost if not entirely abandoned, should be re-emphasized, and the sale of the Eastern and Western Farms is advocated. The courses of study from the self-constituted committee of the Faculty are recommended, two General Courses, Scientific and Classical, Four Technical Courses, Agriculture, Civil Engineering, Chemistry and Physics, and Natural History.

Administrative findings were embodied in a carefully wrought out outline of the duties of the President and an augmenting of the rights and responsibilities of the Faculty in which the famous resolution of 1880 seems tacitly limited. Concluding the Committee finds no evidence of insubordination to the President on the part of the Faculty or other officers and affirms that it is inexpedient at this time to make any changes in the executive or teaching body. However, it is recommended that either the powers of this Committee be enlarged or a new one appointed to consider that question and to report to the June meeting of the Board.

Events moved rapidly, although the Report was read for information and explicitly "not offered for adoption". A peremptory resignation was President Shortlidge's response which was accepted with salary to end of the term. At an adjourned meeting of the Board the same day, the Faculty was called in and the Report read. General Beaver explained the attitude of the Board and the new purpose and plans of the institution, inviting comment and cooperation. Hearty pledges were made and the Faculty retired.

As a climax and at this same meeting of the Board, the Executive Committee was authorized to memorialize the Legislature to investigate the affairs of the College, the last and most searching in this period of institutional adolescence. The Resolution addressed to the Senate and House of Representatives cites that "the allegation has been made in your honorable body that the present management of the institution fails to comply with the requirements of the Act of Congress of July 2, 1862, and the several acts of the Legislature in relation thereto; and recognizing the right and duty of the Legislature to see that the plighted faith of the Commonwealth ... is fully met by the recipient of the Land-Grant fund, respectfully and earnestly request that a Committee be appointed to investigate the affairs of the College." The Board affirms its desire for a thorough and exhaustive study of the institution and suggests that in view of the labor and time necessarily involved, the "Committee be allowed to sit after the adjournment of the present and report to the next session of the Legislature." The discussion brought forth the following premature and amateur bon mot from one of the Solons: "I think for one, that the Agricultural College, and all the various transactions connected with it, is a fit subject for investigation. The history which has brought into existence this agricultural college and the transactions connected therewith are perfectly familiar to any one who has ever given the subject any consideration whatever. I do not think that a greater swindle or greater fraud has ever been perpetrated on the people of Pennsylvania than the transactions which brought into existence this Agricultural College."

A Joint Resolution was approved by Governor Henry M. Hoyt on April 28, 1881, resolving "That a Committee of thirteen be appointed, consisting of five members of the Senate, and eight members of the House, to be appointed by the presiding officers of the respective bodies, to investigate the affairs of the Pennsylvania State College, as prayed for in the Memorial of the Board of Trustees above set forth."

The General Committee organized October 4, 1881, by electing Senator C. T. Alexander, Chairman, and Representative George W. Hall, Secretary. A sub-committee of four together with the chairman was named to take active control of the work and to make a report to the Committee as a whole. Senator Amos Mylin was appointed as Chairman, and the Secretary of the general committee as Secretary. The other members named were Senator John C. Newmyer and Representative William B. Robertson. The committee mapped out a field of inquiry, opened its hearings to all concerned, invited testimony by appealing through the newspapers of the State so that every interest, grievance, prejudice or opinion might find expression. The general plan of the Committee embraced the following points: the present management and its compliance with the organic laws; examination of accounts, appropriations, fees, gifts and their expenditure; and the experimental Farms, income and appropriations, usefulness, etc. The report was approved for submission to the Legislature under date of February 8, 1883. It covered 381 pages, and while it brings into the limelight the debris of hearsay, criticism, or personalities, animosities, jealousies and prejudices, the main current of the stream runs clear, the conclusions and recommendations wise and farseeing.

These may be abridged thus: The committee felt it due to the authorities of the College to say that not only have they placed before the Committee every document or other source of information within their control, but especially that the careful and business-like manner in which the accounts of the College have been kept greatly facilitated their inquiries. As to the educational aim and courses of instruction, the College "in simple accordance with the facts as we find them is furnishing a liberal and practical education for the industrial classes, and that its leading object is to teach such branches of learning as are related to agriculture and the mechanic arts." The practical nature of the work and facilities therefore in agriculture, in horticulture, in the shop, in mechanic arts, and in the field of civil engineering, the admirable condition of completeness and efficiency of the chemical laboratories, and the fine (though still inadequate) collection of apparatuses for the physical laboratory, are stressed. Needs are also referred to in order to render yet more effective the work of the Library and some of the other departments. The testimony as to the character and conduct of the students was so nearly unanimous, the exceptions arise from no conscious purpose to misrepresent the facts. The Committee concludes that the students are "as manly and honorable ... and as correct in their morals, as any similar body of young men in any institution in the State or the country."

The financial management comes in equally for commendation. Differences of judgment, there have been and are, respecting the general management and policy of the institution, but with fullest confidence in the perfect integrity with which all the funds have been expended and accounted for. Considering, the report continues, the well-known financial embarrassments of the institution in its earlier days, and the extent of the interests involved, it is a matter of just pride that no shadow of suspicion of dishonesty rests upon the administration of this great public trust. This is no more than was to have been expected from the known character of the many eminent citizens who have constituted the Board of Trustees; but it is none the less satisfactory and none the less due to them and the State to record the fact.

Upon the subject of Experimental Farms, the Committee found the maximum of perplexity and the storm center of recrimination. Here due recognition is given of the inherent difficulties of the situation; the lack of adequate funds to stock and maintain experimental farms distant from the College, where divided responsibility issued in divided control and "as might naturally have been expected in diminished efficiency and something of mutual criticism." The needs of laboratories and especially of a thoroughly equipped Agricultural Experiment Station are pointed out. The opinion is ventured that the Trustees, if they deem it advisable, be authorized to sell the two outlying farms, the income from the fund to be applied to the support of an experimental Station. Supplementing this fund, annually, by the Legislature and concentrating experiments and efforts on behalf of agricultural knowledge and practice would seem to be sound policy in the interests of economy, efficiency, and ease of control. Concluding this part of the report, it is pointed out that the College has already in use a large part of the appliances and equipment necessary for the successful maintenance of an Experiment Station, that it is now doing valuable work in that direction and publishing its results in a series of popular bulletins.

Under recommendations, a concise statement is made of the conditions (many of which it is true no longer exist) which have caused criticism, widespread distrust, if not hostility toward the College. The causes are analyzed as "extravagant expectations" that a "few months of schooling in an agricultural institution would convert boys who lacked the elements of a sound English education into skilled and scientific farmers." Equally impracticable, if not impossible, is the endeavor to combine compulsory labor with a course of advanced education; that, too, whether the purposes in view are to supplement the scholastic instruction, or to reduce to a minimum the cost of Collegiate training to the student. More immediate rewards in other industries than that of farming have had an influence here and elsewhere in determining pursuits in life, although the Committee finds that the proportion of students who go back to the farm now is as great as when the design of the institution was more exclusively agricultural. Disadvantages in the location of the institution have been pressed upon the Board but these are deemed temporary and relatively unimportant. Considerable emphasis is placed upon the various causes which led to so meagre a realization from the Land-Grant. "Her land-scrip amounted to seven hundred and eighty thousand acres, and it was undoubtedly the expectation of Congress that the lands would bring to the State at least the minimum market rate of a dollar and twenty-five cents per acre. Had this been the case the endowment of the State from that source alone would have been nearly a million dollars ... We do not pass an opinion on others, but we believe it to be the duty of this Commonwealth, having accepted the deed of gift from the United States 'with all its conditions and provisions' and having 'pledged its faith to carry the same into effect,' to restore the land-grant fund to the amount originally intended by Congress."

The Committee further calls the attention of the Legislature, to the need of buildings and equipment, to the advisability of reorganization of its Board of Trustees so as to secure cooperation of the industrial as well as the agricultural classes; and again proposes the sale of the two experimental farms and the establishment of an Experimental Station. With an enthusiasm, which is invariably bred in the mind of one who studies the chart and compass of these peoples' colleges, the Committee concludes: "The need of education for the industrial classes was never so great as now. The vast mining, manufacturing, and agricultural resources and activities of the State demand for their most rapid and economical development all the aid that can be derived from the most advanced teachings of science, and it seems not too much to expect that a State famous for the extent and wisdom of her charitable and reformatory agencies should make full and even generous provision for the higher education of her strong and aspiring youth. In conclusion, the result of a most careful and painstaking examination has fully convinced us that the State College is in good faith fulfilling the trusts committed to it by the State, and that much of the misconception respecting it arises from a lack of easily obtainable information. We believe it has passed its worst days. Its courses of study, in the opinion of experts, are well organized; its facilities good, and in some particulars unusually complete; its faculty is composed of competent, and many of them highly experienced professors; and whatever mistakes it may have made in the past, the entire spirit and work of the institution, as now organized and administered, are directed to the promotion of industrial education... Although in its organization a private corporation, it is in every proper sense the child of the State, and we are strongly impressed with the conviction that the time has come when the State should give it much fostering care as will make it not only an object of just pride, but a source of immeasurable benefit to our sons and daughters."

When this report to the Legislature was authorized at the final meeting of the Committee, February 8, 1883, the leader had already been found who was translating its policies and prophecies into reality and fact. Strangely and significantly it embodies the spirit and even the language of President George W. Atherton as the College moving out from Old Main, finds itself and develops in the third great period of its history.

Part IV

The College Grows

1882—1932

CHAPTER 10

"Moulded by an Idea," The Man and His Task

"The marvelous increase of knowledge and of available utilities which have resulted from the brilliant advances of scientific research, within the present century, have changed not only the physical conditions of human life, but the attitude and direction of human thought. It is patent to every observer, that the principles and methods of scientific investigation today control the intellectual activities of the civilized world, and hence it is not surprising that the men who have imbibed this new spirit should demand that the prevailing systems of education be modified so far as may be necessary to bring them into conformity with the aims and tendencies of the time.

"But while the College will keep this practical aim constantly in view, it will also endeavor to secure that harmonious and symmetrical development of all the faculties which distinguish the thoroughly educated from the half-educated. Not simply the artisan but the scholar; not simply the scholar but the man."

President George W. Atherton
Inaugural Address, June 28, 1883

It has been pointed out frequently that the genius of democracy consists in the fact that with opportunity the man arises. Nowhere is this more clearly exemplified than in the history of our so-called Land Grant Colleges. Senator Morrill, the son of a Vermont blacksmith, read in the sparks that flew from his father's anvil, the principles of industrial training. When the opportunity came to embody those principles in legislation, Mr. Morrill was the man. Abraham Lincoln said in his young manhood, that he believed with his whole heart in education and that he hoped for the opportunity to aid it signally in the future. "For my part, I desire to see the time when education, and by its means morality, sobriety, enterprise and industry shall become more general than at present, and shall be gratified to have it in my power to contribute something to the advancement of any measure which might have a tendency to accelerate that happy period." The opportunity to contribute to this happy end came to Lincoln in 1862, amid the throes of the Civil War, when reason, prudence and economy alike seemed to militate against any measure but the tremendous task in hand, the prosecution of the war. But Lincoln's vision was true and clear. He saw a country re-united; the fratricidal strife past; and industrial regeneration the most pressing necessity. To his prophetic eye, the South was already impoverished, the North severely reduced, the West a virgin territory of unlimited resources. Here was a call to build for the future, an educational foundation, an industrial, constructional unit for every State, an institution of the people, for the people, by the people.

To Dr. George W. Atherton, likewise, came the opportunity to ally himself with these Land Grant Institutions. With prophetic eye, he, too, saw the possibilities and potentialities of these peoples' Colleges, and with opportunity, Dr. Atherton marshaled his forces. In 1868, as a member of the first faculty of Illinois Industrial University, and in close association with its first president, Dr. John M. Gregory, he bore a part in organizing the institution which has become the University of Illinois. After one year, he accepted a call to the newly established chair of Political Science at Rutgers. For fourteen years, he was in almost ideal training, academic, political, legal, public serve to both State and Nation, for the real work of his life. In 1873 he delivered an address before the National Educational Association on "The

Relation of the General Government to Education." He defended these institutions on the broad basis of national policy, as a necessary condition of a full and free suffrage, and essential to industrial development. Fortified with facts, he entered the lists against the vested interests of those worthy antagonists who would limit public education to the elementary schools, who challenged the results wrought by these institutions, and who found in the so-called Agricultural Colleges only a medley of unfulfilled claims and unclear aims. The young instructor came out of the discussion a victor over dogmatic classicism, and over the monopolistic pretensions of an aristocracy of learning. From that time to his death in 1906, Dr. Atherton, more perhaps than any other man, was the champion of these institutions, an active and influential force in subsequent legislation which issued in wider cooperation between Nation and State in their behalf.

Born at Boxford, Massachusetts, June 20, 1837, he was in early years thrown upon his own resources. He learned the primary lessons of life in the cotton mill and on the farm. From the age of twelve, he aided in the support of his widowed mother. By his own efforts, be paid his way at Phillips Exeter, graduating with the class of 1858. There he is remembered as "gentle, manly, and wise beyond his years, bringing to his duties as monitor the kindly uncompromising justice that compelled respect and left no sting behind." He entered Yale College in the Sophomore class in 1860. At the outbreak of the Civil War, he volunteered his services. He was commissioned as Lieutenant in the Tenth Connecticut Division, and was promoted to a captaincy on account of conspicuous bravery and efficiency in Burnside's North Carolina Expedition. His health failing, he returned to Yale, and was graduated with the class of 1863. He was married on Christmas Day of that year, to Frances D.W. Washburn, who with rare devotion labored for her husband's success. Hundreds of teachers and students will generously join in a tribute of esteem and honor to her personal traits and social friendliness which radiated from the President's home for nearly a quarter of a century at The Pennsylvania State College.

His apprenticeship in teaching began in the Albany Boys' Academy in New York. After four years, he was elected to a Professorship at St. John's

College at Annapolis, Maryland, serving during a major part of the year as Acting-Principal. But his real preparation for his life task began with his participation in the initial program of the University of Illinois,[12] followed by fruitful years as Professor at Rutgers. Here his energies and interests reached far beyond his academic chair. He found opportunity, while Chairman of a Commission to digest and revise the tax system of New Jersey, to study law (so closely akin to his social and economic studies), was admitted to the Bar. He was prevailed upon to accept a nomination for Congress in 1876. In a district "hopelessly Democratic," he put such vigor into the campaign as to run appreciably ahead of the national ticket. Dr. Armsby has written that his acquaintance with Dr. Atherton dated from that time when he was a young assistant at Rutgers. He recalls seeing him frequently after a night trip to a political meeting, hastening across the campus to morning chapel with a vigor which the younger men could more easily admire than imitate.

He served, also, on commissions for the Federal Government. In 1873 and again in 1891, he was a member of the Board of Visitors to the United States Naval Academy. In 1875, by special appointment of President Grant, he was on a commission to investigate the charges against the Red Cloud Indian Agency.

It was a matter of tradition that Vice President McKee was the Warwick

---

[12] Allan Nevins writes of Professor Atherton as a member of the first faculty of the University of Illinois in History and Latin. He was also the first teacher of military tactics. He had the entire enrollment for awkward squad. There was no uniform, and the motley headgear in particular tried the heart of the drillmaster, though he refrained from complaining, for he knew how poor were most of the boys. One unhappy wight presented himself at drill one morning in a high silk hat, which was bowled to the ground at the feet of the professor when his neighbor presented arms. Atherton with difficulty concealed his wrath, and thereafter the boys were ordered to wear "some kind of cap." It will be recalled, with what patriotic pride and love for discipline, did Dr. Atherton step into the breach as commandant in 1898 during the Spanish American War, with Major J.W. Andrews of the Board of Trustees in student command.

who turned the attention of the Board to the eminent qualities and fitness of Dr. Atherton in the dire situation confronting the College. Professor C. Alfred Smith, who resigned as Professor of Chemistry in January 1882, and was elected an Alumni representative on the Board in June of that year, presented the name to the Board. He relates that Professor McKee had labored the previous evening and far into the night to persuade Dr. Atherton to allow his name to come before the Board. "I joined Professor Atherton at the morning chapel service and taking him into my study, spent the entire morning, and at the noon hour he yielded." The formal minute under date of June 28, 1882 reads as follows: "On motion, Professor G. W. Atherton, of New Brunswick, New Jersey, was unanimously elected President of the Faculty, at a salary of $3,000 per annum and the use of the President's house and grounds, and $250 were appropriated for expenses of removal."

With the proviso of time to do certain work at Rutgers, to which he felt obligated by his long connection with the institution, he accepted the position in a letter to General Beaver under date of July 31: "prepared to accept the Presidency of the State College and enter upon my duties at once." Four days later, he replied to the expressions of good will and confidence of the President of the Board: "Indeed, my reception on all sides is as cordial and kindly as I could desire, and, I fully appreciate it. Yet, I understand full well that my path is not to be strewn with roses. There will be alert and vigorous criticism and hostility at every step, for a good while at least; but if devotion and hard work, and singleness of purpose can accomplish anything, We will win." With characteristic energy and despatch, he convened the Executive Committee, a fund for advertising was set apart, short courses in Agriculture and in Chemistry outlined. A special circular was, also, issued, setting forth the location, advantages, and prospects of the College, conditions of admission, expenses, scholarships, the preparatory department, not omitting the inevitable "means of access."

Dr. Atherton had a striking physical presence, instinct with energy and commanding attention in any group of men. In England, he was on occasion mistaken for Lord Salisbury. When he faced an audience whether the general public, a group of teachers, or legislative committees, or assembly, State or

Nation, he was easily master. He spoke forcefully because he allied himself to a cause with enthusiasm. He spoke authoritatively because he thought clearly. Methodical and dignified were all his occasions; programs were pre-arranged, they did not happen. Faculty and committee meetings transacted business with despatch. Order and plan, he instilled in the student body—physical habits of posture and bearing, no less than mental alertness and elasticity. Those impressive beginnings of a new term or college year were distinct events and have left an influence upon a generation of students. His ever new interpretative reading of the Ninetieth and Ninety-first Psalms burned their way into the consciousness of his auditors, as the best of literature, the choicest art, and truest inspiration of life. Not by tricks of oratory, not by confusing essentials with electives, not in sentiment void of thought, not by confusing discipline and interest; but by simple, forceful sincerity and earnest straightforwardness, he moulded men and women of Penn State.

An outstanding personal trait, too, was his pride in The Pennsylvania State College. "Moulded by an Idea" wrote Dr. Benjamin Gill in retrospect and memorial. No honor or responsibility could be more challenging than that before administrator and teacher at The Pennsylvania State College. Not the institution as it was (there was enough cause of discouragement in 1882 to test the strongest heart) but the institution that was to be; guided by the needs and intelligence of the people, developed by their bounty, and nurtured by their pride. Many an instructor in those days of wide-spread indifference, and opposition even, to the College was held by faith in his faith, by loyalty to his loyalty in the face of allurements elsewhere. This same spirit engendered in the student body was known as the "State Standard," a genuine but elusive force, a ready reserve, an anchor that held. Even though a smile might hover in its repeated appeals, its effectiveness was undeniable. On repeated occasions did General Beaver, also, make it the rallying point in his enthusiastic talks to the student body—urging loyalty to a greater Penn State, to higher standards of scholarship, more glorious athletic victories, and, better than all else, to true character and manhood.

Dr. Atherton was a leader in the supplementary federal legislation in the interests of the State Colleges and Universities. The Experimental Station Act of 1887, and the Second Morrill Endowment of 1890 were furthered by his marked skill in presenting worthy issues and enlisting support.[13] Later legislation, the Adams and Nelson Grants, also, had the shaping influence of his policies. Throughout his life, he was considered by his co-workers in these industrial institutions as their representative in Washington in all that pertained to their interests. He was the first President of the Association of Agricultural Colleges and Experiment Stations; served a second year, and was an active leader and participant in its policies and deliberations. His address in 1900 at New Haven, at the special request of the Association, upon the Legislative Career of Justin S. Morrill added new evidence of Mr. Morrill's original conception and sponsorship of this class of institutions.

In 1887 by appointment of Governor James A. Beaver, Dr. Atherton was a member of a "Commission to make inquiry and report to the Legislature of Pennsylvania respecting the subject of Industrial Education." He was elected as chairman, and was authorized to visit institutions both in this country and in Europe in the interests of the Commission's task. The Report to the Legislature, two years later, was issued by the State in a volume of nearly six hundred pages, largely the work of his hands. The survey of actual conditions, the principles and possibilities of industrial education, the recommendations for the Schools of the Commonwealth are all so thoroughly set forth, that the Report was on all sides pronounced the most important issued to that time.

The College and University Council of the Commonwealth was established in 1895, and Dr. Atherton was a member continuously until his

---

[13] As early as 1883 and 1885 in the Conventions of "representatives of the different Agricultural Colleges and Allied State Institutions," Dr. Atherton bore a leading part. As chairman of the Committee on Legislation; of the National Advisory Committee; as of its Executive Committee, there is additional evidence of his personal, political, and educational leadership which was crucial to the passage of the Hatch Act after efforts futile and varied (the Carpenter, Holmes, Cullen, and George Bills of 1882 and following years) had failed. It was his call, too, and that of his committee which led to a permanent organization of the Association of American Agricultural Colleges and Experiment Stations, October 16-20, 1887.

death. He was one of the group of three College Presidents who founded the Honorary Society of Phi Kappa Phi, widely influential in the advancement and recognition of scholarship in colleges and universities. Academic honors and titles were not sought by him, and he was not a voluminous writer. His published papers and addresses total, however, some thirty in number. As a labor of love, he issued privately in 1900, a translation with notes of the Magna Carta.

The inauguration of President Atherton was made a part of the Commencement Week of 1883. The Baccalaureate Address was delivered by Dr. William H. Campbell, Ex-President of Rutgers College, at three P.M. on Sunday, June 24. It was held in the chapel on the second floor of "Old" Main, in a room boasting accommodations for "about four hundred," but on this occasion "Holding seven to eight hundred people." Monday and Tuesday were given over to anniversaries of the Young Men's Christian Association, the Washington Literary Society Reunion, the Alumni Association with the annual Address by George B. Loring, United States Commissioner of Education. Wednesday was ushered in by an artillery salute at nine A.M. and the day given over to Meeting of Delegates to elect Trustees; the Cresson Literary Society Anniversary, and to the Alumni Dinner at twelve noon. At this time, the luncheon was held in Bellefonte. In the evening, the Junior Oratorical Contest was held.

Thursday was the "big day." At nine-thirty the program began which lasted at least three hours. The College Choir and Class Quartette furnished music. Addresses by the President of the Board, Francis Jordan and by Governor Robert E. Pattison were first upon the program[14]—with the invocation by the Rev. Robert Hamill, D. D. With "rapt attention, glad hopes and buoyant spirits" the audience listened to the inaugural address of President Atherton. After a five minute intermission the Graduating Exercises, proper were followed by the conferring of degrees and awarding of

---

[14] A note is appended to the effect that "Governor Pattison has promised to be present if his public duties will permit." He was not present on this occasion, the regret the keener as events will subsequently prove.

prizes. Five orations were "pronounced," the Salutatory, "On the Threshold," the Valedictory on "Contemplation," and three orations on "A Modern Philanthropist," Per Gradus ad Metam," and "National Pride." The Class Quartette rendered two selections, "Sunrise" and "Come Where the Lilies Bloom." Commencement day, and none has been more memorable or fraught with greater possibilities, ended with the President's Reception at eight, P.M.

The Inaugural Address was on the "Place of Industrial Training in the System of Higher Education." It was a sane, clear cut and logical discussion of education old and new; advocating training in science and technology as an absolute necessity of industrial progress, of democratic achievement, civic and national. A few quotations will serve admirably as an introduction to the policies and principles under which Dr. Atherton moulded The Pennsylvania State College:

"Let us endeavor briefly to estimate the claims of the old and the new in education, respectively. The starting point of the former is that education in the specific sense of the word is primarily a training of the man for himself rather than a specific preparation for his actual employments.

"It assumes that the powers and faculties of the mind are essentially of the same quality, in all around men, and that they can be trained by a similar process. If this be granted, the question remains, What subjects of study are best adapted to furnish material for that training? and the answer upon which, until recently, the whole system of College education in this country and in Europe has been based, is, "The Ancient Languages, Mathematics, and Philosophy."— The Ancient Languages of Greece and Rome not only embody the thought which more than any other human force has shaped the civilization of the world, but they are the most perfect instruments of expression and models of form that have yet been fashioned by the intelligence of man. In the great fields of poetry, history and philosophy, the ancient writers are still the models and teachers of the world. The youth who becomes familiar with these languages and their literature finds his habit of thought and expression insensibly

219

yet surely transformed. He is wrought upon by a subtle inner force, as by the unconscious influences which come from the presence of beauty in art or from communion with noble thoughts.

"But after all that may be said and admitted in behalf of the old system, the conclusive fact remains, that it was and is designed to train youth only in certain special directions, and that it no longer meets the demands of our actual condition....Modern Industries are coming more and more to avail themselves of the resources of Science, or, to state the same fact in another form, they are being conducted in accordance with the facts and processes which are ascertained by scientific investigation. So necessary has this become, amid the sharp competitions of modern business activities that any branch of industry which fails to use these resources, stands no chance of prosperous existence—it must speedily fall behind or fall out. This wide-reaching truth applies not alone to individual branches of enterprise, but with equal force to nations, and presents some of the most serious problems of statesmanship. A recognition of this has led every government claiming a place in the progressive ranks of civilization to make liberal provision, for the promotion of scientific research, and the maintenance of scientific and industrial education, as the one sure means of material well being...It is sometimes insisted by theorists that this is no part of the province of government, but the stern logic of experience is more convincing than the most skilled argument. For nations, as for individuals, self-preservation is the first law of life. To live they must adapt themselves to their conditions. Those conditions change from age to age, and the education of youth must change with them...The complaint has often been expressed that the institutions founded or aided by this grant have failed to accomplish all that they were expected and designed to accomplish, but, after every allowance is made that truth requires, the fact still remains that this one act has done more, in my deliberate opinion, to promote the interests of liberal scientific education than any other single act of this or any government...These institutions have provided thousands of youth with the means of obtaining a liberal education, fitting them for the useful and honorable careers in life. They have immensely aided the development of the material resources of the country, and they are as yet, only, in the beginning of their beneficent work. Their indirect influence has been, if possible, even greater. They have pioneered in the field of scientific life and industrial education. They have met a want which had steadily increased, and urgent demand; but which the established system of classical instruction did not, could not, and would not satisfy. The result has been nothing less than a revolution in the American system of higher education within the last twenty years. There is not a College in the United States, of any rank, which has not during that period advanced its requirements, introduced new branches of study, improved its methods and its appliances for teaching the old, or as is true in many cases, established new departments, or courses or schools of science... To repeat in short, what I have already said, the new institutions met an active and urgent demand for practical education, education for the work of life, to such an extent as to change the direction, or the methods, or both, of the whole educational thought and force of the country....Note now the words of the law which I have already quoted, and mark how every line is instinct with this spirit. The College shall make its leading object to teach 'branches of learning,' not trades nor arts; but branches of learning, and those not relating to philosophy or art or medicine or law or theology, but relating to Agriculture and the Mechanic Arts. To what end? Not to help especially those who are amply able to help themselves but to promote the 'liberal' education of the industrial classes. Liberal education was a well-defined term. It meant the best that the schools could furnish. But this education was not only to be liberal, it was to be *practical*, that is, was to look to and prepare for intelligent, progressive, successful work. And it was to be as wide as the field of human industry itself. It was to prepare the industrial classes not for one branch of activity—but 'for the several pursuits and professions of life'...Under this broad and magnificent charter, the Pennsylvania State College is now organized. Like nearly every institution of its kind it has passed through a period of trial and experiment, and has only within a comparatively recent time settled down upon an assured basis of organized work. It is now fairly in line with the best experiences and thought of the educational world. We do not at all claim that it is perfect in its methods, and it is far from being complete in equipment....But while the College will keep this practical aim constantly in view, it will also endeavor to secure that harmonious and symmetrical development of all the faculties which distinguishes the thoroughly education from the half-educated. Not simply the artisan, but the scholar; not simply the scholar, but the *man*.

"And now, Gentleman of the Board of Trustees, fellow-members of the faculty, alumni, students, friends; I here pledge anew my efforts to promote in this institution the kind of education which I have so imperfectly touched upon. I invoke your earnest cooperation, and your considerate judgment toward mistakes and shortcomings; and above all, I invoke the favor, the guidance and the blessings of Almighty God."

Policies thus generally enunciated, were made specific in the first annual report to the Board:

1. To make the institution scientific and industrial rather than literary and classical, and especially to teach such branches as are related to agriculture and the mechanic arts, not excluding other scientific and classical studies (and hence including them, Dr. Atherton invariably interjected), and including military tactics,

2. To sell the two outlying model farms and use the income from the principal, plus additional State support for the establishment and maintenance of an Agricultural Experiment Station in the College.

3. To set and maintain high standards of scholarship, even at the risk for a time of reduced numbers,

4. To limit the Preparatory Department to subjects essential to College entrance,

5. To secure the floating debt by a general loan with provision for gradual liquidation.

These policies met a strange and decided opposition from the newly elected and youthful Governor of the Commonwealth, prompted possibly by the exigencies of the political campaign, and as an aftermath of the Report of the Legislature Committee which was made in the session of 1883. The facts must be recalled somewhat in detail, nor merely as a matter of record, but because the subsequent signal friendliness and support which Governor Robert E. Pattison gave to the College reveals his own broadmindedness and his sense of inherent justice when duly aroused. Also the episode peculiarly emphasizes the consummate ability of President Atherton to transmute active opposition into wholehearted support.

The Board at the meeting of January 25, 1884, gave prolonged consideration to the needs of the various departments for apparatus and equipment, trying "to make one dollar do the work of ten." The committee on the Reports of the President and Heads of Departments found legitimate requests aggregating fifteen thousand two hundred and seventy-seven dollars, with not over three thousand dollars available. To meet the imperative needs for salaries and equipment, the committee recommended a modest increase of the floating debt and interest charges. At this juncture, Governor Pattison, not only urged economy, but moved that the number of professors be reduced by one-half. As a skillful counter-move, he was prevailed upon to accept as a substitute motion the appointment of a committee, consisting of the President of the College, the Governor, and one additional member. Dr. E. E. Higbee, Superintendent of Public Instruction was the third member of the Committee. This committee was "to examine the list of Professors and Professorships, and report to an adjourned meeting of the Board, not later than March 25, what changes if any, should be made?"

A majority report signed by Governor Pattison and Superintendent Higbee, and a minority report by President Atherton were received by the

Board. They were discussed at a special meeting held in Bellefonte, March 25, 1884. The minority report dealt so convincingly with the situation as a whole; it brought so true a picture of President Atherton as thinker, administrator, and diplomatist that it as well as the majority report are incorporated here, as documents of perennial interest.

Majority Report

In making the following report, the undersigned have no disposition to reflect upon the past management of the "State College," or to criticize the ability and fidelity of its present body of teachers. We have only taken into consideration, its present financial condition, and its relations to the large agricultural interests of the Commonwealth.

The College has an annual income of 30,000 dollars—three farms, a body of students numbering from 130 to 150, a large building, requiring a considerable amount to put it into repair and proper working order, a faculty consisting of sixteen teachers, and a current debt reported as amounting to some 55,000 dollars.

The farms are widely separated; one in the eastern, another in the western, and another in the central part of the State. The western farm is in no sense a model farm, and is in no condition to throw upon the market. In its present state it is an injury rather than a benefit to the College. It is an advertisement against scientific farming, and not an illustration of its benefits. The eastern farm is in better condition, but is far from being what a model farm should be. The central farm in immediate connection with the College, is all that the friends of agricultural science ought to require.

To hasten the liquidation of the debt, to put the building in proper working order, to supervise the farms, so far removed from the College itself, that as model farms, they may properly exhibit to the people the rich results of modern science applied to agriculture, and to bring the whole work of the College into closer sympathy with the farming and industrial community of the State, we respectfully submit to the Board the following plan, which, in our judgment; will best subserve the ends above mentioned, without detracting from the present professional thoroughness of the institution.

Faculty

I.	President, duties as at present	$3,000
II.	Lecturer on Agriculture and Supt. of the farms	$2,500
III.	Professor of Agricultural Chemistry and Supt. of Experimental Station	$1,500
IV.	Professor of Chemistry	$1,500
V.	Professor of Botany and Horticulture	$1,200
VI.	Professor of Mathematics and Civil Engineering	$1,200
VII.	Professor of Modern Languages (French, German and English)	$1,200
VIII.	Professor of Geology, Zoology and head of the Preparatory Department	$1,200
IX.	Professor of Veterinary Science and Physiology, and assistant in the Preparatory Department	$1,200
X.	Professor of Military Science and Tactics	$500
XI.	Assistant	$500
XII.	Assistant Total cost of teaching Force	$15,500

This plan removes from the work of the College, the Latin and Greek Languages, except so far as the former may be introduced in the study of the French. It adds, as we think, to the efficiency of Agricultural studies by supplying a lecturer on scientific farming, who shall at the same time act as responsible Superintendent of the farms, and also makes room for the important matter of Veterinary Science. These additions we have thought well calculated to answer the wishes of all intelligent farmers, and secure their hearty cooperation.

Moreover it leaves a balance of 14,500 dollars. This balance, we report, should be devoted to the following uses:

Six thousand dollars to be applied to the farms distant from the

Institution, and the remainder to such incidental expenses as may be seen to be necessary to maintain the efficient working of the college.

Respectfully submitted, (Signed)

Robert E. Pattison

E.E. Higbee

Minority Report

The undersigned, regretting to find himself unable to agree with the conclusions and recommendations of his colleagues on the Committee, respectfully presents his views as follows:

The resolution of the Board under which the Committee was appointed, was based upon a proposition to reduce the number of Professors in the College by one half, for which a substitute was offered and adopted that a Committee be appointed "to examine the list of Professors and Professorships and report what changes, if any, should be made." No suggestion was brought forward in connection with either the original action, or that finally adopted, that seemed to contemplate a change in the organization of the work of the College; but the expressed object was merely to make such a reduction of the teaching force as would bring expenditures within the annual income; and it is fair to suppose that the Board contemplated nothing more than was expressed.

The report of the majority of the Committee seems to assume something beyond that, and plainly proceeds upon the idea, without giving it formal expression of so recasting the organization of the College as to make it exclusively Agricultural, and devote, at least one-third of the income of the College, to the maintenance of an experimental and two model farms with a general Superintendent and Lecturer in charge. These propositions involve so sweeping changes in the present status of the Institution, that they should not be adopted without the plainest necessity, or at least, upon well considered grounds and with the most convincing assurance of advantage to the entire industrial population of the State.

The first question before the Board now, and at all times, is, what can be done with the means at command? And the answer to this question is subject to these three limitations:

1. What does the law require it to do?

2. What does public opinion require?

3. What does a sound scheme of education require?

The provisions of law which implicitly control the action of the Trustees have been so often quoted it seems superfluous to refer to them, but it will be a guide to the deliberations of the Board to notice their salient points, which may be summarized as follows:

1. The Institution must be a "College" not a high school, or Academy, or anything else than an institution of the grade indicated by that name which had at the time of the passage of the law, and still has a perfectly understood and distinctive meaning, as an institution for advanced and liberal education.

2. The Institution is to be for the benefit of the industrial classes—including in that term all workers in gainful occupations, and is to be so broad in its courses of instruction as to prepare these classes for the "several pursuits and professions in life."

3. The Institution is to be so organized and maintained as to promote a "liberal" as well as "practical" education. The old Colleges had furnished a liberal education, but not, properly speaking, a practical one. The new Colleges, under the Act of 1862, were to do both.

4. In order to accomplish these ends, the institution is to make it the *leading* object, to teach "such branches of learning as are related to Agriculture and the Mechanic Arts," but "without excluding other scientific and classical studies and including military tactics." In other words these Colleges were designed as agents of the national bounty, in bringing a liberal collegiate education within reach of the industrial classes. And thereas the old Colleges had shaped their courses of study so as to prepare youth for what were known as the learned professions, the new Colleges were to prepare them for *industrial* pursuits and branches of learning which underlie Agriculture and the Mechanic Arts. These two great classes of occupations in Pennsylvania

include fifty-six per cent of the working population, and in the whole United States, sixty-six per cent.

Such being the requirements of the law, how are they to be fairly and sincerely met, with the means at the disposal of the State College? If nothing more can be done, it is evident that the main trunk of its educational course must be strong in the Mathematical, Physical and Natural Sciences, and that the law commands as full provisions to be made for the branches of learning relating to the Mechanic Arts, as those relating to Agriculture. No other course can be regarded as a compliance with the plain mandate of the statute. The report of the majority of the Committee seems to ignore this requirement altogether. Out of eight professorships which it provided for (not including the President or the Professor of Military Science) only the single chair of Mathematics and Civil Engineering and the chair of Chemistry are in any way related to the Mechanic Arts—all the rest relating directly to Agriculture— and these two, especially Chemistry, belong quite as much to Agriculture as to Mechanic Arts.

But the scheme presented is even less satisfactory as a *working plan*, under our present conditions.

1. It makes no provision for specific instruction in the Mechanic Arts and Drawing. The Board is already under engagement to employ Mr. Reber at the opening of the next College year, in this special work and has given him temporary leave of absence for the express purpose of enabling him better to prepare himself for it. This is a contract which the Board is not at liberty to disregard, even if it were desirable to do so. Moreover, the College has just received from a Massachusetts gentleman, a gift of $400 to $500 worth of equipment; and it is a pertinent and striking fact that thirty-six per cent of the working population in Pennsylvania is engaged in Manufacturing, Mechanics and Mining occupations, and only twenty per cent in Agriculture, so that the requirements of the law and the obligations of the Board are more than sustained by the actual distribution of our industrial population.

2. It proposes to abandon Civil Engineering as a distinct department, giving it only such incidental attention as may be included in connection with

the chair of Mathematics. In a state like Pennsylvania this would seem to me a serious mistake. It is now one of the most attractive courses in the College and it does not interfere with any other, since its special studies begin in the Junior year, when young men have gone through the foundation preparation for such particular course as they may select. The chair is held by a gentleman who is thoroughly familiar with the best methods of the profession, and who has, during the past year, done work in connection with the U. S. Coast Survey, which the Superintendent states to be extremely satisfactory. The abandonment of that department would be unfortunate at any time, but especially now that it is so favorably established and so economically maintained.

3. Another important omission in the plan proposed, is that of Principal of the Preparatory Department, except as the duties of that office are assigned to a Professor in the College Faculty. The uniform experience of institutions in general, and of the State College in particular is, that that office is scarcely, if at all, less important to the proper accomplishment of *preparatory* work than the presidency in a College. Situated as we are, with the great body of the students under one roof, consisting of College and Preparatory students, and of both sexes—more than the usual care needs to be given to matters of detail in discipline and conduct. Moreover, in the case of young students, it is absolutely necessary that great attention be given and time spent in training them to the habit and act of study. It would be a great advantage to separate the department wholly from the College, in a building of its own; but while it remains, its successful working absolutely requires a separate and responsible head.

4. An almost equally important omission in the proposed plan is that of Lady Principal. What has just been said as to the Principal of the Preparatory Department applies in this case with the additional and obvious consideration that no such department of the College can be maintained, without a competent Lady in charge of the conduct and deportment of the young ladies in their section of the building. The College is extremely fortunate, at present in having a lady in charge who is not only a highly accomplished scholar and teacher, but a rare example to young ladies of what a sound womanly life and

character should be. The work could not be carried on without a responsible head, and it would be difficult, not to say impossible to fill more satisfactorily than at present.

5. Another important omission in the proposed plan is that of the chair of Physics. This department may well be called vital in any well-equipped modern institution, especially if it aims to secure any recognition whatever for scientific or technical thoroughness. It is an essential to Agriculture as to the Mechanic Arts, and has the widest possible relations to every department of industrial activity. In the State College, it is next to Chemistry, the best equipped with apparatus, and is one of the most important and effective branches of our work. No friend of the College or of thorough scientific education would willingly see it abandoned, or made of secondary importance by attaching it to some other chair.

As a substitute for the distribution of work thus presented I respectfully, and with great deference to the judgment of the majority of the Committee, offer the following:

I.	President—duties as now	$3000
II.	Vice President—Professor of English Literature and Mental and Moral Science	$1500
III.	Professor of Botany, Geology and Zoology and Superintendent of Horticultural Department	$1300
IV.	Professor of Modern Languages	$1000
V.	Professor of Physics	$1500
VI.	Professor of Mathematics	$1200
VII.	Professor of Agricultural Chemistry and Superintendent of Experimental Farms	$1500
VIII.	Professor of Civil Engineering	$1350
IX.	Professor of Chemistry	$1350
X.	Professor of Drawing and Instructor in Mechanic Arts	$520
XI.	Principal of Preparatory Department	$1100

| XII. | Lady Principal | $700 |
| XIII. | Assistant | $500 |

This scheme retains nearly the full completeness of our present organization, supplies the five important omissions above noted, and furnishes a strong and efficient course which does full justice to all the interests which the College was established to promote. The great body of the instruction thus provided relates directly to Agriculture and the Mechanic Arts; only so much provision being made for other studies as is necessary to make instruction in those subjects useful and available and to give a sound preparation for the general duties of life and citizenship; and Greek is abandoned entirely. At the same time, the allowance for payment of Professors and teachers is only $1,,220 more than in the plan proposed by the majority of the Committee.

It is proper to observe, also, that this course of instruction fully and satisfactorily meets the demands of public opinion, as that opinion manifests itself among our patrons and elsewhere. Although we provide a two years course in Agriculture which is made up almost exclusively of technical subjects, and a more advanced course, based upon the first two years for a preparation, there is a very slight demand for either. The truth is, that branches of learning relating to Agriculture are so interwoven in all our work, that no student fails to receive an extensive amount of instruction in them, at the same time he acquires a mental discipline and a learning that prepares him to follow with success any calling for which his native talents may fit him. Is it not the true policy, the wise policy, the policy which the law of Congress contemplates, not to force upon the youth of the industrial classes an education which they do not seek, but rather to provide that which they desire and find they can most profitable use? If the State College is to have students and is to do the work which the law contemplates, it must provide such courses of study as will be attractive to young men and women who wish to make the most of themselves, or, otherwise, such persons will go elsewhere for the advantages which they are denied here.

There are two other points which need to be observed as a permanent

231

guiding principle in any wise and far-seeing plan of administration. One is, that changes in course of study, and schemes of instruction should be adopted with the greatest possible care and deliberation, and so gradually, as to introduce the least possible disturbance of existing conditions. This is due to parents who have sent their sons and daughters to an institution, in confidence that they will be able to complete a course of study, and secure such kind of training and incidental advantages as they had been led to expect. The policy of an institution should have the stability of the oak as well as its capacity for growth and one which makes or is thought likely to make, frequent changes will speedily lose the respect of its best friends and the confidence of the general community.

The other point to be observed is that in order to maintain a high standard of efficiency, Professors must be employed who are masters of their special departments, and not overworked instructors, worn out with the routine of daily duty, and with neither time or energy left for keeping abreast with the knowledge of their day. The advances in every department of science are so rapid and so great, that no man can teach well who is not a daily learner. Such men can not be secured by an institution without the payment of reasonable salaries, in the first place, and the prospect of something like security in their positions.

The adoption of the scheme proposed by the majority of the Committee would seem to me a disregard of these elementary facts. It would disappoint the final expectations of the great body of our friends, and would be a long step backward.

The College is doing sound work, has a strong and efficient faculty, is steadily gaining in public confidence, as its work and aims become correctly understood, and is moving in the line of the best judgment of those who have made educational questions a lifelong study, and of the best experience of other states.

The reductions which are herein proposed in the teaching force, will retain substantially the completeness of our present organization, and will bring our expenditure within our income. The Board is earnestly urged to give it a trial for the next College year. If at the end of that time further changes should be thought desirable, let them be then made with the same conserving care; and thus, instead of a violent and sweeping overthrow of what we have already gained, after long and trying experiment, our growth will retain the best from the past, and appropriate the best from the present and the future.

Respectfully submitted
(Signed)George W. Atherton

***

The Report of the Minority was adopted by a vote of nine to five. An amendment proposed by Gabriel Hiester and embodied in the Majority Report that the chair of Civil Engineering be combined with that of Mathematics was approved.

To complete the narrative and to bring it to its happy conclusion, a minor chapter must be added. Previous to this, on July 5, 1883 in a most caustic message, the Governor vetoed Senate Bill 201, establishing a "scientific agricultural experimental station, appropriating ten thousand dollars each year for four years for maintenance and support." It also provided for the sale of the Eastern and Western Farms, and covering of the proceeds in the State Treasury. The interest at six per cent was to be paid to the Trustees of the College, "to be used by them in maintaining chemical laboratories and conducting scientific experiments on the experimental farm located at the State College, and laboratory tests and investigations connected therewith."

"I cannot, writes the Governor,[15] "give my approval to the costly enterprise authorized by this bill. The past history of the State Agricultural College is not such as to induce the belief that any practical good ever has or ever will come from it. This bill is a partial attempt to re-establish it upon the Government on an enlarged and more expensive scale. It has been a costly and useless experiment from its beginning. Its affairs have twice been investigated

---

[15] For a full statement of these vetoes, see, Pennsylvania Archives-messages and Papers of the Governors.

by committees of the Legislature, and though the majority reports of those committees have fully exculpated the College authorities from any official misconduct, they have demonstrated the absolute uselessness of the institution. It is not necessary now to go over the result of those investigations, but they disclosed that the State was the fortunate possessor of a College that had more teachers than scholars, and that the yearly expense of educating the pupils was sufficient to have bought each of them a farm for himself, and started them in practical, instead of instructing in experimental farming. This College never had the support or confidence of the people. They would not send their children to it, even though the institution has been imploring for pupils and offering most inviting inducements. The farming communities of the State are absolutely indifferent about the existence of this College and do not believe it of any use. My own observations at the meeting of the State Board of Agriculture since I have become a member of it by virtue of my office, and the information I have gained from conversation with the practical farmers in attendance upon those meetings, convince me that that Board, and not the State College, is the body to which the Agricultural classes look with most respect, in which they have the most confidence, and from which they have derived most benefit. Now, this bill, while it places the experimental station, it establishes under the control of separate managers composed in part of members of the State Board of Agriculture, yet locates the station at and in connection with the College, makes the president and professors of agriculture of that institution managers of the station, and interlaces the affairs of the two concerns in most intimate connection. That is to say, while the bill is, ostensibly by its title, for the purpose of creating an experimental station, it is really intended to revivify and re-establish the College on a larger basis, and at a present additional expense to the State of at least ten thousand dollars a year. The introduction of the names of other persons into the management of the station tends to distract attention from the real purpose and effect of the bill. The State College would conduct the station, and it would be a part of the College. The latter probably knowing that the Legislature would not give it forty thousand dollars additional to spend, created this "station" with a separate board of managers. By this bill the money raised from the sale of the two farms is directed to be paid into the

State Treasury. Thus far well, if the bill had stopped there. The bill, however, provides as to this money, "the interest on which at six per cent per annum," the State Treasurer shall pay to the trustees of the College; that is to say, the College converts certain of its property into cash and makes the State borrow it at six per cent. Now, as the State can get all the money she wants at four per cent and sell her bonds at that rate of premium, it is rather remarkable to compel her to borrow her own money from the College and pay six per cent therefore.... When the State wants to spend any additional money in the interest of Agriculture she should do it through the State Board, which I believe to be composed of practical men, and the body to be one which is capable of giving valuable information and suggestions, and largely benefiting the farming community."

A similar bill to establish an experiment station but meeting in some measure the objections of the Governor was passed by the Legislature in 1885. It met a like fate, with a variant note in the theme on our remote location and inaccessibility. The Governor writes:

"The history of the State College is not such as to induce me to look with favor upon any legislation having in view the expenditure of more money upon it or the enlargement of its field of operations. It has not been productive of any practicable results commensurate with its cost. I still adhere to the belief hitherto expressed that any money intended to aid the agricultural interests could be better and more economically used through the State Agricultural Board than through any other medium. That board has the confidence of the agricultural community and its work has been highly satisfactory and done at a moderate cost. To adopt this bill would be to dissipate the resources of the Commonwealth available for agricultural purposes and a permanent experiment to be a yearly drain on the treasury. Moreover if such an enterprise as that intended by this bill is to be established, it seems to me that it would be much better to locate it upon or near the main line of some railroad, where it would be more accessible, than at the remote point now occupied by the State College."

One need be but an impartial student of this episode to glean the important truth that President Atherton had not only an institution to renew, to develop, and to vindicate but an even more critical task to enlighten and educate public opinion, lay and official, in the purposes and possibilities of the State College.

Before and during his second term as Governor, Mr. Pattison became inbued with the spirit and work of The Pennsylvania State College. He candidly revised his judgments by personal study and visitation. He gained what the venerable Dr. J. P. McCaskey described as the "Columbus experience" of every one who sincerely visits the College, a discovery of a new world. To Governor Pattison's individual support and official approval, the College owes its first permanent Engineering building; its department of Mining Engineering; the inauguration of tobacco experiments, one of the earliest cooperative lines of College research; appropriations for campus, roads, walks, residences, and the completion of the Ladies' Cottage. He also sanctioned the principle of proportionate maintenance for all departments of instruction, the College library and athletic field. He, also, signed the bill accepting on the part of the Commonwealth the proceeds of the Second Morrill Act, that of 1890; and approved the Act which added the Secretary of the State Board of Agriculture to the Ex-officio membership of the Board.

This entire episode, early in his administration and in which he "won his spurs" is typical of the indomitable spirit with which Dr. Atherton met opposition, turned foes into friends, won against what seemed insuperable obstacles. Between this and the close of his life work, a period which still largely lies before us for record, he experienced some defeats, but won many such victories. But he "went straight as an arrow toward the goal," with a "singleness of purpose he hewed to the line," so that not only the College finds itself, but finds its constituency also. He was, indeed, moulded by an idea, and that idea transformed the College, secured a loyal body of alumni and students, and an ever increasing attachment and support from the public which it serves.

A tribute from the pen of Dr. H. P. Armsby furnishes a fitting close to the present chapter.

"He was an indefatigable worker, never sparing himself in the server of the College or of the larger public, and he inspired his associates with the like zeal. It has been a common remark of new comers that State College is an exceedingly busy place. It is true, and the secret was in the leader who said not "go" but "come." Firm in maintaining the just prerogatives of his office, he was most generous in acknowledging the labor of others, and was notably free from that petty vanity which seeks to absorb all the credit for progress, and which speaks of "my" College, "my" Faculty, and "my" Board. His ideal was the life of service; and the career of this gifted man must ever put before the students of State a high ideal of what constitutes success in life. During his later years, his multifarious activities overtaxed even his strong physique. Twice leave of absence was almost forced upon him by the Trustees. Returning on each occasion from a European trip, he threw himself unreservedly—I had almost said recklessly—into his work again. Nearly a year before his death he suffered a severe attack of a bronchial disorder, and in the fall of 1905, he insisted upon presenting his resignation, to take effect as soon as his successor should be secured, and on the advice of his physician spent the winter in Southern California.

In the spring, he returned somewhat improved and attempted to take up his work again. A business trip to New York in the uncertain weather of early spring, however, brought on a relapse, and for two weeks his life was despaired of. Later he rallied, and on Commencement Day was able to appear upon the platform and confer the degrees upon the graduating class. This was his last official act. He gradually grew weaker, and on July 24, passed quietly and peacefully away."

He is buried under the shadow of the Auditorium—about which clustered so much of his thought and pride. A monument was placed by the respect and devotion of students, a veritable College shrine where memory may ever turn in honoring worthy achievement and ennobling sacrifice. His real monument is The Pennsylvania State College of all time; not as he found it, confined, walled in, almost entombed in the dungeon-like interior of the real "Old" Main, but as he left it, a somewhat remodeled and reconstructed Old Main, surrounded by a college of spacious campus and buildings, of growing School and responsible Departments.

The story of this hegira from Old Main, the story of the development of a modern College in organization, in habitation, in curricula and laboratory equipment, in internal activities and external relations, in student initiative and life—this is the story that now engages our attention in subsequent chapters.

CHAPTER 11

The Trail from "Old Main," Building a Modern College

"The time seems to me to have arrived when application should be made to the State to provide such enlargements of the College as will meet the original design of Congress and render the Institution more worthy of a great and powerful Commonwealth. The name and credit of the State cannot be wholly separated from the prosperity of the College, and the interests of each should be a care for the other." 1884.

"I trust the time is not far distant when the State College, the Normal Schools, High Schools, and the District Schools of the State may be organized into a harmonious and progressive system, each receiving stimulus, support, and strength from the others." 1892.

"The question is not what shall the State of Pennsylvania do for the State College, but how shall she use the College in such a manner as best to fulfill her contract with the United States and strengthen her own agencies for the promotion of public education." 1897.

Annual Reports: President George W. Atherton

The College in 1882 was practically an institution of but one building, Old Main as it later came to be called, but then known as "the College." All activities of the institution, all its properties and belongings were housed therein except live-stock with the necessary barns and Experimental Farm Barns. In addition there were the dwellings of the President and Vice President, three small structures known as Gate Houses, and two frame residences for Professors. There was, too, an Engine House at the Allen Street Entrance which pumped the water from an artesian well into the reservoir, then, on what is now, New Beaver Field; which in turn supplied the steam heating plant in Old Main, its dormitories and laboratories. In a map of the campus published in 1881-82, the Engine House is called the Mechanic Arts Building, a function which its improvised, half-story garrett did serve from 1881 to 1886. A conspicuous feature of the executive grounds was a barn, housing the single nag, the spanking bays, the cows, chickens and other live-stock of Presidential caliber. President Calder kept a coachman and maintained a handsome turnout—there was a touch of real distinction to the emoluments; while to Presidents Burrowes and Shortlidge, the edible livestock loomed larger as desirable tenants in the executive menage. A College ice-house at the upper pond and subsidiary storage bins provided refrigeration in seasons propitious.

The College enrolled at this time, five resident graduates, forty-seven in four year courses, eight special students, and eighty-five in the Preparatory Department. The total enrollment was one hundred and forty-five, a number slightly exceeded eight times in the previous history of the institution, and not again until the renaissance of 1887. The women students numbered twenty-six, an enrollment exceeded in six out of the eleven years since women were admitted. The institution was fairly provincial, at least one hundred of the total roll came from Centre and immediately contiguous counties. The graduating class numbered nine, a number not exceeded since 1862, and the total list of alumni was one hundred and twelve. The faculty was made up of nine Professors, one of whom was Acting-President, one Assistant Professor, three Instructors, one Assistant, together with a Lady Principal and a Principal of the Preparatory Department; half of whom were graduates of the

College itself.

This was the institution of one building, of dormitories for College men, women and preparatory students; of living quarters for four families of teachers; of museums; of laboratories for agriculture, chemistry, physics, civil engineering and drawing, botany and horticulture, geology and zoology; Armory, Chapel, Library, Faculty Room and College Parlor; Society Halls, Lecture and Recitation Rooms, Administrative Offices, Young Men's Christian Association, Hospital Room, together with gymnasium and room for dramatics. The steam heat plant, coal storage, self-boarding facilities, implement storage, oil and powder supply used the basement. As samples, merely, of contemporary impressions, two are chosen. A report of Delegates from the Agricultural Society of York County in 1872 reads: "Passing up a narrow stairway, ill-lighted all the way, but in one place, utter darkness— thanks to the illustrious architect,—we groped and scrambled our way to the Chapel a mean, low ceilinged room, capable of holding perhaps two hundred people, and either through carelessness on the occasion not ventilated or incapable of being so." A member of the investigating Committee of 1879 is yet more gay and caustic: we "Did go up into the highlands of Centre County to visit the institution," and found "a massive, dungeon-like structure, fit only for a prison or asylum." Its gloomy interior, most forbidding, the very realm of shades and abandonment of hope, one would infer possessed the soul of the casual visitor as he entered its narrow portals.

This multum in parvo was the inheritance of the new president, coupled with the "unsavory reputation" which the institution "enjoyed," the opposition, overt and secret which it experienced, the general distrust and neglect which characterized the public and official opinion of the time. Here, too, was the opportunity to disarm criticism with facts; to inspire hope and instill life into old channels of College work; to build "more stately mansions" for the soul of the new College, with adequate facilities for departments and schools—in short to grow a modern College. Thus began the hegira from Old Main, which did not end until July 15, 1929 when demolition of the ancient and honorable, but long since condemned structure, was vigorously pushed.

Origin and Development of Modern Agriculture at the College

The first and most important fact in the modernization of agricultural instruction was the rise of the Experiment Station.[16] It was the agency that wrought the salvation and regeneration of agriculture. We have seen the attempts to secure support for such a station at the College nullified by the veto of the Governor. Pennsylvania was thus denied the honor of early official establishment of a Station, a project is such close harmony with the purpose of the institution, and one, too, which Dr. Pugh in 1864 had outlined for it. But this did not prevent the beginnings of genuine experiment under Professor W. H. Jordan. There were no students in the upper classes in the course in Agriculture at that time, and Dr. Jordan reports that in the year, 1881-82 he "attended to recitations in Ethics, Evidences of Christianity and Human Physiology." President Atherton immediately arranged that he give his whole time to Agriculture, experimental and extensional. He started a series of general experiments in fertilizers, which have been continued to the present day—the second oldest series in the world. He lectured to farm clubs and agricultural associations, and wrote for the Press. He warmly espoused the cause of an experimental station at the College, and upheld the wisdom of disposing of the Eastern and Western Model Farms, in order, thereby, to centralize and render efficient the task of research. He delivered the bulk of the lectures in the Farmers' Institute Course at the College during the years 1881 to 1885. The addition of short courses and the modification of the main course in conformity with the needs in the State, followed. Dr. Jordan sought to account for the small attendance of Agricultural students at these institutions. He had no illusions respecting the only true means of enlarging interest and effectiveness, through scientific experiment and research. He made a study of eight prominent industrial colleges, with Agriculture as well equipped with men and means as any other department. He found that out of an enrollment of twenty-seven hundred, only sixty-eight were registered in

---

[16] In some Pennsylvania Pioneers in Agriculture Science, published in 1928, Professor Thomas I. Mairs has contributed important and interesting biographical data, and has paid merited tribute to eight leaders in the development of the science and teaching of Agriculture at the Pennsylvania State College.

Agriculture. This, too, in spite of the fact that seven out of the eight states containing these Colleges ranked among the richest Agricultural states of the Union; and that greater effort is made to secure students in Agriculture than in any other line. Experience everywhere demonstrated that the Experiment Station, short courses, extension activities were prerequisites to an increase of students in completer courses. The records here reveal six graduates in Agriculture from 1887 to 1897. From 1896 to 1905, there were twenty-four. These numbers, even, are three times as many as were graduated from 1859 to 1887. Rapid growth everywhere in these lines dates from 1900, the specific reasons, therefore, will appear presently.

General causes, not alone or chiefly local ones, lay back of the seeming apathy toward agricultural instruction; but by making thorough scientific preparation, by furthering experimentation and spreading information, by "keeping the trap set, if you would catch game,"[17] there was a calm confidence in future results. A series of sixteen bulletins was issued; twelve largely the work of Dr. Jordan, the remainder issued under the supervision of Dr. William Frear. These were begun in November 1882, and continued until 1886, when the present series of The Pennsylvania State College Agricultural Experiment Station was inaugurated with Bulletin, Number One, October 1887. In this series to date over two hundred and fifty have been issued, with a mailing list of more than thirty thousand names, in nine major agricultural interests, and reaching about one fourth of the two hundred thousand farms in Pennsylvania.

A change in attitude was response on the part of the Agricultural constituency, and of the Press soon became apparent—the leaders were vindicated by the results of thorough scientific, though delayed preparation.

If an "army travels on its stomach," a College moves on its budget. In 1887, legislation was approved authorizing the sale of the two model farms. An Experiment Station was established at the College, and three thousand

---

[17] This was President Atherton's answer to the plea for retraction of effort on program in the absence of an immediate active student demand. I owe to Dean Watts this characteristic reply of Dr. Atherton to unthinking critics of that day.

dollars appropriated annually for four years toward its support. Meanwhile the Hatch Act had been enacted by the Federal Government, approved March 2, 1887. It required the cooperating acceptance of each State Legislature, or if not in session, temporary acceptance by the Governor. Governor James A. Beaver approved the Act, and it was confirmed by the Legislature in the session of 1889. An annual payment of fifteen thousand dollars was thus provided for the work of each station in the several States. The effect upon Agriculture and Agricultural education has been well-high phenomenal. Jennings in his History of the Economic Progress of the United States writes: "In every State they saved hundreds of thousands of dollars and even millions yearly; and their saving for the country as a whole was in the tens of millions by 1900."

The experimental work which had been carried on by Professor Jordan (and since his resignation in 1885 by Dr. William Frear and others) was merged under the newly established: "The State College Experiment Station." The action of the Board bears the date, June 29, 1887, and the first staff was duly appointed:

> Dr. H. P Armsby, Director
> Dr. William Frear, Vice-Director and Chemist
> Professor Wiliam A. Buckhout, Botanist
> Professor George C. Butz, Horticulturalist.
> William C. Patterson, Superintendent of the Farm.
> H. J. Patterson, Laboratory Assistant.

With the single exception of Professor Harry J. Patterson, an alumnus of the College, who has given distinguished services to Agricultural Education in Maryland, this staff gave their entire lives to the College. There has thus been a continuity of plan and execution in the work of the station, the changes in Directorship being only two, Dean Thomas F. Hunt's important service from 1907 to 1912, followed by a rapid expansion and effective organization of the school under Instruction, Research, and Extension by Dean R. L. Watts, 1912 to date.

The selection of Dr. Armsby was a most fortunate one. The dominant note of scholarliness and of thorough scientific study in agriculture, which characterized the beginnings under Dr. Pugh, Caldwell, Jordan and Frear was extended. Trained at Worcester Polytechnic and Sheffield Scientific Schools, and at the University of Leipzig, he also had a wide experience as teacher and administrator at Rutgers College, the Connecticut Stations, and as Associate Director at the University of Wisconsin. When called from the latter position to The Pennsylvania State College, he had won his doctorate (Yale 1879), and had published scientific papers, as well as his Manual of Cattle Feeding. These issues presaged his chief interest and life work in the problems of animal nutrition, utilization and conservation of animal foods. Genial, fair minded, broad minded, he impressed his personality and methods of work upon the whole College, while he secured the earnest and hearty cooperation of his immediate co-workers. His standards in both respects were always set high. His limitation, if indeed it were such, lay in his distrust of certain popularizing tendency, from whose superficial machinations, he shrank with the unerring instinct of the true scholar and investigator.

The work of the Station was added to the already crowded quarters of Old Main, and from thence, its first bulletins were issued. The first of these contained a summary of experimental activities under three headings: Prior to 1867; the experimental farms 1867 to 1881; and the pre-experiment station period 1881to 1887. Among these early bulletins were studies, also, on Field Experiments, Maintenance Rations, Seed Germinations, Digestibility of Soiling Rye, and Tests of Varieties. The laboratory accommodations of the Station in 1887 "consisted of one room about twenty feet square with the cellar under it, in the main building, while its office, a room about half this size, served both for Station office and Director's study." However, on June 27, 1888, the corner-stone of a new Station was laid. Addresses were made by Professor I. P. Roberts, Director of the Cornell University Experiment Station, by His Excellency, James A. Beaver, Governor of the Commonwealth, and by Director Armsby. The location of the Station in close proximity to the Central Experiment Farm buildings fixed the habitation of the future School of Agriculture. The building was completed April 1, 1889, and the personnel of the Station and College department of Agriculture being largely the same, the transfer quickly followed.

With the Experiment Station as the center of the agricultural research, correlating its findings with those of other agencies; the instruction and extension activities took on a new aspect. Early in 1889, the analysis of commercial fertilizers was transferred to the College by action of the State Board of Agriculture. Dr. H. B. McDonnell and Mr. J. A. Fries were made assistant chemists, the latter holding the distinction of longest term of service in the entire history of the Institution. Other appointments of the late eighties and early nineties were William H. Caldwell as Instructor in Agriculture, 1889 to 1894; Thomas F. Hunt who served one year 1890-91, succeeded by H. J. Waters, 1891 to 1895, all of whom have distinguished records in other places and fields of Agricultural history. Thus wrote Dr. Atherton in the Report for 1892: "During the entire period of its existence, the College has carried on, more or less fully the work of investigation in agriculture, but since the establishment of the Experiment Station in 1887, that work has been conducted with a system, vigor, and efficiency fully in keeping with the advance in other branches of College work. As above indicated, ten men are now employed in that department where only one was employed ten years ago. Among the similar stations in the United States, now numbering nearly sixty, the one connected with this institution is generally recognized as one of the most efficient—a result very largely owing to the zeal and ability of Dr. Armsby, the Director, and his assistants, sustained by a broad and liberal policy on the part of the Board of Trustees."

A creamery and dairy building was erected in 1890, at a cost of seventeen hundred and eighty dollars. It was located south-east of the Station and across the road. This more than modest, but nevertheless noted, structure supplanted the small detached "milk-shed" of the Experimental Farm. Two courses in dairying were organized by W. H. Caldwell; the number and range of the work greatly increased under Professor Harry Hayward 1894-1902. In 1895, the first building for general agriculture was erected, Hemlock Hall, south of the Creamery, at a cost of eleven hundred and sixty-five dollars. It had an honorable career, less stormy than the Creamery, whose bars and locks scarcely thwarted the gastronomic raids of envious studentse, the "non-ags."

Hemlock Hall was agriculture's final gesture of adieu to Old main, and both Dr. H. J. Waters and his successor Professor George C. Watson (1895 to 1907) spoke in glowing terms of the usefulness of even so temporary and improvised a home for the instructional, laboratory, correspondence and general extension lines of agriculture.

The Chautauqua Reading Courses in Agriculture were recommended by Director Armsby in his report for 1891 and were put into operation the following year. They were designed to supplement the work of the farmers' institute and the agricultural press by providing for the farmer in his home more systematic and thorough aids, than these can in their nature afford. It should be recorded that Colonel John A. Woodward, for twenty-seven years a member of the Board, with consistent zeal and support of agricultural education, represented in the institutes of the State, the cause of these Reading Courses. These courses were affirmed by Dr. A. C. True of the United States Department of Agriculture to have been the earliest in the country, widely approved and utilized. Short Winter Courses in Agriculture, in Agricultural Chemistry and Botany, in stock raising and dairying and in veterinary science were maintained at the College, enriched always by the fuller training of the regular course and the program of experiment and research.

Botany and Horticulture made their exit from Old Main when the diminutive block-like brick structure was provided by the Legislature in 1887. The location followed precedent, near the residence, conservatory, and formal gardens of Professor Jacob Whitman, also the nurseries, vineyards, orchards, and hedge rows of Professor William Waring.

Two very important movements, also, aided the School of Agriculture in finding itself and entering its promised land, one within the School itself, the other in the State at large. The one is almost unique, the calorimeter experiments, a sort of fundamental experiment station, dealing with a problem of scientific and practical interest to all the stations. The other, was the enlistment of all the agricultural interests of the State to advance the science and art of rural life but especially to give its educational agency, The Pennsylvania State College, a modern plant with more adequate maintenance.

Let us examine these two briefly.[18] Cooperative experiments with the Bureau of animal Industry of the United States Department of Agriculture were begun in 1898. Many studies had been made in feeding and food stuffs, for these problems were in Dr. Armsby's mind from his earliest contacts with the science of Agriculture. But the determination of the actual quantities relations required the adaptation of a new and immensely complicated apparatus, specially constructed and housed. A building was completed in November 1899, and the two following years were occupied with the installation and perfecting of apparatus, together with preliminary tests and controls. Definite experiments were begun in the winter of 1901-02, "constituting so far as the writer (Dr. Armsby) is aware, the first direct determination of the heat production of cattle."

The calorimeter is essentially a mechanism for registering accurately the inherent potentialities of various food stuffs in terms of their utilization by the animal organization. The character of the work, its scientific approach and method, the results achieved brought international recognition to Dr. Armsby. His absorption in and devotion to these researches led to the establishment of the institute of Animal Nutrition, as an Independent but coordinate branch of the School of Agriculture. The vote of the Executive Committee of the Board bears the date of September 19, 1905, and that of the Board itself, July 1, 1907. Dr. Armsby continued in the directorship of the Institute until his death on October 19, 1921. His successor, Dr. E. B. Forbes, summing up his work, writes: "Scientific journals both of this country and of Europe credited him with larger contributions than those of any other man of his generation to our knowledge of the physiology of nutrition upon which the science and practice of stock feeding are based."

A second movement was inaugurated in 1900 on the part of the agricultural organizations in the State to further the interests of the school. It was a most effective factor in the renaissance of agriculture at The Pennsylvania State College. It was aided, too, by the general atmosphere for

---

[18] An historical and description account may be found in Bulletin 302 of the School of Agriculture and Experiment Station, The Respiration Calorimeter by W.S. Braman.

the improvement and beautification of rural life which characterized the "Back to Nature," "Country Life" emphasis of this period. This brought in its train an increased interest in collegiate instruction of agriculture, in number of students enrolled in all of these institutions. It led to the widening out of the problem so as to include, not only greater production at lessening cost, but to better types of farmer, better surroundings for the women of the farm, better schools for the children, better roads with improved marketing conditions, the introduction of modern inventions to lighten farm labor and to satisfy the longings for the amenities and opportunities supposed to be peculiarly the heritage of the urban classes. Rural life was enriched in every way, a class consciousness was formed which expressed itself in economic, political and education channels. Subdivisions of subject matter, new and highly specialized branches of study arise out of the broad and ill-defined term, agriculture in the Colleges, and these new disciplines found themselves welcomed into the inner circles of the exact sciences. In short they became sciences, which agriculture in its generic sense is not.

On June 4 and 5, 1900, upon invitation of the State Board of Agriculture, delegates from the State Department of Agriculture and Board of Agriculture, the Department of Public Instruction, the Grange and Alliance, the State Agricultural Society, the Dairy Union met at the State College. Other organizations included in the call and meeting were those of Horticulture, the Jersey Cattle Club, the livestock Breeders, the Guernsey Breeders, and the Poultry Association at The Pennsylvania State College. The Allied Agricultural Organizations of Pennsylvania was formed, with Dr. N. C. Schaeffer, Superintendent of Public Instruction as President and Dr. H. P. Armsby, Secretary. Executive and legislature committees were named, and much consideration was given to the expressed purpose of the conference, which was: "to consider the present condition and needs of Agricultural Education in all its branches in the Commonwealth." Resolutions framed and legislation urged included the introduction of nature study in the public schools, with provision also for carrying this and the Township High School Act into effect. There was urged also a "sufficient appropriation for the erection and maintenance at The Pennsylvania State College of a suitable building for the teaching of the different branches of Agriculture, including Dairying and Forestry."

Efforts in the session of 1901 failed of full accomplishment. The Allied Organizations continued their activities. Enlarged to a representative body of sixteen State organizations, a second conference was held in Harrisburg, January 21, 1902. The program was broadened to include permanent improvement of public roads; and "one or more Summer Schools for the benefit of teachers who cannot attend our State Normal Schools or The State College." Again, emphasis was placed upon the needs of the School of Agriculture for buildings and maintenance. Plans for immediate needs were formulated. These were urged by representatives of the Allied Organizations, by the Board of Trustees and by friends of the College throughout the Commonwealth. A beginning was made in the provision for a Dairy Building, the first unit in the modern agricultural group, the harbinger of better facilities for all departments of the School. The building for agriculture followed, not without delays consequent upon partial veto by the Governor in 1905 on the ground of insufficient State revenue. The appropriation to complete the building was approved by the Session of 1907.

Thus at the close of President Atherton's administration, Agriculture was moving in a definitely modern direction, its research agencies established, its Experiment Station and Institute of Animal Nutrition, the plant taking permanent form. The second Morrill Act of 1890, and the Adams (1906) and Nelson (1907) Amendments to the Federal Enactment of 1862, added to the resources and facilities of the College in which Agriculture largely profited. Instruction was offered in a general course in Agriculture and in three options, Agricultural Chemistry; Dairy Husbandry; and Horticulture including Forestry. Short courses during the winter months in a variety of subjects, a creamery course, correspondence courses under thirty-one subjects and enrolling in 1905-06, twenty-five hundred persons, were given. The school, also, participated continuously in Farmers' Institutes Extension group fairs, and other Agricultural gatherings. Eighteen Freshmen were entered in the four year course in the fall of 1905, a significant increase. Agriculture had found itself, it had "gone out from Old Main building" and set up for itself.

The Story of Engineering.

From practicum carpenter and blacksmith shop to instruction in mechanic arts; from drawing as an indoor diversion in plotting gardens as an outdoor recreation; from surveying (the College since 1871 proclaims ownership of a transit, compass, and chains) in the department of Mathematics to Civil Engineering (the first graduate in 1885); from Mechanic Arts and Civil Engineering to fully organized schools of Engineering, with research and experiment stations, extension centers and activities, such in brief is the story of engineering. The initiative was taken by the Faculty, June 19, 1880, in appointment of a Committee to prepare a mechanical practicum during the next session. The plan was approved, but owing to the chaotic conditions of the year 1880-1881, an instructor was not secured until the spring session. Mr. John H. McCormick, a recent graduate of Ohio State University arrived at the College on March 25, 1881. In a letter under date of April 1, 1927, Mr. McCormick writes: "There had evidently been no preliminary preparation or even planning for the work I was to carry on. All communications came to me through President McKee. A living room in the one College building was assigned to me, also a classroom in which I started class in free hand and mechanical drawing, about evenly divided in number between young ladies and young men, but not large at that, I was then given space above the pumping station, located on the road and a little to the west of the College building, in which work benches were installed and about six sets of hand wood-working tools purchased and placed in boxes above the benches. The capacity of the little shop was at once tested. The work seemed popular with the students throughout the term, when compared with the classes I had started in, at Ohio State." An exhibition at the Commencement of work done by the students was arranged in the College parlor at the right of the main entrance. It called out the "interest and approbation" of the Board in a special Resolution adopted on June 30, 1881.

In a report to the Board, the character of the work may be gleaned. "In wood-working, instruction is first given in the proper care, use and grinding of the tools. Exercises in sawing follow including the making of plane surfaces, correct angles and true forms, also, in framing, jointing, pattern work, and the finishing of such work with sand-paper, oil and varnish. In mechanical drawing, the first work is tinting plane surfaces and shading cylinders, by parallel lines, thus securing practice in the use of the right-line pen. The class then proceeds to outline and shade simple forms, in projection and perspective." Mr. McCormick urges the need of proper drawing desks, and recommends the addition of "metal working shops including forge work, iron bench work, and machine tool work. Moulding in brass could be introduced at small expense by building a pit-furnace in connection with the engine house stack." He suggested that a building large enough to accommodate these shops be annexed to the engine house, and estimated as necessary for building and equipment in the sum of fifteen hundred dollars. Thus were foundations laid, and in some respects a program evolved for the immediate future. Throughout the year 1881-82, one of retrenchment and uncertainty, Professors Louis. H. Barnard, Professor of Civil Engineering 1881 to 1893, and Josiah Jackson, Professor of Mathematics 1880 to 1893, carried the work in drawing and mechanic arts. The following year L. E. Reber, then in charge of the military department was appointed Instructor in the Preparatory Department and in drawing. Under contract with the Board, he was on leave during 1883-84 to prepare himself to take charge of the department of mechanic arts. The history of engineering from that date until his resignation as Dean in 1907 is intimately bound up with him. Here as in Agriculture, there have been but three changes in the Deanship of the School, John Price Jackson serving from 1907 to 1915. The former created and organized the division of extension at the University of Wisconsin, the latter resigned to enter Governor Tener's cabinet as Director of Labor and Industry. Both are alumni who have brought honor to their Alma Mater at home and abroad.

In the fall of 1884, the work was reorganized by Mr. Reber, as Professor of Mechanical Drawing and Instructor in Mechanic Arts. Students were attracted and the department at once outgrew its improvised quarters. Plans for a building were drawn, and the first exclusive academic structure supplementing the College building was dedicated on February 10, 1886. It was a two story, frame structure, located east of the engine house and facing College Avenue. The cost of the building itself, was sixteen hundred and fifty dollars, and the equipment, in addition to donations, aggregated eighteen hundred dollars. The funds for this modest, yet significant beginning were not due to legislative aid. General Beaver revealed that "a small fund accumulated under the direction of the President of the College, and by the skill and industry of one of its professors in securing and performing scientific work— furnished a fund which has been expanded under the direction of the Executive Committee of the Board of trustees." A brief description follows of this sturdy landmark, until 1930 in use as the eastern-most and least grotesque of the old mining futurist group: "The building is of wood, but very neatly and substantially constructed. The apartments consist of four rooms, a forge and lathe room on the first floor, while on the second floor is a turning and carpenter shop. All the tools and appliances used are of the best that could be procured anywhere. The course is designed to afford such students as have had the ordinary common school education, an opportunity to continue the elementary scientific, and literary studies, together with mechanical and freehand drawing; while receiving a theoretical and practical instruction in the various mechanical arts. The instruction in shop work is given by means of exercises so planned as to cover, in a systematic manner, the operations in use in the various trades, and only such constructions are made as cover principles without undue repetition." The course embraced bench and machine work in word, pattern making, iron and steel forging, vise and machine work in iron and metals, drawing and designing preliminary to construction. A mechanic arts course of three years was offered in 1884, growing into a Mechanical Engineering course, first outlined in 1887-88, from which the first student graduated in 1890.

A pardonable pride in these early prospects and achievements led to an elaborate dedication of the Mechanic Arts Building, held in the College Chapel on February 10, 1886. An address by Professor John Hamilton on the new education as based upon "the desire to construct" was followed by General Beaver. On behalf of the Board he reviewed the progress of the building, the difficulties overcome and the hopes centered in it. The keys were turned over to Dr. Atherton (in the absence of Colonel Jordan, President of the Board), who responded in "a logical yet happily practical address." The keynote was: "Given these high natural endowments, these boundless resources, nothing but an adequate system of industrial education is requisite to give us pre-eminence in the sciences and arts of life, as we already hold it in the science and art of government. As a means toward this great end, the department of Mechanic Arts in the State College is to be religiously used.... But beyond this and in all his relations, we mean never to lose sight of the fact that the student is a man, and a citizen—that he is not to be trained as a mere machine, however perfect, but as an intelligent and responsible being, destined to perform his part and to exercise his influence in our great system of free institutions."

Under the new conditions, interest and numbers grew rapidly, the shops and laboratories were overcrowded. In 1892-93, the Engineering courses, Civil, Mechanical and Electrical, enrolled eighty-one, out of the total of one hundred and sixty-four students in the four year courses. Work in Mechanic Arts was incorporated in all the College courses and was justly popular. A Summer Session (the progenitor of all our sessions) of eight weeks in "Mechanical Drawing and Work, and especially designed for teachers" was authorized on January 13, 1888. A series of lessons, with detailed illustrations, in carpentry and joining, in forging, in vise work, in machine work in wood and iron were included in the Report of the Pennsylvania Commission on Industrial Education. A working model of a horizontal engine made entirely by students was also featured. These were widely reproduced and favorably commented upon, in one instance in a discussion of technical education in the English Parliament. The introduction of electric lighting in 1887, and the erection of the first central heating and power plant in 1889, north of the Mechanic Arts Building added to the laboratory facilities. The Mechanical Engineers "took turns in running the plant," and when the "great" triple-expansion Corliss engine was installed in the basement of the new building of 1893, both the College and the public were duly impressed and awed by the manipulations, simple and compound, under varying loads, of this hippogriff of experimental machinery which propelled only its own gigantic mechanism. As an engineering calorimeter; it ante-dated, however, both the animal calorimeter and the "illuminated digestion" of the famous and comfortable bovine, Jessie, "with a window in her stomach." Some other engineering features of special importance by way of experiment, which, too, have had their day and ceased to be, are the Experimental Trolley Line; the Lifting Power of Planes under changing conditions of speed and air; Tunnels and Shafts, the miners' studio near the old frame mining group, and the Steel Wireless Tower.

The second stage in Engineering began with the provision in 1891, for a more permanent housing of the departments of Civil, Mechanical, and Mining Engineering. One hundred thousand dollars was the amount appropriated for a building, and Governor Pattison signed the Bill. Ground was broken in June 1891. It occupied the site, essentially, of the present main engineering structure, and was built of red pressed brick, with trimmings of brownstone. Its Saracenic, dome-like capping added variety. A conspicuous feature was the stone arched entrance, supported by short, cylindrical columns on either side and extended above into a projection from the rooms of the different floors. The building was three stories, with basement, and a rear wing, one story and attic. It had a frontage of two-hundred and sixty-six feet and a depth of two-hundred and eight feet; a total of fifty thousand eight hundred and twenty four square feet or about one and one-seventh acres. Within its walls, the statistician continues, one may tread over two and one-third acres of floor space; surrounded by four million brick. Or, having made complete tour of the building, he will have been in fifty-seven different rooms. Need we wonder that the great heart of General Beaver, who, as he himself once phrased it, "furnished the rousements," swelled with pride as he handed over these "two and one-third acres—*acres*"— to Dr. Atherton. Equipped from top floor to basement, crowded and soon overcrowded with the various branches of engineering, there came to the entire institution a new sense of pride and responsibility. Engineering, too, was finding itself.

In replying to General Beaver, this note was happily stressed by Dr. Atherton in the thought that "The Pennsylvania State College by the equipment, the increased and improved equipment which it is receiving, and by the increased hold it is acquiring upon the affections and confidence and pride—I may justly say—of the people of Pennsylvania The Pennsylvania

State College is coming into a position of responsibility to the present and to the future that cannot belong to any private institution, however magnificently endowed. This is the child of the United States Government, a government whose first President declared that in order to perpetuate free government, there must be an intelligent citizenship. And this institution is also the child of the State which has, in these later years, shown a generous pride in making it worthy of this worthiest of Commonwealths. By that fact this institution stands, whether it will or not, in a relation of responsibility to the whole public school system of the State that no other institution holds or can hold and for the right exercise of which it will be held—whether it will or not and whether man will it or not—it will be held to a just and severe accountability. The public schools of the world have not given birth to universities, but have been children of the universities, and while the logical order would be from the bottom upward, yet the actual order has been from the top downward; and there never has been and never can be a sound system of public education which is not inspired and vitalized by a sound and vigorous system of higher education. The public school system of Pennsylvania with its magnificent group of Normal Schools, has needed, now needs and in the future will still more need, the inspiring and helpful influence which The Pennsylvania State College (or when the time shall come, The Pennsylvania State University,) may give to that system; and so, I say every step in advance brings to us a more serious and deep responsibility."

At this formal opening on February 22, 1893, recognition of this new opportunity and responsibility was given in the remainder of the exercises. Governor Pattison[19] spoke of the State and Higher Education. General Francis A. Walker of the Massachusetts Institute of Technology represented higher education; and the Secretary of the Interior, John W. Noble, who by

---

[19] President Atherton always tactful and diplomatic on public occasions was at his best. Upon the conclusion of the Governor's rather guarded and impersonal address, Dr. Atherton said: "I must ask leave (and I am sure our friend, the Governor, will not misunderstand me) to supplement his speech by just one single thought. He says he hopes he shall live to see the educational system of Pennsylvania include the primary school, the high school, and the university. I want to add, and that *this* shall be the university."

his message represented the National Government, was commissioned by the President of the United States to bear greetings on this dedicatory occasion.

Electrical Engineering was first taught under the direction of the department of Physics. The latter was set up, as already noted, as an independent department in 1879, and graduates in Physics and Electrotechnics appeared on the Commencement Program until and including 1893. Action by the Board, January 23, 1893, established the department of Electrical Engineering in the School of Engineering and John Price Jackson a member of the class of 1889 was placed in charge. After two years of practical engineering work he had returned to his Alma Mater as Instructor. For twenty-four years thereafter, he developed the department of Electrical Engineering to one of the first in point of numbers and efficiency. He also served as Dean of the School. Some of the men who collaborated with Professor Jackson in developing Electrical Engineering were Messrs. Lardner, Reed, Frankenfield, Thompson, Wood, Dennington, Arney and Godard.

Civil Engineering, as has been indicated, is the oldest of the Engineering subjects at the College, but with a more definite status of identity and growth dating from 1893. The department heads virtually cover the period from that time, Professors Fred E. Foss and Elton D. Walker, a period of consistent growth. Alumni, too, will recall the names of Breneman, Beyer, Butts, Kirkham, Shattuck, Webber, among others, in this development when Civil Engineering was finding itself and professionalizing its work.

Mechanical Engineering, as a department, is identified with Professor L. E. Reber from 1882 through the period under consideration. A list of co-laborers follows whom alumni will gladly honor such teachers as the Navy details, Lieutenants Pemberton and Kinkaid, Messrs. Griffin, Heisler, Lenfest, Harding, Hunter, Wood, Resides, and certainly, also, those practical masters of machine field, and shop management, Messrs. Dunkle, Towle, and Parker, whose very eccentricities or characteristics were corner stones of genuine influence and of character.

Mining Engineering was established in 1891, with provision for the technical work later in the new Engineering building. The courses at the outset were in close correlation with those of Engineering and Chemistry, as well as incorporating the identical subjects of the first two years of all courses. In 1894, the first student was graduated and when the schools were organized in 1896, the department was accorded the status of a School, under Dr. Magnus C. Ihlseng as Dean. An enthusiastic group of young men was appointed, Messsrs. Pond, Stoek, Shedd, and Hopkins. Through the interests of the latter, the experimental polylith was placed upon the campus, and a series of studies and surveys of the mineral resources, brownstones, clays, etc., of the Commonwealth published. These were preceded by a series of semi-popular bulletins and lecturers on mining and geology from 1893 to 1898, among the earliest of College experiments in extension teaching of technical subjects. In 1900, the School was again merged with Engineering, but six years later re-established in a series of temporary structures to which were joined other more temporary structures. These were erected largely by the personal solicitation of funds by General Beaver. Under Deans Marsham H. Wadsworth, Walter R. Crane, Elwood S. Moore, Elmer A. Holbrook, the School has had an increasing prestige but scarcely consistent growth. The Mining Experiment Station and Mining Extension revival, as well as the organization and provision for a great School of Mineral Industries is part of a necessarily later study.

The story of Engineering as a whole culminates in 1906, the end of a distinctive and most important period of College development, in an enrollment of two thirds of the student body and with the stage set for greater things to come.

Physics and Chemistry

The completion of the earliest building for Physics and Chemistry in 1889 marks another stage in the flight from Old Main. The need of differentiation in a growing body of technical students led to an increase in courses and laboratory facilities. In 1893, Professor M. M. Garver came to the Staff. The history of the department to 1907, the retirement of Professor I. T. Osmond is virtually the record of these two men. The well-nigh unparalleled growth of the work in more recent years is another story, but has its counterpart in current revolutionary advances in this most ancient, seemingly rigid, conservative science.

Chemistry was emphasized in all periods of the College, but received a new program and marching orders in the earliest report of Dr. Atherton. The man to work out and perfect these policies was not found at once, the immediate predecessors of Dr. G. G. Pond, serving only for periods of three years each, Charles J. Bell, 1882 to 1885 and William H. Herrick, 1885 to 1888. In the last named year, a young Amherst Bachelor of Arts of 1881, who had studied abroad and had served his Alma Mater as Instructor in Chemistry was appointed Professor of Chemistry. He lived and taught in Old Main for two years, but moved the department with two young instructors to the new building in May 1890. For a total service of thirty-two years with rare energy and devotion, he helped to lay the foundations of the real Penn State. Nor will the fact be denied that Chemistry "found itself" as it, too, moved out from Old Main. Over ten thousand individual students came under his personal instruction, and of the graduates of the four year courses in Chemistry, ninety-seven per cent followed that profession. They are teachers in Universities and Colleges, in High Schools and Academies; chemists, technicians and industrial leaders in all parts of the country. Not only <u>was</u> he a real teacher, a builder of specialists but also of men, but he still lives in the memory of grateful students; and even yet more securely, in the permanent and sacred traditions of our institutional life. Were evidence needed, let that tribute in 1918 suffice, and of which later.

If we turn to the first report of Dr. Pond, we discover the convictions, methods and ideals which his life progressively realized. Of the beginnings of chemical instruction, he wrote: "But nothing must cause us to lose sight for a moment of the fact that the importance of our work—consists in building a broad and solid foundation in the science, and hence *no inferior work can* be accepted here—and we shall at no point allow ourselves to lose sight of our main purpose, namely, that only complete mastery of the groundwork of an extensive study can form a true and enduring inspiration for its continued pursuit." Thirty-two years of passionate, unswerving devotion to that sound principle has been one of the strong moral forces at Penn State. Of the laboratory, he said: "The teacher should never be absent, but should be always on the alert to see that no time is lost, no opportunity is omitted to drill in forming habits of accuracy and cleanliness." The laboratory and all advanced instruction must develop a good manipulator and technical worker, yet "the real object lies far deeper than this, and is not reached short of a severe discipline upon every faculty of the mind, such as very few branches of study can achieve." If that doctrine savors of educational puritanism one may imagine the reply of Dr. Pond would have been, "make the most of it, its true."

Concerning department plans and ideals, the same report continues: "I see no reason why we should not expect, in the very near future, to have here as perfect and successful a chemical department as is to be found in any institution, and to offer to our students every opportunity that can be afforded in any institution in the land." The handicaps were many, the disappointments often keen, the facilities not what he craved, yet in the real sense in which the teacher is fundamental, the same in which Zoology was Agassiz; Botany, Gray; or Psychology, James; Chemistry had a creative and vital source in the personality of Dr. Pond.

The Armory and Gymnasium

The combined armory and gymnasium of 1889, supplied with movable apparatus brought another desertion of Old Main. With its improvised annexes, brick encased temporary dormitories, it has served, with the addition of the Track House built in 1903-04 at a cost of nine thousand dollars, to provide for a wide variety of uses. The Armory has witnessed innumerable contests, military drills and formations, alumni banquets and reunions, balls formal and informal, mass meetings and class scraps, some of which fairly rocked the "stately tower" itself. It still stands to serve, although its ivy vines can neither hide the inherent ugliness of its walls, nor militate against the error in not having it face the rising sun. The whole architectural ensemble (I almost wrote scramble), its necessity and utility granted, is a living example of the genuine things Penn State has done with meager resources.

Women Go Out from Old Main

Provision for women marks an important step in this new institutional expansion. The Free Lance in January 1889 comments in glowing terms upon the array of new buildings; but voices the need for a "Female Seminary and a Preparatory Building. As it is, Prepdom occupies the east third of the Main College Building, and the west third is occupied by the ladies and several families. Thus the College department is confined to the central third of the building receiving jars from both sides." In June 1889, the "jar" from one side is to be allayed, and the undergraduate response is true to form: "Our co-eds are to have a cottage all to themselves with big porches, cozy rooms, and lots of hammocks_____m_____m." As a preparation for the "larger freedom" in the offing, the rules relax so that the "College Parlor is open to both sexes, Wednesday evenings from the close of Rhetoricals to nine P. M. during which time the ladies without special permission can meet their friends."

The credit for the beginning of proper, in the sense of non-primitive, conditions for women is due to the coming of Miss Harriet McElwain. The title of Superintendent of the College Parlor and of the Culinary Department had given way to that of College Matron. It was followed by Preceptress, and in 1877 by Lady Principal. To the latter post and instructor in History, Miss McElwain was appointed in 1883. It was her consistent presentation of the need of better conditions for women students that finally issued in results. Her plea to the appropriations committee in 1889 led to the erection of the Ladies' Cottage. It functioned, as our modern terminology has it, as a model home, in which Domestic Economy was lived, rather than taught. Home Economics proper, really dates from 1907. But the arts and refinements the social amenities and the cultural use of leisure were enforced in the Cottage, and through the recommendation of Miss McElwain, the curriculum for women was enriched by opportunities for the pursuit of art and the study of music. The establishment of Industrial Art under Miss Anna E. Redifer in 1889 brought to the entire College, through the years, a sense of the pervasiveness of beauty and art in all conduct and life.

A minute of the Board of Trustees upon the retirement of Miss McElwain after nineteen years of service will best show how her work and influence affected the College during this important period. "During her earlier connection with the Institution, besides having charge of the Women's Department in close and insufficient quarters, she had done her full share of teaching—with a clearness, intelligence and breadth of view that rendered her work among the most conspicuously successful of any in the College. With the growth of the Institution, her duties as Secretary and Registrar and as in charge of all the general correspondence of the President's Office demanded more and more of her time until she came to be the central source of information and direction with regard to all the details of administration.... It is difficult, if not impossible to overestimate the importance of her services to the College during the period of its rapid development, which began soon after her appointment to the Faculty. Her conscientiousness and fidelity in the performance of every duty, her quick and intelligent sympathy with the interests of the body of students, every one of whom she knew by name and character, and her high standards of what a true College life should be, were all a constant source of inspiration and help to those with whom she came in contact, and it is safe to say that the students who were connected with the College during her term of service regard hers as the most helpful single influence exerted upon them during their student life."

Old Main Resents the Exodus

During this period of building a new College, six dwellings were erected, which in turn released additional dormitories and room in Old Main. Alterations in the interior were, however, made to provide for College activities which perforce remained in the building but which had outgrown their quarters. Thus the chapel was enlarged in 1887-88, by uniting the two floors, the lower the original dining room and later gymnasium, with the original chapel on the second floor. What is well described as an "almost magical change" is made by the removal of the dark and forbidding box stairways, the object of so many uncomplimentary remarks, and the erection of others, broad and ample, and abundantly supplied with light by windows cut through the solid stone walls of the central and eastern wings. The lighting of the entire building with "incandescent electric lights" in 1887 "has also proved a great convenience." Nine years later, a new roof of diverse architecture was put on, the circular tower was replaced by the familiar serial box-like structure, said by the super-imaginative to be replica of the tower on Independence Hall. Old Main was beginning to lose her identity, but at the same time was bidding for the perpetuity of sentiment.

The new chapel, just mentioned, seated six hundred, and considerable enthusiasm was expended upon its rather "ornate ceiling, massive pillars," and particularly its "opera chairs." There seemed to be a breath of cosmopolitanism, enhanced by the folding seats and the commodious wire hat-holders, each seat numbered as it was by what appeared a silver check. The spacious platform amply seated the Faculty, the center and left tiers accommodated the student body, while the right row of seats provided "splendid isolation" for the department of women. The gallery was reserved for public occasions and bell room, until about 1900 when the growing student body forced the Freshmen to the upper floor. The seal of the Commonwealth and the portraits of some of the worthy founders of the College looked down from the surrounding gallery, while a semi-transparent curtain over an offset of the platform told its mute tale at morning chapel of properties and rehearsals of coming dramatic events.

From Chapel to Auditorium and Library Rooms to Carnegie Building.

The Commencement of 1902 marks an important stage in College annals, since it brought the first unconditional gift of a building to the Institution. Plans were drawn and prints were distributed to the audience for a projected enlargement of the Chapel. An annex with spacious platform, organ chamber, auditorium with ante-rooms was to be added to the north side of the Old Chapel. Incorporated with it, the seating capacity would be increased to twelve hundred exclusive of galleries. Prophecy and imagination gave substance to the enthusiastic belief that the uncomfortably crowded conditions on any public occasion, as well as the daily needs for larger quarters for chapels and assemblies would bring a response from the friends of the College. Since 1893, the maintenance costs had so greatly increased, that the legislative appropriations for buildings ceased for a time. An appeal to the public was the natural way of relief, particularly so for those welfare and student buildings which the State could scarcely be expected to furnish. In

1902 and again in 1904, Dr. Atherton had a list of needed buildings and endowments, privately printed and circulated with the hope of enlisting the interests of donors. These lists ran into the millions as the vision splendid grew; and efforts were made to realize them. Indeed their partial realization are an earnest of what the later years have brought in Booster Campaigns, Alumni Fund, the Welfare Building Campaign, and the Bond Issue, which succeeded while it failed.

Mr. and Mrs. Charles M. Schwab were present at that most famous Commencement of 1902, when Mr. Schwab delivered the principal address. Leaving his seat upon the platform, he consulted with Mrs. Schwab for a moment, and generously offered to carry out the plan of enlargement. His keen and clear grasp of the situation led him to see the temporary and insufficient relief which the plan at best afforded. A second consultation followed while the audience waited in breathless, dramatic suspense. Soon came the announcement of the splendid gift, an auditorium, a separate building, adequate and fitting for the Institution, and Institution which has ever called out the loyal support and counsel of Mr. Schwab as an honored member of the Board of Trustees. The Auditorium was dedicated June 16, 1903, the only regret being the wholly unexpected and wholly unavoidable absence of the donors. Personal representatives, there were; and this message signed by Mr. and Mrs. Charles M. Schwab was read: "Though absent, we are with you in spirit today. We wish you all every happiness. We trust that the future will hold for us health, and conditions that will make it possible for us to realize our hopes and wishes for State College." President Atherton in accepting the trust responded as follows: "I accept these keys, and the custody of this noble and beautiful building, with a deep sense of gratitude to the generous donors, and of responsibility to trustees, to faculty, to students, to alumni, and to the Commonwealth of Pennsylvania. And I here dedicate this Auditorium to the cause of sound learning; to the advocacy and promulgation of truth in every department of human thought; to loyalty, patriotism, and unselfish consecration to public duty; to the service of Religion, pure and undefiled." Appropriate acknowledgements of gratitude were voiced in Resolutions of the Board, tendered in casket of artistic design and locked with a golden key. A loving cup from the student body to Mrs. Schwab carried something of the meaning of this gift to them. For the faculty, Professor F. L. Pattee spoke the Dedication ode, The Message of the West. A few stanzas from this noble epic must suffice to show how interwoven are industry and spiritual achievement, material progress and cultural advance in art, work, and religion:

"Ah who shall say!
When souls are quivering with the thoughts of God,
When speed and light and power
Obey man's little hour
And tremble at his nod;
When lightning and fire
Are slaves to his desire;
When earth is shaking neath his rush and roar;
When East and West are one,
And Time has been undone,
Ah, who shall say we have no makers more?

Whoever finds the way
From dust and din one jot to set us free,
To ease one jot the trammels of the clay,
Our prophets, poet, evermore shall be.

All honor to the men who make,
The men, who toiling low upon the clay,
Seek out the easier way
For us to take;
But he supreme our seer and poet is

Who, standing firmly upon the things of earth
And knowing well their worth,
Points to eternities,

Points to the world unseen
That towers o'er human pile and mere machine.

Then was it not,
A seer's, a poet's thought,
Here in the path of eager youth
In quest of truth,
Of tool and toil in quest,
The strong new learning of the rising West,
Here at the cross-roads where the thronging feet
Of youth and duty evermore shall meet,
To build this shrine, this white and silent dome,
For higher things the home?

Who founds a College hall devote a Truth
Builds on eternal youth,
Who builds where dawning manhood peers
With measuring eye adown the years,
Who raises by the path a shrine
To higher strivings dedicate and things divine
Builds for eternities,
And makes for evermore the future his.
This solid dome shall last
When thrones and kingdoms have been overcast.
Old shall it be,
Old as the crumbling marbles over sea,
Lintel and step shall wear at length away,
Girder and wall shall sink in slow decay.

But ah, before that day
What mighty lessons shall these shades convey!
What teeming tide on tide and file on file

Shall surge from age to age adown this aisle!

Forever young,

Young hearts forever here,

No age in this fair hall, no dole and tear,

But hope eternal,—joyous anthems flung

Upon the freshness of the morning air,

And courage, brother love, and visions fair:

Forever shall it be,

The Alma Mater is forever fair."

Through the generosity of Mr. Andrew Carnegie, the Library, too, made its exit from Old Main. As a Trustee of the College, Mr. Carnegie served from 1886 to 1916 and had shown a genuine interest in its development through his own activities and by enlisting other public men in its behalf. In an official Manual of the Public Benefactions of Andrew Carnegie, his donation to this institution is cited as among the earliest of his gifts to Colleges, and was motivated by his friendship and regard for President Atherton and General Beaver. From these somewhat personal beginnings, the scope of his benefactions, and the Manual continues, to educational institutions began to broaden until they vitalized higher education in practically every State in the Union.

On January 26, 1899, the Board of Trustees received a communication tendering the sum of one hundred thousand dollars for the erection and equipment of a library building on condition that the State make an annual appropriation of at least ten thousand dollars for maintenance. "The College," he wrote, "is doing such a great work for the State that I do not think any individual should contribute money to it for additional buildings, unless the State agrees to maintain them. It is a duty which the State owes to its bright young men who attend the College of their own State instead of going to other States for their education. Born Pennsylvanians, they grow up Pennsylvanians." The practical and legal difficulties in the way of a continuously binding Legislative guarantee, led to the Board's assuming, in a manner satisfactory to Mr. Carnegie, the responsibility for adequate library maintenance. The amount pledged was increased by the donor to one hundred and fifty thousand dollars, and the present building was erected and furnished.

The library itself had passed through the usual stages of comparative neglect, inaccessibility, and lack of organization. In an inventory of 1857, it is credited with one hundred and ninety volumes, augmented by the opening of the College in 1859 to some fifteen hundred volumes. The first librarianship consisted in acting as custodian of the key. Later under the watchful eye of a busy teacher librarian, it was open an hour per day, and "at a time convenient to teachers and students not otherwise occupied in the regular duties of the School." During the decade 1879 to 1889, with slight student assistance, Professor Charles F. Reeves, of the chair of Modern Languages and Librarian increased the service and secured added support. During the College year 1889-90, the library was "moved into enlarged quarters, in the central wing on the second floor, and a reading room added." Here it remained until 1903. Organized and classified, however, and in charge of trained assistants, it became from 1890 on an integral part of all instruction. The professional services and personal devotion of Miss Helen M. Bradley, Librarian from 1895 to 1909; and Miss Anna Adams MacDonald, Assistant Librarian 1895 to 1907, brought the work to a high state of efficiency. The need for more adequate quarters, for larger book funds and staff, means to meet the widening opportunity for service to students and faculty, were urged. Much credit must perforce be given to those who labored under well-nigh impossible conditions to achieve results. Books, maps, charts, government documents were stored and stacked in various parts of Old Main, thus restricting their use in quarters never adapted to modern library usage.

The appointment of Mr. Erwin W. Runkle as Librarian in 1904, and the consequent organization of the library in the newly erected building, led to consistent advance in facilities, budget, staff, and service. The library grew from fifteen thousand volumes to nearly one hundred thousand, the Staff from two to twenty members; the budget increased more than five-fold. An historical collection of Penn State material, letters, documents, personalia, etc., was begun, and a museum opened for the display of items of interest. The George W. Atherton Library of Political History, and the James A. Beaver Collection of Pennsylvania History were established. A Summer School for Librarians was initiated with the cooperation of The Free Library Commission of the Commonwealth. Responsible departmental organization of the activities of the library was instituted, and the urgent need stressed, line upon line, precept upon precept, of a more adequate, better planned building, better facilities for work, and a radical adjustment of the budget for the library.

Mr. Runkle relinquished direction of the Library for full time teaching in 1924, the appointment of Miss Sabra W. Vought, has but accentuated the problems and needs incident to an increased student body, the demands of instruction and research; the development of a Graduate School. That these responsibilities and demands have been so successfully met in a building erected twenty-five years ago, and no more than fairly adequate at that time, is a tribute to personal efficiency, to professional mastery of library detail, and to a loyal staff. Special recognition is due to Miss Gladys R. Crammer who came to the Staff in 1921, and whose work as Assistant Librarian (and 1930-31 Acting-Librarian) has signally contributed to the contacts and many sided relations which a College Library perforce assumes.

The dedication of the Library on Pennsylvania Day, November 18, 1904 was a distinctive occasion in every way. The special guests included Mr. and Mrs. Andrew Carnegie, Mr. and Mrs. Charles M. Schwab, Governor and Mrs. Samuel W. Pennypacker, State Librarian, Thomas Lynch Montgomery, Deputy Attorney General, Frederic W. Fleitz, Major General Charles Miller. An Anglo-American brilliancy was cast over the exercises, also, by the valid hope that Mr. John Morley, as the honored guest of Mr. Carnegie would be the honored guest of the College, but unforeseen and unavoidable conditions intervened. In the forenoon, addresses were delivered in the Auditorium on Pennsylvania by Mr. Fleitz, and on Pennsylvania Libraries and their place in Education by Mr. Montgomery. Messages of congratulation to Mr. Carnegie and to the College followed from Governor Pennypacker and Mr. Schwab. A luncheon was served in the Armory to upward of five hundred guests, and at two o'clock, the exercises were resumed in the Library Building.

President Atherton voiced the happiness of all, the sense of fruition which this occasion brought, "the great working laboratory of the living soul of the institution," Mr. Carnegie responded in both a humorous and sober vein. Addressing Dr. Atherton, he said: "I wish to congratulated you, Mr. President upon the presence of the Governor here today. I judge that he has been sleeping as I was (laughter) and that he has awakened to the fact that of all the appropriations that he has approved none is capable of affording more good for this State than that to the State College.... If the teachers of mankind be right, from Homer to Washington, then the only solid foundation upon which can be erected a society marching ever upward, and where the right of Democracy can be maintained, must be the universal education of the people. How noble then your vocation and that of your fellows: to be laying well and deep the foundations upon which human society alone can rest.... it remains for me to perform the ceremony of handing over this library to you, Governor Beaver, as President of the Board of Trustees, and this I do in the earnest hope, nay the confident belief, that year after year it must be of greater and greater usefulness to the students of this institution, with the hope that in communing with the teachers of mankind you may not only become educated men but that here may be implanted within you the fruitful harvest of high ideals, from which, gentlemen, we expect you to press ever upward to the truest of all wisdom, the best. And what is the test of the best? That one may render precious service to his fellows, to his State and to his country.... General Beaver, I hand you this key. Take it, Sir, from one who loves Pennsylvania, who loves State College, who loves the people of the United States and who would serve them all well."

Expressions full of emotion and gratitude welled forth from General Beaver and Dr. Atherton, the depth and sincerity of which can only be appreciated by those who struggled with the difficulties, meager resources and growing responsibilities, which these gifts so wisely helped the institution to meet. The Trustees, the Faculty, and Students gave visible token of their appreciation by appropriate Resolutions, and with "the aid of the artist a fitting casket to contain them, striving thus to convey more fully what we could not ourselves express." The Student Body had its part in the day in presenting, a specially designed and made loving cup, by their representative, Mr. F. J. Saunders of the Senior Class. Mrs. Carnegie responded in words of such eloquence and simplicity, as easily to rank first in a day redolent of golden speech: "My ambition in life is to be the silent wife of my husband, the silent partner; to hold up his hands as far as I can and help him to do his work in the world; but out of the fulness of my heart I am obliged to speak today and tell you how deeply I thank you for this very great and unexpected honor that you have conferred upon me. I thank you very warmly."

Dormitories go out from Old Main.

In sharp contrast to generous private provision for some of the activities are the straits to which the institution was forced in providing dormitory accommodations for those outside of Old Main. The growth of the student body from eighty-seven in 1882-83, to two hundred and eighty-seven in 1892-93, and to six hundred and two in the next decade led to the erection of emergency dormitories. The Bright Angel[20] was built in the autumn of 1903 and Devil's Den and the Old Track House, the following year. These were comfortable, barrack-like structures of a single story (with exception of the Track House), with a narrow hall the full length of the building, from which opened the hermetic, scholastic cubicles. They housed about one hundred students, the track house serving as the forerunner of Varsity Hall, the others as the progenitors of McAllister Hall (1905), and later offspring Watts and Frear Memorial Dormitories. One may still observe the strains of service, angelic; and physiognomy, satanic of these forebears in the brick veneer annexes to the Armory, and in the Infirmary and Forestry Buildings, and until recently in the Old Mining Collection. One section was utilized, also as a Stores and Service Building until supplanted by the present one of steel and brick. Units constructed as units may be incorporated and built into harmonious and enduring structures, but the topsy-like growing of a series of temporary "sheds" (which circumstances forced to spring up like mushrooms)

---

[20] More euphoniously and perhaps more academically and scholastically they were known, also as Beta Alpha and Delta Delta.

are sad blots, now happily vanishing, upon a campus of otherwise inherent beauty and charm.

Thus have we followed the hegira from Old Main during the period in which The Pennsylvania State College was finding itself under the leadership of Dr. Atherton and General Beaver. These outward fortunes had also an inner history of changes cyclic and kaleidoscopic, to which the next chapter is to be devoted. A few words, however, will serve to complete the picture of Old Main, as she finally ceased to serve, deserted with only an immortality of memories which will never fail. Only administration, the general subjects of instruction and biology, headquarters of the Alumni Association, the Young Men's Christian Association, student dormitories and the Head Janitor, remained in Old Main to share its too evident decline. Liberal Arts accomplished its partial hegira in 1915-1916, in its first independent, unit structure, while biology tenanted a part of McAllister Hall ere it inherited the outgrown domain of botany. Music more and more, with dramatics a close second, domiciled within the Auditorium. The back wash and overflow from all parts of the new campus continued to use the facilities of the Old Chapel, Lecture Rooms, etc., and the newly formed School of Education defied the law of impenetrability in finding temporary quarters for its work in 1923. The unsafe conditions of the building led to the closing of its upper floors, entirely as dormitories in 1924, and it was abandoned for all or any classes four years later. The last guard of its cherished history and prepotent memories, General Administration, capitulated in July 1929, when the work of demolition began upon, with one exception, the only visible link between the College of 1859 and the "Colleges" of today.

CHAPTER 12

Administration, Instruction, and Student Affairs

"All that any educational institution needs is a good teacher and a good student, by which I mean the student who is earnestly and sincerely seeking what the College can give him. Anything in our entire system which will bring good students and good teachers together is good, and anything which tends to keep them apart is bad."

Professor C. L. Kinsloe

"This is my indictment: the enormous emphasis put of late years upon the "log" in American College and university education has unseated "Mark Hopkins" and rendered all but extinct the type which Garfield designated the "student."

Professor F. L. Pattee

We have now detailed the personality and task of Dr. Atherton as the College found itself and moved out from Old Main and through Old Main to a modern institution. We have traced the plants from College yard to Campus; from one building to twenty-one; from a student body of less than one hundred to one of over eight hundred; from a faculty of sixteen, to one of eighty-six; from a graduating class of three, to one of nearly one hundred. There remains to be considered the more hidden and intimate changes, in administration, personnel, courses of study, physical and social activities of student body. Entrance conditions were progressively raised, a select list of Normal and High Schools made up, graduates of which were provisionally admitted to the Freshmen class in lieu of examination. The minimum age limit for entrance was raised to sixteen years. In 1895, the lower or B. Preparatory was dropped. The College was beginning to set standards for the schools of the State. The sub-freshman class of one year was "retained until such time, only, as the requirements for entrance to College could be reasonably met." Provision for advanced standing was made in 1902, based upon the completion of entrance credits, and equivalent course work pursued within two years of application. New courses were added as follows:

1882-83, Latin Scientific
1883-84, Mechanic Arts
1884-85, Ladies Course in Literature[21]
1886-87, Mechanical Engineering
1887-88, Physics and Electrotechnics
1890-91, Biology
1890-91, Mining Engineering
1893-94, Electrical Engineering
1893-94, Mathematics
1895-96, Sanitary Engineering
1895-96, Classical

---

[21] Evidence that this course did not lead, necessarily, in the line of least resistance is shown by a faculty minute in 1889 in which a young lady was permitted to substitute Determinants for Junior French, Integral Calculus for Horace, and Quarternions for English Literature.

1896-97, Philosophy
1903-04, Industrial Chemistry
1903-04, Modern Language and Literature
1905-06, Forestry
1905-06, Electro-Chemical Engineering

Prizes and rewards were offered for excellence in entrance examinations for scholarship and, achievement, chief of which were Roberts' Military Prizes; and the McAllister and Orvis Prizes; the President's Award; the Agricultural, Physics, Natural Science, and Biology Prizes. But the most signal recognition came in 1902 through the establishment of the John W. White Fellowships and Scholarships. The donor is one of the most distinguished of Penn State Alumni. Dr. Atherton characterized this gift as "not only in itself an occasion for profound gratitude, but is made doubly precious to the College because it is to serve as a memorial to the donor's father, the Reverend John W. White, who was, for many years, one of the most beloved and acceptable preachers at the College." In 1904-05 the Trustees established the ten Freshmen Scholarships for the highest general averages for admission. The Louise Carnegie Scholarship Fund supports since 1905, twelve annual awards. The Phi Kappa Phi of which Dr. Atherton was one of the founders, established a chapter at the College in 1900, the forerunner and potent incentive of some twenty other scholarship organizations on Campus. The early nineties marked an effective interest in and provision for the general courses. The classics were dropped in 1885, but re-established within a decade. Separate chairs and departments of English and Rhetoric, Modern Language, History, Economics, Art, Music, Philosophy, appear. In the President's Report for 1894, it is asserted that the "rapid growth of the technical departments has absorbed all available resources, and heretofore it has been impossible to maintain the general courses with the same breadth and efficiency. Not all students wish to become engineers or chemists. The demand for extended courses of instruction in biology, history, languages and literature, economics, and the whole range of political and social science is active and urgent among our students, and the number desiring to take such courses leading to the degree of Bachelor of Arts increases every year. The

State Institution which fails to provide as amply for that class of students as for those preparing for the industrial professions does an injustice to a great body of its youth by rigidly limiting and narrowing their choice of studies, and disregards the highest interests of the State itself." The bare enumeration of the outstanding teachers who began their work in this decade shows the increased provision for non-technical training; the real origin of Liberal Arts in the College; as well as the enrichment of the technical courses themselves: E. E. Sparks, H. T. Fernald, Anna E. Redifer, Jennie J. Willard, Benjamin Gill, W. C. Thayer, F. P. Emery, J. M. Willard, E. W. Runkle, F. L. Pattee, J. H. Tudor, C. D. Fehr—the list lengthens impressively, J. H. Leete, I. L. Foster, A. H. Espenshade, H. K. Munroe, N. C. Ridge, Carl L. Becker. The next decade added for years of service, as well as many for briefer periods, Miss L. V. T. Simmons, H. F. Stecher, T. C. Gravatt, J. H. Frizzell, P. O. Ray. For briefer but equally important services, the list must include Miss Nichols, Miss McFeely, Miss Snyder, Messrs. Field, Powell, Trenholme, Grumbine, Ansart, Babb, Calkins.

The formation of the Schools was a most noteworthy step in Institutional consciousness. As early as 1874, a committee consisting of President Calder and Professor McKee was named by the Board "to consider the propriety of division into Schools." Evidently the time was not propitious, as no report seems to have been made. However, in the year 1894-95, Standing Committees of the Faculty are emphasized, followed naturally by Division or Course Officers. There fell to these the duties of scheduling, care of absences and to some extent discipline. This served to relieve for a time the pressure of details in the Executive Office; and also the Faculty Minutes from that plethora of "cases" so prodigal of time and energy. These were Deans in training. Early in the year 1895, the Executive Committee approved the organization of the College into seven schools as follows:

School of Agriculture, H. P. Armsby, Dean
School of Natural Science, G. G. Pond, Dean
School of Mathematics and Physics, I. T. Osmond, Dean
School of Engineering, L. E. Reber, Dean
School of Mines, M. C. Ihlseng, Dean

School of Language and Literature, Benjamin Gill, Dean
School of History, Political Science and Philosophy, George W. Atherton, Dean

On January 3, 1896, the Board of Trustees confirmed the form and personnel. The Schools were less autonomous in those early years; in no sense legislative; advisory and academic rather than administrative. The General Faculty was still a unifying agency, an all inclusive body, the seat of final authority. The Deans had not acquired the halo of distinction which the years have brought. Even as Deans, "Poppy," "Lordy," "Swampy" and "Ike" were bandied titles more honored by students than the more dignified academic ones. Teachers, too, had that intimacy of contact which led to friendly relations indicative of genuine influences. Thus "Herby," "Peeny" "Sir Michael," "DeltarX.," "Baldy," "Gravy," "Unser Karl," "Freddie," "Frenchie," "Doc," and others were known and respected in their sobriquets, and no other identification was necessary.

The nineties were marked, too, by the multiplication of Faculty Organizations. Chess and whist clubs had existed and also sporadic attempts at dramatic expression and cultivation. A Shakespeare Club became the Friday Club in 1892, continuing until 1907. A Faculty Newspaper Club under the inspiration of Professor E. E. Sparks and Thomas W. Kincaid flourished, alternating with the Scientific Association. The latter was formed on November 29, 1893, and left a record of one hundred and sixty-one meetings; before it succumbed to the disintegrating forces of more specialized groups, departmental and professional organizations. Its last meeting was held on November 1, 1904. Science was liberally interpreted in its deliberations, and after the piece de resistans, the paper of the evening has been delivered, many an academic problem or situation came in for a thorough airing. In 1896, the Literary Club was formed. Dr. Benjamin Gill was its founder, and until his death, its choicest spirit. This, the oldest of existing College organizations, has virtually emphasized by its activities in the College Community, the fellowship of scholarship and the practical value of ideals.

Repeated expressions of undergraduate sentiment led in 1892 to the shortening of the College year to thirty-six weeks. Seven years later the semester division of the College work went into effect. From 1892, the change of Sunday Chapel from afternoon to morning, "to conform with other Colleges," was made permanent. A system of demerits, administered during the seventies by the Military Department was replaced in 1883 be censure marks. Definite penalties were tabulated against the majesty of College regulations, and when the accumulations reached the danger point, the Faculty records became clogged with requests for remittance, excuses and claims of error, pleas for reduction within the safety zone. Sixty censure marks were accompanied by a notice to parents. This called out vigorous denunciation of the system as a whole in student quarters, as "antiquated, fossilized, and provocative of violations." The undergraduate post voices the sorry state of affairs to his sensitive soul in measured and more temporate language:

> We walk no more in the forest,
> We talk no more in the hall,
> But censure marks by the hundred
> Are hanging over us all."

The result was that the cut system replaced the mark system in 1890, with a variegated history of success and failure, with much matching of wits in defining and utilizing them, not only during term time as privileges or necessities, but before and after vacations to the manifest discomforture of the calendar. In 1907, the present regulations of "expected" attendance on all scheduled exercises, with the responsibility placed upon the instructor for a judicious application, superceded the cut system.

Material improvements, too, began to break up the splendid isolation and drab exterior of the Campus. On June 22, 1883, telephone connections were established. One of the neighboring town papers comments to the effect that "messages to and from the institution are quite numerous." Electric lights, as we have noted, were turned on the Fall of 1887, a small Edison Plant (three hundred and seventy-five, sixteen candle power lamps) was contracted for on August 10, 1887, at a cost of thirty-eight hundred dollars. Twenty-five acres were added to the campus in 1887 and the entrances improved by "handsome self-opening gates." "Patent pavement" replaced the path from Old Main entrance to the avenue in 1889, and in the same year a tunnel was constructed on the west side of the road, carrying steam pipes and electric wires from the first Power House north of the Mechanic Arts Building to Old Main and the laboratories. The hedge between the Ladies' Cottage and the Main Building was removed in 1890, the vineyard west of the Armory followed, orchards and timber made way for buildings, athletic fields and grass plots. One landmark only survives, and that but partially, in the botanical gardens; the ghost walk and the snarled and ancient wind-break along the roadway to the west of the Mineral Industries building were felled so recently as 1929.

Railroad accessibility was measured in the Sixties and Seventies by Spruce Creek, Lewistown and Bellefonte. In the Eighties were added Scotia, Lemont and Krumrine Crossing. The catalogue for 1885 projects the Beech Creek Line, "to pass through Bellefonte and thence into the Nittany Valley within one mile of the College. There is, accordingly, every promise that the College, in the course of a few months, will be one of the most accessible points in the central part of the State." As early as 1883, the Bellefonte and Buffalo Run Road was featured for early completion, but it was not until January 1892 that the right of way through College ground was finally secured. On Saturday April 2, 1892 at 1:30 P. M., the first train on the Bellefonte Central to the College was operated. A special excursion was run. Students, distinguished citizens, and presumably some teachers left the College at two, P. M. and arrived at Bellefonte at three. With recovery from the fatigues of rapid travel, the metropolitan celebration of the event and submission of the entire caravan to the art preservative, the express returned at five P. M.[22] On the following Monday, the regular schedule went into effect, with three trains a day—

---

[22] The author of "Chronicles" in the Free Lance writes of this junket; "But lo as the train approached its destination, great trouble fell upon the people, for the men-slayers had greased the tracks, yea, the rough and rocky men from State College had poured soft soap upon the rails. But forbearance was with the people, and sand failed not for the engine, and at the last hour of the day amid great rejoicing and commendation the people came out of the train."

modified during the years into a somewhat variable, highly flexible, betimes irregular schedule. Passenger service retreated as the inevitable competition of auto and truck became more acute; but in these latter days blowing a more lusty whistle as its cargoes of freight arrive; and the new vision of a main line outlet once more dangles before the eyes.

The town, too, responded to the new life and improvement on the campus beginning in 1887, but it did not become an incorporated borough until 1896. Bucolic specimens no longer ranged in its streets, and piggeries were banished, though not without both opposition and diplomacy. Fences were removed and sidewalks were replaced by permanent ones; both processes aided materially by the athletic celebrations and their "illuminations" which had their reptilian age in the nineties. Throughout their entire history, the College and town had paralleled in growth so that there has always been a community of interest. The population of the town in 1896 was approximately three hundred. There were one hundred houses, and the student body numbered three hundred and thirty eight. In 1900 the town had eight-hundred and fifty-one inhabitants; in 1910, fourteen hundred and twenty-five, in 1920, twenty four hundred and five, and in 1930, forty-three hundred and forty-eight. The College enrollment in the last named year was four thousand and forty-four, exclusive of the Summer Session. The streets have come out of the mud, two main thoroughfares paved, civic and public utility needs met, financial and business blocks erected, park and recreational facilities provided. Churches which would be distinctive in almost any city have been constructed in cooperation with State and National organizations interested in their student affiliations. Since May 12, 1898, The Times, a weekly paper has been issued. With the present forward looking community of more than ten thousand (citizen and students), every effort is being made to realize the modest slogan: "The Ideal Residence Town and Home of The Pennsylvania State College."

The College was a boarding school in its early days, with all the insularity and paternalism which that carries with it. In the early seventies, however, private clubs were formed, first in the basement of Old Main and later in the village. The College Dining Room under the Chapel became in 1877, the

Armory; and the basement under it the gymnasium; still "free fuel" and "use of cook stove" was as late as 1879 an inducement to students boarding themselves. Some of these clubs going out from Old Main developed a genuine spirit and individuality, adopted names and instituted "yells." The Duquesne was eminently practical, "I roar for the bread, more bread I roar." The Cottage incorporates as its Aegis the haste for morning chapel: "I dash for hash, for hash I'm rash." The P. S. C. Club builds its favored menu before our very eyes: "Buckwhe__buckwhea__buckwheat cakes," while the Delmonico wields a more subtle rhyme: "Rub-a-dub-dub, three men in a tub, the place to get grub is the Delmonico Club."

Of one fact there can be no doubt, these eating clubs did foster student spirit and early rivalries. They were the nurseries of the fraternities. They were the forerunners, too, of other student changes, activities, organizations, etc., which the famous classes of 1889 and 1890, more than any others, inaugurated and developed. During the seventies and early eighties, the sentiment of both Faculty and Board of Trustees was hostile to fraternities. During a part of that time, as noted, a pledge was exacted of entering students to refrain from forming or holding membership in a secret fraternity. The Board on at least two occasions commissions the President and Faculty to take steps necessary to dissolve existing organizations and to prevent their recurrence.

In 1872, a chapter of Delta Tau Delta was in existence at the College, but it surrendered to official disapproval. A chapter of Q. T. V., a society originating at the Massachusetts Agricultural College in 1869, was more or less active from October 1884. A general convention of this Fraternity (the first ever held at the College) met in May 1888. Following much activity upon the part of members of the classes of 1889 and 1890, together with prominent Alumni, the Faculty voted on October 13, 1887 to recommend to the Board that the rule prohibiting secret societies be rescinded. With some misgivings and much deliberation, the petition was held under advisement until June 29, 1887, when approval was voted. The response of the student body was no less deliberate, and it was not until April 19, 1888, that a request from certain members of the College to form a Chapter of Phi Gamma Delta was received by the Faculty. The inevitable committee was called into action, and a favorable report made a week later. The committee consisted of Professors Osmond, Buckhout, and Reber. Under date of May 17, 1888, the Q. T. V. Fraternity requested official recognition, and now with the usual proviso that the question of regulations be deferred, the application was granted. On October 4, of the same year, the sanction of the Faculty was sought for a chapter of Beta Theta Pi. Referred with power to Professors Osmond, Reber, and Pond; the minutes of October 11 record formal approval.

President Atherton welcomed the fraternities, and enlisted them in support of scholarship and college spirit. The first two fraternities, Phi Gamma Delta and Beta Theta Pi, secured houses for themselves the second year of their existence, and in the Report of the President for 1889, their enterprise and influence were strongly endorsed. "The enterprise of two of the College fraternities is worthy of special mention. They have within the last six months, taken possession of new and handsome cottages specially erected for their use, thus furnishing an important relief to the pressure upon the College rooms, and at the same time creating a change in the habit of social and domestic life among the members of those fraternities, and, indirectly, among other students, which is, in every way, as far as I can judge, beneficial and healthful." From these beginnings, there was a consistent growth; and at the end of the Administration, there were twelve fraternities, eight social and national, two professional, and two local.

College Colors, dark pink and black were adopted by the student body in October 1887; and the first College Yell a year later. It goes thus:

> Yah! Yah! Yah![23]
> Yah! Yah! Yah!
> Whish–wach! pink, black –
> P! S! C!

In 1890, the Athletic association voted to change the College colors to Navy Blue and White. The Yell is transformed, too, into one commendably

---

[23] Also printed Whish-whack.

brief: P.S.C. Yo! He! Hep! Rah! Ra! Boom! Rah!

Length dominated the succeeding Yell: some eighty words, and with vain and heathen repetitions. These were gradually ironed out into the preset euphonious form:

> Ss! Boom! Ah! Coo! Penn State!
> Yell! Yell! Yell! Again!
> We're from the land of William Penn!
> State! State! State!

The so-called "new" Yell and "Locomotive" Yell are worthy of transcription in our glandular history:

> Yah! State! Yah! State! Yah! State!
> Hoo-rah Penn State! Hoo-rah Penn State!
> P–E–N–N–S–T–A–T–E
> Penn State! ! !
>
> Rah! Rah! Penn State!
> Rah! Rah! Penn State!
> Rah! Rah! Penn State!
> Rah! Rah! Rah!
> Rah! Rah! Rah!
> Penn State! ! !

Of College Songs, first place goes unreservedly to Alma Mater, composed by Professor Fred Lewis Pattee in April 1901. It was printed anonymously in the Free Lance. The article affirms: "State is fortunate in one respect, she has an air which by tradition and by a natural process of evolution has become distinctly her own peculiar property. The stirring hymn by Converse, "Lead me on," first made prominent at Penn State by the Class of '95 who insisted on singing it on the Commencement platform, is now the logical State College song.... it lacks only words. With considerable hesitation I would suggest the following. May others follow until the true State College song has been found." The general sentiment of approval grew rapidly, and at the Alumni Dinner in June 1901, the Presiding Officer, General Beaver announced its adoption as the Official College Song, Alma Mater. Its reproduction here is a glad tribute to both the author and the song—the influence of which will outlive marble halls or stately towers of stone. Blue and White by F. E. Wilbut, and Victory[24] and the Nittany Lion by J. A. Leyden are other songs into whose lines thousands have poured tender sentiments and lasting devotions of College life. Special mention is, also, made of the Commencement Hymn by President Atherton, sung at every Commencement occasion from 1903 to 1924. Dedicated to the Class of 1903, it deserves a perpetual dedication to all classes, past and future:

"God of our fathers, by whose hand
Nations and men securely stand,
Vouch-safe to us Thy blessings now,
As in Thy presence here we bow.

Our fathers saw the "inward light
Of truth and duty, freedom, right;
When a harsh mother drove them forth
As wandering exiles o'er the earth.

On these fair shores their bars found rest,
The homes they builded Thou hast blest,
The tree they planted spreads its shade
O'er every valley, mountain, glade.

Through changing scenes of changing years
Through stress and toil, through hopes and fears,
The cloud by day, the fire by night,
Preserved their faith and courage bright.

The starry ensign they unfuried

---

[24] "Victory" was written by Mr. Leyden in response to an offer of a prize by President Sparks in 1913-14 for the best foot-ball song. It has ninety-nine out of the one hundred essentials of a perfect score.

Has flung its radiance o'er the world;
The slave goes free, th' oppressed look up
The nations sing a song of hope.

Help us to keep alive the fires
Enkindled by those honored sires,
Here consecrate the strength of youth
To hear aloft Thy banner, Truth;

And, as we face the future fair,
Guide Thou our steps with heavenly light;
Inspire our hearts to be like them -
Servants of Duty, Truth and Right."

Athletics prior to the nineties were largely spontaneous and unorganized. Such games as were arranged both at home and abroad were preceded by specific faculty permission. The earliest sport seems to have been Cricket, sponsored by urban students sent to the Farm School in the mountains to develop physique and to reform their ways in a temptationless environment. The first faculty action occurs under the dates of March 16 and 23, 1866 when there was granted "A Play Ground twenty-four rods by twenty rods, with the pale fence of the nursery as one of its shorter sides, and to the clump of trees east of the College." This was a sport of outdoor gymnasium, with parallel bars and other improvised apparatus. In a perfectly riotous fashion, it was voted on March 17, 1871 to allow as much of College grounds as needed for base-ball ground." Before the end of the decade the enthusiasm grows so as to call for Legislation on the use of the front campus, times at which games may not be played, and even holding the students "responsible for the conduct of their guests when invited to play upon College grounds." In 1872, a petition for an indoor gymnasium is laid before the faculty. With genuine foresight, the student point to a rare opportunity to secure apparatus from a nearby town. The faculty countered by deciding "to let the students take the matter in hand and see what they can or will do."

The earliest base-ball games were with local teams, Lock Haven, Bellefonte, Boalsburg. The faculty minutes of June 16, 1866 record a gracious permission to the Union Base-ball Club to play at Lock haven, July 4. From this time, frequent references to base-ball occur. The game developed its traditional hero in "Monte" Ward whose pitching defied all known laws of gravitation and of delivery. Harmless entanglements in academic discipline, or difficulties with the intricate demands of class room routine engendered then as later those familiar defenses mechanisms of undergraduate loyalty to the team. Community and College sentiment were upon occasion organized to keep these antediluvian heroes of athletics upon their pedestals. The champions of Centre County in 1875, bear proudly upon their bosoms, P. S. C. On June 27 1879, the "College Club" as it is called played by permission with a "picked nine of Bellefonte," described as "full of conceit and perhaps a little, just a little beer." The outcome as a matter of important record is that "the College catcher suffered a severe injury in the eye, and has to retire." The urban encounters, some of the details of which may be apocryphal, were a preparation for College contests, the first of which appears in the faculty minutes authorizing a game with Bucknell University at Williamsport in June 1882. Four years later, the College Club joined the State Association of College Base-ball Clubs.

To President Burrowes must be awarded, as we have seen, the palm for the earliest mention of foot-ball. The Report for 1870 contains these lines: "No death occurred, and there were few cases of indisposition, except those arising from slight hurts at work or play—base-ball and foot-ball having received a due share of attention at leisure hours." Kicking and carrying a foot-ball about on the front campus, even when it calls out special faculty favors and regulations scarcely assumes sufficient vigor, however, to constitute the beginning of football at the College. Nor, perhaps, those two match games with Bucknell in November and December 1881. Express faculty permission was secured for the game at Lewisburg, the number of players, the time of departure, and of return. The minutia, always relatively unimportant were "inadvertently violated," and when the return game at the College was under discussion, the guilty players were first penalized, but later absolved, conditions in extension being both exceptional and critical. Both games were won by "our team." The Bellefonte Watchman describes the "boys as returning home in high spirits. They say they were most courteously treated by the University fellows, who lustily cheered them on leaving Lewisburg."

The officials of this contest were, according to a letter of J. P. McCreary '82, J. G. White, Umpire, J. P. Mcreary, Referee, and G. C. Butz; Scorer, the team, William Bruner, C. S. Chadman, J. M. Dale, Robert Tait, J. H. Hollis, C. C. Chesney, R. F. Whitmer, P. D. Foster, W. R. Foster, J. D. McKee, M. E. Baldwin. The Bucknell Mirror spoke of the Penn State team as "well uniformed and disciplined, whereas our boys, although having considerable practice, were not up to all their dodges." The score was nine to nothing in favor of State, and "Old Billy Hoover," tailor and confectioner of the Shingletown Gap made the togs."

Between this and the organization period of athletics in 1887, no record of a foot-ball team or of games played is to be found. The point of contact was evidently not lost, for in 1887, the first regular foot-ball squad finds a worthy opponent in Bucknell. A game at Lewisburg was played on November 12, and a return game at State College on November 19. Both games resulted in victories for our "first eleven, the first touchdown came within two minutes after the game had been called...The teams were well matched in size and strength. Neither side could gain anything by what is called rough playing, and all the points scored were made by the skillful playing of "tricks," the best of which was the one so frequently played by our half-backs." That team, by virtue of priority, its guilty knowledge of the precarious success of "rough play," and still more by the stellar role of its ingenious half-backs who could so frequently turn the trick, merits amply a place on the roll of honor:

Quarter-Back—Linsz, G. H.
Half-Backs—Jackson, J. P., Mitchell, J. G.
Full-Back—Mock, J. G.
Rushers —Leyden, H. R., Rose, J. R., Hildebrand, C. C., Kessler, R. H., Weller, J. S., McLean, H. B., Barclay, W. L.

This is the team that caused the Free Lance of November 1887 to break forth: "At last a foot-ball team has been organized. "Now, "let her go. P. S. C. Hep! Hep! Hep! Boom!" Since which time "she has gone and with a fair 'lion's' share of victories, defeats, and loyalties.

The schedule for 1888 included games with Dickinson, Lehigh, and Bucknell, and the year following with Swarthmore and Lafayette—Dickinson canceling. From these beginnings the schedule lengthens and broadens to include contests with the principal Colleges of the East, South, and of the mid West—with post season games on the Pacific Coast. The formation of the Pennsylvania Inter-Collegiate Foot-ball association was effected in the Spring of 1891, the inspiration of which goes to Colonel J. F. Shields, now the honored President of the Board of Trustees of the College. The League was made up of Franklin and Marshall, Swarthmore, Haverford, Bucknell, Dickinson, and Penn State. Promptly, Penn State won the pennant, and upon the occasion of bestowing the honors, miniature silver foot-balls with "State Champions, P. S. C. 1892" were awarded. The coveted "S" on the sweater, Blue and White, as a distinctive reward followed in 1894. But the "Lion" looked for yet more strenuous conflicts outside the league. The series with the University of Pennsylvania began in 1890. Although it was not until nine years later that a near victory, a tie score, was secured. The team of 1911 "turned the trick" and the following year repeated the record. The series with the University of Pittsburgh was opened in 1893, with a decisive victory for Penn State. Throughout the years of amicable but strenuously fought contests, the Lion sharing both reverses and victories, there is a proud record of institutional loyalties and broadmindedness. The record of the Pitt-Penn State series at the close of the season of 1930, is Won by Penn State, twelve: Won by Pitt nineteen; Tie Score, two. The date of first games with some of the larger institutions are, Navy, 1894; Cornell, 1895, Princeton, 1896; Army, 1899; Yale, 1899; Harvard, 1913, Dartmouth, 1917. Fate has occasionally served up a clean slate as the goal of goals, and while Penn State has always "emphasized the team," individual "stars" shine out in fond undergraduate hearts. Names like Randolph, Cartwright, Ruble, Murray, Wood, School, Very, Mathe, Miller, Bebout, Berryman, Dunn, Forkum, Hewett, Harlow, McCleary, Higgins, Way, Haines, Killinger, Robb, Conover, Bedenk, Wilson rise spontaneously. Let the Dean of American Foot-Ball, however, acclaim our local hall of fame Penn State on the All American Teams 1889 to 1924."

All American Teams of Walter Camp 1889-1924.

1898: 3rd Team—Randolph, Guard

1906: 1st Team—Dunn, Center

1911: 2nd Team—Very, End

1912: 2nd Team—(Very), End

1913: 3rd Team—Miller, Quarter

1915: 2nd Team—(Higgins), End

1915: 3rd Team—Berryman, Fullback

1919: 1st Team—Higgins, End

1920: 1st Team—Way, Halfback

1920: 3rd Team—Haines, Halfback

1921: 1st Team—Killinger, Halfback

1921: 2nd Team—Bedenk, Guard

1923: 1st Team—(Bedenk), Guard

1923: 2nd Team—Wilson, Halfback

"Pulling in the team" was one of the minor sports of the nineties. The tales of the game, a rehearsal of collective and individual achievements developed more oratory than Rhetoric 21, as coaches and players brought the glowing, burning news from the front. Most memorable was that the tie game with Harvard on October 24, 1914, when Penn State was gallantly granted the ball and when the inevitable celebration on the following Monday evening resulted in near tragedy. The votive offerings of wood were piled too high, the inflammatory oils too generously applied; the consequent explosion broke the silence of Old Nittany.

The dates for the inauguration of other sports at Penn State are as follows:

Inter-Collegiate Track, 1897

Basketball, 1896

Wrestling, 1910

Tennis and Soccer, 1911
LaCrosse, 1913
Boxing, 1919
Golf, 1922

From a proud record of athletic prowess, two events are chosen as outstanding and typical of the everwidening scope of competition, and the slogan of fair play under which the Penn State Spirit carries on whether to victory or defeat. The Seventh Olympiad Records in hurdles and track by Harold Earl Barron and Marion Lawrence Shields in 1920 exemplifies the first of these. The second has been described as "the finest spirit of sportsmanship ever displayed on Franklin Field." The Relay Races of 1920 at the University of Pennsylvania furnished the stage and "Larry" Shields the actor. As briefly portrayed by Graduate Manager Fleming, "an accidental foul at a turn of a race caused a Georgetown man to stumble and fall." Mr. Shields (sensing both accident and his own absolute innocence) "stopped and helped the Georgetown runner to his feet and started him on his way again, thus losing the race, but winning more for Penn State and for himself by this act, than he could ever have won by simply winning the event."

Somewhat informal organizations for the different sports preceded the formation of a general Athletic Association in 1888. Under the President of Gilbert A. Beaver, there were committees on General Athletics, Base-Ball, Foot-Ball, Cricket, and Tennis. Increased supervision here as elsewhere has accompanied the rapid growth of interest in physical training in our Colleges. But prior to 1894, the student body frequently raised and discussed the questions: Why do not the Faculty and Alumni take more interest in Athletics? Games are finances by subscription; by contributions from the players themselves; by a series of lectures and entertainments (for example, the first Masque Ball in 1891) for the benefit of athletics. However, in 1894, a Faculty Committee on Athletics was appointed. Article nine of the Constitution of the Athletic Association adopted February 6, 1894, provided for an Alumni Advisory Committee. This group was to consist of five members, elected by the Athletic Association at the beginning of each winter term, the chairman to be a resident of State College. The duties of the

Committee were "to devise ways and means for raising funds for the development of the several branches of athletics; to control expenditures and issue directions under which the Athletic Association shall disburse all funds." Subsequent revisions met the gaps and problems in divided responsibility and oversight between student managers and committees, the Graduate Committee, and the Faculty. An important amendment was enacted in 1899, whereby the separate auditing committee for the several sports were merged in "an advisory committee of three members who shall be alumni and two members who may be members of the Faculty (including instructors)." Later the demand arose for a permanent office and head of graduate interest in athletics, and in 1908, George R. Meek, of the Class of '90 was installed as the first Graduate Manager of Athletics. Others who have served either independently or as combined with the office of Alumni Secretary are P. E. Thomas, R. H. Smith, and since 1918, N. M. Fleming.

The earliest official coach was Nelson E. Cleaver, a graduate of Dickinson College, an assistant from 1887 to 1889 in the Preparatory Department of The Pennsylvania State College. Two years later, April 30, 1891, a petition "to found a chair of physical culture" was presented to the Board of Trustees. It was signed by ten Seniors, nineteen Juniors, Twenty-three Sophomores, thirty Freshmen, and by thirty-seven from A. and B. Preparatory Classes. The petitioners agreed to pay one dollar per student per term, not less; the said sum to be collected by the Business Manger of the College with other fees. It is of interest to note that the Committee which drew the paper was A. C. Read and J. E. Quigley, both subsequently members of the Board of Trustees, whose effective support of physical education persisted. The reason urged upon the Board were both characteristic and illuminating.

1. A healthy body is needed to maintain a healthy mind.

2. Without an instructor, there is greater danger of wrong use of the gymnasium.

3. There is need of constant responsible oversight of apparatus and equipment.

4. A great necessity exists of having a good trainer for our foot-ball and base-ball teams.

5. Good standing in athletics would widen the reputation of the College.

6. Such action as petitioned would put us in line with other prominent Colleges.

A minor prophet might readily portray the response to this appealing logic. In 1892, George W. Hoskins was appointed as the first instructor in Physical Education. Her served for four years, formulated physical exercises for all students, instituted physical measurements by classes. He offered four cups as prizes, reconditioned Old Beaver Field for general athletics, and trained teams that began to participate in contests with some of the larger Colleges. The question of playing the Coach was the occasion of the first storm to rock the academic calm—the faculty agreeing to a temporary concession provided that the practices were definitely known to our opponents.

"General" Hoskins as he was familiarly called was followed by Dr. S. B. Newton who visioned a department of student health and hygiene. He carried into effect a period of all student participation in physical training and widened the scope of inter-collegiate competition. In 1900, N. W. Golden, "Pop" as he was universally known, began a service of twelve years, in which the rapidly growing student body demanded increased facilities. Inter-class and fraternity contests were multiplied in the interests of physical training for all. Contacts with Secondary Schools were encouraged. Trustee (and as they grew to be athletic) Scholarships were increased. The teachers, even were envisaged in a scheme of training, which should iron out the kinks of asceticism and smooth the pedagogic brow. Mr. Golden saw Old Beaver Field outgrown, and during the early years of 1900 urged a second and third field. Just before the close of the administration of Dr. Atherton, a re-survey of the campus, immediate and future requirements was on the boards. With the aid of specific legislative appropriation and the cooperation of the Board, New Beaver Field was laid out in 1907-08. Following the resignation of Mr. Golden in 1912, separate coaches for the principal sports were named. Foot-ball particularly was in its golden age. Victories were the rule, if not commonplace, and the State was basking in that phase of athletic prowess wherein she consciously sought a first-line schedule. In 1918, Hugo Bezdek was called to the Physical Directorship—academic recognition given to physical education, Varsity and Recreation Halls erected.

Social affairs assumed a larger place, when on January 23, 1890 the ban against dancing in the College buildings was removed by the Trustees. Agitation began when the Armory floor was in prospect in 1887, but successive appeals were negatived. Though the students announced the action as "permitting hops at least three times a year," the principal event at Commencement received the more dignified title of Junior Reception or Assembly. The Senior "Hop" of the preceding April was a gala affair with fully two hundred and fifty people in attendance. "One hundred electric lights lit up the Armory till it shone and sparkled like a crystal palace." Carriages conveyed the guests coming by special train, from the station at "Krumrine Crossing" on both occasions. The second Assembly was described as "socially brilliant but not financially." It continued to be the climax of the undergraduate social occasions until the reconstruction of the Commencement Program in 1922.

Chapel at the College has always been more than an academic requirement, more even than a religious exercise. Chapel was the College expressing its spirit, its essential unity. It was one of the traditions, maintained (with the single exception of the period of the Great War) from 1859 to 1927. Saturday Chapel was abolished on January 13, 1881, and in recent years during examination week all Chapel exercises were suspended. Student wit has frequently directed itself to these suspensions from which there ensued no dire calamity. So also, many have been the militant campaigns to abolish compulsory Chapel, abolish it for Seniors at least. In several instances, in order that the camel might get his nose under the tent, a beneficient campaign to excuse the faculty from attendance was heartily sponsored. The increase in the student body made double Chapel necessary. Attempts to enrich it, to vary it with serious talks and spice it with peppy mass meetings failed. The old order was ineffective, the tradition was dead. A new and vital responsibility came with the abolition of Chapel in 1930, and of compulsory Sunday attendance in 1931.

Class scraps have had an almost "sacred" place in student life, with the ever recurring plea of how without them to keep alive and maintain College spirit. The cane rush seems to have been one of the most hazardous combats. It was abolished in 1901, because of possible injury to athletic prospects. It had a successor in the clash of classes following the first meeting of the Freshmen, and this persisted as late as 1923. The Picture Scrap, too, resulted unusually in destruction of property in which the innocent bystander and the enterprising photographer suffered along with the Freshmen. As late as 1908, six classes in two weeks were broken up by false alarms of an impending Freshmen picture. The Freshmen Banquet furnished the occasion of some of the fiercest inter-class battles, but also some of the keenest bits of strategy and subterfuge. It was definitely abolished in March 28, 1910. The Cider Racket was the occasion of a more general melee, but how to get the cider on the Campus without detection was the problem that worried the poor Freshmen. It was solved betimes by the ruse of empty barrels, or barrels filled with water, only; in hope of diverting attention or marshalling effort in the wrong direction. In one case the real cider barrel came upon the Campus innocently embedded in a family laundry basket, seemingly destined by its rural purveyors in ramshackle conveyance for one of the professorial domiciles.

But the distinctive Penn State Class encounter was the Flag Scrap. It had a continuous history from 1886 to 1916. In its Inception, the flag was placed upon Old Main Tower, the fight a sort of simultaneous wrestling match taking place on tower stairs and platforms with the accompaniment of generous dashes of water. Later the Armory was used or essayed to be used. The Class of 1895, first erected a pole, a practice continued. With small classes, it was a good, clean scrap, and needed no rules to guarantee both fairness and safety. But as numbers increased, abuses multiplied. The Campus was guarded for months to thwart the erection of the Freshman pole. Machines of wondrous construction, rivaling the modern tank, to charge withal were brought forth. Flour, soot, and even noxious fumes were utilized.

Persistent efforts to regulate and so perpetuate the scrap were unavailing. A contemporary description of a typical battle will serve to show, (though with some pardonable exaggeration) the hold which this traditional scrap had in the mind of the undergraduate. "Late Friday night the Freshmen were busy making arrangements for the hoisting of their flag, when it was discovered by the Sophomores, who kept up a vigil throughout the night, and succeeded in foiling the attempt of their antagonists to raise their flag pole on the Campus. The Freshmen then resorted to other means of displaying their colors, and unfurled them between the Cottage and the main building on a telegraph wire, near a role to which it was fastened. When the Sophs discovered this, a rush was made, the wire cut and the flag fell to the ground. A thirty minute scrap and the Sophs had half the flag, the freshmen half, and both had bruises, black eyes and sore muscles.... On Tuesday, the Sophs appeared in Chapel with the boutonnieres of the Freshmen Flag and the Freshmen retired out of class order to the Hall and awaited the Sophs. A general conflict ensued, but of short duration owing to the number of peace-makers who had assembled in great haste from the rostrum....Third days battle began at one P. M. on Tuesday, and the Sophs in minority gave over the colors coveted.... Thus ended one of the most hotly contested class fights ever witnessed at P. S. C. Tailors were in demand, the odor of arnica was distinguishable throughout the community and the quarters of the participants might have been taken for apothecary shops." With the old era of unlimited scraps declining as to a hazardous; set, organized and regulated contests appeared. Push Ball, Barrel, Tie Up, Sand Bag, Pants, and Tug of War have had their innings; with the fertile imagination of the collegiate body adding such "feats" of Freshmen discomfiture as Spirit Week and Poverty Day.

General hazing had its disquieting story, here as elsewhere. It resisted faculty and trustee edicts and lived its full and nine lives. Abolished for a season, when a pledge was the open sesame to the restoration of a luckless culprit under suspension, it flamed with renewed vigor. In the College year 1912-13, the Sophomore Class voted to abolish indiscriminate hazing. Poster Night was instituted, and the entire student body accepted the new policy of every man a square deal. Poster Night has evolved into a glorified Stunt Night, the Freshmen furnishing the entertainment, instead of those weary, all night marches and celebrations which harried the surrounding towns and country-side. Customs have become a matter of grave and serious concern, and a Tribunal has since October 22, 1913 sat in solemn state upon the Freshmen who does not know his "bible."

Green or blue caps have so firm a place in identifying the neophyte, that it is a matter of surprise that the custom dates but from March 8, 1906. The two upper classes with prudent oversight of Sophomores "voted the green caps for Freshmen." The editorial hope is expressed, "that the Freshmen will be favorably inclined to whatever the upper class committee decides upon." On May 3, 1906, the announcement is forthcoming; "the Freshmen Caps are here. They are a pleasing green in color, and although they are not striking, they are characteristic enough to distinguish the wearer." Not to be outdone in being characteristic and meek, one week later, the Freshmen Co-Eds are showing their class spirit by wearing green caps."

The rival literary societies as we have noted fostered debating, dramatic, and other literary activities. Rhetoricals were also a feature of extracurricular moment from the earliest days—presided over as was Chapel by the Faculty in order of seniority in academic rank. Later young instructors, of even non-linguistic subjects, earned their spurs by keeping the peace in Rhetoricals while Horatius held the Bridge, or Napoleon fought the Battle of Waterloo. With the decline and final disbanding of the Literary Societies in 1895, class debates and inter-collegiate contests multiply. President Atherton and Dr. Pond offered prizes in inter-class debates. Believe it or not, the competitive spirit was intense, and in those days reached the entire student body. In 1898 for a debate with Dickinson, a special train carrying a hundred passengers was run from Bellefonte. Dr. Atherton presided in place of General Hastings, detained by the exigencies of the Spanish American War. In 1902, a debating league was formed, and the fruits of victory were gleaned by such founders of debating at Penn State as Braucher, Wentzel, Groff, Borland, Lama, and the lamented Morrell Smith.

Organized dramatics date from 1897 with the formation of the Thespians. In the Cottage near the north entrance of the Ghost Walk on October 22, F. L. Pattee and J. H. Leete met with Andrews, Diehl, Beaver, Reed, Neubert, Strohm, and Yundt, to form a dramatic club. With laudable ambition and noteworthy achievement, classical plays first held the boards. The Rivals, She Stoops to Conquer, The School for Scandal, and Lend Me Five Shillings preceded the musical comedies of later years. The Penn State Players organized in 1920, and that it has become a real laboratory of dramatic art may be inferred from the performance in 1930 of its one hundredth play. The first German Play was given in 1909 and dramas in French, nine years later. The women of the College have also given occasional dramatic performances as special benefits, while the Christmas Party and May Day Celebration are annual fetes to which much artistic skill is devoted.

Class Memorials had their origin in a suggestion of President Atherton that the circular space in Old Main tower was left for a clock, and not for class numerals. The Class of 1904, in the Sophomore year nurtured the suggestion, and as a Class Memorial donated the Tower Clock. I transcribe, as historically important, the formal acknowledgment:

> Committee of the Class of 1904: C. S. Bomberger, Chairman) Chas. L. Armsby) R. W. Wray) I. P. Thompson) P. J. Morissey) M. J. Rentschler) Wade H. Barnes)

> June 20, 1904

Gentlemen:

I am directed by the Board of Trustees of The Pennsylvania State College to acknowledge on its behalf and place on record the gift to the College by your Class of a tower clock, and to express the very warm appreciation and thanks of the Board of Trustees, together with the pledge of the Board to preserve and maintain the clock both as a memorial of your class and for the uses for which it is designed.

This acceptance and acknowledgment that has been already

expressed to your class in public, but the Trustees especially desired that the act should become of the public records of the College. For myself, personally, I do not need to assure you how deeply I appreciate the gift, both in itself and in its far reaching significance. It will always be not only a memorial of the fine loyalty of your class to the interests of the College, but a stirring incentive to those who will come after you.

George W. Atherton

Secretary of the Board of Trustees and President of the College.

This was the beginning of a series of Class Gifts and Memorials,[25] a list of which follows:

Class of 1904: Tower Clock

1907: Atherton Alcove

1909: Headstone—Grave of President Atherton, Hospital fund $500

1910: Library Clock,

    Student Aid Fund $1000

1911: Granite Boulder in Open Air Theatre

    Base Ball Grand Stand (Assisted by Messrs. Hamill, White, and Shields of Trustees.)

1912: Wireless Tower

1913: Front Terrace to Old Main

1914: Pipe Organ

1915: Sun Dial, Front wall

1916: Auditorium Lamps

    Memorial Gateway

1917: Liberty Bonds, East Gate Memorial

1918: Liberty Bonds, East Gate Memorial

1919: Improving Open Air Theatre

---

[25] Honorable mention should be made of the Pugh Memorial Volume and Portrait by the Class of 1861; the Oil Portrait of Professor Josiah Jackson by the Class in 1892.

1920: Insurance

1921: Insurance

1922: Projected Swimming Pool

1923: X-Ray Outfit

    Building Fund

1924: Grand Piano, Building Fund

1925: Memorial Gate

1926: Building Fund

Classes of 1927 To 1931: Arboretum and Winter Sports

Religious instruction was coincident with the founding of the College consisting of Sunday afternoon services, faculty-taught Bible Classes, and later Young Men's Christian Associations and other Voluntary Groups. The transfer of the Sunday Service to the morning led to a wider choice of speakers. It also brought men like Dr. J. M. Gregory, Gerald Stanley Lee, Dr. Lawrence M. Colfelt for protracted periods of residence at the College, enriching our student life by many contacts. But best of all, it led to the pulpit ministry of Professor Benjamin Gill, who from 1899 to 1910 was College Chaplain, as well as teacher and Dean from 1892 to 1912. A volume of Sermons and Addresses printed by the College contains sections from one hundred and forty-eight sermons preached in the Old Chapel and in the Auditorium. The topics show a keen and sympathetic approach to the problems of life—some of them truly historic in the annals of the Institution. "The Problems of Life solved by Worship," the last service in the Old Chapel; "come let us reason together" on occasion of the "Strike;" or his last message on "Some Practical Bearings of a Belief in a Future Life" are indicative of their interest. The opening addresses of each College year reveal in a vital way the thoughtful care with which he chose his themes. Uncertainties and Success; Leaving Home; The Call of Religion; Under Changed Conditions; Symmetrical Manhood; Passing on the Torch; Academic Foundations; Picking up Religious Experience; Honoring One's Name; these are some of the subjects. Who cannot see in these a keynote for the year to come. As Professor F. L. Pattee writes in the Preface of the volume, the series as a whole "reflect in a remarkable way the spirit of the College life during the era they cover.... it is a series of sermons that is a part of the splendid history of the College and as such should be jealously guarded in its most sacred archives." Dr. Gill possessed a true literary sense, and such addresses as Opening Young Eyes; Values inherent in a Friendship; The Evil Tendencies of a Good Life; The greatness that is right above us; A Man is worth what he can think; Lead Kindly Light; The Pronoun I; The Only Reasonable Form of Prayer contain genuine literary inspiration forged in the fires of a love for Penn State and of its student body. Thrice fortunate the institution that has such spiritual forces builded into its religious history. Supplemented as it has always been by a free pulpit, by volunteer labors and sacrifices, and by organized campaign movements of outstanding religious figures, it has issued in a type of social and moral leadership at Penn State in which we take just pride—a leadership such as what embodied, for example, in a "Dick" Harlow; a Bill Wood; a "Pete" Weigel; and Abbie Dorward; a Hugh Beaver; a "Daddy" Groff; or a Tom McConnell.

There would certainly be genuine interest on the part of a large group of Alumni and friends in quotations from some of Dr. Gill's addresses. For its historic value its insight and pathos; its rare blending of a matchless tribute to Dr. Atherton, with a self-revelation of the author's range of mind and depth of soul, I incorporate a part of Dr. Gill's Memorial Address, Moulded by An Idea delivered in the Auditorium, May 26, 1907.

"Very, very impressive was the face of our dead President as he lay here in his casket last summer. It seemed not of flesh but of marble, chiseled by some contemporary of Phidias, and seasoned somewhat by the lapse of time.

It showed us plainly this: that nature is a sure and effectual sculptor, that the thoughts and emotions of men gradually chisel themselves on the form and in the features. The ugly face of Socrates was made attractive by his inner thoughts.

In some of the faces of the early Caesars you can read the grandeur of the Roman Empire. Dr. Atherton was an unusually impressive

300

personality. In a body of assembled College presidents he was second to none in this respect. An idea contributed to this distinction of personality; the presence and constant operation of this idea rendered him an object worthy of careful study.... The idea I refer to was this: He thought of himself constantly as the President of The Pennsylvania State College.... That thought moved, swayed, ruled, and— toward the end—controlled and wholly absorbed him. And let me impress this fact: He was not the President of The Pennsylvania State College which he found here, but of the College *which was to be here*; the College which he was gradually been bringing here; the College, which, in spite of slow legislation and opposition *is* here, and is here to stay. A man coming here to a College so remote, so little known, so small, might easily have found it no great inspiration. But he came to this little village, call it a bunch of houses rather, with as much pride as he would have gone to Cambridge or to the presidency of his own college at New Haven, because he saw from the first, not the College that was, but that was to be.... Pennsylvania was to his thought an empire. This was the most ideal location in it. From the start, he dreamed of its extending avenues and walks and its noble buildings and thronging scholars. It was his Oxford, rather say, his Jerusalem, The Pennsylvania State College. I came here to see the College on the Saturday before commencement, 1892. For two hours and more, busy as he was, he went with me over the campus and among the buildings. He said: "I want you to go to my Mt. Pisgah," and he took me up to the top of "Old Main" and showed me "all the land of Gilead unto Dan." But what entertained me most was that I never saw in any man a greater enthusiasm for an idea than I saw in him that day. I have seen him on a thousand occasions since and I never saw him when this idea was not in his thought or when it could not be fanned suddenly into a flame. Furthermore, if you came as a member of his faculty, he wanted the same idea to take form in you,.... He quickly resented comparisons where there was the least disparagement of State.... For the last seven years of Dr. Atherton's life I was thrown into very close and tender relations with him. I saw his heart laid open scores of times as no other person did. I had the opportunity to test the sincerity of his motives and the nobility of his convictions.... I believe that he felt himself president of this College, under God, and sought to be ready at any moment to give an account of his stewardship.... in the silence of his office he was quietly and unselfishly making a College and making a village while others were studying how to make something out of the College or out of the village. In his conduct as a president his ruling idea was always to the fore. At Sunday service he presided with a quiet dignity uniform on all occasions, almost to the least motion. No outside matter of announcement was allowed to mar the order of service. The doctor of divinity or the plain parson alike spoke without any introduction, even on commencement occasions. In that way each service was a worship of God, not of men. It was the divine service of The Pennsylvania State College, in dignity and orderliness unsurpassed anywhere in the land. The same was true of the daily Chapel. He never failed to attend it and it was a source of much pain to him that any one needed to be exhorted to attend this service of a great brotherhood worshipping the divine Father....

The position of such a man, seeking to convince legislatures, to guide the counsels of trustees, to harmonize the differences among schools and departments, to coordinate departments in such a way that each shall have its related place and share, to bear with as well as to instruct the great body of students, to keep in sympathetic touch with the patronizing public, such a position requires great generalship, and herein his ruling idea served a noble purpose—He passed into the shadows embodying until the last, the idea which had controlled him and which sees us here today. He had never brought shame upon that idea, but always honor.

It was that idea that carved the lines of strength and grace upon his features; and that same idea, ruling in us, students, and teachers, and trustees, and friends of the College, will make us an institution honorable and to be honored."

Student publications have a varied past, but real history begins with the late eighties. They grew out of the ventures and adventures of the two literary societies—first as unprinted (and often unprintable) papers read before the members. The earliest was termed, "the Anonymous," whose motto was "Catch me if you can," issued in 1859 in diverse handwriting and containing enough wit, wisdom, and caricature to come under the ban of faculty censorship. The Weekly Argus and later the Spectator were like undergraduate papers in manuscript, the latter, however, attaining to the dignity of a printed title page. Annuals and special programs of anniversaries, inter-society debates and dramatic performances fed the fires of student publicity. The Cresson Annual, Volume I, November 14, 1873, makes it bow as "the first printed paper ever published at the Agricultural College of Pennsylvania; modestly but hopefully we tender this our effort, asking indulgence for its errors and a generous consideration of its merits." It was a two page sheet, one set solidly, both sides, with advertisements, the other giving a prominent place to the "Fourteenth Anniversary Program of The Cresson Literary Society, Agricultural College, Pennsylvania." This was embroidered with contributions on "Can Gravity Act Through a Vacuum;" Literary Societies; Home: Be Sociable; also a column of Jokes, another of Squibs, and a third, Facetiae. The second issue is increased in size but remains true to form except that its contributions are distinctly labeled, "Four the Cresson Annual." The issue of 1874, spurred the Washington Literary Society to issue, The Photosphere a twenty-four page paper. Editorial pride avers, "Of its kind, it is the first ever issued at the institution we feel assured our friends will accept this, the result of our inexperienced effort, with all due consideration." Pages sixteen to twenty-four are solid advertising, yet the editors bewail the fact that although the Photosphere is "the latest thing out," the editors are also "out, too, out of pocket."

The immediate forerunner of College Journalism was the Students' Miscellany, issued Friday, February 4, 1887, published by The Cressons. The editorial voices the value of a journal by students in the interests of the College. It hurls a stirring challenge to the student body: "Yale, Harvard and

Cornell have their dailies; Princeton, Dartmouth and even Allegheny at Meadville, and Bucknell at Lewisburg have their monthlies; why should we not follow their example? Can our inefficiency be due to lack of brains? In intellect we hold ourselves to be the equal of any College in the land. Can it be lack of numbers? We are more numerous than our neighbors at Bucknell. Can it be lack of College pride? Judging from all expressions on this point we can answer with an emphatic, "No." Energy and initiative only are lacking, the editors, Grace M. Moore and A. A. Patterson pledge the hearty support of the Students' Miscellany[26] to "any student who has the grit and energy to work this matter up."

A joint Committee of the Literary Societies accepted the challenge; secured the consent and cooperation of the faculty on March 7, 1887. There was issued the first genuine College periodical at The Pennsylvania State College. The Free Lance, Volume I. Number I bearing the date April 1887. The editorial board of this monthly publication admirably conceives its mission as an additional means on the part of students to make the ministry of the College more complete. It is to be a training for citizenship in the broadest sense. The ideals of the board are set forth thus: "The College paper should be a triple (?) bond of union: as an organ of the students it sums up their individual sentiments into a "collective will," whereby they may assert themselves; to the Alumnus it keeps fresh the memory of his Alma Mater; between Colleges it promoted friendship and wholesome competition. With these points in view the Free Lance launches on the College ocean. She hopes to be cordially received at all foreign ports, advocating in this respect "free trade." She will join in any alliance to rid the sea of pirates; she will consider herself responsible for all matter found on her deck and all property entrusted

---

[26] A sample gem or two may be tolerated: "Osaac was in the flood- but he was not drowned. He still pays the Highest Cash Price for Hides of all Kinds," "My stock of shoes, saved from the fire—though not damaged—I will literally give them away, at lower than Philadelphia Prices." The "Small Talk Column" contains such items as, "Merely say, Harrisburg" and Lieut. Pague smiles audibly, "The Professor of Chemistry raises a Herrick-cane in class occasionally," "The College Library is like a Sepulcher—once closes, it is never opened," "The right man in the right place— George W. Atherton."

to her care; and, above all, the great cause of inter-collegiate commerce demands her share of influence toward securing that perfection of our System of Education which holds out to every American Youth the means to the highest possible freedom, enjoyment and manhood." Comment is unnecessary, College student journalism has found itself. The Free Lance was issued until April 1904, ending with Volume XVIII, Number I. It was succeeded by the State Collegian published weekly, Volume I, Number I of the date of September 29, 1904. The name was changed to Penn State Collegian in 1911, and since September 1902, it has been issued semi-weekly. It has altered its size and form, adopted its activities and policies to the needs of a growing College. It has printed a Summer Collegian, extra issues when occasion demanded—in short leading in as well as following the principles and spirit of Penn State.

The Class of 1890 issued the first *La Vie*, as a Junior year book. Thirty-one volumes have been printed, an increasingly interesting and valuable portrayal of College life. Some of the annuals have such merits as literary and artistic productions as to receive the award by competent judges in contests of national scope. The 1930 *La Vie* is the latest issued by the Junior Class, a supplement of lesser scope to cover the Senior Year was brought out by the Class. With the academic year 1930-31, the *La Vie*, therefore, passed into the hands of successive Senior Classes. The *La Vie* of 1890 is a small volume of one hundred and twenty-seven pages. It opens with "Greeting" to its Friends to whom it is dedicated, and expresses a desire "to establish a custom which shall be followed by each succeeding class upon its advent to the Junior Year." It aims both "to enlighten and entertain." "Faculty Failings" and "Grinds," the closing pages, furnish the latter; while enlightenment comes with College and Class histories, followed by a record of fraternities, associations, publications, social, musical, gastronomic, chess and whist clubs, prizes, and honors. The Athletic section is complete, and literature is represented in a series of biographical sketches of the faculty, and poetic effusions on "The Old Stile," "The Studious Freshman," "To the Faculty." It is credit to the class, and fits in well with the brilliant record of the Class of '90.

As a backwash from the Strike, to be presently detailed, the Lemon, a semi-anonymous, irresponsible and rather scurrilous publication appeared in seventeen numbers during the years 1906 to 1908. It took itself, it must be confessed with sufficient seriousness to announce a somewhat definite program, to herald a larger participation of student wish and will in College affairs. It also, plumed itself as the exponent of a more cosmopolitan outlook on the part of both the College and the town. The Lemon Board was instrumental in the adoption of the Nittany Lion as the College emblem. It pledged its profits to the general welfare, and cooperated with Colonel T. H. Nay, Commandant, in securing a distinctive College flag. The Board also, sponsored a movement to change the name of the borough, with its inevitable confusion worse confounded, from State College to Atherton, Pennsylvania. Here was euphonious, wise, merited, and in every way desirable change, but it failed partly because it did not seem fitting to take the Lemon seriously. Perhaps its best service was unintentional, the bringing out of the latent humor of our College life, and the need for a responsible and permanent medium of expression. This medium has been met by the Froth, the Penn State Froth, the College monthly of wit, humor, and life established in June 1910. With the exception of the War Period, the Fall of 1918 these two representatives of our general collegiate life, Penn State Collegian, and Froth have continuously carried on. How successfully these rank as training for after life may be gleaned from the records of some sixty editors and staff writers of the Free Lance and Collegian. About one half are engaged in teaching; one fourth in law or business; one fourth in engineering practice and management. In the group are to be found nine College Professors, three writers of international reputation, one in general literature, one in finance writing, and one in engineering. Five are members of the Board of Trustees and one is the President of the Board.

The principal department journals and issues may be recorded in this connection. The Journal of the Engineering Society was the pioneer, but it printed only three issues, Volume I, Number I June 1890; Volume I, Number III, June 1891. The Engineer appeared from 1908 to 1910, suspending with Volume III, Number IV, May 1910. The third, the Penn State Engineer has a successful record from Volume I, Number I, May 1920 to date, an increasingly creditable and valuable review of general Engineering and school projects. The Penn State Farmer is the oldest of these special student publications in continuous issue. It was founded in January 1908, and its program "to promote the welfare of the Agricultural School and Agricultural Society and to further the cause of scientific Agriculture in Pennsylvania," is being carried out with marked success. The human interest in faculty, students and alumni has been incorporated in its files and its influence is felt in other Schools of the College. The students in mining issued a quarterly during the years 1914 and 1915. Two temporary endeavors in Liberal Arts preceded the Old Main Bell, May 1925 to date. Eldorado, in spite of its name, lived one year, four numbers were issued in 1920. It was succeeded by Blue and White, 1920 and 1921, five issued of a single volume. Lion's Tale, a journal for women students had a brief existence, December 1924, to June 1926. Other, somewhat irregular organs of Schools or Departments are Penn State Educator, Penn State Patron, Commerce Comments, Chemistry Leaflet, Engineering Extension News, Mineral Industries serve to keep other interests of College work before the public. The most recent accession to the list is The Headlight, issued five times a year by Librarian Lewis and Staff. The Young Men's Christian Association has distributed a Handbook every year since 1894. A Woman's Handbook appeared in 1924. The College Directory was a student enterprise from 1908 to 1924, when it became an official College publication. The Faculty Bulletin, weekly, during the College year has been printed since October 1921.

Two events of diverse import remain to be chronicled. In 1904, a change in the reckoning of the College was approved by the Board. The date of the actual opening of the academic work, 1859, had hitherto been the point of departure. By a change to 1855, the date of the Charter, the Semi-Centennial Celebration took place at the close of the College year 1904-05. All entered with enthusiasm into a fitting recognition of the anniversary, a distinct climax and fitting tribute, too, to the achievements of Dr. Atherton for the institution. Commencement furnished the occasion, and the following papers and addresses were presented on Monday, June 12, 1905:

Erwin W. Runkle

In the Auditorium, Morning 10:00 o'clock to 12:00 o'clock

Early Steps leading to the Establishment of the Farmers' High School and its subsequent Development—General James A. Beaver— State College as a Pioneer in Scientific Education, Dr. Albert H. Tuttle, '68.
The Administration of the first President, Dr. Evan Pugh, Professor C. Alfred Smith, '61.

Dr. G. G. Pond

Dr. Pugh as a Chemist
The Relation of the Farmers' High School to Agricultural Education and Research,

Dr. H. P. Armsby

In the old Chapel—Afternoon, 2 o'clock to 4 o'clock

The Place of the State College in the System of Publican Education
Dr. N. C. Schaeffer
The Development of Engineering in The Pennsylvania State College
Professor D. C. Jackson '65
Historical Sketch of the College from 1855 to 1905-
Dr. Wm. A. Buckhout, '68
The Relation of the College to Military Education-
Professor John Hamilton, '71
The State College and the Military Service-

John I. Thompson, '62.

In the Fall of 1905 occurred "the great strike," the causes trivial, the results important. The system of "cuts" in absences from classes led naturally to the husbanding of these privileges (although termed necessary absences in the regulations) by the good students. By using them just before and after vacations, these periods were artificially extended. The poor or improvident student could not resist the temptation which the sigh of his more favored brothers presented, thus the work of the College was seriously crippled. The adoption of the proviso in the first semester of 1903, that these "cuts" for necessary absences shall not apply within twenty-four hours preceding or succeeding vacations or other suspensions of College work brought a vigorous protest, a rising tide of emotion fed by imaginary sources, and finally issued in precipitate action. From Monday, November 27 to Wednesday, December 6, students absented themselves from practically all classes. Daily mass meetings were held to consider overtures, air new "grievances," and prevent breaks in the ranks. Unwisely, let it be said, the faculty betimes declined to treat with students suspending themselves, until they had returned to duty. The students were loath to return to classes until assured of the assent to their demands. Most unwisely must it be said, student opinion was stamped by fancied abuses. When a Committee of the Board, the alumni, the faculty, and the student body met, conciliation was an easy matter. The wisdom of the stand for academic standards was upheld; the so-called abuses were seen in the wrong perspective. Let the historian of the Class of 1907 voice the student view;- "Never was a strike conducted in such a quiet, orderly fashion,—although there was naturally considerable feeling engendered on both sides; it was wonderful, yet natural, how the atmosphere cleared, and our daily regimen of College work was resumed with better understanding among all concerned. The fact remains that few Colleges in our country possess a student body capable of carrying through such a movement in such a truly American way; and such events as this have served to strengthen our spirit as College men and American citizens."

To criticism (sic) of administration, which could not have been more than specious pretense, had not President Atherton been gravely ill, let the faculty reply: "There has been no criticism of the things that really count in a College administration. Dr. Atherton's great executive ability, his far seeing wisdom, his unswerving loyalty to one great ideal, his unfailing optimism, his power to unify and coordinate forces, his genius in judging, and directing of men, his commanding personality,—in short those well known qualities that in twenty-four years raised State College from an unknown and discordant little training school to a great university recognized as one of the real forces of

American education—these have none of them been criticized."

The hope, that although broken in health and necessitating protracted absence each year, was treasured by the Board and his fellow teachers, that the institution might yet continue to profit by, and the world of scholarship be enriched by his labors. This said General Beaver on behalf of the Board is "the silver lining to the darkest cloud which I have ever seen hang over this institution." But such was not the fate the future held. The workers are buried, but the work goes forward. The cloud perforce lifted as the choice of leadership fell upon one who had known Penn State as a teacher, who had shown so vital an interest in student life, social athletic and academic, who embodies something of the sanity and idealism of President Atherton. With the advent of Dr. Sparks, an era of extension and of popularization of Penn State began. A genial personality and persuasive address made him pre-eminently the students' beau ideal, the students' "Prexy," to this period our story now turns.

CHAPTER 13

Era of Good Feeling, Extension Activities, and Rapid Growth

"If I should come to The Pennsylvania State College, I pledge to the institution my full time, and strength, and thought; to the Board of Trustees my unwavering loyalty to their policy and fidelity to the trust they put in me; to the Faculty the sympathetic cooperation of long-standing friendship; and to the students my highest sense of sympathy, help, and impartial justice."

Dr. E. E. Sparks, November 16, 1907.

After an experience of five years in The Pennsylvania State College, I venture to formulate a policy for the future. It should be the aim of the institution:

1. Not to aspire to the much-abused title of "University," since professional and graduate schools are not feasible owing to the location, but to aspire to be the most thorough and, perhaps, largest College in the United States.

2. To cultivate the family feeling of unity among students and faculty so readily fostered by the isolated location; to make mutual helpfulness the keynote of College Spirit.

3. To take advantage of the isolation to work out the relation of mind-making to character-making.

4. To modify and adjust the courses of study to the shifting demands of public life and occupation; at the same time not to lose sight of the cultural and higher ideals of life.

5. To hold fast to fixed courses of study for undergraduate work, with set tasks for preparation, daily recitation and regular habits of work.

6. To search for every channel of usefulness to the people of Pennsylvania; to benefit in some way every tax-payer of the state; and to make the College the vital center of radiation for the information and resulting progress of the Commonwealth.

7. To bind together all persons who have at any time attended the College into a brotherhood of devotion to the institution, a jealous zeal for her good name and a realization that her reputation is simply a reflection of theirs.

8. To use every effort to foster state pride in the College, and not to be content until a permanent means of income is provided by the state.

9. To continue the policy of uniform support for all schools and departments of the College, taking into consideration the number of students and consequent needs.

President E. E. Sparks—January 1914.

Upon the death of President Atherton, Judge James A. Beaver became President, Pro-tempore, with Professors W. A. Buckhout and J. H. Leete caring for local administrative interests, pending permanent changes. Dr Atherton had for years borne too great a burden of executive duties; the institution was emerging unheralded from a small to a large College. His long and unique service made it difficult to relinquish any oversight which his care and thought had so closely woven into the life of the College. However plans had been matured for a larger division of tasks and responsibilities in which he should have general and advisory control, being relieved of such details as manifestly belonged to other agencies. Critical illness and subsequent demise reopened the matter, and Judge Beaver reported to the Board a plan for the separation of public and academic functions from the financial, together with suggestions and recommendations for changes in internal administration. The desire of Dr. Buckhout to devote all his energy to his department and to the School of Agriculture, and the resignation of Professor Leete, made a still more complete reorganization imperative.

A Council of administration consisting of the Deans of Schools and the Heads of the Departments of Mathematics and of English as an advisory board in all matters of College administration was instituted. College finances became a separate, (though not independent) agency. Dr. Judson Perry Welsh, was elected as Vice President, Business Manager, Financial Agent, and Registrar. To this plethora of duties were added Professor of Pedagogics and Director of Summer Session. Budgets were to be recommended by departments to the Deans; reviewed by the Financial Agent; referred to the President; and finally approved by the Board of Trustees. A system of purchases by requisition, annual inventories, and many clock punching details of daily vocation and avocation activities were recorded on blanks. The catalogue, a none too modest document of three-hundred and sixty-seven pages was swelled by one-hundred, with a shower of fascicule in its wake. A sky-rocket of university status and name lent a temporary brilliance to things academic.

A student board consisting of three Seniors, two Juniors, and one Sophomore was appointed, with the privilege of appearing before the Council of Administration or Faculty when cases of discipline or changes in rules affecting the student body were under discussion. The board was to act, too, as a clearing house for all requests from the student body or the several classes, thus taking the initial steps in student government so happily utilized and developed by President Sparks.

There followed rapidly a series of other changes, the ground work of which had been laid, the execution delayed, only, by the serious illness of the President. Annex Number One was divided between an infirmary and a building for Forestry, the latter receiving an additional twenty-five hundred dollars for an attached, temporary structure. Thus Forestry "to which Dr. Atherton had given much attention, even to mapping out a Course," was begun under Dr. B. E. Fernow in 1907, succeeded by Dr. H. A. Baker, 1907 to 1912. Lectures in Forestry had been a part of the training in Agriculture for more than twenty years, first under Dr. Rothrock and later by Dr. Buckhout, Enrollments, however, in a complete course covering four years were authorized by the Executive Committee in September 1905. The first two years of the course were virtually identical with those in general agriculture, so that specific provision for professional forestry came later as indicated. Dr. T. H. Hunt accepted the Deanship of the School of Agriculture on November 22, 1906 and a vigorous administration and growth of the School ensued. Nine departments and courses of study were organized, and a newly completed Agricultural Building dedicated on November 22, 1907. Home Economics (alias Domestic Economy in the Ladies Cottage since 1889) was provided for in the basement of "Old Main," the rising chimney surmounted by a veritable periscope was one of the scenic wonders of that monstrous roof. The cooperation of the women of the State was specifically enlisted under the influence of Miss Kate Cassatt McKnight, President of the Woman's Federation. This body met at the College October 16 to 18, 1906, and took steps toward scholarships for women, and sponsored an enlargement of the Ladies Cottage. The Alumnae Club of State College, also, issued a pamphlet in June 1906 setting forth the new opportunities for women at Penn State. Since which time lack of facilities has been the only retarding factor in the yet more rapid growth of the number of women. Increasing and more adequate provision owes much to the interest of Miss Florence Dibert and Mrs. Clara C. Phillips, both in service on the Board of Trustees, and throughout the Commonwealth. Miss Louise Waugh was the first instructor in Home Economics, a work which rapidly developed, under Miss Sara C. Lovejoy, and especially under the direction of Miss Edith P. Chace, in lines of domestic science, art, vocational home economics, and institutional management. The department was incorporated in 1923 with the School of Education.

Engineering F. a frame structure erected from funds solicited by Judge Beaver saved the basement of "Old Main" from housing a portion of the Electrical laboratories, unwise as such an arrangement must have proved. The Chemistry Annex (euphoniously Bull Pen) was another hastily executed makeshift; while the Woman's Building, a camel's hump addition to the Cottage of earlier vintage was prompted by the demands for dormitories and laboratories for women students. An important interim action was the restoration of the mining department to school status and the brief but vigorously personal services of Dean M. E. Wadsworth. A new impulse to the Agricultural Extension was given by the appointment of Professor Alva Agee, and for this wider program for Agriculture begun in the closing years of the Atherton Administration, much credit is due to Colonel John A. Woodward. The first comprehensive plan of Campus and grounds was formulated under the stimulus of the exodus from Old Main. The Lowrie Plan was issued in a handsome booklet financed by Trustee James L. Hamill. While many modifications have been made, the general lines of the "layout" have proved permanent. The Report officially adopted by the Trustees, June 1, 1907 is thus one of the important landmarks in the development of a campus orderly and beautiful.

In a protracted and earnest search for a successor to Dr. Atherton, the sentiment of the younger members of the Board was more and more centered upon a former teacher of the College. The kind of leader needed at that important and even critical juncture was one who, while realizing that the foundations were laid, equally seemed the immediate task of extending the influences and activities of the institution to every part of the Commonwealth. The institution was still a somewhat local one, colloquially the Centre County College, near Bellefonte. Its scholastic standing was known by the competent to judge as second to none. Its graduates, especially in Engineering and Chemistry, were taking leading places in those industries; while Agriculture was just garnering its forces for its brilliant advance, but in spite of these new horizons and achievements, the masses of the people of the Commonwealth neither realized that or what The Pennsylvania State College purported to be. It needed "to be sold" to the people of the State. It needed that intelligent backing of our industrial democracy, not alone to make its work more effective, more responsive to the needs of the people, but to roll up a tide of public sentiment which should be irresistible and which should issue in a more adequate legal and financial responsibility and support. The College had "found itself" and was ready and anxious to meet the enlarged opportunities—the type of man to lead must be found. He must be the scholar, the executive, but above and beyond all, the magnetic personality, the man who could win the allegiance of both classes and masses to a cause by his own contagious and enthusiastic devotion. The College must popularize, in the best sense, its program. It must justify its truly democratic traditions. It must serve not only the few, the leaders to be, but the people themselves, on the farm, in the factory, in the counting room, in the school-room, everywhere, in the several pursuits and professions of life.

Nature, training and experience conspired to fit President Sparks for such a task. He graduated from Ohio State University, with an early interest and bent toward American life, and with an already acquired experience and facility in reporting and interpreting that life, journalistically. An educational apprenticeship in both High School and Academy, plus a decided talent and leaning toward the forum as a teaching agency was prophetic of his later life.[27] Five years as head of the Preparatory Department at The Pennsylvania State College brought him into contact with the work and aims of a growing State College. His plans for his own department were well conceived and wisely

[27] A study of the early years of Dr. Sparks has been made by Albert J. Gares, Penn State 1929, as a thesis for the Masters Degree. Mr. Gares has access to autobiographical and other manuscript material, and he has added to the knowledge of the formative influences of Dr. Sparks' youth and College life.

executed, as the Reports of 1890 to 1895 reveal. But more significant was his interest and effectiveness in every line of College activity. In committee assignments and tasks, Dr. Atherton relied upon his young, ambitious co-workers and Dr. Sparks, left and impress upon the College during the first period of service by a keen sympathy with physical training, interest in a better teaching of English, in press bureau and extension lectures, and in a genuine zest for leadership in social activities for both faculty and students. He believed the College should touch the whole man, and much of his later administrative success was due to the way these secondary but contributory academic interests were utilized in developing responsible self government in the student body.

Resigning the principalship of the Preparatory Department in 1895, he entered the University of Chicago, won his doctorate in 1900. As teacher, extension lecturer, writer, and administrator in the University, he was all unconsciously preparing for a new call to The Pennsylvania State College. On November 22, 1907, the Board of Trustees elected Dr. Sparks as the eighth President of the College, and five days later, an acceptance was received by the Board. Active duties were to be entered upon before the close of the College year, and a formal inauguration was planned as part of the Commencement Exercises in June 1908. The students, however, did not await the formal induction, but staged a spontaneous welcome, no less effective because so speedily arranged and executed. Dr. Sparks arrived on Monday May 11, and two days later a reviewing stand had been erected near the Auditorium, and the President-elect with the Deans duly installed thereon. The College exercises of the forenoon were suspended, an additional flavor to the tone of-prevailing good feeling. At nine-thirty A. M., monster parade, led by the Band and Cadet Regiment marched past "in column of platoons, making an excellent appearance with their line extending fully three hundred yards." The athletic division followed with base-ball team and bats at "carry arms," and agriculture with "almost every animal Noah saved in the Ark" in line with floats and representing "sterilized milking" and "sowing wild oats." "Swamp Angels" with characteristic effectiveness dispensed the black arts and alchemy of Chemistry, while the "Electricals" satirized the Not-Any Traction

317

Company, then periodically building a line to metropolitan centers from State College. The "Mechanicals" Hot-Air Engines belched forth fire and smoke under the caption "Watch for the Sparks." "Miners" had their Mule-Cars, the Home Economics float dispensed to the groundlings cakes and other culinary tid-bits. Forestry enacted a visible drama of the beauty of forest life, and the Civil Engineers portrayed in action a frontier surveying corps. The College steam roller added a ponderous, cacophonic touch as it brought up the rear, Dr. Sparks protesting that this climax and finale bore no real or symbolic reference to the incoming administration.

The formal exercises of inauguration, much more pretentious than formerly, took place on Commencement Day, June 17, 1908. For the first time, representatives of other institutions were present. Two special addresses were delivered at an afternoon convocation by President Alexander C. Humphreys on The Engineer as a Cultured Specialist, and by Dr. Paul Shorey on The Service of Humanistic Studies to the Technical School. The morning exercises included addresses of welcome from the student body by William B. Geise, '08; and from the Alumni by Richard W. Williamson '93. The faculty was represented by Dr. William A. Buckhout '68, and Judge James A. Beaver spoke for the Board of Trustees. The inaugural and commencement address by President Edwin Erle Sparks took the theme, The Economic Obligation of Public Education. In the interests of simplifying the program, the "customary orations" by members of the Senior Class were omitted, only the Valedictorian, W.F.H. Wentzel in an impressive and thoughtful way represented the class. His tributes, every reader who knows and loves Penn State, will surely echo. Turning to General Beaver, he said: "Of all hearts there is none bigger than yours, of all faces there is none more welcome than yours. Of all men, there is none who has meant more to us and to our Alma Mater during our undergraduate history. From the very beginning you inspired us and ever since you have appealed to our inner sense of manhood...We felt that you always had that love that "leaned hard," the words that sank deep, and the censure that demanded our hearty approval. In you, the faith of Dr. Atherton had surely found a receptive heart, in which it is reflecting itself with added sympathy. You surely have done your share in making possible the success of

Dr. Atherton, first by backing him up in all his efforts, and then by your devoted service since his death. With honor have you held the reins and with honor have you laid them down. We recognize you for what you have done for our manhood, for clean ideal sentiment, and for the square deal." Addressing President Sparks he continued "almost in one breath we must say welcome and farewell.... You have already created a harmonious spirit and a promising future. In all confidence we believe our hopes will be realized. We look up to you as the proper successor of General Beaver and of Dr. Atherton. In your hands we leave the immediate destiny of Penn State, the guardianship of her equipment, the supervision of her instruction, and the reputation of our Alma Mater. May your success redound most richly to the welfare of the sons and daughters of our College and the service of our State."

The rapid growth of the student body is the dominating feature of the period 1908 to 1920. From an institution of less than one thousand, the number grew to nearly forty-five hundred, the graduating class from one hundred and thirty-one, to four hundred and sixty-eight. By 1909 only two unassigned seats remained in Chapel, the Freshmen were delegated to a separate service in Old Main. Five years later, in part motivated also by a strong student desire to abolish Chapel, two assemblies were held in the Auditorium, on alternate mornings of the week. A Wednesday morning general mass meeting further reduced the odium theologicum which seemed to adhere to the traditional Chapel. By 1914, a limitation on the size of the Freshmen Class was enforced, and the College had become, as was modestly boasted, strictly as a College, the largest in the United States.

As numbers grew, old customs and traditions wavered, new ones took their places. "Freshmen must speak" lent an air of friendliness and comradeship. If it became too perfunctory, spirit week had great powers of revival. Vicarious activities served, too, to tone down the rather rugged bucolics of the "small college." Thus wrestling takes the place of the Campus rush; fire drill instead of inspection (long a bone of contention); the tribunal, for indiscriminate hazing; stunts, sings, and rules instead of unorganized and hazardous mass scraps. A masque ball or all College dance instead of Halloween pranks lost nothing by exchange; while Memorial Day honors at the grave of Dr. Atherton instead of the outworn "professional graveyard" of unsavory memory, was a most fitting arrangement. Ornamental lights at buildings, commencement chair, and drinking fountains instead of the parious symbols on the tower of "Old Main," bulletin boards instead of trees, and "Please" instead of "Keep off the Grass" bore their part in a campus beautiful.

More attention was paid to wholesome entertainment for the student body. A free lecture was provided, moving pictures and other forms of amusement arranged.

Chapel speakers were chosen with a strong appeal to youth; and music, mass singing had a genuine renaissance. Campus singing was stressed by Dr. Sparks, he believed in a singing College. In the fall of 1909, a week was specially set apart for campus songs under an expert leader. The appointment of C. C. Robinson in 1912 as Music Director marks a distinct stage, too, in the provision for the place of music in the curriculum. The new interest in orchestra and bands, which have contributed so much to academic pleasure and profit have unbrokenly flowed since 1914 from the enthusiasm and skill of Band Master Thompson, as his friends, and they are legion, love to speak of him. That pervasive, evasive thing called College spirit was ever in the mind of Dr. Sparks. In cooperation with the President of the Board, a prize was awarded on April 10, 1918 for the best definition to Mr. J. A. Allard of the Class of 1920. Under the keynote of loyalty, it reads: "To be loyal to our College, to our daily work, to our ideals, to our sense of honor, to our fellows, to our country, and to our God."

Fraternities grew from nine in 1905-06 to thirty-eight in 1919-20. Social and living conditions were improved, and withal, scholarship was enhanced. Socially, Dr. Sparks gave himself without stint to the students; their interests were always his first concern, and he became the very inherent expression of a genial, generous personality, the beau ideal of the student body. Peradventure, some may have felt that in the eternal triangle of trustees, faculty and students, the affections of the President played too luridly about the students, it was not that he loved Caesar less but Rome more. He was fairly intoxicated by the loyalty and good sportsmanship that radiated from the staccato chorus of "Rah! Rah! Prexy," and an almost transcendent and transfigured parenthood suffused his countenance as he spoke of "my boys, and my girls."

But academic as well as personal agencies fostered the new student regime. The Freshman advisor system brought direct and helpful relations between teachers and new students. It emphasized the broad and fundamental training underlying all the work of the College; stressed the need of the best teaching for the lower classes; and furnished a most favorable environment in which the student might "find himself" before the choice of a professional course was thrust upon him. Here was a genuine educational experiment, which still has its devotees as wiser than the immediate enrollment in the several schools and departments, with a consequent loss of Collegiate, scholastic, and class integrity.

Character building, a professorship of personal administration was another of President Sparks' educational experiments. Dr. Arthur Holmes came to the College in 1912, and he gave seven fruitful years of service as Dean of the Colleges. He was adept in private counsel, provokingly inspiring in public address, but always made moral values emerge from a thoughtful criticism of academic traditions, prejudices, and "hobbies." He was succeeded in 1919 by Dean of Men, Arthur R. Warnock, the first to hold that specific and increasingly important post in our academic life. An honor system for the entire College, long advocated (and indeed used in some departments, notably, Electrical Engineering) was adopted March 3, 1915. The vote stood eleven hundred and forty, for; and four-hundred and fifteen, against. Despite the large sentiment opposed to any so-called "system" of honor, every effort was made to ensure success both by precept and by example. As loopholes and weaknesses appeared in the regulations, changes were instituted. From multiplicity of causes, the bare mention of which would provoke partisan discussion, the "system" proved impracticable. On May 30, 1921, it was definitely recalled. The initiative, here as in its adoption, came from the student body, friends and foes alike.

Student health and hygiene received added attention, when the plan for a College physician was broached. An infirmary (part of Bright Angel) was set up in the woods in the rear of the athletic field to care for any cases of contagious diseases. Agitation for a student hospital went on. The Woman's Club of State College added to the fund, and donations were solicited from friends of the College. On January 15, 1915, the Health Service was opened in the "Ihlseng" house, and a residence erected for the physician in charge. Dr. Warren E. Forsythe was the first incumbent, succeeded after two years by Dr. J. P. Ritenour. The latter was shared in the Welfare Building Campaign, so that his "plant" embraces a permanent well equipped hospital, together with a dispensary, offices, laboratories, and staff-rooms in Old Main.

Scholastic changes consistently followed the rapid growth of the student body. The unit system of entrance was adopted in 1907-08 with fourteen required units, and with flexibility as applied to diverse courses increased to the standard of fifteen units. An English Composition increased to the standard of fifteen units. An English Composition test was instituted in 1912-13; and placing the responsibility for adequately prepared Freshmen upon the schools of the Commonwealth, the College also dropped its Preparatory or Sub-Freshmen Class. The seven schools were combined into "Five Great Schools" as the familiar form of publicity voiced it. The merger was effected by the union of the lesser arts units, the languages, literatures, historical and philosophical sciences into a School of Liberal Arts. The School of Mathematics and Physics was apportioned to other schools; mathematics to Liberal Arts, and physics to Natural Science. Other collegiate divisions were grouped as the Institute of Animal Nutrition, ranking as a School; and as unattached departments, Home Economics, Industrial Arts, and Physical Education. To these should, also, be added the Engineering Experiment Station established in 1908; and the Mining Station ten years later.

The Summer Session for Teachers dates from 1910; in part consequent upon a series of resolutions adopted by the State Teachers' Association in 1908. Summer School work was first offered in 1888, as noted, an eight weeks course in mechanical drawing and practice intended especially for teachers. In 1893, the facilities of the new Engineering building in manual arts were featured for summer students. Five years later a general summer session was announced with Dr. M. G. Benedict as Director. The Trustees encouraged the project by opening all the facilities of the institution, including the free rent in the dormitories. With no available funds for salaries, advertising and other expenses, owing to a lean legislative year, the attempt proved abortive. The following year, however, a somewhat enlarged program was offered beginning July 5 and ending August 16 with Dr. G. G. Pond, Dean of the Summer Courses. The tentative almost hesitant nature of these beginnings is shown by the announcement: "These courses are not intended to interfere or compete with any of the established "Summer Schools," but to serve certain specific purposes, namely, Manual Training, improvement of teaching in industrial and agricultural courses, and in better preparation for entrance to College." These attempts are important, however, for their early recognition of the responsibility of the College to the teachers of the State, and of its rightful place as the crown of the Free Public School System of the Commonwealth. From its beginnings, as an appeal to teachers, only; it has become an essential part of the entire instructional and research work of the College. The first session enrolled one hundred and forty-six; it grew during the administration of President Sparks to ten hundred and forty-five. High School Principals' Conferences; Superintendents' and Rural Pastors' gatherings; Institutes special and general have become integral parts.

In the College a diversification of courses attended by necessity the increase of numbers. Mining was differentiated into two divisions: Mines, and Metallurgy, and a course in Industrial Engineering added in 1908-09. The following year Landscape Gardening, Architectural Engineering, Pre-Legal and Pre-Medical courses were organized. In 1910-11, Highway, Milling, and Railway Mechanical Engineering; Mining Geology; Botany, and Natural Science courses appear. The following year Commerce and Finance was organized, and in 1913-14 Agricultural Education and Industrial Education was added; while Home Economics becomes Domestic Science, Domestic Art, and under the Smith-Hughes Act, later, adds Vocational Home Economics.

Women students increased from nineteen to two hundred and sixty three, and McAllister Hall was converted into a dormitory for women in

September, 1915. The Cottage system of housing prepared the way for closer associations and sororities. Maple Lodge, Everyn Cottage, Edgewood, Hilcrest, Practice House are euphonious titles for former prosaic professorial domiciles. Women's Student Government was formulated in 1915, and elaborated into the present form of Senate and House of Representatives in 1920. Deans of Women serving during this period were Sara Lovejoy 1907 to 1918, and Margaret A. Knight to 1923.

The College faculty increased nearly five-fold during this little more than a decade, and the turn over was unusually high. In engineering, Dean R. L. Sackett succeeded in 1915, Professor John Price Jackson, the latter resigning to become a member of the cabinet of Governor Tener. Department heads, Diemer, Kinsloe, Kocher, Harris, and Keller began their work, and teachers like Govier, Light, Isenberg, O'Donnell, Stavely, Torrence, Dedrick, Markle, Broderick, Woodruff, Patterson, Nesbit, Bradford, are added to the classrooms and laboratories. In agriculture, Dean Hunt's removal in 1912 to the University of California brought R. L. Watts, Professor of Horticulture since 1907-08, to the Deanship. A bare enumeration of typical names of the faculty beginning their labors during this period bespeaks the kind of men who have helped to bring the School of Agriculture to its rightful place in relation to the College and to the State at large. They are: Baker, Larsen, Gilmore, Goodling, Stewart, Noll, Tomhave, Gardner, Myers, Ferguson, Cochel, Hibshman, Weaver. The list continues, Stoddart, Borland, Nissley, Havner, Dickey, Fagan, Cowell, Orton, Green, Kern, Wilde, Holben, Blasingame, Edwards, Swope. The list closes, Kelly, Overholts, Hill, Fletcher, Rasmussen, Bentley, Knandel, Lisse, Nixon, Parkinson, Bressler.

In the School of Mines, following Dean Wadsworth, Deans Crane, 1907 to 1918, Moore 1918 to 1922 served the College, and Messrs. Bonine, Honess, Chedsey, Robinson, Knight, MacFarland succeeded that noteworthy first group of Stoek, Shedd, Hopkins, Linville, and others. In Natural Science, Dean Pond continued his work until his death in 1920, and some of his co-laborers during the preceding decade are Chandlee, Meyer, Duncan, Ham, Davey, Mason, Keach, Smith, W, Parks, Currier, Olewine, Cryder. The School of Liberal Arts as re-constituted by President Sparks was headed by

Deans S. E. Weber, 1910 to 1914 and T. C. Blaisdell, 1915 to 1920; President Sparks and Dean Holmes served during the transition periods. Some of the names new to the school are Boucke, Burrage, Marquardt, Harris, C. O. Harris, M. M. Robinson, Reichard, Marshman, Van Riper, Pierce, Hasek, Martin, Herman, Merrill, Dye, Anderson, Dotterer, Rhoton, Mason and Gibbons. The School too has pride in that group of young men at various times on its staff, who elsewhere as College Presidents and University Professors are achieving distinguished careers, men like Rowe, Zook, Collings, Taliaferro, Smith, Trenholme, Curl, Becker, and Ray.

Such an unusual growth of student instruction placed a heavy burden upon the administration for facilities, buildings, and equipment. Maintenance appropriations increased from a half-million to nearly two and one-half millions. Twelve hundred acres were added to the land holdings. Four buildings, Green House (1910-11), Dairy Barn, Stock Judging Pavilion, and Horticultural Building (1913-14), were erected for the School of Agriculture. Units E. and D. Engineering were built in 1912-13 and 1913-14. But special burdens placed upon Engineering during the war were multiplied by the calamity which hovered. On the memorable evening of November 25, 1918, the Main Engineering Building burned. The partial destruction of the light and power plant complicated the disaster, and for a time it seemed as though the activities of the entire institution were paralyzed. Temporary arrangements were speedily made; equipment was procured; exchanges of subjects and time adjustments were effected. At the end of the Christmas vacation, the work of the various departments was proceeding almost normally. Three new units, C, B, and A were constructed during 1919-20, relieving some of the congestion in laboratories, lecture rooms, and offices. During the period under consideration, unit structures were also erected; on the East Campus, the so-called Mining building; the lower Liberal Arts unit, and the Pond Laboratory in Chemistry.

In 1910, the Pump House and Foundry, unsightly structures in an unsightly main Campus entrance were torn down. The materials (a thing which has characterized the College, using to the utmost its meager physical plant) were utilized in the layout of the Engineering Experiment Station. The enlarged plantings of the landscape department, ivy and shrubbery helped to hide the sordid bareness of some of the time-worn, outworn buildings. The front and west terraces on "Old" Main, the open air amphitheater (a happy product of the Summer Session), all contributed to a better campus. Also the front wall, Senior benches, (though of brief duration), and the Memorial Gateway brought added dignity to the College approaches. The gateway has been modified, but at one time, it was surmounted by two lions, rampant; inartistic relicts of Pennsylvania Exhibits at World Fairs. By the untutored these were known as "Pa" and "Ma", and it seems to cling as a sort of tradition ever since, that the making of graven images of the Nittany Lion is a hazardous undertaking. In 1914, the Patriotic Order of the Sons of America donated the flag staffs that dominate the front campus.

The town kept step with the enlarging College, the population increased four-fold in the period under discussion. A telegraph station became a reality and a free mail delivery instituted. The good roads movement continued to react adversely on the local railroad, but brought the borough streets out of the mud. A paved College Avenue in 1920 was the forerunner of a whole series of civic improvements.

A Press Club and Country Clubs carried the news of the College into every part of the State. These activities at first purely voluntary and uncoordinated were brought together in a Publicity Department established in June 1914. A. O. Vorse was the first College news editor, followed by D. M. Cresswell in 1919, who has developed a department of public information, a University Press to be, a veritable clearing house for the manifold activities of the institution, academic, administrational, promotional, and scientific.

Improved methods of efficiency in the Office of the Registrar began with the re-organization work of Professor A. H. Epenshade in 1909. College entrance, scheduling and recording were responsibly centered; and in 1916 with the marked increase of candidates for advance standing, a College Examiner was appointed. Buildings and grounds brought together, previously, illy-coordinated agencies, under Professor R. I. Webber in 1918. Surveys of the administration of the College, its executive, financial, service, and accounting activities authorized in 1917, led to the appointment of a Comptroller. On May 1, 1918, R. H. Smith was elected, and an efficient and broadly visioned service (which we have noted previously in alumni, athletic, and collegiate promotion lines) is accruing, helpful to all phases of College activities.

Extension was consonant with the foundations and aims of the College, and there never was a time, from the addresses and memorials of Frederick Watts to the people of Pennsylvania, up to the present day, when the College did not have in view its responsibilities to this wider public. Through Chautauqua Reading and Correspondence Courses, through experiments and publications, Agriculture has done pioneer work; while Engineering, Mining, Chemistry, Economic Zoology, and other fields made their numerous contacts through lectures and in bulletins. A more distinct recognition of the need and importance of this work for and by the College, led to the formulation of the slogan, Our Campus the Commonwealth. Ideas, as Dean Sackett happily expressed it, were now to be transformed into institutions. A report to the Board of Trustees reviewed the work in 1910 by the several schools and divisions. Agriculture records eight industrial trains operated through forty counties of the State. Over three hundred addresses by staff members reach fifty thousand people. Correspondence Courses enroll twenty-five hundred; while exhibits, prizes, as well as the more organized cooperation in teaching elementary agriculture in the normal and public schools have brought marked results in practical agriculture. The School of Engineering reviews the trail of the Good Roads train, vocational classes in the Pennsylvania Railway shops in Altoona, and organized provision for drawing and other industrial subjects in other cities. An experiment is detailed in furnishing lessons by Correspondence, supplemented by occasional meetings with the instructor. The first bulletins of the Engineering Experiment Station are also issued. Through institutes, Mining as a School reports fully ten thousand miners reached, while lectures on accident prevention and other practical subjects were delivered in the bituminous and anthracite regions of the State. The Department of Home Economics details forty-eight meetings and addresses and urges that interest awakened would justify demonstrations on purchasing and preparing foods, on household decoration, on dress making, etc., in every community.

The Committee having carefully considered these "ventures" in the field of extension concludes with the following recommendations:

1. The trials made in this College as herein noted show that Extension work is both demanded and feasible.

2. Experience shows that regular class room work suffers when instructors are called upon frequently to be absent on Extension work. A special staff of lecturers and demonstrators is absolutely essential to the proper conduct of this outside work.

3. The funds for the support of this work should not be taken out of the regular maintenance of the College. The sum should be sufficiently large to command the very best talent or the work should not be undertaken. This report was adopted and ordered printed by the Board of Trustees on November 11, 1910, an important step in the program of President Sparks to take the College of the State to the people of the State."

If agriculture, here, had blazed the way by the extension zeal of Pugh, Burrowes, Hamilton, Colonel Woodward and by the appointment of Alva Agee as Superintendent of Agricultural extension in 1906-07, she was also the first division of the College to be properly supported in the work. Here a federal enactment made the work secure and its development rapid. The Smith-Lever Bill in 1914 and its acceptance on the part of the Commonwealth is second only in importance to the Morrill Act itself. The underlying principle is systematic, continuous contact in self-help and community service by putting the technical information and inspiration of specialists into the hands of County Agents and experts in Home Economics. These by the Cooperation of Federal, State and County Agencies reach every rural or rural-urban farm and home. The Federal Appropriation is based upon percentage of rural population to the total in each State, and is conditioned upon the grant of equal amounts by the States themselves. In Pennsylvania, the County Commissioners are authorized to cooperate. Thus County

Agents, Home Economics and other experts and demonstrators are at work in every part of the Commonwealth, bringing the science and the art of rural life to the people. The Director, M. S. McDowell has been associated since 1909 with this division, and since 1914 as its Head.

Engineering, Mining and other forms of Extension are supported by budget allotments and fees. Instruction is given under class room conditions and standards, in evening schools, and by lecturers and conferences. Dean L. E. Reber, who resigned in 1907, to head the Wisconsin Extension Service, had repeatedly urged that means be provided for carrying the results of Engineering Experiment and research to the industries. His successor, John Price Jackson, organized the first definite instruction in 1909-10. This work was directed by Professor J. A. Moyer, head of the Department of Mechanical Engineering until 1915, when he was called to extension service by the State of Massachusetts. Under the administration of Dean R. L. Sackett a vigorous growth followed, extension was first recognized as a separate or independent branch by the appointment of Mr. N. C. Miller as Instructor in Engineering Extension. Additional centers were established, and instruction by correspondence and by conferences in elementary engineering, industrial, and collegiate subjects provided. Professor J. O. Keller, since 1925 head of the Engineering Extension Division has districted the State, and in many new centers established courses in industrial management, foremanship and business personnel. By cooperation with the resident faculty, the field of correspondence instruction was widened, not only in technical lines, but in Economics, English, History, Psychology, etc. Viewing this work in its larger perspective, it not only carries the College to the industries, it reacts upon the spirit and instruction of the College itself. It may be but slight exaggeration to say, that greater benefits accrue at home than in the field in keeping the College in touch with its primary purpose and aims, the training of the industrial classes in the several pursuits and professions of life.

The third major field of extension is that of teacher training, vocational and industrial education fostered by the Smith-Hughes Act of 1917. With the Summer School, this factor receives emphasis in extension work, viz:- intensive and restricted attention to one subject or part of a subject may be brought to yield results comparable to a longer pursuit of a group of subjects. Actual situations and problems are met by definite projects and solutions, the student's laboratory is the student's professional experience itself. As organized by Director A. S. Hurrell, it aims to bring College training within the reach of the sufficiently earnest student, but with due regard for standards of entrance and credits for graduation, as well as for the essential residence requirements.

A marked extension of service during the administration of Dr. Sparks was that of expert assistance and cooperation between the College and the State. Agriculture and Engineering were represented in the Governor's Cabinet and as advisors and consultants in Economic Entomology, in landscape Architecture, in Education, in Industrial Training, and in Economics, the service of the College was then, as always since, noteworthy. Dr. Sparks in an early report called the attention of the Board to "duplications" in College and State Agencies, and advocated forcibly the wisdom of the use by the State of the aid and counsel of College experts, facilities and operations wherever possible. He maintained, rightly, that the College was both obligated and anxious to render such service, and if "College teachers in all those lines are not qualified to pass practically upon public works, they are not qualified to teach students from whom the experts are to come."

Thus cooperating, all departments of the College are extension departments. In the words of President R. D. Hetzel, "the extension services have made opportunity for educational universal. Every postal route, every rural delivery box is an extension of the College itself. Adult education is reaching millions." The radio has accepted the challenge, is holding up the torch, brining "more light" under the auspices of the College.

A larger and more effective student enlistment of the Alumni in the progress of the College is, too, noted. The period of service of R. H. Smith from 1911 to 1918 as Secretary of the Alumni Association and Graduate Manager of Athletics was marked by constructive work in both fields. Mass athletics, subordinated to the true aims of physical training, enlarged facilities in equipment and playing fields were urged. The "Booster Campaign" as it was called, for a "bigger and better Penn State." A non-political publicity movement spread from an awakened and enlightened alumni to every part of the State. The newspapers, public libraries, civic clubs and chambers of commerce were enlisted. Penn State "movies" in cities and towns carried the message of the campus to the masses. Crystallized and enforced by direct and personal appeal by alumni and faculty to leading citizens in the State and to the responsible governing bodies, the issue was inevitable. Information led to responsibility, responsibility to more adequate support. Governor J. K. Tener concisely voiced this rising sentiment in every part of the Commonwealth by affirming that after the public schools which are always first, Penn State does and should come next. Here, too, in these campaigns were laid the foundations of the general alumni fund, the welfare buildings movement, and the phenomenal results achieved by the "bond issue" in later years.

Faculty activities and organizations became more numerous and varied under the inspiration of the administration. A series of faculty dinners were held with conferences and addresses of general import; while the schools and even the departments held grave and learned, if not the sophistic, discussions of academic and administrational problems. However, this brought about a more virile expression of faculty thinking, and the committees of the faculty became less perfunctory. A representative of each school set in the councils of every school, and the minutes of the Council of Administration were read for information in faculty meetings. A faculty exchange was opened in the "lobby" of the "Old" Main business office. In 1908-09 the University Club was organized, and six years later the present building was erected on the site of the University Inn, which had reverted to the College campus. There was, also, much agitation, through with hopes deferred, for a social hall, with the net but important result of club rooms in "Old" Main and the organization of a Student Union in 1919 under Dean Warnock's leadership. Once there was held before the vision, a "Gigantic" gymnasium, a transplanted and transformed relic of the Great War. Contributions were called out, and rare collegiate enthusiasm, a prophecy, however, of things yet to be.

Events, celebrations of personal achievements, as well as buildings mark an institution's progress. Some of these must find record in these pages. The interest in College history was furthered by the reunions of fifty year classes beginning with the Commencement season of 1911. The assembly of "Stateana" by the Librarian, begun in 1904, was enriched by the labors of the Committee on successive reunions under the chairmanship of Dr. G. G. Pond.[28] Professor J.H. Tudor, whose conscientious industry was proverbial, markedly succeeded in a collection of pictures of former teachers. General James A. Beaver deposited the McAllister-Beaver Correspondence, papers and documents of priceless value in the history of the College. Enlarged during the years by the Watts, Waring, and Pugh letters, papers, diaries, administrational and scientific data, the College has just cause for pride in the prophetic reach of its Founders, for "There were giants in the days of "The Farmers" High School of Pennsylvania."

Even more personal and intimate academic occasions crowed for the mention. The honoring of Professor I. T. Osmond, signaling his long service to the College, by an emeritus relationship met a hearty response among faculty and alumni. A reception and testimonial to W. C. Patterson was a genuine tribute to a rare personality. It was a recognition, likewise, of the fact that not all those who teach in an academic community are "on the Faculty." His long and faithful services, smoothing the ways for work, taking the "kinks" out of academic situations, a spontaneous refuge in almost any emergency, such are the encomiums that seek expression by all who shared in his life. To town and gown, alike, the familiar "one horse shay" and its genial lovable, omnipresent driver was a veritable vision of an ever hovering providence. Trustees, faculty and friends joined, too, in a memorable occasion at the University Club, in doing honor to the thirty years on conspicuous service to the College and to the advancement of science by Doctors H. P. Armsby, G. G. Pond, and William Frear. The reception was held on April 18, 1918, and served to show that even in the midst of the war's alarms, the

---

[28] The Pioneers of Penn State, the issue of the Penn State Alumni Quarterly, Vol. VI, Number 3, April 1916, is a permanent record of the painstaking labors of Dr. Pond, as well as a genuine contribution to the history of the institution.

classical note of the victories, the greater victories of peace may be celebrated.[29]

More noteworthy, if possible, was that unannounced event on the Commencement platform, April 24, 1918. W. H. Teas of the Class of '97 and later a trustee of the College, addressed the audience in part as follows: "He spoke, as he announced, for Dr. W. H. Walker, "our most distinguished graduate chemist, unavoidably absent in chemical warfare work."

"President Sparks, Men and Women of the State College: It is my privilege today to represent some four hundred alumni of old Penn State who have graduated from its courses in Chemistry during the last thirty years; and we appreciate the opportunity granted us by your program committee to present to you a matter of great interest to us. There are certain times of the year, and certain occasions when we are accustomed by habit to do definite things. Certain events call for special celebrations upon their recurrent anniversaries. But once in a while, there springs up spontaneously, as it were, a movement which by its very earnestness sweeps rapidly to success. An idea is announced so pregnant with truth that it swiftly carries conviction to the minds of all it reaches. Such indeed was a chance remark dropped some months ago by a Penn State chemist when in a group of his fellows. It was in effect a desire to express to Dr. Pond in some tangible form a small fraction of the affectionate regard in which he is held by his own students, and the ever deepening sense of gratitude to him for the generous help which is manifold ways and at all times he has bestowed upon them. No seed was ever dropped on more fertile soil. A responsive chord was struck in the heart of every Penn State chemist, and at once there rolled back an anthem of approval and delight. I lack the power to condense in a few sentences the volumes of love and gratitude which every man expressed."

---

[29] May it not be fitting to add a merited tribute in this connection to long and faithful service in less well-known ways to Benjamin Beaver, "Johnny" Carrigan, and Percival Rudy,—and among the living, to Jacob Krumrine, whose campus work covers the period from Dr. Atherton to the present? Nor shall alumni, faculty and students look in vain, also, in this record to find informal recognition of the skillful devotion and ever growing adaptability with which Miss Mary T. Nitsky has served, as Secretary, with four successive administrations and three interregnums, covering nearly the entire period of the institution's real growth.

There follows a tribute which any real teacher might justly covet, together with an explanatory statement, "a committee with William H. Teas at its head soon had a fund commensurate with the purpose," a gift permanent, recurring and of inherent values. "Happily, he continued, there exists an object in which are reflected all these requisites. I have a series of steel engravings entitled Bonds of Friendship and Loyalty which shall grow ever stronger as the years go by. "But, Beware of the Greeks bearing gifts." In accepting this testimonial Dr. Pond incurs an obligation. He must agree to spend for the pleasure of Mrs. Pond and himself the value of the coupons as they mature twice a year. In the realization of this pleasure the donors ask only, that in whatever form it may be derived, the fact he recognized that there are present in spirit four hundred loyal Sons of Penn State to do them honor; that four hundred hearts bear in synchrony, and as many lusty voices wish them added years filled to overflowing with duties faithfully performed, and gratitude doubly earned. It is, therefore, a real privilege, Dr. Pond, on behalf of your chemical graduates, to present you five thousand dollars in Liberty Bonds as a token of our gratitude and of our affection."

The response of Dr. Pond, as well as the address needs no interpretation or comment; the occasion was an honor to the College, to the alumni, and to the whole profession of teaching, as well as to Dean and Mrs. Pond. His reply was fitting and characteristic of the man. "If anything could have been arranged as an anniversary celebration which could overwhelm Mrs. Pond and myself with astonishment and delight to a greater extent than this, my imagination is not sufficiently fertile to enable me to dream what it might be. Splendid as the donation is, from the point of view of its intrinsic value, we weigh the fine spirit behind it, the sympathetic and loving appreciation, the hearty endorsement of long-time policies, as of infinitely greater worth. From the bottom of our hearts, we thank you, and we hope that we may have many more years in which to continue our life work with such cordial friends as this demonstration shows that we posses."

But two years of added service was granted Dean Pond. In the midst of the added duties and cares as acting Executive (owing to the nervous breakdown of President Sparks), on May 20, 1920, he died after an illness of but a few hours. He left a rich legacy in over ten thousand students who had come under his instruction,[30] a loyal band of chemical graduates, many of them in the very forefront of chemical science and practice. The Priestly Memorial Museum at Northumberland is in large part a memorial to him from his men, as well as a tribute to a world renowned scientist. The Pond Chemical Laboratories are outwardly memorializing his achievements, which College history and traditions will ever be the richer on account of the permanent place accorded to him, among the builders of Penn State.

The record of the College in the Great War bears an important place in the chronicles of the administration of President Sparks. It is a story of the proud achievements on the part of Trustees, Faculty, Student Body and Alumni, while it bears no whit less its sombre side in gallant sacrifice of life on battle field, in camp, and at home.[31] Professor Fred Lewis Pattee in an Ode dedicated to the Class of 1917 has embodied, for all time, the spirit which animated and instigated every effort the College put forth, the glory of unselfish endeavor and the mead of undying sacrifice. "Business as usual," "War is temporary, education is permanent," inevitability gave way to The Call of the Hour;

"Oh glorious midst circling hills
Our Alma Mater Stands,
The guardian of our tenderness,
The future in her hands;
But now from out her quiet halls,
There rings a voice to-day,
The nation's rousing bugle call
To battle's stern array.

---

[30] Arranged before his demise but carried out on Commencement, the ten thousandth student entered upon his roll book in Chemistry received a gold watch appropriately inscribed.

[31] The College has published an account of the means and agencies used, honors achieved, and work done in all divisions of the College during the World war. It is credited by Alumni Secretary, Edward N. Sullivan and is dedicated to "The Men of Penn State who made the Supreme Sacrifice in the World War."

That bids us speed to fields unknown,
    By duty's hard decree,
To toil and plan with those who stand
    For God and Liberty;
No more to dream, no more to play,
    No more to view afar
The toil and tumult, and the joy
    And agony of War.

We're with thee, O dear Native Land,
    Thou glorious and free;
Here at our Alma Mater's feet
    We give ourselves to thee;
For Motherland, America,
    Deep laid with tears and pain,
If thou dost fail, then Freedom fails
    And all have died in vain.

Thou canst not fail, America,
    Thy years have just begun;
The light in all the world to-day
    Is from thy rising sun.
That glorious hope shall never die
    Nor tyrants trample thee,
While loves on soul of us to strike
    And die for Liberty.

Events followed in bewildering succession. The fundamental law of the State Colleges and Universities included military training, and since 1863, the College was in some sense preparing for any emergency, national or state that might arise. There was an almost unbroken line in the federal detail of Army

Officers from the times of Lieutenant Walter Howe in January 1877 to Captain Arthur E. Abrends at the outbreak of the World War. The College was thus possibly more quickly responsive to "war's alarms," and with the greater difficulty held the educational keep firm in those trying days. However, pleas for peace, for civilization and for honor without war as well as efforts to avert it, found a free and sympathetic forum here. Preparedness, too, had its Cassandra voice of direful warnings, while to the observant, a growing sense of responsibility for leadership, a more sober appreciation of the values of a moral, world citizenship were forming in the student body. When, therefore, diplomatic relations with Germany were broken on February 3, 1917, in two days, the student body had acted making history. Words were translated into deeds, and up to June 2, 1917, nearly a thousand students had been granted leave of absence. A page from the records reports that: "In a short patriotic demonstration which would rival the spirit shown by our grandfathers in the days of '61, the Penn State student body assembled in Mass Meetings on Monday Night, (February 5, 1917) adopted with a great cheer the following resolutions, which are entirely indicative of the true Penn State Spirit:

"Whereas, The students and alumni of The Pennsylvania State College have for the past sixty years enjoyed the privilege of an education supplied largely by the beneficence of the State and Nation, and

"Whereas, these students and alumni during these years have been instructed in military science for the purpose of being prepared to defend both State and Nation in the event of a crisis;

"Therefore, Be it resolved, speaking of the male students of the College, 2300 in number, That we tender our services, in whatever capacity they can be used, to the President of these United States, and to the Governor of this Commonwealth for preserving the national rights of the Country a giant foreign aggression, and the protection of her citizens in their free use of the seas; Also, Resolved, That we tender to Woodrow Wilson, our unqualified support as President of these United States."

The following replies were immediately received by Cadet Colonel.

A. W. Roberts:

February 6, 1917

The White House

Washington

My dear Colonel Roberts:

May I not thank you for your kind telegram of February 6, and tell your students of the Pennsylvania State College that I am gratified and heartened by your generous assurances.

Cordially and sincerely yours,
Woodrow Wilson

Colonel Archie W. Roberts
State College, Pennsylvania

***

February 6, 1917

Executive Chamber
Harrisburg

Colonel A. W. Roberts
State College Cadet Regiment
State College, Pa.

My dear Colonel Roberts:

The Governor has asked me to acknowledge with thanks the receipt of your telegram of the 6th instant, tendering to the Commonwealth the services of the twenty-three hundred men students of the Pennsylvania State College, trained in military science, for the preservation of our National rights, and to express his high appreciation of the patriotic spirit thereby manifested. Your communication has been referred to the Adjutant General with the request that it receive early attention and consideration.

Yours truly,

W. H. Ball, Private Secretary

***

Definite action was taken toward mobilizing the resources of the institution by the appointment of a Research Committee composed of the Directors of the Agricultural, Engineering, and Mining Experiment Stations, and the Division of Chemistry. A canvass of the upper classes was carried out to determine in "what capacity each is willing to serve in case of emergency." First aid units, wireless telegraph corps, field hospital, and rapid gun fire corps were organized for instant service. Use of College buildings, campus, and athletic fields was tendered to the War Department, and to the National Guard of Pennsylvania for drill grounds and training camps throughout the year. Summer training camps were recommended, and the men of the Summer Session added military instruction to their schedules; the women, first aid and hospital training. With the declaration of war on April 6, 1917, the College had, therefore, both fundamental and temporary emergency measures under way. Thereafter Engineering took care of a continuous stream of group classes in accounting, store-keeping, inventory, disbursement, and transportation. Shops and laboratories did double duty by special training for field and trench, telephone and signal corps, automobile mechanics, and in the work of aviation. Barracks and mess halls were erected near Old Main, and upon Old Beaver Field, the campus was transformed into a veritable army post. At one time, over eleven hundred men without high school education were under emergency training, the trade school and college functioning side by side.

Agriculture doubled and re-doubled its energies in food production, in conservation of soil fertility, in crop adjustments, in eliminating waste, inferior seeds, stock, etc. Farm Bureau and Extension representatives emphasized "war gardens" everywhere; increased dairy and beef products, while home economics leaders carried the "gospel of canning the surplus that nothing be lost." Mining and Chemistry bore their respective parts in training and research upon gases and explosives, tunneling and excavating, map making, topographic and geological, the search for new clay, coal and other deposits.

Lectures on mathematics and the physical sciences, on the historical and economic factors in the war we given by members of the faculty, topics ranging from ballistics to morale. The Library was designated as general receiving and distributing station for books and magazines in barracks, mess halls and in hospital quarters. Cooperating with the American Library Association, the library aided in raising funds, gathering books and magazines for the united library work with the Army and Navy at home and abroad. Special collections on war, strategy, adventure and daring were gathered, and the library was the distributing center for War Posters, War Loan Circulators, Food and Win the War Campaigns.

Thirty officers of the regular Army were stationed at the College, and as President Sparks write their "authority is extended until little is left of the old regime." The upper classes were largely depleted before June 11, 1917, and there was an appreciable falling off on the part of the entering class. The S.A.T.C. unit, the Student Army Training Corps, was sworn into the regular service at an impressive mobilization on the front campus on October 1, 1918. Participating therein were sixteen hundred students; two hundred and sixty three in vocational section; and two hundred and fifty members of the Faculty. Henceforth, if not before, was it apparent, "Old Penn State" as the students phrased it, "She ain't what she used to be. She's in the Army now." College customs had "winked out;" there were no green camps; nor was green grass taboo, could you find any mid the tramp of marching feet. Bugle called at sunrise and taps sounded after fifteen hours of drill and study. Fraternities were barracks, and social functions were not only under a ban, they actually were not. No member of the Student Training Corps was on the street after eight thirty in the evening, and at ten thirty lights went out. Setting up exercises were held on the street before each barracks at seven A. M. College periodicals lapsed; compulsory chapel was abandoned; athletics had all the intercollegiate inflation drained off; students marched to and from classes; a serious air invaded everything. "Over the top," trench warfare, bayonet practice lunging on more or less life-like and hated effigies; hand grenade throwing, gave an air of reality, not the play at war.

The Armistice brought no greater med of joy anywhere than upon the College Campus. Demobilization began December 10, 1918, the College resumed its accustomed work, chastened through suffering, and ready to do its full quota in reconstruction and rehabilitation. Official records reveal that nearly eight thousand students, alumni, faculty, and service men went out from Penn State. Twenty-two hundred and four alumni, including forty-nine from the faculty enlisted. These were grounded in thirty-two branches of the service. In addition, the Student Army Training Corps had under orders nearly fifteen hundred. The roll of commissioned officers numbered ten hundred and thirty-nine. Citations and decorations, both from foreign governments and from the United States, cause just pride to all who cherish brave deeds; while the tablet in honor of those who made the supreme sacrifice, seventy-four men of Penn State, shall ever teach the lessons of the cost of human liberty and the undying glory of its uttermost gift.

The retirement of President Sparks in June 1920, broken in health but not in love for Penn State was part, too, of the toll of war. The Resolutions of the Board of Trustees pay a merited tribute: "Doctor Sparks realized all that was expected of him both as an educator and as our Chief executive, but in the charm of his delightful personality, and by his power as an eloquent and forceful public speaker, he was able to add much to the name and reputation of Penn State throughout the State and Nation. Dr. Sparks was always at home and the peer of any present in the Councils of Educators however distinguished.... Such achievements in so short a time could be accomplished only at a heavy price, and the price our President paid was the sacrifice of his health and strength."

By invitation of the Board of Trustees and the suffrages of his fellow teachers, he remained at the College until his death on June 13, 1924. As Lecturer on American History, he kept the academic faith; while his interest in scholarship and the fraternity of Phi Kappa Phi as its Regent General led him to carry the gospel far and wide. Dr. Thomas affirmed that he was one of the best known figures on the American College campus, and testifies that "in all our relations, which might have been trying to a less generous spirit, he lived perfectly by the Golden Rule." His place in the history of Penn State and in the affections of all who love her is secure.

CHAPTER 14

The Present Decade, A Public Institution in the Service of Commonwealth and Nation: The New Penn State.

"As I see it now, the goal of our effort should be the development of the College into the Pennsylvania State University, directly owned and controlled by the State, with Colleges of Agriculture, Engineering, Mining, Liberal Arts, Education, Home Economics, and a Graduate School located at State College, and the affiliation of such other professional and technical Colleges located elsewhere as will give to the State of Pennsylvania a State University comparable in breadth of program and in direct relation to the State system of education to such Universities as Wisconsin, Minnesota, and Illinois."

President John Martin Thomas, April 29, 1921

"It seems to me that by law, by tradition, by practice, by necessity, by every test that be applied, The Pennsylvania State College is proved a public institution of higher learning. This institution is by these tests to Pennsylvania, potentially if not actually, what the public colleges and universities are to their respective Commonwealths.... There can be no question as to the character of the Institution... Neither am I now concerned what name we shall bear so long as it shall be an honorable one. I have the faith to believe that our people will name us according to our deserts, and if at any time our virtues outgrow the inference of our present title, that they will confer upon us one that is adequate."

President Ralph Dorn Hetzel

For a successor to Dr. Sparks an extended and prolonged search was made. A study was undertaken by a Committee of the Board together with the Comptroller of the directions of growth, the increasing demands upon the institution, the imperative necessity of a more secure and adequate financial basis, as well as the kind of an executive demanded at this particular period of its history. "Growing pains" must be alleviated; more satisfactory provision must be realized for plant, teaching force, and student life. On January 25, 1921, the President of the Board, Judge H. Walton Mitchell reported for the Committee, and authorization was granted to tender the Presidency of the College to Dr. John Martin Thomas of Middlebury College. Happy and markedly successful in his direction of this New England institution, his own Alma Mater, it was with reluctance that these ties and associations were broken. He gave significant expression, however, to the call of a larger opportunity and of a wider service opening before him. He frankly confessed that he believed heart and soul that the future of American Education is in the hands, largely, of the State Colleges and Universities. He affirmed that it could only have been an opportunity thus to identify himself with such an institution, of large and undeveloped possibilities that he could be tempted from his own beloved College and its life.

Dr. Thomas took up his work on April 15, and with a directness born of a love for action outlined a policy for the institution, seeking university status and recognition on the basis of its history, achievements, present standards of scholarship and organization. Changes in internal government, realignment of departments, and the formation of several new schools were also projected. Formal inauguration was postponed until October 13, to 15, 1921, the most elaborate of all Penn State's installations.

The ceremonies were grouped about three ideas:

First, Educational Conference Day whose aim was to bring together some of the best counsel here and elsewhere upon the problems of vocational, industrial, and professional training.

Second, Inauguration Day which centered in the message of Dr. Thomas, and

Third, Alumni Home Coming Day.

Sectional conferences were held during the day on Thursday closing with a general convocation in the evening.

In Agriculture, two topics were discussed: Progress in Rural Life by Dean A. R. Mann of Cornell University; and the Outlook in Agricultural Research by Dr. R. W. Thatcher, Director of the New York Agricultural Experiment Station at Geneva.

In Engineering, the discussions were grouped about the Relation of the Technically Trained Man to the Development of Industry, Economy of Production, and the Relation of the Technical School of Industrial Research. These subjects were presented by Mr. L. W. Wallace of the Federated Engineering Societies of Washington, D. C., by Frank B. Gilbreth, the well-known economy engineer, and by Alfred D. Flinn of the National Research Council.

The Mining Conference stressed research in Mining, Metallurgical and Ceramic Industries. R. A. Holbrook of the United States Bureau of Mines, Dr. Charles H. Warren of the Massachusetts Institute of Technology, and Dr. George H. Ashley, State Geologist of Pennsylvania were the principal speakers.

In Industrial Chemistry and Chemical Engineering the speakers were Dr. Charles H. Herty and William H. Walker.

The Conference of Women emphasized the Education of Women, the Need of Teachers in Home Economics, and Social Significance of Training in the Household Arts. Addresses were made by Miss Florence M. Dibert, President of the Federation of Pennsylvania Women, by Mrs. Henrietta Calvin of the United States Bureau of Education, and by Miss Mary B. Breed of the Carnegie institute of Technology.

Education confirmed its discussion to Financing of Education, the principal speakers were Dr. Thomas E. Finnegan, Professor Edwin R. A. Seligman, Superintendents Edwin C. Broome of Philadelphia and Samuel E. Weber of Scranton.

The closing assembly in which all sections and the public joined was addressed by Mr. Charles M. Schwab. He reaffirmed his friendship for Penn State, and his hearty approval of her work. He expressed his pleasure in speaking in the Auditorium (his much appreciated gift to the College) for the first time. He forcefully argued that the only cure for industrial depression was the resumption of work, rigid economy, and a cheerful facing of the future. In his always optimistic sprit Mr. Schwab affirmed that "at present the United States is only at the beginning of industrial development, and the student of the present day is to be envied because of his opportunities." He insisted that such an investment as the Commonwealth of Pennsylvania has in The Pennsylvania State College is of inestimable value if the State is to continue its lead in American Industry.

Friday, Inauguration Day, began early with a College Parade and ended late at night with the Student Celebration on New Beaver Field. Between these came the chief of inaugural occasions, the installation of Dr. Thomas and the Inaugural Dinner.

The parade was headed by the Military Regiment, the World War Veterans and Rehabilitation of Men; and was followed by exhibits, floats, operations, and projects of all divisions and activities of the College. Agriculture, Engineering, Mining, Natural Science, Liberal Arts, Home Economics, Music, Athletics, Alumni Association, Froth, Collegian and Dramatic Organizations were represented. Many of the exhibits had a distinct educational value since they showed processes in operation. These ranged from mining coal to baking cakes; from vitamin-fed rats to blooded stock; from market quotations to a Sixteenth Century Drama; from the "big bug" of the Entomology Department to the "Say it with Flowers" of the Department of Horticulture.

The Judges were Honorable E. T. Stotesbury, Judge J. W. Kephart, Commissioner L. S. Sadler, and B. D. Coleman, Esquire, and prizes were awarded as follows:

Individual Floats:

> First Prize, Music
> Second Prize, Forestry Camp
> Honorable Mention, Mine Drift.

Group Floats:

> First Prize, Department of Electrical Engineering.
> Second Prize, Agriculture.

The Inauguration Ceremony, the crowning event of the week, followed immediately upon the parade. The Processional was a brilliant spectacle. Representatives from one hundred and twenty Universities and Colleges, and from forty-four Learned Societies were in line. The Auditorium presented an array of eager, happy faces in a setting of bright colors and harmonious decorations. Earnest and befitting addresses were delivered by representatives of the Faculty (Dean Watts), the Alumni (Mr. Shields), and the Student Body (Mr. Overdorf).

Judge H. Walton Mitchell on behalf of the Board of Trustees spoke of the future growth of The Pennsylvania State College, and of the absolute confidence of the Board that the right leader in that future had been found. He formally inducted Dr. Thomas into the office of the President of the College, and the Oath of Office was solemnly administered by Robert Von Moschzisker, Chief Justice of the Supreme Court of Pennsylvania. The introduction of President Thomas was made by His Excellency, William C. Sproul, Governor of the Commonwealth. In fitting words, Governor Sproul welcomed President Thomas on behalf of the State as the new servant and leader of one of its greatest educational institutions.

The inaugural address followed—a scholarly summary of the history and genius of the Farmers' High School, the Peoples' College of 1885, as it is developing by "manifest destiny" into the University of the People of Pennsylvania. President Thomas outlined the immediate, forward steps to be taken, and the practical means necessary to attain these ends. The inaugural was a "brilliant forward pass" as Dean Sackett characterized it, an address which championed a cause with the vigor of the prophets.

The Inaugural Dinner was served at noon in the Armory and toasts were responded by the Governor William C. Sproul, Dr. Thomas E. Finnegan, and by Presidents W. O. Thompson of Ohio State University, David Kinley of the University of Illinois, and Robert E. Vinson of the University of Texas. The addresses were not only felicitous and happy expressions of congratulation to the College and of good-will and best wishes to President Thomas personally, but notably so, were they commendatory of his State University program. The ideals and aims of the State University were ably expressed by President David Kinley, and this brief quotation may be taken as the keynote of all the speakers: "A State University properly conceived is an arm of the State that should be treated as coordinate and not subordinate to the ordinarily accepted political divisions—executive, legislative and judicial. It is the developmental arm of the State. It is the branch of the state government whose main business is the discovery of the path of progress which the people may best follow and the training of men to lead the people in that path. The University should appeal directly to the people, stating its aims and work, in order to let them decide, through instructions to their representatives, how great and large they wish the development arm of the state to be. The University renders three lines of service, residence teaching, research and extension."

The auditorium was packed to the utmost on Friday evening, when President Thomas was duly installed into the fellowship of Penn State students, and his ideals and plans for a great institution were enthusiastically received. Lack of room to accommodate the students in the morning was atoned for by the enthusiasm of this student celebration. Addresses were also made by Dr. Sparks, The Hon. E. T. Stotesbury, by Governor Sproul and Lieutenant Governor Beidleman.

The day closed with an outdoor celebration on Beaver Field. The Band and Glee Clubs furnished music. Freshman Stunts were staged, and Alma Mater was sung to the glow of hundreds of flash lights, rhythmically pulsating in unison as the chorus rolled across the field from stand to stand, and echoed in the distance. A display of fire works closed the evening, with a climax in a set piece of President Thomas accompanied by a salvo of bombs.

One comment from outside must suffice for the many which might be quoted. President Arthur A. Hamerschlag wrote: "I have heard so many favorable comments upon your inaugural exercises that I want to couple them with my own and tell you that the parade of the students, the address of Mr. Schwab, and the simple dignity and deep feeling of the inaugural ceremony comprise a group of addresses and events which mark them as unique in a year in which many similar functions are occurring."

After but four years of forward carrying, rugged, energy, consuming, sacrificing labor for the institution, and out of well-nigh clear sky came the resignation on June 13, 1925. The action of the Board, itself, reads: "Our reluctant acceptance of Dr. Thomas' resignation is caused only by the letter itself not leaving the Board any discretion in the premises. But in so accepting the Board of Trustees of the Pennsylvania State College feels compelled to express its deep regret at this most unexpected termination of Dr. Thomas' labors on our behalf: And to express further its sincere appreciation of the value of his service with us; of his eminent fitness for the position from which he is now voluntarily retiring; of his loyalty, zeal, breadth of vision and sympathetic attitude toward all departments of education; and above all of his splendid personality, his Christian character and broad human sympathies." His own statement at Commencement may best express the sentiment of Dr. Thomas himself: "I have lost none of my confidence in the steady growth and ultimate development of The Pennsylvania State College, but under present circumstances I believe I can do a more constructive service in New Jersey. For many years legislative appropriations to the Pennsylvania State College have been far below the careful estimate prepared by the institution. It is not the hard work a man does which wears him out, but the good work which ought to be done which he cannot do owing to circumstances beyond his control. Both Dr. Sparks and Dr. Atherton my immediate predecessors, broke down before they were sixty years of age.... The state of New Jersey is in urgent need of greater facilities for higher education, and the opportunity at Rutgers for sound development on a large scale in the immediate future presents and appeal which I cannot resist, particularly as New Jersey is my old home state, where I began my professional work and lived for fifteen years. I shall leave Penn State with deep regret. There is no dissention in the institution and entire harmony prevails both in the Board of Trustees and in the faculty. I have had most loyal and hearty support from trustees, faculty, alumni, students and the many friends in the State, all of whom I shall remember in deepest gratitude."

There is much of solid achievement for the College in those four brief years, keyed as it was the most sanguine ideals of expansion. Surely, rarely, does an inaugural so capture the imagination, and call out so vivid a response. There could be no uncertainty or misunderstanding of the program for Penn State as it was conceived in the mind and heart of Dr. Thomas. Brighter skies presaged a new institution, prophecy seemed almost actuality. The justice and courage of the appeal spread to all parts of the Commonwealth, and was echoed, even in national quarters. Its literal realization pales into insignificance when compared with the forces set in motion and the forward direction given to them in the Penn State of today. Let the closing paragraphs of Dr. Thomas' inaugural attest some of these forces; "I am not unaware that the program I have sketched is exceedingly large and difficult. The building of an adequate and worthy state university in the Commonwealth of Pennsylvania is a tremendous undertaking. My friends, I cannot build such a university. The trustees and faculty and alumni of this State College have not the power and ability to build it. If we could, it would not be the Pennsylvania State University. The university must be built upon the conviction and by the will of the nine million people of this Commonwealth. If it be their desire and judgment that on the foundation laid by a handful of earnest farmers sixty-seven years ago an institution of the people and for the people shall be erected to crown the free public education of the Commonwealth, nothing can prevent it. Whether such be the will of the people of the state, I do not know. But these things are clear. There has been a steadily deepening conviction on the part of the people of Pennsylvania for many years that the state should complete its system of public education by university owned by the Commonwealth and entirely under public control. Plans for the erection of such a university by other means than the expansion of this College already owned by the state have not met with favor and have been abandoned.... An educational program adequate to the needs of the state in all except higher education has been undertaken with enthusiasm. The Supreme Court has rendered a decision precluding further state appropriations to sectarian institutions. This State College, founded on the model which has developed state universities in twenty-three other Commonwealths, protected of Almighty God through a half-century of penury and adversity such as almost no other American College has endured, has advanced steadily, and in recent years rapidly, in attendance and influence, and in the good-will and confidence of the people of the state. Everywhere it is spoken of as the people's College. It has students in numbers from every county in Pennsylvania, far and away the most representative student attendance of any College in the state. The Youth of Pennsylvania believe in it, and besiege us with pleas for admission. The farmers believe in it, the business men believe in it, the people generally believe in it; its courses of study are more complete than those of many state universities now existing. Its educational program requires but few additions to make it one of the best rounded state universities in the nation. It needs only the change of one word in its name to take its place with the most noble product of American democracy—the American state universities. I have taken today the only position as to the future of this institution which can be taken consistently with the spirit of its founders and the steady advance of the College to its present power and influence. The guiding of Providence and the steady push of events, in other institutions not less than our own, have been toward the establishment of Pennsylvania's University here. Humbly before the opportunity and responsibility, we tender all we have and our utmost effort in the future to the good people of this state and loyally await their will."

The increase in the student body during the period just under review had been so marked, that plant, facilities, teaching force, financial support were all outgrown. Nowhere were the buildings or laboratories adequate to the numbers, who despite limitation of the entering classes, thronged the campus. Garrets and basements were utilized, temporary structures, precariously housing valuable and significant apparatus and equipment, continued to be used. Even the colosseum-like Old Main was condemned as unsafe, while dormitories, lecture rooms and offices were not available in her stead. Chemistry, physics, botany, zoology were carried on under conditions that sorely tested at times both teacher and students. Engineering was experiencing a phenomenal growth, its facilities foreshortened even by calamitous fire. Dairy and animal husbandry, agricultural chemistry, and bacteriology were cabined and confined; laboratories in some instances doing duty as offices and lecture rooms as well. Arts and letters, the library, stores and supplies, student organizations and activities; all were handicapped by the conditions and necessities of the time. Student publications had more than once dangerously bordered on truth in "viewing with alarm" the increasing tide of temporary structures or in more accurate terms "shanties"; while a tempered criticism and warning of the loss of worthy teachers because of inadequate maintenance and salary budgets, struck a yet more significant note.

But be it said with emphasis, there is not the least tinge of criticism or blame implied locally in these facts. The conditions were such when Dr. Atherton and Dr. Sparks assumed the presidency, and they were accentuated by the very success which attended their labors. In the first report of Dr. Sparks, we find him deploring the fact that "much of our work must continue to be done and our valuable equipment continue to be housed in temporary frame buildings; which are little short of a disgrace to the wealthy state of Pennsylvania. A stranger viewing some of these disfigurements on the fair slope of our Campus might imagine that this State College represented one of the newest and poorest states of the Union, instead of one of the oldest and richest.... The greatest need of the College at present is additional buildings.... The general condition may be likened to that of a child who has outgrown its clothes; one part of the garment is scarcely let out until discomfort is manifest in another place. In addition to recitation rooms, shops and laboratories, there is great need of buildings for purposes lying outside recitations or practicums. The extensive athletic field is not as yet supplemented by a gymnasium for winter exercise. A playground fitted for every kind of outdoor sports yet lacking facilities for bathing cannot be considered complete. Also there is demonstrated each day the need of a student club house. Between recitations the students living in the village must return to their rooms, and this means a growing inconvenience and a loss of time as the village extends its limits. The student body has no home for its social life."

Here was a program and a challenge, both of which became more insistent with the passing years. They reached the breaking point at the opening of the last decade, and the story, especially of the last five years, makes history read like romance.

This challenge was met by the College and Alumni in the campaigns to set before the legislature and the people of the state the actual, imperative, even crucial needs of the institution. An alumni fund which should appeal, also, to the friends of the College was undertaken to meet some of the emergencies that confronted the new administration. The alumni endowment fund movement of June 1920, grew into the Welfare and Emergency Building Campaign essaying to raise two million dollars. The minute of the Board of Trustees reads: "In harmony with the resolution on alumni contributions adopted April 29, 1921, the Trustees approve an effort on the part of the alumni and friends of the College to raise a building fund of at least two million dollars to be expended when secured approximately as follows:

> Track House or Varsity Hall $125,000
> Recreation Hall, Gymnasium and Swimming Pool $500,000
> Hospital $150,000
> Residences for Women $150,000
> Home Economics Laboratory and Cafeteria $150,000
> Library Additions $350,000
> Restoration of Old Main $175,000
> Penn State Union $400,000

With the outlook so auspiciously dawning, campus plans were revised. The College architects were commissioned to adopt a permanent plan looking toward a College of at least ten thousand resident students. The Lowrie plans of 1907 as modified in 1914 were to provide certain basic features in working out present needs, while a larger and more thorough provision for the future growth and expansion was to be made. Preliminary consideration was, also, given to residence halls for men, and for an early reconstruction of Old Main as an administration and student activities building. A standing committee on College architecture was named by the trustees, consisting of the Presidents of the Board and of the College, and Messrs. McCormick, Hamill, and Shields.

Plans for the campaign were made in the spring of 1922 and prosecuted in what was termed the "busiest summer in the history of Penn State." Expert direction in such campaigns was secured, and the expenses underwritten. An executive committee upon whose shoulders fell the immediate direction and correlation of effort consisted of Dr. Thomas, Messrs. R. H. Smith, J. F. Rodgers, E. K. Hibshman, E. N. Sullivan, and Miss L. V. T. Simmons. Organizations were formed in every county; alumni clubs, faculty, students, summer session, extension workers, every arm and agency of the College was an organ of publicity and solicitation. The Parents Association formed in May 1922 became a "booster" for the emergency campaign. President Harding, Governor Sproul, and an advisory committee of prominent men and women of the Commonwealth endorsed the movement. Flying squadrons of faculty and alumni speakers covered the State, and human ingenuity seemed exhaustless in the flow of striking and varied means of publicity. One of the most effective forms of appeal was the publication by alumni and friends of the College, of a pamphlet, The Faith of the State. It set forth the organic facts of the relation to the Commonwealth, federal and state support, organization, needs and plans for the development of the institution. It portrayed graphically what the alumni and friends of the College were doing by way of self-help in the two million dollar emergency building campaign, thus enforcing the opportunity and obligation of the state for necessary academic structures and for more adequate maintenance.

A huge thermometer was erected which reached to the top of Old Main to register the rise in the flow of gifts. Under the genial warmth of the early stages of the campaign, the subscriptions rose rapidly, but as newer and more distant sources had to be tapped, and the frosts touched the campaign, the ascent was more difficult. In all essential respects, however, the movement succeeded, its secondary results are abiding. A report of the Comptroller for June 30, 1927, solicitations having practically ceased, gives the following as the total pledged including accrued interest, one million six hundred and ninety four thousand eight hundred and seventy four dollars and sixty-two cents. The aggregate of collections is, however, nearly a half million short, which with expenses of campaign reduces the sum actually realized to about one million. The fruits have been (extending to the present (1932) and in part only attributable to the fund) Varsity and Recreation Halls, dormitories for men, the Hospital (Potato Growers Association of Pennsylvania), and the Grange Memorial Dormitory for women.

The Bond issue was a second large constructive measure urged by the College, and given hearty support by President Thomas. The law prohibited the use of any federal grants or funds for buildings, the sates were wisely to provide these. In the fulfillment of her pledge, the faith of the state, the Bond Issue would carry a guarantee of funds over the term of years, with the advantages of careful planning for present emergencies and the needs of the immediate future. A constitutional amendment therefore passed the Legislature in the sessions of 1923 and 1925. Its second adoption was unanimous in both houses. It would, therefore, have come up for approval by the voters of the state at once, had not an opinion of the Supreme Court intervened. The last revision of the constitution was made in 1923 and since revisions may be submitted to vote only after intervals of five years, the College bond issue with others was relegated to 1928. The sequel to this is a later story and of signal interest.

Four internal changes of major importance were the institution of the College Senate; the establishment of a graduate school; a school of education; and a realignment of chemistry and physics so as to constitute practically a new school.

The College faculty had become too large a body for legislative purposes. The growing consciousness and individuality of the several schools were leading in the direction of more autonomy and differentiation in academic actions. Initiation at least lay with the several school faculties. There was, therefore, a dominant reason for a representative body of instruction and administration which should harmonize, adjust and correlate the legislative

355

interests of the College. A College Senate was authorized by the trustees, June 12, 1921 to be composed of deans, directors and department heads, general administrative officers and three representatives elected from each school. It was constituted the sole legislative body on all questions that pertain to the educational interests of the College and on all matters that concern more than one faculty, subject to the jurisdiction of the Board of Trustees. The list of committees was revised, and added responsibility placed for the widest acquaintance with the best practices and solutions of problems elsewhere, as well as for the execution of policies and principles agreed upon and become matters of legislation. The committees as originally blocked out were those of educational policy; courses of study and curricula; admission; graduation requirements; honors and scholarships; College calendar; and regulations affecting students.

Graduate instruction was given as early as 1862, two students were enrolled with Dr. Pugh. One was a graduate of the College in its first class, C. Alfred Smith, the other Augustus King,[32] a graduate of Columbia College. Instruction and investigation were carried on in individual ways, under the direct stimulus of the teacher. Administration was simple in form but under the general guidance of a committee with its chairman. Thus Presidents Pugh and Fraser, Dr. Buckhout, Deans Pond, Holmes, Moore, and Holbrook directed graduate study until the school was formed in 1922. To that time, nearly nine hundred students had been enrolled; there was a distinct place for more centralized and yet more cooperative endeavor in improving graduate study. Dr. F. D. Kern was appointed as Dean, and an organization of the new

---

[32] A distinctly human touch is given in a footnote of the catalogue as follows: "It is our painful duty to record the death of this promising young man, who by his goodness of heart and gentlemanly demeanor had endeared himself to all his instructors and associates during his residence with us. He left College about the 1st of August, apparently in good health, to be with his venerable father, (Pres. King of Columbia College), for a few days, as he said, to solace him in view of the danger to which his brother (Gen. King) was exposed in the Army of the Potomac. He arrived at home somewhat indisposed, though not thought to be seriously so; but after some days his case developed into Diphtheria, and finally ended with Typhoid fever, of which he breathed his last. His friends may assuredly feel that the loss of a friend upon earth has been his gain of many in heaven."

school was effected at a meeting held November 6, 1922. The school had an enrollment in its initial year of one hundred and seventy-three. The College has a proud record of awarding degrees for work done, only; and has consistently maintained high standards of scholarship for its graduate honors. On April 18, 1924, the Executive Committee of the College, on recommendation of the Graduate faculty voted to approve the granting of the degree, doctor of philosophy. Its first bestowal was upon Marsh W. White in June 1926, the dissertation was "A Study of the Energy of High Velocity Electrons."

A third important internal step was the establishment of a School of Education in 1923. Dr. W. G. Chambers, appointed as Dean, had come to the College two years earlier as director of the summer session and of educational extension. In this school were brought together teacher training and psychology from Liberal Arts, Agricultural or Rural Education[33] and Industrial Education from the schools respectively of Agriculture and Engineering, and certain unattached departments, home economics, and nature study or as later denominated nature education.

The fourth major action relates to the school of Natural Science. The report of the committee is important not only for the settlement of immediate issues, but for its bearing upon the whole question of the relation of the sciences to the arts or technologies. A considerable body felt that the time had come for a strong, dominating, traditional school of Arts and Sciences, perhaps allocating to its ample fold and stray waifs in other schools. The whole problem was referred to a committee appointed by the Trustees, consisting of Messrs. Walker, Shields, Mitchell, Dr. Stoddart, and the President of the College. A few excerpts from the report will best resumé the situation, alternatives, and conclusions arrived at: "Your committee has been unable to obtain authoritative information as to the motives which controlled the division of the sciences which would normally come under the head of "Natural Science" among the three Schools of Natural Science, Agriculture

---

[33] This department has, however, been reunited with the School of Agriculture since 1925.

and Mines. This division took place some twenty-five years ago, and the reasons for the present organization rather than the more logical one of combining all the natural sciences into one school are not easy to determine. Since the death of Dean G. G. Pond on May 20, 1920, the School of Natural Science has been administered by Dr. Charles W. Stoddart, who is Dean of the School of Liberal Arts.

At least four possibilities present themselves:

> A. Reallocate the subjects which are normally classified as natural sciences, now located in the Schools of Natural Science, Agriculture, and Mines, and thus establish a School of Natural Science in line with the organizations found elsewhere in analogous institutions.

> B. Allow the School of Natural Science to remain as now constituted, but combine it for administrative purposes with the School of Liberal Arts.

> C. Retain the present division of natural sciences among the three schools but provide a separate Dean for the School of Natural Science.

> D. Abandon the name, "School of Natural Science," and establish a new school under the name School of Chemistry and Physics."

The latter course is deemed the wisest as the various reasons and interests are unfolded. The selection of Gerald W. Wendt as Dean brought vigorous life to the School in the directions of a cultural pursuit of pure science; in a division of industrial research, and in the application of science to the industries generally. These results are being markedly strengthened and extended by Dean Frank C. Whitmore who succeeded to the deanship in July 1929.

Enrollments during the term of Dr. Thomas in both regular and summer sessions increased by six hundred each. The faculty grew from four hundred and ten to seven hundred and sixty, the increase largely attributable to extension and research; and provided for in supplementary federal legislation to the Morrill and Hatch Acts. Appropriations from the State, however, were less in the bienniums of 1923 and 1925 than in 1921; needs meanwhile becoming greater and the emergency more acute. Four new buildings were erected, the Mechanical Laboratory, Watts Hall, Beef-Cattle Barn and Varsity Hall. To relieve intolerable conditions in office space in Old Main, the last internal alterations were made in 1922, and the offices of the President, Comptroller, and Purchasing Agent were moved to the second floor. Lecture and recitation rooms, the School of Education, and Teacher Training Extension brought congestion again in the quarters vacated. The dormitories, themselves, were definitely closed in the interests of safety in June 1924; a few years only of a stately silence in the topmost floors and a sporadic use by what were termed the "lighter classes" of these hazardous quarters remained ere the final trek from Old Main was completed.

Additions to curricula were made as follows: Farm Machinery, Poultry Husbandry and Highway Engineering in 1920, Architecture, a year later. Agricultural Economics was organized in 1923, with Ceramics and Chemical Engineering, the following year. Special institutes were featured in the Summer Session in French, English, Education and more recently in Music and Physical Education. Among the chief personnel changes in this first half of the decade was the appointment of Dr. Stoddart as Dean of the School of Liberal Arts. The School has had a rapid growth second in numbers in the entire institution.[34] The work has been coordinated into three main types of curricula: Arts and Letters, Commerce and Finance, and Journalism. The cultural aims and practices have been given both edge and definite direction. Deans Holbrook of Mines, Chambers of Education, and Ray of Women became new school heads. Forbes succeeded Armsby in Animal Nutrition;

---

[34] The enrollment in the School of Liberal Arts has increased from 420 in 1920 to 990 in 1931; the faculty from 82 to 113. Approximately sixty per cent of the instruction in the school is for students in other schools. Every student in College averages two and a half courses in Liberal Arts each Semester, and of the grades recorded in the office of the Registrar each Semester, Liberal Arts turns in 10,000 out of the approximate College total of 35,000.

while men like Moore in Education, Dutcher in Biochemistry; Grant in Music; Owens in Mathematics, Everett, Hechler, and Kaulfuss in Engineering are notable additions to the staff. In 1923, a new alignment of work in the School of Agriculture under instruction, research, and extension was effected. Vice Deans were charged with the separate divisions, while oversight and general direction lodged as before in Dean Watts, who is also Director of the Experiment Station. William G. Murtoff was elected as Treasurer of the College in 1924, and together with the Comptroller, and Purchasing Agent, a modern and efficient system of College finance has ensued.

Scholarship Day was established on April 27, 1922. Its celebration at first semi-annually, brings a notable address, and the announcement of scholarships and fellowships, prizes and awards, student and faculty honors, and the elections to honor societies, of which there are now some twenty. A Committee of the Senate on instruction in the sciences was added in 1924, while the same year the honor point system was adopted. Both have resulted in raising the general level of scholarship, and in holding out a more distinct appeal to outstanding ability and industry.

The functions of the Freshman Advisor System have gradually reverted once more to the several schools. A more general acquaintance with the institution and the work of the several departments has, however, been achieved by Freshman Week. The first session was held in September 1925, with Dr. Fraser Metzger, College Chaplain since 1923, as chairman. The types of work were assemblies, school meetings, lectures, classes, mass meetings, and miscellaneous. The schedules were filled to overflowing with mental tests, military organization, singing and cheer practice, instruction in the use of library, and how to study. Student conduct, cultural objectives, character building, and vocational guidance, also, had their repeated part in the role of events. The first program, perhaps attempted too much, it was too rich and varied. There was no time for digestion and assimilation. Simplified and coordinated under the inspiration of the Dean of Men and others, it has continued to justify itself. It is accordingly realizing what Dean Warnock has described so concisely as the primary purpose; "to enable the Freshman to do his College work more efficiently from the start."

Some important changes in the means of publicity are to be noted. The Faculty Bulletin begun in 1921 carries weekly news, and forecasts the academic weather. The annual report was issued in a new form the following year, its accustomed statistical contributions to science and art printed elsewhere. Broadcasting as a College "activity" also began in 1922; "sawing the air" is no longer a mere professorial caricature. Cooperation with organizations and agencies within the State was furthered. It is invidious to cite but one instance of so many. However a survey of the College by the State Chamber of Commerce resulted in a valuable report which that organization sponsored and widely circulated. The Trustees gave cordial expression of gratitude, therefore. The rulings of the Attorney General's Department on the status of the College as a State Institution, upon the questions of insurance; inheritance, income, and gasoline taxes; and the State Employees Retirement Act are also noteworthy as directions of public moment and concern.

Memorials in several directions call for brief record. From James Gilbert White, whose previously mentioned gifts have enhanced scholarship, came two loan funds of twenty-five thousand dollars each. The Mary Beaver White Loan Fund and the James A. Beaver Loan Fund are signal memorials, as well as the perpetual means of meeting the needs of worthy students. The Edwin Erie Sparks Memorial Library of American History owes much to friends of Dr. Sparks, everywhere. It was established in 1925, and will continue to enrich the resources of the College Library in the lines so effectively served by the scholarship of President Sparks. The John Hamilton Fund established in 1921 from legacy of John Hamilton for endowment of religious work and purchase of evangelical religious books for the library, also carries a memorial of long time service to the College.

With a Delphic prescience of the rapidly approaching senescent doom of Old Main and a Stoic-like surrender to fate, the passing of the "Old Willow," Old Main's lonely sentinel, has poignant interest. So lone the "picture of loveliness and stately grace," it is as much a part of Penn State as buildings or men. Tenderly nurtured and sentimentally guarded, it was given hearts of stone and anchors of chains to prolong its life. But it stood at the parting of the ways, and on April 26, 1921, the south branch fell. Two years later August

21, 1923, the remainder of the tree succumbed. Mr. L. H. Dennis of the class of 1912, writing in the Penn State Farmer, lamenting the fact that "repairs" had not been undertaken earlier, threw out the fertile suggestion that a shoot be started from the old tree as a successor. During the Commencement season of 1921, a cutting nurtured by Treasurer and Mrs. W. G. Murtoff was transplanted near the site of the Old Willow, where today it bids fair to rival in beauty and affection, its progenitor.

The 'Old Willow' has been the recipient of boundless sentiment, of many poems of praise, and of myriad photographs. The La Vies of 1916 and following years contain splendid reproductions, both real and in artistic embellishment, showing that even in its declining years, it wore the garb of beauty and continued to hold a genuine place in the hearts of Penn State men as our oldest natural tradition. Who planted it? Tradition answers variously. William G. Waring set it out. Some workmen in the College placed it as a marker for a fork in the roads. Dr. Pugh brought it, a "bit of England," a "scion from a willow on the poet Pope's grounds at Twickenham." One tradition connects it with the willows that wept with Napoleon at St. Helena, and a certain mythical tales have attributed to it a sort of spontaneous generation. Suffice it to say, it was planted about 1859, and its most likely sponsor is that self-same first horticulturalist and superintendent of farms and "College lot," an artist-enthusiast in his profession, who did have in the College nurseries as many as sixty varieties of growing willows to display to admiring visitors.

Foregoing the attempt to assess historic import; and content to recount some of the progress and activities of this fruitful decade, we turn now to the last five years, a short time in the life of an institution. Yet so crowded is the stage, so varied and multiplied the forces at work, that only trends may be indicated, only selected achievements detailed. Narrative perforce lags while history is being made and remade. The passing of the Old Willow, just described, is but nature's illustration of the fact that men, their institutional work and handicraft must also pass. Call the roll of the decade, how the ranks have been decimated, beginning with Pond, and continuing with Armsby, Frear, Stecker, Willard, Sparks, Thompson, Hamilton, Tudor, Webber, Foster, Anderson, Crockett, Wood. A college that can suffer such losses has regal cause to honor, such as these, if her heritage is spiritual. Pass in review the landmarks on the campus ripe for the harvest; Old Main, Old Track House, Old Beaver Field, Old Mining Sheds, Old Flour Mill Group, Old West Barns.[35]

Follow the expanding view as giant trees fall upon the front campus, receding to right and to left, while a fit environment, a setting of sweep and beauty, emerges with the new Old Main. Mark the disappearing Ghost Walk and its funereal array of ragged pines and hemlocks, while friendly vistas of "Ag Hill" and "Pond Lab" open up. Scan fraternity row, rescued from its blanketing of hedge that in age vied with that of the institution itself. Behold a campus whose sparse walks were tunnel coverings or bare trunk-line connections, metamorphosed into a criss-cross and maze of convenient, time-saving ways. Recount the last athletes to gambol and race on Old Beaver Field, now flanked by Botany, number one, with the serried ranks of official parking where cinder paths once held away; while across the road where cabbages were kings; the Hospital and Grange Dormitory for Women now reign. Watch Liberal Arts annex another expanse of old orchard for Unit number two, while it is still remains the most congested, most thronged of all the academic abodes. Hear the wall of falling oaks as they make way for Recreation Hall, Frear Dormitory and the Nittany Lion Inn. See utility joined in a symphony of light, heat, and power, splendid supplanter of the old College avenue mining group; while Mineral Industries under Dean Steidle has begun to appropriate the pre-empted domain of a military field. Note, well a new Engineering building, commanding as of yore the main campus entrance; while the old railway station has taken to itself wings to become a suburban ornament instead of a metropolitan blot. Better than all, mark Allen and Pugh

---

[35] That destruction and replacement have followed dire necessity and emergency, only; let such remaining temporary and outgrown, outworn and out moded structures, the survival of the least unfit, attest. Such for example are the frame forestry layout, the armory and improvised annexes, the old botany and chemistry block-houses, frame Engineering F. the existing or resisting scraps of the ninety-one power plant that survived the fire of 1918, and the little oil and powder house whose utility has long since been relegated to archeology.

Streets barred from the Campus, while a mall or malls are extending a stately beauty farther and farther northward to the central and pivotal quadrangles of the institution, the Arts and the Sciences. In these very latest days, observe the disentombment of the cemetery of debris from the Engineering holocaust, to furnish a site for Home Economics; while Dairying has gone just over the brow of the hill, to a most commanding spot there the broad acres of the College demesne, its flocks and herds, from Dan to Beersheba, may be surveyed.

Putting this in plain terms, in five years, fifteen major structures and units were erected, beside a Veterinary Hospital, Sheep Barn, Poultry Range, and an addition to the Dairy Barns, Calling the catalogue of ships, they are Service and Stores, Hospital, Recreation Hall, Mineral Industries, Engineering, New Old Main, Frear Dormitory, Pond Laboratory, Grange Dormitory for Women, Botany Unit, Power Plant, Liberal Arts Unit, Home Economics, Dairy, Nittany Lion Inn. Physical improvements in other structures and a veritable transformation of the Campus, itself, bring the total new investment in the physical plant during the five years to over five and a half million.

The real significance for Penn State of this increase of facilities and plant betterment, the relation to the larger plans for the College, and to the service it renders are brought out clearly in a recent address of Dr. Hetzel, Forces Moulding Penn State. I quote: "Unfortunately, failure to make provision for the development of the institution over a period of many years made it imperative that most of this has had to go into replacement of buildings inadequate in the beginning and exhausted by long and heavy service. But this development of the Campus has made it possible for us to see the physical beginning of the great Penn State.

"If you will study these buildings and improvements carefully, you will discern a hint of the extent, the beauty and the logical and efficient inter-relationship which will be the glory of future days. You will need a goodly measure of faith to catch the full vision of the future; you need only an open mind and a sense of the fitness of things to share the rapidly improving facilities and the growing beauty of the Penn State of today.

"Let me illustrate more concretely both the plan and the faith of which I speak. When the officials of the State called for the estimates of funds needed for buildings at the College during this present biennium, there was submitted a carefully studied and a fully supported estimate exceeding in total the sum of eight million dollars. A little less than one million was granted, but it was not denied that eight millions were needed. Let me give you a kaleidoscopic view of what Penn State would have been in physical form at the end of the year 1933 had this request been granted.

"In addition to the diary building and the home economics building, now under construction, [36] there would have been a new forestry building, a building for the housing of agricultural biochemistry, a farm machinery laboratory, an electrical engineering building, the completion of the liberal arts building by the construction of the central unit, a building for the housing of a modern journalistic and printing plant, the completion of the Pond chemical laboratory, the construction of the first two wings of a physics building, a home for the orphaned School of Education, dormitories for women capable of housing three hundred persons, a second unit of the Recreation Building which would contain a swimming pool and adequate and proper facilities for lockers, a gymnasium and activities building for the women students of the institution, and in addition to these there would have been provided many seriously needed green houses and farm and other service buildings. This is not the greater Penn State of fifty years hence, but what is

---

[36] Since the above was written, an added note may find place..The Home Economics Building has been completed, and was first used during the Summer Session of 1932. On August 26, 1932, the Dairy Building was dedicated. The Commonwealth was represented by Clyde L. King, Secretary of Revenue who was personally commissioned by Governor Pinchot to make the Presentation address, and by the Secretary of Agriculture, John A. McSparran who gave the Dedicatory Address. College speakers included, among others, President J. Franklin Shields of the Board, President Hetzel. The outdoor staging of the celebration was especially fitting. Emphasis was placed upon the opportunities and certainties of yet larger and better service to the Commonwealth by the more adequate facilities for instruction and research in Dairy Husbandry and Production thus provided.

sorely needed now to meet with reasonable adequacy the demands that are being made upon the College.

"I have used the physical plant as the major vehicle in presenting the picture not because I consider it the most important factor, but because it is the best medium for picture making. More important, much more vital is the quality of the men and women who will study and teach, investigate and inspire. And of equal importance with this is the quality of those gathered here to learn. In the accepted scheme of things, both of these eclipse in importance and in the provisions of the larger plan the consideration given to the physical plant.

"But why a larger Penn State? I am compelled to answer that if Penn State is a public institution and maintained in order to serve the vital needs of this great commonwealth, it must take on the proportions necessary to the task. This implies no sacrifices in quality of service, in fact the plan calls for constantly advancing standards. The handwriting is already upon the wall. Entrance requirements now demand a greater evidence of capacity and disposition to profit from college training. There is being set up more and increasingly efficient research. There is a growing emphasis upon the field of graduate study, the encouragement of productive scholarship, insistence upon higher standards of conduct; in short, the gradual development of an educational environment of the highest order. The very fact of increasing excellence in quality will bring increasing demand for enlargement of out-put. The world needs much of quality education rather than little. A measure of the virtue of a small house may be in its smallness, but if a large house is needed, smallness ceases to be a virtue. If Penn State is to give in quality and in quantity what is now being asked, and what will be demanded in increasing measure of the Penn State of the future, it must be prepared for the tasks both in the quality and the scope of its service."

But narration of achievement has outrun chronology. We must retrace our steps to the resignation of Dr. Thomas.

To an administrative committee consisting of the three senior Deans, Watts, Sackett, and Stoddart, with the President of the Board, Judge Mitchell, and R. H. Smith, Executive Secretary, was entrusted the direction of College affairs. Judge Mitchell who was approaching his twenty-fifth year of membership on the Board, and as its chairman since General Beaver's death in 1914 was a guarantee that no essential interests of the institution would be overlooked while a successor to Dr. Thomas was sought. The committee functioned wisely and harmoniously, and won the gratitude of the Board, faculty and student body. Unusual thoroughness and deliberation, therefore characterized the search for more than a year for the right man to guide the destinies of Penn State. The committee of the Board, Judge H. Walton Mitchell, Chairman, Vance C. McCormick of Harrisburg, James L. Hamill of Columbus, Ohio, W. S. Wise of Meadville and John F. Shields of Philadelphia brought a unanimous recommendation, which received like action by the Board. The call was extended to Dr. R. D. Hetzel, and on September 25, 1926, the acceptance which is meaning so much to The Pennsylvania State College was received.

The youngest but one in the entire panoply of Penn State's presidents, his training and experiences were most ideal. A graduate of the University of Wisconsin, both academic and in law, he was connected with Oregon State College as teacher of political science and later as director of the extension division. He was President of New Hampshire State College during nine years of growth, reorganization, State support and guidance into university status. He possesses an enthusiasm for research which in common life as everywhere is basing conclusions on facts; and is singularly free from any of the taint of officialism. With a positive gift for leadership, equaled by a genuine spirit of cooperation, of enlistment and cordial recognition of mutual endeavor, Penn State is in very truth happy in its increasing tasks and responsibilities under his inspiration.

Dr. Hetzel entered upon his duties on January 1, 1927. Already installed and adopted into the family of Penn State, a simple dignified, and fitting inaugural occasion followed in June in connection with the regular Commencement Exercises. Dr. Hetzel's address was an inspiring review of the Land-Grant movement, its significance for State and Nation. The comment of the Alumni News shall be taken as representative, "one of those fine rare documents well delivered, impressing all with its depth and sincerity of purpose, with no frills, but containing the elements of strength and resource, those very elements needed to give confidence for the future of Penn State."

Impressive as is the initial physical regeneration of Penn State, it is only a part of the story of change and progress; of "unfinished business" finished, though clinging sometimes like barnacles to the Penn State craft; of new business transacted under fresh "sailing orders" to more strenuous seas but happy harbors. We detail some of these, the record is crowded with achievement, full of promise for the future, instinct with hope.

The Bond Issue was unfinished business of large moment. The electorate of the Commonwealth was to have its first direct opportunity to record its will for the College. Right royal was the response viewed in the light of the conditions—a distinct example of the success of failure. Of the five bond issues at the election of November 6, 1928 the College polled the largest vote by a quarter of a million and carried thirty-eight counties out of the sixty-seven. It lost eight counties by less than a thousand; fourteen by less than five thousand and in only six counties was the negative vote over that figure. The total minority was but twenty-six thousand five hundred and sixty one. Defeat rested squarely upon the conviction that current funds in the State Treasury were adequate to meet the needs. The Pittsburgh Post Gazette voiced the public sentiment of all parts of the Commonwealth; "Who can doubt that a bond issue proposal as popular as that would have won sweepingly, if there had not been the implied assurance that the needs of the College would be met adequately by the next State budget."

Publicity was "home made," the campaign College managed; the organization reaching out to every county and town of the State. Of one little brochure, "For the Future of the Youth of Pennsylvania—Give your vote," a million and a quarter were distributed. For the statistically minded, these laid end to end would reach nearly a hundred and twenty miles. Radio talks, whirlwind campaigns, slogans of reason and rime, reminders wrapped with bread deliveries, every maxim and axiom of art and science had its innings. One of the pleasant features was the way sister institutions and student bodies "lent a hand" for "your Penn State bond issue." The whole campaign was without a note either of rivalry or bitterness.

In all essential respects, the new physical education movement of which Penn State is justly proud, and in which the College pioneered is "a sport for every man" individually and collectively keyed to health of body and vigor of mind. The situation remedial has been described by Dr. Hetzel in these words: "Intercollegiate athletics at Penn State, as was the case in the great majority of the Colleges and Universities of the country, grew up as an orphan child. College faculties and trustees did not see fit to concern themselves seriously with it, and so it was farmed out, nursed in its infancy by the students and handed over in its troublesome maturity largely to the alumni. In fact, however, this orphan took on such proportions and such vigor that it ceased to be controlled either by students or alumni and became a victim of circumstances. Athletic contests became so spectacular that they quickly and in alarming measure attracted the attention of the public. Gate receipts grew, and gate receipts at institutions whose teams won the greatest number of games, exceeded the gate receipts of other institutions. This seems to make it desirable that there should be set up at each institution every possible facility designed to increase the chances of victory. Competition became keen for skilled coaches. Salaries for these men mounted in direct relation to their success in winning games. Great stadiums were built, involving millions of dollars. The time and the energy of student players were so completely absorbed that they remained students in name only. Pressure was brought to bear upon institutions to offer subsidies to promising young athletes. Serious abuses developed form which students suffered and which compromised the character and reputation of American Colleges and Universities. The spirit of good sportsmanship departed. The futility and viciousness of the whole situation soon began to be apparent to all thinking persons."

Not all these abuses characterized Penn State, her "isolated position" rendered her immune to some forms of athletic contagion, and at the same time fostered a more marked development of intramural games and contests. But guilt was the proper confession long before committees began "finding out" what they and the College body already well knew, or before subsidized foundations turned their batteries upon the commonplaces of athletic codes and practices. Self-complacency has been the besetting academic sin, while reforms when honestly undertaken, and they are many, have been justified by their fruits. Hints of over-emphasis of football, too much concentration on teams, over-stimulation and production of specialists in sports, and too little attention to facilities for mass athletics and general physical development began to be heard. The multiplication of so-called athletic scholarships (perfectly defensible if administered in the spirit of their inception) became a storm center of criticism. Increased to a maximum number, in their golden age, to seventy-five, they had become not incentives to and rewards of scholarship with athletic proclivities, but "baits" for the latter, and rewards, mayhap, for lack of the former. Varsity Hall, too, had until 1928 when it was made an open part of the men's dormitory system, a considerable scope for the attraction of athletic prowess; while the "training table" could, without couvert charges, make a rather tempting, attractive, convenient, and flexible appeal.

A group of committees at about the same time took up the general problem, a perennial one in our academic life. The original action in the latest reformation seems to have come from the Council of Administration when on May 10, 1926, it was voted that an investigation be made of the present method of athletic control and recommendations submitted to the Senate and Trustees. On May 20, the Senate named a committee consisting of Holbrook, Bressler, Duncan, Martin, Hurrell, and Kinsloe. The alumni on June 14 adopted the following resolution: "that a committee of alumni be appointed by the President of the Alumni Association for the purpose of making a survey of the relations of athletics activities to the student body, faculty and alumni with recommendations lending toward closer cooperation and any changes necessary therefor." The first report was made to the association on October 22, 1926, the final one on February 26, 1927. The stress on needed cooperation in the original resolution of the alumni was affected by adjusting and harmonizing the findings and reports made, finally, by representatives of the Board, Faculty, Alumni and Students. The result, a School of Physical Education and Athletics has been established with a Director "given the same status and same responsibilities, ad Deans of other Schools, and effective July 1, 1930. The finances of intercollegiate athletics were budgeted within the School, the members of the coaching staff were given rank and status as members of the faculty of the institution. *All subsidies to students, granted because of athletic skill, were abolished...* The councils, generally composed of alumni and students became not the governing bodies, but advisory bodies. The final responsibility for athletic policy and procedure was vested in the officers of the institution."

Compulsory chapel was another of those academic waifs left upon the presidential doorstop of Dr. Hetzel. It, too, has received settlement in the light of the new era at Penn State. Maturity of mind and desire to express it in such intimate problems of life made wider freedom inevitable, but in no degree lessened the obligations and responsibilities of the College. These are met by a voluntary chapel service, led by speakers with real messages; by unifying the undergraduate religious interests and activities in a Penn State Religious Association; by series of special conferences with faculty representatives and outside speakers, and particularly by stressing the character forces that are best developed by doing well the daily tasks as they arise. Under the ministrations of Chaplain J. H. Frizzell, youths' religious life is being nurtured into one of worthy worship. A more wholesome relation also exists in student affiliation with local churches, since there is no longer a premium on mere attendance. A genuine spirit of helpfulness and cooperation has developed.

Compulsory military drill is another academic puzzle, upon which more heat than light has been thrown in the past. It is under process of adjustment; essentially with due regard to the organic and moral obligations of the Land Grant colleges, while at the same time adapting that obligation to changing conditions and to the better fulfillment of the aims of military instruction itself. Specialized training, aptitudes and professional life plans are a better point of departure for national defense, than the uniform lock-step of the drill ground of obsolete or traditional set-up.

The relation of Forestry service and training at Penn State and at Mont Alto was an academic knot which happily has been untied. Contraction of the work of Penn State's excellent courses and training in Forestry could not be justified on any count, while the expansion of Mont Alto would have involved an expenditure even greater, since the Commonwealth already had in the several schools at The Pennsylvania State College, the contributory subjects essential to a well-rounded training in Forestry. Legislation in 1929, providing for consolidation in certain branches of State activity enabled Forestry and the Foresters to get together. Mont Alto is the ideal training ground for the first year men; the work of the three upper classes is pursued at Penn State. This relation is proving eminently successful. The school at the College has just celebrated its twenty-fifth anniversary, a record of efficiency in academic training in which Professor J. A. Ferguson has had large part, as member and head of department since 1908. Accomplishment has been in the face, too, of a meager physical plant, a small frame two-story domicile, with the inevitable frame annexes, erected in 1907. It is still Forestry's Old Main, and the "oldest forestry building continuously in use in the United States."

The widening and deepening of the influence of the Alumni, of which we have found increasing evidence led to a reorganization of the Association in 1930. The town meeting stage had done its work, in which the voice of the loudest and most dogmatic oft dominated. A well-districted, representative leadership has taken its place, while the acceptance of E. K. Hibshman of the direction of the affairs of the association has brought with it a rich experience and wide acquaintance with men and public relations in the Commonwealth. Constructive service and criticism of every field of College activity are urged upon the Alumni by Dr. Hetzel. In his earliest meetings with the association, he sketched the ideal alumnus thus:

> "I feel that the Alumni have an unusual opportunity to contribute to the larger interests of the College by helping us to maintain and to strengthen the campus influences which make for efficient scholarship, intellectual integrity and high moral character. No generation of College students has ever been so alert and so challenging, so genuinely anxious to know true values, as is the

present one. The Alumni can make a positive contribution of far-reaching significance by so adjusting their contacts with the undergraduates of the institution as to strengthen the growing conviction on the part of these young people that law and order, and morality, and serious effort and intellectual accomplishment are consistent with true manhood and in harmony with the most acceptable ideals for which the College stands. In other words, my suggestion is that the Alumni should think, even more than Alumni are accustomed to thinking, of the College as a place where the most valuable and sacred product in the world is being influenced and moulded and that this is the most sacred obligation that rests upon their College. This may require that at times the Alumni shall try to overcome the confusion which apparently obtains in some quarters, as between their Alma Mater and their club. This may seem to you to be a bold suggestion but I feel very keenly that I could not be true to my trust if I did not state honestly my conviction.

"Things have changed and things are changing; as a matter of fact, change at The Pennsylvania State College like change in business and in professions, in commerce and in agriculture, in banking and in building, means progress. If Alumni are to be increasingly helpful they must keep fully abreast of advancing thought and accomplishment on the College Campus. What I suggest I hope you will not think to be unreasonable. We should like to have you bring to our assistance the trained intellects, the matured minds, the seasoned and experienced judgments which you use in the service of every other cause with which you are concerned. It would help us more even than we are now being helped if you would bring this equipment to bear upon the question of scholarship, the question of proper student conduct, the question of athletics, the great problem of adjustment, the task of bringing the institution into a position where it can prosecute with skill an adequate program of scientific research. Lend us these talents to aid us to put it into position to give the fullest and best type of instruction to the deserving youth of our

State; to help it to so expand its influence and its agencies as to reach every person and every enterprise of merit with constructive ministry, whether they be on the campus or off."

Thus the whole round of academic activities has felt the reflex effects of the new era for Penn State. The appointment of Adrian O. Morse in 1929 as Executive Secretary to the President has been a real factor in facilitating the myriad contacts, preliminary counsels, and weighing of measures that tend betimes to overwhelm an academic program. Other outstanding accessions to the Faculties include Champlin (Educational), Peters (Research in Education), Gauger (Mineral Industries), Pilcher (Architecture), Sperry (Bacteriology), Banner (Journalism), du Mont (Romance Languages), Taylor (Ceramics). There is, also, to be chronicled a marked trend toward responsible, centralized administration of research in Agriculture, Engineering, Chemistry, Mineral Industries and Education. There is a new freedom to teach and to learn; responsible initiative is stimulated; results are appraised in the light of genuine values. The group Insurance and Permanent Disability Plan which went into effect on April 1, 1932 is indicative of this new spirit of co-operative responsibility. It is but the harbinger of other measures to render the worker and teacher more independent and secure as he gives single and undivided service to the institution.

There is a more conscious dropping of mere display occasions at the College, and more support given to groups and associations in conferences and discussions. A new kind of adult education is thus being fostered, a continuous year round process. The College has been carried to the people, now they come in larger measure, also, to the College. "Experts" meet practitioners, and research workers view with men who "know," both are benefited. Scarcely a day without its announcement of some group, gathering both to hear and to tell of new things, new processes and methods, hoping to catch an inspiration from our no longer "isolated location." Nittany Lion Inn, fit survivor of University Inn, here finds its real reason for being and receives honorable mention among the extension agencies of the College.

The rather severe and drab advertising of other days has given way to illuminating, artistic forms; the preliminary announcements and summer session bulletins are particularly noteworthy.

Limitation of the size of the Freshman Class has become a more genuine, progressive selection. A fair standard of elimination according to relative rank is applied, thus securing better qualitative groups each succeeding year.

Increased provision for women in dormitories and group houses has since 1926 brought admission of sororities, and nine national organizations are now established.

The College library has had a much belated physical rehabilitation and under the eager skill and direction of Librarian Willard P. Lewis, a new era dawns for the Library.

A live chapter of the American Association of University Professors has given positive, constructive support to the new College, and indirectly at least, real contributions have been made. Studies which might be cited are group insurance; annuity and retirement provisions; leave of absence; teaching load; the quarter system; etc.

In recognition of graduate school standards and research activities of the College through many years[37] a chapter of Sigma Xi was established in 1930.

---

[37] A resume, Seventy-five years of Research, was issued in 1930, by the Council of Research as a contribution to the celebration of that occasion. Too modest has Penn State ever been in "celebrating" conspicuous investigations, from Pugh to Armsby, from Waring to the wizards and searchers of today. Research in Progress 1930-31, Bul. Vol. 25, No. 17 lists 438 projects, and "most of them have an important application to the welfare of the State." Publications of the Agricultural, Engineering and Mining Experiment Stations, the Institute of Animal Nutrition are evidences of research activities over a long period of years. Pioneer investigations in Wireless Transmission, Lifting Power of Planes, An Experimental Trolley; Mine Tunnels and Safety Devices; Oil and Gas Engines are noteworthy, while Soil Tests and Crops; Researches like those on Standards of Nutrition, Vitamins; Pennsylvania Wheat 44; Marketing Crops; etc., etc., have returned to the people of the State but conservatively reckoned more than the entire cost of the Institution from its foundation. More recent studies by departments of Chemistry, Botany, Physics, Zoology, (continued)

As a public institution, with a clearly defined relation to the Commonwealth, the College has also accepted membership in the National Association of State Universities. Yet more significant is the opportunity for large constructive service to the Commonwealth in the drafting by Governor Pinchot of Dr. Hetzel as chairman of the Greater Pennsylvania Council, authorized by the Legislature in 1929.

That significant occasion which garnered the old and pledged it to the new Penn State, the Seventy-Fifth Anniversary Celebration, October 23 to 25, 1930, calls for comment. Three-quarters of a century of service to the Commonwealth was itself ample cause for commemoration. It might have been a mere glorification of the past. Old Main reborn and reconstructed might easily have engrossed the attention and furnished all the stimulus needed for a family gathering of Alumni and friends. Twelve buildings to be dedicated, and improvements to plant campus, and equipment at the expenditure in three years of over four and a half millions might have made it a glorification of a merely physical Penn State. But it was none of these. Governor Fisher, with simple dignity, on behalf of the Commonwealth transferred the custody of these new buildings to the Board of Trustees. Mr. Shields besought the President and Faculty to share with the Board in this great public trust. To which Dr. Hetzel replied: "The President and Faculty are proud to accept the trust which the custodianship of these buildings implies. We hereby dedicate these buildings to the welfare of the Commonwealth and the Nation, and rededicate ourselves to the high purpose of this College."

A committee, C. W. Stoddart, Chairman; the Deans, and R. H. Smith, D. M. Cresswell, G. R. Green, A. O. Morse, E. B. Stavely, S. K. Hostetter, D. C. McLaughlin, President of the Senior Class, arranged a celebration which extended over three days. Education Day opened with conferences on admission problems and personnel practices. An evening convocation brought greetings from the American Land Grant Colleges, by Dr. W. O. Thompson

History and Political Science, and Education are abundant indications of the need of a genuine College Press and of more adequate publication funds.

of Ohio State; from Pennsylvania Colleges by President Hanson of Gettysburg; from the State Department of Public Instruction, Superintendent James N. Rule, and from Secondary Schools by Principal John H. Tyson. Pennsylvania Day followed with a student activities parade, and luncheon to official guests. In the afternoon, Recreation Hall held a record attendance while Mr. Shields gave a thoughtful address on the Genesis of Penn State. Governor Fisher spoke last and in a happy, congratulatory tone: "You have a splendid past. Your background is an inspiration. We have been thrilled today by the narrative given by Mr. Shields of the record made by this College and by its great leaders who saved it from rack and ruin; but let us turn our faces to the rising sun. The glory of State College is not in the past. It will be seen when State College shall reach out and has become what it shall be, a great university open to admission to every boy and girl that desires to step from the high school into an institution of higher learning."

The third day was devoted to the alumni and students, with a house warming in the new Old Main that dissipated any lingering traces, if such there were, of mistaken loyalties to the mere form or substance of an historic structure. A real feature, too, of the celebration was the exhibit in the Armory of the activities and achievements of the College, a truly informative picture in miniature and composite form of the institution. This multum in parvo brought as great surprise and comment from those who thought they had competent knowledge of Penn State, as from those who were neophytes.

Thus may our story and record fitly close with more than three-quarters of a century of public service in instruction,[38] research and extension, in

---

[38] Briefly and statistically in 1931-32 Seven Schools offered residence instruction in forty-six different curricula to 4390 resident students, not including 3640 in Summer Session attendance nor 249 in two-year and winter courses. Extra-mural students numbered 17,597, in Extension Courses in Engineering, Industrial Education, Mining and Teacher Training; in Correspondence Courses in Agriculture and Home Economics, in Engineering, in Teacher Training, and in Industrial Education. This brought the total enrollment for the year to 25,720. The Administration, teaching, research, and extension staff numbered 1053. The State appropriation, which has been continuous since 1887 when it began at $10,000 was for the current biennium $5,060,000 supplemented by Federal Funds, income from fees and sales.

building and carrying the Penn State spirit into the life and thought of the Commonwealth, the Nation, yes, the whole wide world. The future cannot but be secure because Nation and State have united to build these institutions for democracy; because increasing public service to the Commonwealth is a sure guarantee of support and recognition; because the "way" of Penn State, of which we spoke in the Preface, is the way of education to, in and for real life, and because finally, students, faculty, alumni, administration, and friends are united by our Penn State spirit of "absolute and complete loyalty to the highest objectives and ideals of the College."

EPILOGUE

The aftermath of the Great War, the startling contrasts of immediate expansion, subsequent depression, and tardy recovery brought new problems, responsibilities, and tasks to education. Students phenomenally increased, directions of training multiplied, new courses and facilities were urgently demanded and supplied. As was to be expected, educational institutions were among the first to sense the approaching changes. To advance while seemingly forced to retreat, to economize while holding fast to essentials; to anticipate situations which were to become actual and be ready to meet them; in short, to transform emergencies into opportunities; such are the most recent achievements of Higher Education.

In this adjustment, The Pennsylvania State College has an enviable record. Not content to do less with less, but to do more with less—the College initiated its own survey. It studied critically, sympathetically, the whole round of its activities, separately by departments, schools and divisions, and weighed the results in the light of the essential aims and functions of a Public Service Institution, an Institution of the Commonwealth. No outside agency could have turned more thoroughly and constructively the searchlight of fact and value upon it than the College has itself done. From this, have issued a better coordinated conception of education, a more earnest student body, a more sacrificing type of teacher, a keener sense of responsibility to the public. Secondary but no less important results, have been a renewed sense of awaiting opportunities and yet unrealized directions of service, research, and instruction. The physical plant has been modernized in part, only. The arts and the fundamental sciences, the libraries and laboratories, research personnel and publication agencies, sadly need an adequate physical plant and greatly increased faculties, without which genuinely creative teaching and research are in jeopardy. Proud of the three-quarters of a century of academic instruction, research, and public service attained on February 16, 1934, The Pennsylvania State College confidently looks to the Commonwealth and its

379

entire citizenship, to alumni and friends everywhere for that enlightened support which ensures an ever greater and better Penn State.

February 16, 1934

APPENDICES

A. The College and the Civil War

    John I. Thompson, Jr.
    Class of 1862

B. Presidents of the Board of Trustees, of the College, and the Trustees.

C. Organic Laws:

    Chartered by the Commonwealth   (1855)
    Constituted by the Nation   (1862)
    'The Faith of the State' pledged   (1863)

The College and the Civil War.

Extracts from an address prepared by John I. Thompson, Jr., '62 for the Semi-Centennial of the College, 1905.

When the shot, fired from the rebel gun at Charleston upon Fort Sumter on that memorable Spring morning in April 1861, sent a wave of indignation and anger surging throughout the length and breadth of the Northern States, the little body of students within the walls of what is now called "Old Main" at the Farmers' High School, nestling amidst the foothills of the Alleghenies, in common with vast multitudes in city and town, in village and hamlet, in field and in forest felt the shock of that mighty wave.

Previous to that moment political feeling ran high and the students had been sharply divided into two parties, but the fearful tidings that the flag has been fired upon, brought by swift messenger from Bellefonte obliterated party lines, and cemented them into one compact band. They were no longer Democrats, they were no longer Republicans, they were loyal Americans.

When three days later President Lincoln's call for 75,000 troops was received, the excitement was indescribable. It seemed that nothing could hold the boys to their school duties, and that the Farmers' High School, was, for the time doomed.

At this juncture President Evan Pugh, assembled the students in the chapel and by a kindly talk, somewhat allayed the excitement.

After 44 years my impression of that address is, that it was skillful, adroit, masterful. No *words* that day spoken by Dr. Pugh, remain in my memory, and of that wise and tactful pleading only two thoughts can I recall. One was that the war would not be fought out by the 75,000 men just called, that it would not be ended in 90 days, that it was to be a struggle for years, and that all who were there assembled could remain and continue their education, as far as the Farmers' High School was able to take them, and still have ample time to do their duty to their country in the mighty conflict just commencing.

The other thought advanced by his was, that at no time in the life of a young man is he so dear to his mother, as between the ages of 16 and 20. Then when manhood is almost upon him, the mother pictures for him a splendid career. A few years later she frequently and perhaps generally realizes that the career is not destined to be attained, that her splendid boy is growing to be a man, very much like other men. For the sake of their mothers they should keep out of the war until they had passed the 20 year line.

Dr. Pugh's words of caution and advice had the effect of somewhat settling the unrest, but as the weeks sped on through that eventful summer, one after another quietly left for their homes, there to enlist in the Union Army. This gradual melting away continued throughout 1861, 1862 and well into 1863, as student after student succeeded in gaining the reluctant consent of his parents. In the meantime, I think it was in 1862 a number of students, while preparing themselves for the battles of life, decided to prepare themselves also for fighting the battles of their country when their services should be required.

They therefore organized a military company, purchased a flag, and drum, and as all muskets were then in active demand at the front, each man had a wooden musket, after the old Harpers Ferry pattern, made by Jonas C. Trozel, Carpenter and Superintendent of the Work House Department, whose carpenter shop stood near the cottage now occupied by Professor Foss. We drilled upon some spots on the campus not covered with nursery or stone piles, and learned the manual of arms with those wooden guns.

I have no recollection of the organization of the company, I cannot recall its name, not the name of the captain, or any of the other officers. The whole thing seems like a dream to me, but I know it was not a dream for I still have my wooden gun.

In June 1863, General Lee and the Army of Northern Virginia, began their march northward with the intention of carrying the war into Pennsylvania.

A call was issued by President Lincoln for 100,000 men—50,000 of them for Pennsylvania. The call was at once re-echoed by Governor Andrew G. Curtin.

Upon receiving this call, the students of the Farmers' High School, (which had then been rechristened The Agricultural College of Pennsylvania) who were of proper age, without obtaining or indeed asking the consent of parents or faculty, immediately enlisted; some going at once to their homes, to join companies being formed there, and the remainder numbering 31 uniting with the men of this vicinity to form a company of 100 under the command of Captain John Boal of Boalsburg.

The call of President Lincoln was dated June 15, 1863. The company in which the students had enlisted left Bellefonte via the Bald Eagle Valley R. R. for South Western Pennsylvania, June 17 or 18.

I cannot refrain from mentioning one incident which occurred on the march from Johnstown to Berlin.

Somewhere between Berr's Creek Furnace, and Stoyestown in Somerset County, the day being very hot, Captain Boal had ordered a halt for rest at a roadside grove through which flowed a fine stream of cool water. As we rested there enjoying the water and the shade we were startled by the sound of a drum in our rear beating regular marching time—tap—tap—tap—tap. As the sound of the drum drew nearer, all crowded into the road, expecting to see a company of soldiers come around the bend, when to our surprise we beheld a solitary man, marching Southward through Somerset County, evidently going to the defense of his country, with no weapon but a tenor drum. It was one of the students of the Farmers' High School, who being at his home when the others left the College and who upon returning, had hunted up the drum which belonged to the wooden gun company—followed by rail to Johnstown—and then on foot until he found us. He was determined not to be left behind.

From the time when Johnny Martin in 1861 laid down his life for his country—when gray haired Professor David Wilson in 1862 led a company to Chambersburg to assist in repelling the invasion of Maryland, which threatened Pennsylvania, when all in the School who were old enough enlisted in 1863—to the time when Tellico Johnston with his 100 days men marched away to the war in 1864—each student of the Farmers' High School stood ready for service at the beck and call of his country.

They were in all the divisions of all the Armies of the Union and the roll of the battles in which they participated, is the roll of the battles of the War.

I know nothing of what was done by the larger Colleges in the War for the Union. They no doubt did their duty, many may have done as well as the Farmers' High School, none could have done better. They with their thousands of students contributed of their abundance—like the poor widow who threw her two mites into the Treasury—the Farmers' High School of Pennsylvania, cast in all that she had.

Presidents of the Board of Trustees.

Frederick Watts, 1855—1874
James A. Beaver, 1874—1882
Francis Jordan, 1882—1898
James A. Beaver, 1898—1914
H. Walton Mitchell, 1914—1929
J. Franklin Shields, 1929 -

Presidents of the College.
(Dates of election, resignation or death)

Evan Pugh: December 7, 1859—April 29, 1864 (Died in Office)
William H. Allen: June 15, 1864—September 5, 1866
John Fraser: September 5, 1866—March 14, 1868
Thomas Henry Burrowes: November 20, 1868—February 25, 1871 (Died in Office)
James Calder: March 21, 1871—January 22, 1880
Joseph Shortlidge: May 27, 1880—April 8, 1881
George W. Atherton: June 28, 1882—July 24, 1906 (Died in Office)
Edwin Erle Sparks: November 22, 1907—January 22, 1920
John Martin Thomas: January 25, 1921—June 13, 1925
Ralph Dorn Hetzel: September 24, 1926

Erwin W. Runkle

Trustees of The Pennsylvania State College.

February 22, 1855 to July 1st, 1933

Key

Ex-officio—Office given

Appointed—By the Governor

Elected—By Alumni or by Agricultural and Engineering Societies.

Adams, Harvey S., 1926-1931, Elected

Affelder, William L., 1927, Elected

Africa, J. Simpson, 1883-1887, Secretary of Internal Affairs

Ailman, J. T., 1911-1913, Elected

Allen, William H., 1864-1866, President of the College

Allison, Dr. T. H., 1879-1881, Elected

Andrews, J. H. M., 1915- , Elected

Atherton, George W., 1882-1906, President of the College

Balderston, R. W., 1924- , Appointed

Banes, Col. Charles H., 1886-1887, President of Franklin Institute

Banks, John N., 1881-1885, Elected

Barlow, Thomas W., 1907-1920, Appointed; 1906-1910, Elected

Bayard, E. S., 1910-1924, Appointed, 1925- , Elected;

Beaver, James Addams, 1873-1887, Elected, 1887-1891 Governor of the Commonwealth; 1891-1914, Elected; 1906-1907, President Pro-Tempore of the College

Becht, J. George, 1923-1925, Superintendent of Public Instruction

Benedict, John G., 1930- , Elected

Bergner, Charles H., 1906-1910, President of the State Agr. Society

Biddle, Craig, 1859-1867, Elected

Birkinbine, John, 1897-1905, President of Franklin Institute

Bissell, William S., 1879-1882, President of the State Agr. Society

Blight, George, 1867-1869, Elected;

Brown, Henry D., 1915-1926, Appointed; 1927-1931, Appointed; 1932- , Elected;

Brown, Maj. Isaac B., 1895, Secretary of Internal Affairs; 1903-1905, Secretary of Internal Affairs.

Browne, George B., 1858-1859, Elected

Brumbaugh, Martin G., 1915-1919, Governor of the Commonwealth

Burrowes, Thomas H., 1869-1871, President of the College

Calder, James, 1871-1880, President of the College

Calder, William, Dr., 1877-1881, Elected

Callery, J. D., 1911-1914, Appointed

Campbell, Curtis G., 1855-1888, Elected

Campbell, Gen. Jacob M., 1877-1886, Elected

Carnegie, Andrew, 1886-1916, Elected

Chadwick, Samuel, 1864-1866, Elected

Chalfant, Edla S., 1831-1932, Appointed

Chess, Moses, 1862-1864, Elected

Colfelt, Lawrence M., 1898-1906, Elected

Conard, M. E., 1902-1908, Elected

Cosgrove, John C., 1922- , Elected

Counter, Maj. Richard, Jr., 1906-1909, Elected

Creasy, William T., 1909-1920, Elected

Critchfield, N. B., 1903-1915, Secretary of the Board of Agriculture.

Crow, William E., 1918-1922, Elected;

Curtin, Andrew Gregg, 1855-1858, Secretary of the Commonwealth; 1861-1867, Governor of the Commonwealth

Darlington, Henry T. , 1876-1878, Elected

Darlington, J. Lacey, 1875-1876, Elected

Deike, George H., 1925- , Elected

Dewey, P. H., 1925-1927, Appointed

Dibert, Moronce M., 1931- , Appointed

Diehl, Ambrose N., 1916-1934, Elected

Dorsett, E. B., 1929- , Appointed

Downing, George M., 1906-1927, Elected

Downing, Samuel R., 1884-1902, Elected

Doyle, James B., 1888-1891, Elected

Dubois, John   , 1876-1877, Elected

Dunkle, A. K., 1879-1883, Secretary of Internal Affairs

Eby, Jacob R., 1872-1875; Pres. of the State Agr. Society

Edge, Thomas J., 1880-1884, Elected; 1893-1899, Secretary of the State Board of Agr.

Ellis, B. Morris, 1865-1871, Elected

Elwyn, A. L., 1855-1858, By act of 1855

Endlich, John, 1878-1879, Elected

Eyre, Joshua P., 1857-1860, Elected

Finnegan, Thomas E., 1919-1923, Superintendent of Public Instruction

Fisher, John S., 1923-1927, Elected; 1927-1931, Governor of the Commonwealth

Fox, Cyrus T., 1891-1903, Elected

Frantz, Samuel O., 1908-1911, Appointed

Fraser, John, 1866-1868, President of the College

Fuller, Frank M., 1903-1905, Secretary of the Commonwealth

Gearhart, Peter, 1919-1922, Elected

Geary, John W., 1867-1873, Governor of the Commonwealth

Gordon, Cyrus, 1876-1901, Elected

Gowen, James, 1855-1857, Pres. of the State Agr. Society

Greenland, Gen. Walter W., 1892-1895, Adjutant General

Greer, John M., 1898-1904, Elected

Griest, William W., 1899-1903, Secretary of the Commonwealth

Guthrie, Gen. Pressly N., 1883-1887, Adjutant General

Goger, Farman H., 1926- , Elected

Haas, Francis B., 1925-1927, Superintendent of Public Instruction

Haldeman, J. S., 1860-1862, Pres. of the State Agr. Society

Hale, Jas. T., 1858-1865, Elected

Hamill, James L., 1905- , Elected

Hamilton, A. Boyd, 1865-1869, Pres. of the State Agr. Society; 1869-1872, Elected

Hamilton, Hayes, 1867-1869, Elected

Hamilton, John, 1884-1890, Elected; 1899-1903, Secretary of the State Board of Agr.

Hammond, John W., 1877-1879, Pres. of the State Agr. Society

Hans, John T., 1934- , Elected

Harrity, William F., 1891-1895, Secretary of the Commonwealth

Hartman, J. H., 1881-1884, Elected

Hartranft, John F., 1873-1879, Governor of the Commonwealth

Harvey, Henry T., 1876-1879, Elected

Hastings, Daniel H., 1887-1891, Adjutant General; 1895-1899, Governor of the Commonwealth

Herr, Joel A., 1886-1901, Elected; 1903-1906, Elected

Hetzel, Ralph D., 1926- , President of the College

Hiester, A. O.   , 1855-1874, By act of 1855--Elected

Hiester, Charles E., 1860-1863, Elected

Hiester, Gabriel, 1879-1912, Elected

Hiester, Wm. M., 1858-1861, Secretary of the Commonwealth

Highee, E. E., 1881-1889, Superintendent of Public Instruction

Hildrup, Wm. T., 1874-1880, Elected

Hill, William F., 1901-1913, Elected

Holstein, Wm. H., 1874-1876, Elected

Hood, George W., 1886-1898, Elected

Hoyt, Henry M., 1879-1883, Governor of the Commonwealth

Huff, Lloyd B.   , 1906-1911, Appointed

Hutchinson, George G., 1906-1927, Elected

Jackson, John Price   , 1915-1916, Appointed

Jessup, William, 1855-1858, By act of 1855

Johnson, Alba B., 1922-1927, Elected

Jones, E. E., 1920-1924, Elected

Jordan, Charles G., 1927-1931, Secretary of Agriculture;

Jordan, Francis, 1867-1873, Secretary of the Commonwealth; 1872-1898, Elected; 1882-1883, Secretary of the Commonwealth

Kaine, Daniel   , 1863-1879, Elected

Kapp, Amos E., 1869-1870, Pres. of the State Agr. Society

Keith, John A. H., 1927-1931, Superintendent of Public Instruction

Kelly, James, 1866-1880, Elected

Kendall, J. L., 1915-1923, Appointed

Kiess, Edgar K., 1913-1930, Appointed

Knoche, Frank, 1888-1891, Elected

Knox, Thos. P., 1862-1865, Pres. of the State Agr. Society

Latta, Gen. James W., 1875-1883, Adjutant General; 1895-1903, Secretary of Internal Affairs

Lewis, Robert R., 1927- , Elected

Linn, John Blair, 1878-1879, Secretary of the Commonwealth

Longenecker, Jacob H., 1890-1891, Secretary of the Commonwealth

Lowry, Milton W., 1907-1924, Appointed

Lyons, Hannah McK., 1931- , Appointed

M'Candless, Gen. William, 1875-1879, Secretary of Internal Affairs

McAllister, Archibald, 1858-1867, Elected

McAllister, H. N., 1855-1873, By act of 1855--Elected

McClelland, Capt. William, 1891-1892, Adjutant General

McCormick, C. S., 1881-1886, Elected

McCormick, John H., 1930-1931, Appointed

McCormick, Vance C., 1908- , Elected

McDowell, John, 1888-1899, Pres. of the State Agr. Society

McFadden, L. T., 1914-1924, Elected

McFarland, Maj. Irvin, 1978-1881, Elected

McKee, James Y., 1881-1882, Acting Pres. of the College

McSparran, John A., 1924-1931, Elected & 1931- , Secretary of Agriculture

Martin, David   , 1897-1899, Secretary of the Commonwealth

Mellon, W. L., 1927-1932, Elected

Menges, Franklin, 1910-1913, Elected

Miles, James Sr., 1855-1868, By act of 1855

Miles, James Jr., 1876-1884, Elected; 1883-1885, Pres. of the State Agr. Society

Milholland, James, 1930- , Elected

Miller, Maj. Gen. Charles, 1904-1910, Elected

Mitchell, A. W., 1916-1926, Elected

Mitchell, H. Walton, 1902-1929, Elected

Moore, D. Glen, 1934- , Appointed

Morris, John C., 1870-1872, Pres. of the State Agr. Society; 1882- , Pres. of the State Agr. Society

Munce, R. L., 1913-1925, Elected

Musser, Boyd A., 1927- , Elected

Mylin, Amos H., 1884-1902, Elected

Nick, Edwin W., 1931- , Elected

Olmsted, Marlin E., 1906-1913, Appointed

Orvis, Ellis L., 1901-1925, Elected

Orvis, John H., 1875-1893, Elected

Packer, Wm. F., 1856-1861, Governor of the Commonwealth

Parrish, Charles, 1876-1877, Elected

Patterson, William H., 1908-1917, Elected

Pattison, Robert E., 1883-1887, Governor of the Commonwealth; 1891-1895, Governor of the Commonwealth

Patton, Charles E., 1915-1919, Secretary of Agriculture

Paxon, J. A., 1887-1888, Pres. of the State Agr. Society

Pennypacker, Samuel W., 1903-1907, Governor of the Commonwealth

Pettebone, E. R., 1914-1925, Elected

Phillips, Clara C., 1926-1934, Appointed

Piolett, Victor E., 1878-1884, Elected

Pinchot, Gifford, 1923-1927, Governor of the Commonwealth; 1931- , Governor of the Commonwealth

Pollock, James, 1855-1858, Governor of the Commonwealth

Poole, Ernest J., 1930- , Elected

Price, Charles S., 1912-1914, Appointed

Pugh, Evan, 1859-1864, President of the College

Quay, M. S., 1973-1882, Secretary of the Commonwealth; Excepting May 2nd, 1878 to January 30, 1879

Quigley, James, 1907-1915, Elected;

Rasmussen, Fred, 1919-1925, Secretary of Agriculture; 1923-1925, Appointed

Read, Augustus C., 1906-1916, Elected

Reeder, Eastburn, 1885-1888, Elected

Reeder, Frank, 1895-1897, Secretary of the Commonwealth

Rhone, Leonard, 1880-1886, Elected

Robb, James F., 1890-1896, Elected

Roberts, A. S., 1855-1857, By act of 1855

Roberts, Capt. Charles W., 1887-1895, Elected

Roberts, Wm. B., 1871-1874, Elected

Rogers, R. R., 1875-1878, President of Franklin Institute

Rothrock, William P., 1924-1930, Elected

Rule, James N., 1931, Superintendent of Public Instruction

Schaeffer, Nathan C., 1893-1919, Superintendent of Public Instruction

Schwab, Charles M.   , 1902-1932, Elected

Scott, George, 1875-1877, Pres. of the State Agr. Society

Scott, Col. T. A., 1876-1877, Elected

Shields, J. Franklin, 1905-   , Elected

Shortlidge, Joseph, 1880-1881, President of the College

Sickles, Gen. T. H., 1881-1882, Elected

Slifer, Eli, 1861-1867, Secretary of the Commonwealth

Slocum, George W., 1932- , Elected

Smith, Dr. A., 1876-1878, Elected

Smith, Prof. C. Alfred, 1882-1885, Elected

Snodgrass, James M. K., 1856-1862, Elected

Sparks, Edwin Erie, 1907-1920, President of the College

Sproul, William C., 1919-1923, Governor of the Commonwealth

Starkweather, S. W., 1877-1886, Elected

Stenger, William C., 1883-1887, Secretary of the Commonwealth

Stewart, Thos. J., 1887-1895, Secretary of Internal Affairs & 1895-1905, Adjutant

General

Stone, Charles W., 1887-1890, Secretary of the Commonwealth; 1894-1908, Elected

Stone, William A., 1899-1903, Governor of the Commonwealth

Stuart, Edwin Sydney, 1907-1911, Governor of the Commonwealth

Strohm, John   , 1855-1858, By act of 1855

Taggart, David, 1857-1860, Pres. of the State Agr. Society

Tatham, W. P., 1879-1885, President of Franklin Institute

Taylor, A. Wilson, 1872-1878, Elected

Teas, Wm. H., 1929-1930, Elected

Tener, John K., 1911-1915, Governor of the Commonwealth

Thomas, John M., 1921-1925, President of the College

Thomas, Col. R. H., 1896-1903, Elected

Turner, Joseph C., 1869-1875, Elected

Tyson, Chester J., 1912- , Elected

Walker, R. C., 1855-1856, By act of 1855

Walker, William H., 1907-1927, Elected

Waller, D. J., 1890-1893, Superintendent of Public Instruction

Wallis, J. T., 1913-1922, Elected

Warriner, Jesse B., 1925-1926, Elected; 1927-1931, Appointed

Watts, Frederick, 1855-1875, By act of 1855--Elected

Weller, John S., 1896-1902, Elected

Wickersham, James P., 1875-1881, Superintendent of Public Instruction

Wilhelm, A., 1885-1887, Pres. of the State Agr. Society

Willits, Frank P., 1923-1927, Secretary of Agriculture; 1927- , Elected

Wilson, Joseph M., 1887-1896, President of Franklin Institute

White, H. V., 1886-1919, Elected; 1920-1923, Appointed

White, Gen. Harry, 1868-1872, Elected

White, James D., 1903, Elected

Wise, W. S., 1924-1928, Appointed

Woodward, John A., 1884-1911, Elected

Young, Hiram, 1900-1906, Pres. of the State Agr. Society

Zook, Ralph T., 1932, Appointed

Chartered by the Commonwealth

An Act to Incorporate the Farmers' High School of Pennsylvania.

SECTION 1. *Be it enacted by the Senate and House of Representatives of the Commonwealth of Pennsylvania in General Assembly met, and it is hereby enacted by the authority of the same.* That there be and is hereby erected and established, at the place which shall be designated by the authority, and as hereinafter provided, an institution for the education of youth in the various branches of science, learning, and practical agriculture, as they are connected with each other, by the name, style, and title of the Farmers' High School of Pennsylvania.

SECTION 2. That the said institution shall be under the management and government of a board of trustees, of whom there shall be thirteen, and seven of whom shall be a quorum, competent to perform the duties hereinafter authorized and required.

SECTION 3. That the Governor, Secretary of the Commonwealth, the president of the Pennsylvania State Agricultural Society, and the principal of the institution, shall be each *ex-officio* a member of the board of trustees, and they, with Dr. Alfred L. Elwyn and Algernon S. Roberts, of the city of Philadelphia, H. N. McAllister of the county of Centre; R. C. Walker, of the county of Allegheny; James Miles, of the county of Erie; John Strohm, of the county of Lancaster; A. O. Hiester of the county of Dauphin; William Jessup, of the county of Susquehanna, and Frederick Watts, of the county of Cumberland, shall constitute the first board of trustees; which said trustees and their successors in office, are hereby enacted and declared to be a body politic and corporate in law, with perpetual succession, by the name, style, and title of the Farmers' High School of Pennsylvania, by which name and title the said trustees, and their successors, shall be able and capable in law to take by gift, grant, sale, or conveyance, by bequest, devise, or otherwise, any estate in any lands, tenements, and hereditaments, goods, chattels, or effects, and at pleasure to alien or otherwise dispose of the same to and for the use and purpose of the said institution: *Provided, however*, That the annual income of the said estate so held, shall at no time exceed twenty-five thousand dollars; and the said corporation shall, by the same name, have power to sue and be sued, and generally to do and transact all and every business touching or concerning the premises, or which shall be necessarily incidental thereto, and to hold, enjoy, and exercise all such powers, authorities, and jurisdiction as are customary within the colleges within this Commonwealth.

SECTION 4. That the same trustees shall cause to be made a seal, with such device as they may think proper, and by and with which all the deeds, diplomas, certificates, and acts of the institution shall be authenticated, and they may at their pleasure alter the same.

SECTION 5. That at the first meeting of the board of trustees, the nine named, who are not *ex-officio* members shall, by themselves and by lot, be divided into three classes of three each, numbered one, two, and three; the appointment hereby made of class number one, shall terminate on the first Monday of October, one thousand eight hundred and fifty-six; number two on the first Monday of October, one thousand eight hundred and fifty-seven, and number three on the first Monday of October, one thousand eight hundred and fifty-eight; and upon the termination of such office of such directors, to wit; on the first Monday of October in every year an election shall be held at the institution to supply their place, and such election shall be determined by the votes of the members of the executive committee of the Pennsylvania State Agricultural Society, and the votes of three representatives duly chosen by each county agricultural society in this Commonwealth which shall have been organized at three months preceding the time of election, and it shall be the duty of said board of trustees to appoint two of their number as judges to hold such election, to receive and count the votes, and return the same to the board of trustees with their certificate of the number of votes cast, and for whom, whereupon the said board shall determine who have received the highest number of votes, and who are thereby elected.

SECTION 6. That on the second Thursday of June after the passage of this act, the board of trustees, who are hereby appointed, shall meet at Harrisburg, and proceed to the organization of an institution and selection of the most eligible site within the Commonwealth of Pennsylvania for its location, where they shall purchase or obtain by gift, grant, or otherwise, a tract of land containing at least two hundred acres, and not exceeding two thousand acres, upon which they shall procure such improvements and alterations to be made, as will make it an institution properly adapted to the instructions of youth in the art of farming according to the meaning and design of this act. They shall select and choose a principal for said institution who with such scientific attainments and capacity to teach as the Board shall deem necessary, shall be a good practical farmer; he with such other persons as shall, from time to time, be employed as teachers, shall comprise the faculty, under whose control the immediate management of the institution, and the instruction of all the youth committed to its care, shall be subject, however, to the revision and all the orders of the board of trustees; there shall be a quarterly meeting of the board of trustees at the institution, and as much oftener as shall be necessary, and they shall determine; the board shall have power to pass all such by-laws, ordinances, and rules as the good government of the institution shall require, and therein to prescribe what shall be taught to and what labor performed by the pupils, and generally to do and perform all such administrative acts as are usually performed by and within the appropriate duty of a board of trustees, and shall, by a secretary of their appointment, keep a minute of the proceedings and action of the board.

SECTION 7. That it shall be the duty of the board of trustees as soon and as often as the exigencies of the case may require, in addition to the principal, to employ such other professors, teachers, or tutors as shall be qualified to impart to pupils under their charge a knowledge of the English language, grammar, geography, history, mathematics, chemistry, and such other branches of natural and exact sciences as will conduce to the proper education of a farmer; the pupils shall, themselves, at such proper times and seasons as shall be prescribed by the board of trustees, perform all the labor necessary in the cultivation of the farm, and shall thus be instructed and taught all things necessary to be known by a farmer.

SECTION 8. That the board of trustees shall annually elect a treasurer, who shall receive and disburse the funds of the institution, and perform such other duties as shall be required of him, and from whom they shall take such security for the faithful performance of his duty as necessity shall require; and it shall be the duty of said board of trustees annually on or before the first of December, to make out a full and detailed account of the operations of the institution for the preceding year, and an account of all its receipts and disbursements, and report the same to the Pennsylvania State Agricultural Society, who shall embody said report in the annual report which, by existing laws, the said society is bound to make, and transmit to the Legislature on or before the first Monday of January each and every year.

SECTION 9. That it shall be lawful for the Pennsylvania State Agricultural Society, to appropriate out of their funds to the object of this act, a sum not exceeding ten thousand dollars, whenever the same shall be required, and to make such further appropriations annually, out of their funds, as will aid in the prosecution of this object, and it shall be the duty and privilege of said society at such time as they shall deem expedient by their committees, officers or otherwise, to visit the said institution and examine into the details of its management.

SECTION 10. That the act to incorporate the "Farmers' High School of Pennsylvania," approved the thirteenth day of April, Anno-Domini one thousand eight hundred and fifty-four, be and the same is hereby repealed.

APPROVED – The 22d day of February, A. D. 1855.
James Pollock, Governor

Constituted by the Nation

Law of Congress.

An act donating public lands to the several States and Territories which may provide colleges for the benefit of agriculture and the mechanic arts.

Be it enacted by the Senate and House of Representatives of the United States of America in Congress assembled, That there be granted to the several States, for the purposes hereinafter mentioned, an amount of public land, to be appropriated to each State a quantity equal to thirty thousand acres for each senator and representative in Congress to which the States are respectively entitled by the apportionment under the census of eighteen hundred and sixty; *Provided,* That no mineral lands shall be selected or purchased under the provision of this act.

SECTION 2. *And be it further enacted,* That the land aforesaid, after being surveyed, shall be apportioned to the several States in sections or sub-divisions of sections, not less than one quarter of a section; and whenever there are public lands in a State subject to sale at private entry at one dollar and twenty-five cents per acre, the quantity to which said State shall be entitled shall be selected from such lands within the limits of such State, and the Secretary of the Interior is hereby directed to issue to each of the States in which there is not the quantity of public lands subject to sale at private entry at one dollar and twenty-five cents per acre, to which said State may be entitled under the provisions of this act land scrip to the amount in acres for the deficiency of its distributive share; said scrip to be sold by said States and the proceeds thereof applied to the uses and purposes prescribed in this act, and for no other use or purpose whatsoever: *Provided,* That in no case shall any State to which land scrip may thus be issued be allowed to locate the same within the limits of any other State, or of any Territory of the United States, but their assignees may thus locate said land scrip upon any of the unappropriated lands of the United States subject to sale at private entry at one dollar and twenty-five cents, or less, per acre; *And provided further*, That not more than one million acres shall be located by such assignees in any one of the States: *And provided further*, That no such location shall be made before one year from the passage of this act.

SECTION 3. *And be it further enacted*, That all the expenses of management, superintendence, and taxes from date of selection of lands, previous to their sales, and all expenses incurred in the management and disbursement of the moneys which may be received therefrom, shall be paid by the States to which they may belong, out of the treasury of said States, so that the entire proceeds of the sale of said lands shall be applied without any diminution whatever to the purposes hereinafter mentioned.

SECTION 4. And be it further enacted, That all moneys derived from the sale of the lands aforesaid by the States to which the lands are apportioned, and from the sales of land scrip hereinbefore provided for, shall be invested in stocks of the United States, or of the States, or some other safe stocks, yielding not less than five per centum upon the par value of said stocks; and that the moneys so invested shall constitute a perpetual fund, the capital of which shall remain forever undiminished, (except so far as may be provided in section fifth of this act.) and the interest of which shall be inviolably appropriated, by each State which may take and claim the benefit of this act, to the endowment, support, and maintenance of at least one college where the leading object shall be, without excluding other scientific and classical studies, and including military tactics, to teach such branches of learning as are related to agriculture and the mechanic arts, in such manner as the Legislatures of the States may respectively prescribe, in order to promote the liberal and practical education of the industrial classes in the several pursuits and professions in life.

SECTION 5. *And it be further enacted*, That the grant of land and land scrip hereby authorized shall be made on the following conditions, to which, as well as to the provisions hereinbefore contained, the previous assent of the several States shall be signified by legislative acts:

First: If any portion of the fund invested, as provided by the foregoing section, or any portion of the interest thereon, shall, by any action of contingency, be diminished or lost, it shall be replaced by the State to which it belongs, so that the capital of the fund shall remain forever undiminished; and the annual interest shall be regularly applied without diminution to the purposes mentioned in the fourth section of this act, except that a sum, not exceeding ten per centum upon the amount received by any State under the provisions of this act, may be expended for the purchase of lands for sites or experimental farms, whenever authorized by the respective Legislatures of said States.

Second: No portion of said fund, nor the interest thereon, shall be applied, directly or indirectly, under any pretense whatever, to the purchase, erection, preservation, or repair of any building or buildings.

Third: Any State which may take and claim the benefit of the provisions of this act shall provide, within five years, at least not less than one college, as described in the fourth section of this act, or the grant to such State shall cease; and said State shall be bound to pay the United States the amount received of any lands previously sold, and that the title to purchasers under the State shall be valid.

Fourth: An annual report shall be made regarding the progress of each college, recording any improvements and experiments made, with their cost and results, and such other matters, including State industrial and economical statistics, as may be supposed useful; one copy of which shall be transmitted by mail free, by each, to all the other colleges which may be endowed under the provisions of this act, and also one copy to the Secretary of the Interior.

Fifth: When lands shall be selected from those which have been raised to double and minimum price, in consequence of railroad grants, they shall be computed to the States at the maximum price, and the number of acres proportionally diminished.

Sixth: No State while in a condition of rebellion or insurrection against the Government of the United States shall be entitled to the benefit of this act.

Seventh: No State shall be entitled to the benefits of this act unless it shall express its acceptance thereof by its Legislature within two years from the date of its approval by the President.

SECTION 6. *And be it further enacted,* That land scrip issued under the provisions of this act shall not be subject to location until after the first day of January, one thousand eight hundred and sixty-three.

SECTION 7. *And be it further enacted,* That the land officers shall receive the same fees for locating land scrip issued under the provisions of this act as is now allowed for the location of military bounty land warrants under existing laws: *Provided,* Their maximum compensation shall not be thereby increased.

SECTION 8. *And be it further enacted,* That the Governors of the several States to which scrip shall be issued under this act shall be required to report annually to Congress all sales made of such scrip until the whole shall be disposed of, the amount received for the same, and what appropriation has been made of the proceeds.

APPROVED, July 2, 1862.
A. Lincoln.

"The Faith of the State" Pledged

An act to accept the grant of public lands by the United States to the several States, for the endowment of agricultural colleges.

WHEREAS, By an act of Congress, passed the second day of July, one thousand eight hundred and sixty-two, a grant of land was made to the several States and Territories, which may provide colleges for the benefit of agriculture and mechanic arts, equal to thirty thousand acres for each Senator and Representative in Congress to which the States are respectively entitled, by the apportionment under the census of one thousand eight hundred and sixty, which act of Congress requires that the several States, in order to entitle them to the benefit of said grant, should within two years from the date of this act, express their acceptance of the same:

And whereas, the Legislature of Pennsylvania has already shown its high regard for the agricultural interests of the State, by the establishment of the Agricultural College of Pennsylvania, and by making liberal appropriations thereto; therefore,

SECTION 1. *Be it enacted by the Senate and House of Representatives of the Commonwealth of Pennsylvania in General Assembly met, and it is hereby enacted by the authority of the same,* That the act of Congress of the United States, passed the second day of July, one thousand eight hundred and sixty-two entitled "An act donating lands of the several States and Territories which may provide colleges for the benefit of agriculture and the mechanic arts," be and the same is hereby accepted by the State of Pennsylvania, with all its provisions and conditions, and the faith of the State is hereby pledged to carry the same into effect.

SECTION 2. That the Surveyor General of the State of Pennsylvania is hereby authorized and required to do every act and thing necessary to entitle this State to its distributive share of land scrip, under the provisions of the said act of Congress, and when the said scrip is received by him, to dispose of the same, under such regulations as the board of commissioners hereafter appointed by this act shall prescribe.

SECTION 3. That the Governor, the Auditor General, and the Surveyor General are hereby constituted a board of commissioners, with full power and authority to make all needful rules and regulations respecting the manner in which the Surveyor General aforesaid shall dispose of the said land scrip, the investment of the proceeds thereof in the State stocks of this State, and apply interest arising therefrom as herein directed; and in general to do all and every act or acts necessary to carry into full effect the said act of Congress; *Provided*, That no investment shall be made in any other stocks than those of the United States or of this Commonwealth.

SECTION 4. That until otherwise ordered by the Legislature of Pennsylvania, the annual interest accruing from any investment of the funds acquired under the said act of Congress is hereby appropriated, and the said commissioners are directed to pay the same to the Agricultural College of Pennsylvania for the endowment, support, and maintenance of said institution, which college is now in full and successful operation, and where the leading object is, without excluding other scientific and classical studies, and including military tactics, to teach such branches of learning as are related to agriculture and the mechanic arts.

SECTION 5. That the said Agricultural College of Pennsylvania shall, on or before the first day of February of each year, make a report to the Legislature of the receipts and expenditures of the said institution for the preceding year.

APPROVED—The 1ˢᵗ day of April, A. D. 1863.
Andrew Gregg Curtin, Governor

About Erwin W. Runkle

Dr. Erwin William Runkle devoted much of his life to preserving and documenting the Penn State story. His seminal work in assembling the earliest collections of school history earned him the title, "Father of the University Archives."

Runkle was born on May 20, 1869 in Lisbon, Iowa to parents Adam and Malinda. He remained in the Hawkeye State through the end of his undergraduate education, earning his B.A. in 1890 from Toledo, Iowa's Western College (which would eventually merge with the modern Coe College). Three years later, Runkle was awarded his Ph.D. from Yale University, where he served as a lecturer in history of philosophy. In September of 1894 in Polo, IL, he was married to May Middlekauff, with whom he had one child, Lawrence.

Runkle arrived in Happy Valley in 1893, when he was appointed an instructor of philosophy and ethics at the Pennsylvania State College. He also served as the part-time college librarian for 20 years, from 1904 until he was chosen to head the school's new department of philosophy in 1924, a post he held until his retirement as professor emeritus in 1935. Runkle organized a large collection of letters, reports, manuscripts and other information pertaining to Penn State history in recognition of the College's 50th anniversary in 1905. He also served, even beyond formal retirement, as Penn State's first official historian, from 1926 until 1938.

During his career, Runkle authored several studies and papers on psychology and philosophy. He was a member of the American Psychological Association and the American Philosophical Association as well as a fellow of the American Association for the Advancement of Science. Runkle was a member of the Phi Kappa Phi national scholastic honor society and the social science honor society, Pi Gamma Nu.

Erwin Runkle died as a result of hemiplegia on February 14, 1941.

About George T. Henning, Jr.

George Henning earned his B.A. from The Pennsylvania State University, College of the Liberal Arts in 1963 and an MBA from Harvard University in 1965. As a student at Penn State he participated in many activities and served as president of Men's Residence Council and a member of Student Government Assembly. His academic and leadership accomplishments were recognized with membership in Lion's Paw, Omicron Delta Kappa, Skull & Bones, Androcles, and Phi Eta Sigma.

Henning's business experience has included executive positions at five publicly traded companies. Coming out of retirement in 2009, he served as Interim CFO and later Interim CEO and President of Aventine Renewable Energy, Inc. of Pekin, IL, through March 2010.

Henning served Penn State as a member of the Board of Trustees from 2004 through 2010. He also served two terms on the Penn State Alumni Council and was active in Penn State chapters in Boston, Pittsburgh, Houston, Cleveland and State College. George and his wife, the former Susan Young ('63HEc), have lived in State College during retirement. They co-chaired their class's 40th and 45th and 50th Reunions and participate in Penn State alumni, cultural and support groups.

George and Sue enjoy extensive interaction with student groups on campus and in their home. In 2011 they were named honorary Lion Ambassadors. USA Today, the magazine W, Town & Gown, YouTube and WPSU-TV have featured their Penn State memorabilia collection and spirit. In 2011 the Penn State All-Sports Museum presented some of Henning's memorabilia in an exhibition titled "A Fan's Journey." They are members of the President's Club, Mt. Nittany Society and Nittany Lion Club and are Alumni Association Life Members. George continues his service to the State College community through service on community non-profit boards including the Renaissance Scholarship Fund, Schlow Centre Region Library, the Penn State All-Sports Museum and the Friends of the Palmer Museum.

About the Publisher

The Nittany Valley Society fosters a spirit of community across time for Penn Staters, Central Pennsylvanians, and friends through a knowledge of our past, an appreciation for our present, and an affection for our spirit as a living treasury for our future. This finds expression through virtue, vigor, and soulfulness apparent in acts of honor, the cultivation of customs, and the Old State Spirit.

The Nittany Valley Society is a 501(c)(3) corporation in State College, Pennsylvania that serves as a cultural conservancy for the Nittany Valley, helping people to discover its many treasures and better share the story of this special place. Visit nittanyvalley.org to learn more and discover our other books, including:

The Legends of the Nittany Valley by Henry W. Shoemaker

Conserving Mount Nittany by Thomas A. Shakely

Is Penn State A Real University? by Ben Novak

Reminiscences of Dr. F. J. Pond by Francis J. Pond

The Birth of the Craft Brew Revolution by Ben Novak

www.ingramcontent.com/pod-product-compliance
Lightning Source LLC
Chambersburg PA
CBHW030412100426
42812CB00028B/2928/J